DRAMA IN THE RENAISSANCE

COMPARATIVE AND CRITICAL ESSAYS

Drama in the Renaissance
AMS Studies in the Renaissance: No. 12

ISSN: 0195-657X

Other Titles in This Series:

1. Hilton Landry ed. *New Essays on Shakespeare's Sonnets.* 1976.
2. J. W. Williamson. *The Myth of the Conqueror: Prince Henry Stuart, a Study in 17th Century Personation.* 1978.
3. Philip C. McGuire and David A. Samuelson, eds. *Shakespeare: The Theatrical Dimension.* 1979.
4. Paul Ramsey. *The Fickle Glass: A Study of Shakespeare's Sonnets.* 1979.
5. n.p.
6. Raymond C. Shady and G. B. Shand, eds. *Play-Texts in Old Spelling: Papers from the Glendon Conference.* 1984.
7. Mark Taylor. *Shakespeare's Darker Purpose: A Question of Incest.* 1982.
8. Kenneth Friedenreich, ed. *"Accompaninge the players": Essays Celebrating Thomas Middleton, 1581–1980.* 1983.
9. Sarah P. Sutherland. *Masques in Jacobean Tragedy.* 1982.

DRAMA IN THE RENAISSANCE

COMPARATIVE AND CRITICAL ESSAYS

EDITED BY
Clifford Davidson
C. J. Gianakaris
John H. Stroupe

PREFACE BY
C. J. Gianakaris

AMS PRESS
NEW YORK

Library of Congress Cataloging-in-Publication Data

Drama in the Renaissance.

(AMS studies in the Renaissance, ISSN 0195-657X ;
no. 12)
   Includes bibliographies and index.
   1. English drama--Early modern and Elizabethan,
1500-1600--History and criticism. 2. English drama--
17th century--History and criticism. I. Davidson,
Clifford. II. Gianakaris, 1934-   . III. Stroupe,
John H. IV. Series.
PR653.D73 1986   822'.3'09   83-45277
ISBN 0-404-62282-8

MANUFACTURED IN THE UNITED STATES OF AMERICA

AMS Press, Inc.
56 East 13th Street
New York, N.Y. 10003

Contents

Preface

This book of critical essays is the second of three volumes in a
series which treats the major periods of Western drama after the
Greeks. The first volume examines the medieval era—an age
spanning more than 500 years and producing masterpieces as
diverse as *Everyman*, the plays of the Fleury Playbook, and the
great Corpus Christi cycles of England. A third volume explores
modern dramatic literature from Ibsen to our own day. This present
volume, however, brings together a planned group of essays about
Shakespeare and his contemporaries—the theater of the Renaissance—which had its beginning even while the medieval mysteries
were still playing on the civic stage.

The essays to follow, reprinted from *Comparative Drama*, acknowledge the dramatic heritage of Renaissance drama. But in
addition to the continuity which has been established between
medieval and Renaissance drama, the latter period also involves
forms which, in Jonas Barish's words, imply a unique "multiplicity
and comprehensiveness," and it is those characteristics that primarily are revealed in the papers in this volume. The critical modes of
the essays are deliberately various, having been selected not only for
intrinsic excellence and for their coverage of many desired works
and authors, but also because they reveal a broad range of
methodologies and insights which well illuminate poetic drama.

The broad range of the essays will become evident as one reads
through the twenty articles comprising this collection. But a few
specific remarks about one or two of the papers may be suggestive
of the diverse means of these scholars in sharing their special
perceptions of Renaissance drama, especially concerning Elizabethan and Jacobean plays. These approaches involve iconography, ritual elements, allegory, statistical analysis, phenomenology,
philosophical groundwork of drama, language and image, staging,
collaborative technique, and the adaptation of Renaissance plays to

vii

film. In addition, a few essays have been included concerning drama on the Continent to indicate parallels and differing processes operating there in the Renaissance theater.

Huston Diehl, for example, discusses iconography and the unique manner in which Renaissance society perceived its world and art. She states, "In these plays, as in so much of Renaissance art and culture, visual icons provide a key to understanding the way a specific individual partakes of an ideal form." Well-considered philosophical and metaphysical positions are argued in the essays by Leonard Tennenhouse, Norma Kroll, and R. J. Kaufmann. For instance, in discussing *The Atheist's Tragedy* Kaufmann traces the special tragic world created by Tourneur which leads to drama displaying "aberrant energy in forms of social activism." Additionally, the papers by Carol Rosen and Peter Anderson provide yet another perspective when they apply the contemporary theories of such writers as Lévi-Strauss, Merleau-Ponty, and Artaud. Statistical research techniques are employed by Judith K. Gardiner and Susanna E. Epp in their computer study of Ben Jonson's comedies in order "to draw conclusions based on an entirety of information." Meanwhile, Raymond Pentzell provides insights into matters of production, and Marvin Felheim urges scholars to allow artistic freedom to screen-adapters of Shakespeare's plays.

A reading of the essays in this collection would lead one to agree with Barish's useful conclusions in his initial paper: "Through repetition, through simultaneity, through its insistence on doing everything at once, [Elizabethan drama] tries to keep us in touch not with a limited and a local reality, but with the totality—with everything that is, everything that has been, and everything that can be imagined to be, all at one and the same time."

C. J. GIANAKARIS

The Editors are grateful to those who have assisted in various ways in the preparation of this volume. We especially wish to acknowledge Mr. Michael Schulze for his conscientious work in preparing the index for this book.

The Uniqueness of Elizabethan Drama

Jonas A. Barish

Elizabethan drama might be considered to be unique in a number of ways, but I should like to speak only of a single familiar way, the full uniqueness of which may perhaps be easy to overlook. I refer to its multiplicity or comprehensiveness, and I would contrast it rapidly in that respect with three of its main rivals in the theater of Western Europe: the drama of the Greeks, that of neoclassical France toward the end of the seventeenth century, and that of modern Europe in its first or naturalistic phase as pioneered by Ibsen, Strindberg, and Chekhov.

We can start with the physical stage. Whether the Elizabethan theater derives from pageant wagons, or the trestle stages of traveling fairs, or from gaming houses, or inn-yards, or architectural structures like city gates and funerary monuments, or from the baldachinos and pavilions in Renaissance paintings, what evolves is a complex playing area, with a central platform, an alcove or discovery space at the rear, flanked by doors, a trap door leading to a cellarage below, a balcony or balustraded space above, with possibly a second level above that, and on the platform itelf a pair of great columns that divide the stage. We have a versatile, multiple playing space which can represent locales such as a field, a castle, a city wall, a ship's deck, a forest, a desert, a cave, a cell, a tavern, a hall of state, or a street, in free alternation or succession. Characters can wander in from one door and out another, lean out of windows or emerge from the alcove, skulk behind pillars or peer from over arrases, and they may occupy two or more parts of the stage simultaneously. One of the most striking effects in Elizabethan drama comes from this last-named feature, as in the parley scenes in historical plays, when besieging armies stationed on the platform challenge the defenders of a town or castle situated above, or

1

scenes of overhearing, in which characters lurking above, or behind pillars, eavesdrop on others—perhaps, as in Act V of *Troilus and Cressida,* being themselves eavesdropped on in turn —or scenes in which something is going on below stage as well as at platform level, like the cellarage sequence in *Hamlet.*

If we compare all this with the fixed scene, or *skaena,* of the Greek theater, often representing a palace door, as in *Oedipus,* or with the fixed scene of the French neoclassic stage, usually an antechamber of the palace, as in *Britannicus* or *Bérénice* or *Phèdre,* into which come and go only those characters who have essential business there, or with the tasteless bourgeois parlor of Ibsen, with its expressive clutter, perhaps permitting a bare glimpse of some world beyond—a fjord, a mill-stream, a town-scape with steeple—we can see that in these other cases the fixed stage creates a sense of high focus. The action with which we are concerned is locked to the place on which our gaze is fixed, and whatever occurs elsewhere will have to be reported by messenger or some similar device of secondary narration.

On the Elizabethan stage, even when the action takes place entirely on a single island, as in *The Tempest,* it still suggests fluidity and dispersal rather than concentration. It moves us hither and yon over the island, refusing to fasten itself to one spot. Probably *The Alchemist* comes closest, of Elizabethan plays, to confining itself to a fixed site, yet it does so for a special and highly eccentric purpose: to create a sense of abnormal pressure, of something bursting at the seams and threatening to explode. The rascally alchemists use the stage doors as places into which they can thrust inopportune clients, so as to make room for new arrivals who cannot be put off, so that what we see is not so much the confinement of a story to its natural locus in a single room as a multiple action deliberately *crammed* into a smaller space than it can naturally occupy, with the result that at length, like the overheated furnace and burning retorts themselves, the whole plot goes up *in fumo,* in a terrific cata-clysm, after which the outside world at length comes pouring in, taking its comical revenge on the absurdity of the unity of place.

Spatial restriction, on the Greek and French and modern stages, entails (or imposes) severe temporal restriction. As the action unfolds before the single palace door, or in the palace peristyle, or the bourgeois parlor, it tends to limit itself sharply in time to what can be presented as a more or less continuous process, unfolding before our eyes with a minimum of gaps. This produces the brevity and intensity of what we may call Aristotelian drama. We start close to the climax. We learn about the past through devices of recapitulation and retrospection. We encounter the action only when it has become white-hot. There is no time left for digression or excursion, only for the swift completion of what is already in motion, the speeding of an arrow, long since shot from its bow, into its target—only the few hours in which the fate of Oedipus is decided, or that of Antigone or Philoctetes, or in which Britannicus or Phèdre meet their dooms, or the few days in which Nora Helmer or Mrs. Alving or Hedda Gabler come to terms with their lives and take their resolutions for the future. We need hardly recall Sidney's whimsical lament over the geographical licentiousness of the theater of his day and its promiscuous ways with time, or Ben Jonson's raillery about York and Lancaster's long jars, or Shakespeare's apology for the temerity of his epic enterprise in *Henry V*. What is plain, when we compare Elizabethan habits with those of other stages and other epochs, is that the shameless Elizabethan stage tries to do everything. It refuses to recognize anything as beyond its powers. It crushes decades into minutes and shrinks great empires to a few feet of square board with godlike casualness.

It must be partly this voracious appetite for space and time that gives it such a striking affinity for magic, as in *Friar Bacon and Friar Bungay,* or *Doctor Faustus,* or *Old Fortunatus,* or *Macbeth*. With the literalizing of dreams of flight, of fantasies of transformation, of clairvoyance and clairaudience, and of invisibility, with the annulment of time through the conjuring up of past and future, the whole spatial and temporal universe is brought within the compass of the playhouse. The spectators are invited to share, along with the characters, the dizzying exhilaration of traversing the cosmos in a matter of seconds, of visiting the remote past and journeying into the indiscernible future from a position of absolute security. The other theaters aim at compression and selectivity, at making a little stand for a lot. The Elizabethans wish to drag the whole lot bodily onto the stage. The other theaters hedge themselves about with exclusions and taboos. The really exciting actions, the violence, the sensationalism, the amorous encounters, the magical occurrences, all happen, as Victor Hugo complained,[1] frustratingly offstage. Only the Elizabethans, with their split-level stage, their dumb shows, gods, and ghosts, their gluttony for spectacular effects, try to make everything at once visible, audible, and palpable.

Their plays tend, in consequence, to use large casts of characters. An average Greek tragedy will contain half a dozen or so speaking parts plus a chorus. Racinian tragedy rarely exceeds seven personages—three principals, three confidants, and a slave or servant or messenger. In the modern theater, Strindberg's *The Father* contains eight characters, *Miss Julie* three. *Hedda Gabler* has six, *Uncle Vanya* nine. *Henry VI, Part II*, by contrast, includes somewhere in the neighborhood of forty-five designated roles plus a bewildering array of supernumeraries: lords, ladies, attendants, petitioners, aldermen, herald, beadle, sheriff, officers, citizens, prentices, falconers, guards, soldiers, rebels, and messengers. The Elizabethan stage specializes in crowd scenes. The choruses of Greek or Senecan drama can hardly be said to constitute a crowd, such as we find at the Capulets' ball or at the court of Denmark. Still less do they compose a mob, such as we find in the street scenes of *Julius Caesar* or *Coriolanus*. Crowds and mobs, interestingly enough, in Elizabethan plays tend to individuate themselves, to decompose into Hob and Dick, First and Second Citizen, so that we feel them both as a horde, with an almost oppressive group identity, and also as collections of discrete individuals, each with his own passions and idiosyncrasies. When Racine needs a crowd, as in *Bérénice,* or Ibsen, as in *An Enemy of the People,* they keep them as severely off-stage as would Sophocles or Seneca.

The craving for completeness leads Elizabethan playwrights to differentiate their characters not only temperamentally but also socially, to make a practice of including representatives of every social level and mingling them freely on the stage. Final scenes in Shakespearean comedy bring the whole community, from king to commoner, together for some climactic recognition or some communal festivity, while in tragedy the society is likely to be gathered together at some point to witness or perform some painful, crucial rite, as in the forum scene of *Julius Caesar* or the play scene in *Hamlet*. Jonson's comic endings involve the community in a judgment scene, in which rewards and penalties are meted out by some high tribunal before which the rest of the cast is assembled, while in Jacobean tragedy it becomes nearly formulaic for an authority figure such as a Duke or a newly crowned heir to march in and restore order at the end. The effect at such moments is always to enlarge the focus, to expand the vision, to create a sense of plenitude and inclusiveness, whereas in the other kind of play the tendency is for the focus to narrow to only those characters who are central and indispensable to the story: Prometheus alone on his rock, Thésée bending over the lifeless body of Phèdre, Mrs. Alving staring helplessly into space as Osvald demands the sun, or Chekhov's three sisters clinging in desperation to one another as the regiment marches off to its new quarters.

The copious cast of an Elizabethan play, moreover, spanning the social spectrum as it does, is characteristically set to performing actions both numerous and complicated, to the point where after 1600 a play without a double plot becomes almost anomalous. Even when one cannot find a multiple plot according to strict definition, one nevertheless finds a play to be loaded with incident, swollen with episode and subsidiary scene and secondary characters. And again we can set this alongside the tight, spare construction of classical plays, with their preference for the single line, their avoidance of episodes that don't grow inevitably out of each other, or of French plays, with their even closer concatenation of events, or of Ibsenian drama, with its unrelenting pressure of passion and revelation. Most traditional drama, indeed, works by trying to maintain and step up the pressure. Elizabethan drama deliberately throws itself let-up punches, interrupts linear movement in order to go off on tangents, interferes with the single mood by introducing not only the social mixtures deplored by Sidney, the mingle of kings and clowns, but also the mixture of tones, the mingle of hornpipes and funerals which more Aristotelian kinds of drama will not tolerate.

Now this multiplicity of plot and character and stage space, of times and tones and conditions the mixture of genres, also, which produces the hybrids and crossbreeds catalogued by Polonius—is reflected in the verbal medium. Greek tragedy utilizes its hexameters, varying the long speeches from time to time with bouts of stychomathy, and punctuating the dialogue at regular intervals with choric odes. French neoclassic drama adheres with singleminded fierceness to the Alexandrine couplet. Ibsen, once past his youthful days of experiment with poetic drama, adopts a realistic prose as his standard idiom. But in the Elizabethan drama every kind of verbal style jostles every other. We have both prose and verse: a prose ranging from the most unkempt and colloquial to the most loftily ceremonial, from the most syntactically disordered to the most artfully symmetrical, and a verse which, along with the staple, blank verse, includes rhymed pentameter couplets, octosyllabic couplets, doggerel couplets, lyric and stanzaic and strophic forms, all combined and recombined in endless permutation—as, for example, in *A Midsummer Night's Dream,* with the blank verse of Theseus and Hippolyta, the pentameter couplets of the lovers, the octosyllabic couplets of Robin Goodfellow, the songs and lullabies of the attendant faeries, the clownish prose of Bottom and his associates, and the even more clownish stanzaic verses they recite in their playlet of Pyramus and Thisbe.

Elizabethan dramatic language, moreover, runs heavily to wordplay, and more particularly, to puns. Puns involve precisely the exploiting of the mutiplicities in language, the unlocking of two or more meanings imprisoned in a single word. One could compile a lexicon of words that nearly always contain a punning sense in Elizabethan dramatic dialogue—like crown, royal, noble, angel, cross, face, grace, kind—and a goodly number also that along with the explicator of ambiguity, William Empson, we would designate as complex—like blood, sense, honest, or fool—which cover a range of meanings too wide to be easily schematized. The verbal medium is a kind of three-piled texture, and the dramatists are constantly seeking to unravel the weave, to hold the words up to the light so as to discover the strands of sense woven into them. Racine, by contrast, works with a notoriously tiny vocabulary, where the words sometimes acquire a high expressive charge, and attain the status of symbols, but never the unstable, skittish, multiform identities of their Elizabethan counterparts. In this sphere as in others, where the non-Elizabethan drama presses toward clarity and economy, the Elizabethans long for total inclusiveness. They try to jam a whole linguistic universe into a word or a phrase or a line, bewildering us with the treasures they have to offer, until we are tempted to follow M. H. Mahood's advice, who, after distinguishing four equally valid possible readings of a line in *Romeo and Juliet,* ends by recommending that with "cormorant delight" we simply "swallow the lot."2 The Elizabethan mode, in all of its manifestations, approaches surfeit, prompting not only cormorant appetites like Miss Mahood's but also fastidious shrinkings like that of Edmund Wilson, who complained of *Bartholomew Fair* that there is in it "so much too much of everything that the whole thing becomes rather a wallow of which the Pig-woman and her pigs are all too truly the symbol."3

As a final consideration one might mention the dialectical and open-ended nature of Elizabethan drama, as exponded by critics like Norman Rabkin, who sees Shakespeare's plays as marked by "complementarity"—which is to say that they are multiple in meaning and irreducible to a single formulable argument.4 Shakespeare, in this view—and, I would add, often the other Elizabethans as well—does not encourage us to assign a final interpretation to the events of his plots, does not opt for one among two or more conflicting points of view, but presents them all pitted against each other, each with its own irrefutable force and weight, requiring us to hold them in suspension in our minds as unresolved simultaneities.

Now, obviously, any of the features I have pointed to may be found outside the Elizabethan drama, but it is only there that one finds them in such dense conjunction. Restoration drama, for example, uses the double plot relentlessly, almost mechanically, but shows little of the multiple stagecraft, and less still of the linguistic multiplicity, of the Elizabethans. Words, in the Restoration, are being programmatically stripped of their richness, puns downgraded as "clenches" and disapproved for serious purposes. In the craft cycles of the Middle Ages, to revert to the origins of the Elizabethan stage, one finds a high degree of inclusiveness, but of a relatively linear kind. One hallmark of Elizabethan multiplicity is simultaneity: the contrapuntal effects achieved when two or more plots interlock with each other and interinanimate each other, when two or more areas of the stage are occupied at the same time so as to cast ironic cross-lights on each other, or when two or more meanings spring unexpectedly from a single word. The mediaeval drama tends by contrast to be agglutinative, compound rather than complex.

It may perhaps be objected that I have been using as a control group a neo-Aristotelian form of drama that has prevailed only for relatively limited periods in the history of the European theater, and that especially since the Romantic revolution the stage has fallen heir to an abundance of just such loose and baggy monsters as the Elizabethans specialized in, engulfing vast tracts of time and space, employing panoramic techniques, and so forth. But this phenomenon is itself inspired by Elizabethan example. With the early Goethe, in *Götz von Berlichingen* (1771), with Victor Hugo in *Cromwell* (1827) or *Hernani* (1830), with Pushkin, in *Boris Godunov* (1836), or Büchner, in *Danton's Death* (1835), or Hebbel, in *Agnes Bernauer* (1852), we find a self-conscious return to the methods of the Elizabethans. These authors all grasp the fact that to free themselves from the tyranny of classical form, with its simple, mythic, monodirectional plot, is to embrace precisely the multifariousness of Shakespeare and his associates. Even so, they tend to avoid double plots and most of the other devices of simultaneity I have been trying to signal. What they capture of the earlier drama, especially of the historical drama, is its power to suggest large-scale historical processes working through individual lives. Their plots bulge with subsidiary characters and digressive incidents, and speeches that enrich the texture without advancing the story, but they rarely display the kind of inner intricacy we find in plays like *King Lear* or *The Silent Woman* or *A Chaste Maid in Cheapside*. The effect is often more mediaeval than Elizabethan. It suggests a series of pageant wagons rather than the image of a complex, intricately ordered cosmos.

When we turn to the Elizabethan stage revival at the end of the nineteenth century, we find a clear though unacknowledged retreat to classical principles. William Poel, its pioneer, understood that you could not properly perform an Elizabethan play except on some variety of platform stage, that it was necessary to dispense with movable scenery, proscenium arch, and the other staples of nineteenth-century theatercraft. But he did not see that the older stage went hand in hand with a certain kind of dramaturgy, and precisely with the expansive, multiple, discontinuous, spatially and temporally stretched-out kind of play we have been describing. He thought of Elizabethan dramatic technique as barbaric, reflecting the incapacity of untutored playwrights to construct a well-knit plot. And so, for his own production of *Arden of Feversham,* he simply rewrote the entire text, gave it a new title, *Lilies that Fester,* and remade it into a snug one-acter, set from beginning to end in the manor parlor and consisting of action made continuous in the best neoclassic maner. If leisure served, one could demonstrate that something very similar happened when Maeterlinck, in France, adapted *'Tis Pity She's A Whore,* and later, *Macbeth,* for performance, or when Jacques Copeau mounted his famed production of *A Woman Killed with Kindness* to inaugurate the Vieux Colombier in 1913. In every case we have either the outright suppression of a second plot or else the removal of a host of subsidiary incidents that are thought to be "doubtful, obscure, and parasitic," to borrow Maeterlinck's terms for the portions of *Macbeth* he deleted from his acting version,5 a peeling away of the layers of complexity, a stripping off of the alleged excrescencies and redundancies that we have no reason to think did not, for their original creators, belong to the very heart of their inspiration.

The same would apply, *a fortiori,* to the hundreds of closet dramas written throughout the nineteenth century in antiquarian imitation of Elizabethan models. The authors of them are interested in the psychology of violence, in crimes of passion and politics and revenge, in thunderous confrontations between legendary historical personages, but they show little concern for the density of texture that makes the older drama what it is. Ruskin, in *The Stones of Venice,* finds one cardinal feature of Gothic architecture to be its redundancy6—the tendency for the creative impulse to spill over in a torrent of expressive detail, repeated and varied in carved capitals and wrought drain spouts, in painted altars and ornamental pulpits, in stained-glass windows and sculptured choir stalls. Some such tendency seems to be at work in the Elizabethan drama, giving it the massive and exuberant character we all recognize in it. Through repetition, through simultaneity, through its insistence on doing everything at once, it tries to keep us in touch not with a limited and local reality, but with the totality—with everything that is, everything that has been, and everything that can be imagined to be, all at one and the same time.7

NOTES

1 Preface to *Cromwell,* in *Oeuvres complètes,* ed. Jeanlouis Cornluz, XI (1967), 31.

2 From *Shakespeare's Wordplay,* in Laurence Lerner, ed. *Shakespeare's Tragedies: An Anthology of Modern Criticism* (Harmondsworth, 1963), p. 26.

3 *The Triple Thinkers,* rev. ed. (New York, 1948), pp. 216-17.

4 *Shakespeare and the Common Understanding* (New York, 1967).

5 *Macbeth,* trans. Maurice Maeterlinck, in *L'illustration théâtrale,* no. 123 (August 28, 1909), p. 3.

6 Vol. II, Part II, Chapter 6, "The Nature of Gothic."

7 This essay was originally read as a paper before the Drama Section of the Modern Language Association in New York, December 29, 1976.

Iconography and Characterization in English Tragedy 1585 - 1642

Huston Diehl

Even though the characters of Renaissance drama are more highly individualized than their medieval predecessors in the morality plays, and are more closely "drawn to nature," they have not altogether lost their symbolic function. With a new psychological complexity, these characters present an illusion of reality, but at the same time they often function as symbols of higher moral reality. Because of the psychological orientation of our own post-Freudian culture, however, readers of Tudor and Stuart plays today tend to emphasize either the psychological *or* the symbolic aspects of Renaisance characters; there is a tendency, in other words, to see these characters either as modern and naturalistic or as medieval and allegorical, but not to see them as both. Critics who argue that the characters of the English Renaissance stage resemble real individuals usually focus on the playwrights' desire to "imitate nature" and the actors' desire to bring their roles to life on the stage. Andrew Gurr, for instance, argues that "Street reality obscured nature's ideal forms, so far as the theatre was concerned, to the extent that the players actually intensified the individuality of the characters they were impersonating." On the other hand, critics who argue that the characters of the English Renaissance stage are primarily symbolic reject the assumption that these characters are either psychologically consistent or even particularly verisimilar. Irving Ribner, for example, emphasizes the characters' symbolic function: "These dramatists are always more interested in mankind than in individual men . . . they rarely hesitate to sacrifice the consistency of character portraiture to the needs of the larger symbolic statement."[1]

Both sets of conclusions about Renaissance dramatic char-

11

acterization assume a dichotomy between the representational
and the symbolic. This dichotomy, however, is a modern, not a
Renaissance creation. This modern tendency to divide what the
Renaissance saw as indivisible may be illustrated by a seventeenth-century painting by Jan Vermeer which depicts an artist
painting a woman dressed as a personification of fame. Some
modern art historians title this work "A Painter in his Studio"
and stress its naturalism; others, however, title it "Allegory of
Fame" and stress its symbolism. The painting is, of course, a
brilliant fusion of naturalism and symbolism, its artist associating himself with the fame he desires, but our modern minds want
to divorce the two, acknowledging either one or the other. Although it is apparently difficult for us to see how a character
can simultaneously be a realistic individual and a symbolic
abstraction, the Renaissance mind nevertheless continually plays
with this very simultaneity, this fusion of real and ideal.

The idea that the individual embodies the universal is widely
manifest in the culture of Renaissance England. Men of letters
embraced Neo-Platonic philosophy, with its system of correspondences, its belief that the physical things of this world par-
take of ideal forms. Courtiers sparked the *imprese* craze, adopting symbolic pictures to express their own personal desires. Poets,
artists, and musicians created lavish masques in which court
personages dressed as personified abstractions and acted out
allegorical narratives which played upon a curious double reality.
Even Queen Elizabeth nourished and exploited a cult in which
she was simultaneously woman and goddess, queen and ideal
monarch, unmarried virgin and chastity personified. Nowhere
is this interconnectedness of individual and ideal more telling
than in Renaissance portraiture, an art form where we would
expect to find the desire to "imitate nature" far greater than the
desire to create symbolic abstractions. Yet Elizabethan portraits frequently combine the physical likenesses of real persons
with symbolic images which associate the human subject with
concepts such as faith, justice, and chastity. Marcus Gheeraerts'
"Rainbow Portrait of Queen Elizabeth I" is an illustrative example; it depicts not only the monarch's physical features, but
also images of eyes, ears, a serpent, and a rainbow which suggest her Platonic essence—political reason and imperial power.[2]
It is my contention that the Tudor and Stuart playwrights also
routinely fuse individual character with Platonic essence, there-

by satisfying both the tendency to individualize and particularize and the tendency to personify and typify. Sir Philip Sidney in his *Defense of Poesie* focuses on this very fusion of particular and universal when he argues for the superiority of poetry over philosophy: "Anger, the Stoics said, was a short madness. Let but Sophocles bring you Ajax on a stage . . . and tell me if you have not a more familiar insight into anger, than finding in the Schoolmen his genus and difference."3

These relationships between the real and the ideal were most often expressed visually. Visual expression was favored because of the Neo-Platonic belief that visible things could lead one to the invisible world and also because of the Aristotelian belief that the sense of sight was superior to the sense of hearing.4 In her dress, her progresses, her pageants, and her portraits, Queen Elizabeth, for one, clearly demonstrates her belief in the power of the visual medium; she astutely employs visual details to associate herself with ideas such as power, wisdom, and chastity. Dramatists, too, used visual details to illustrate how their individual characters embodied universal ideas. Although the visual elements of the Renaissance stage are often ignored by modern readers, playwrights and aestheticians in sixteenth and seventeenth-century England repeatedly emphasize that drama appealed to the eye as well as to the ear. John Webster, for instance, argues that "An Excellent Actor" is so closely involved in visual communication that he is by nature a painter. Owen Feltham likewise recognizes the drama's use of visual, as well as verbal, elements, and he praises the unique power of the visual to aid the memory and move the soul: "The *Stage* feeds both the eare and eye," he tells us, "and through this latter sence the *Soule* drinks deeper draughts. Things *acted* possesse us more, and are, too, more retainable than the *passable tones* of the tongue."5 We should, therefore, be aware of the ways these playwrights used the visual medium of drama. One way was certainly to define character. Like the master myth-maker Elizabeth—and the imprese-makers, the masque-writers, the portrait painters— Renaissance dramatists repeatedly employ visual icons, drawn from a rich public symbolism, to associate individuals with abstractions. I would like to examine here some of the specific ways the visual—through symbolic reference—illuminates character in the English tragedies written betwen 1585 and 1642.

Actual pictures, emblematic in nature, brought in and

described on stage, sometimes help to define a dramatic character by illustrating his essential nature. The *imprese* or device often functions this way; its symbolic icon and enigmatic motto reveal something central about the character to whom it belongs. Sometimes the effect is comic, as in Marston's *Antonio's Revenge* where Balurdo describes an *imprese* identifying him as an impotent fool. More often, such devices express in a concentrated and highly symbolic way the tragic circumstances of the characters they identify. Such is the case in Marlowe's *Edward II* where Mortimer and Lancaster defiantly describe the *impreses* they will bring to the courtly triumph; both devices— one featuring a cedar tree, the other a flying fish—challenge Edward's supremacy and threaten Gaveston's life.6 Emblematic needlework, when it is shown and discussed on stage, also elaborates character in these Renaissance tragedies. As with the *imprese,* its symbolic icons associate an individual with an abstraction. Perhaps the most outrageous example occurs in Tourneur's *The Atheist's Tragedy;* there an intricate piece of needlework minutely described by two prostitutes visually conveys the destructive power of female sexuality and ironically expresses the perverted nature of these bawds. Needlework also universalizes Aspatia, the wronged woman of John Fletcher's *The Maid's Tragedy.* She closely identifies herself with the mythical figure Ariadne whose story is being wrought in an embroidery, and she demands to serve as the model for this image of "Sorrow's Monument," as she herself calls it.7 However individualized, particularized, and "real" such characters are, then, their connections to these symbolic pictures reveal what is universal in their nature and apply their particular experiences to all mankind.

Another technique the Renaissance tragedians use to reveal the universal essence of a particular character is the popular masque-within-a-play. There the allegorical role a character plays and the iconographic detail used to define that role actually identify his basic nature. Like the courtly masques which they imitate, these play-masques exploit the connections between allegorical role and character acting the role, between illusion and reality. The possibilities for dramatic irony are consequently great. In the anonymous tragedy *Alphonsus,* for example, the character of Hedewick appears in a masque as Lady Fortune, *"drawn on a Globe, with a Cup in her hand, wherein are Bay leaves, whereupon are written the lots."* What the visual globe and lottery cup suggest about Fortune—her fickleness, her instability, her indifference—also extend to the situation of Hedewick who is ruled by fortune and, metaphorically as well as literally, on an instable globe. The audience sees and understands more than the characters participating in this masque do, certainly more than Edward who pronounces Hedewick/Lady Fortune "Empress" and symbolically embraces her. Although this allegory may seem too contrived and artificial to the modern reader, it is important to see how its personification of Fortune provides a central visual image which illuminates the specific actions of the play. A more elaborate example of this technique occurs in the final masque scene of Middleton's *Women Beware Women*. There the main characters take part in a wedding masque, many assuming allegorical roles which ironically reveal their true nature. The bawd Livia, for instance, ironically plays Juno, the goddess of marriage and protectress of woman. The peacock feathers she wears as an emblem of Juno, however, expose her duplicity by linking her with pride and its fall:

> *Fabrito.* Look, Juno's down too . . .!
> What makes she there: her pride should keep aloft:
> She was wont to scorn the earth in other shows:
> Methinks her peacock's feathers are much pulled.[8]

Like these masque roles, disguises often express visually the inner nature of the characters who don them. To the audience, in other words, a disguise often reveals, rather than conceals, a character's essence. An interesting example of this technique occurs in Webster's *Duchess of Malfi* where Bosola, disguised as an old man, announces to the Duchess "I am come to make thy tombe."[9] At this moment Bosola functions simultaneously as the malcontented individual he is, the man who is prepared to kill the Duchess, and as a personification of death itself, an abstraction which defines and comments on his particular character and action. This technique may also operate in *Hamlet* where the disguise of madness actually expresses the turmoil of Hamlet's soul, where disguise and reality become indistinguishable.

Perhaps the most pervasive disguise used in the Renaissance tragedies to reveal inner self is the habit of a fool. A traditional icon for human folly,[10] the fool's motley and coxcomb ironically define character in Marston's *Antonio's Revenge* where the hero disguises himself *"in a fool's habit with a walnut shell and soap to make bubbles."* Announcing to the audience that, in order to escape detection, "I put on the very flesh/ Of solid folly," Antonio actually serves as an emblem of human folly; his childish delight in the bubbles he blows symbolizes folly's—and his own—attraction to the transitory world of human endeavors. Likewise, both Antonio in Middleton's *The Changeling* and Roseilli in Ford's *Love's Sacrifice* disguise as fools in order to be with the women they love and, in the process, become the incarnation of foolishness in love. The visual habit of the fool comments on their particular behavior and universalizes their particular stories. "Keep your habit, it becomes you well," Isabella explains to her would-be lover Antonio when he tries to tell her his fool's garb is only an exterior, "For all this while you have but play'd the fool."11

Even the costume a character wears or the property he carries when he is not hiding behind a disguise or acting in a masque may serve as an iconographic sign, identifying the individual with an abstraction. Surely the *sight* of a mower and men carrying "Welch hookes" evokes the ideas of time and death in Marlowe's *Edward II* and relates the suffering of the doomed king to the universal human condition.12 Although such icons are usually commonplaces, familiar to any student of the Renaissance, the extent to which the Tudor and Stuart playwrights employ them and the way in which they illuminate character have not been adequately recognized or fully explored. My examples of this technique are too numerous to elaborate, but a brief mention of some of them will serve to illustrate the point. The moneybag, a traditional icon of avarice, for instance, associates Barabas in Marlowe's *Jew of Malta* and D'Amville in Tourneur's *Atheist's Tragedy* with the sin of covetousness and thus universalizes their specific acts of miserliness and greed.13 Similarly, conventional icons like the bed in which Evadne ties the king in Fletcher's *The Maid's Tragedy,* the mirror in which Lucretia gazes in Barnes's *The Devil's Charter,* and the blindfold Tymethes ties over his eyes in Drue's *The Bloodie Banquet* associate these characters with the sin of lust. Even though the king makes light of Evadne's binding him to the bed, ironically insisting "I'll be thy Mars. To bed, my queen of Love," and Lucretia gloats over her alluring beauty reflected in the mirror, and Tymethes eagerly accepts both physical and moral blind-folding, the audience is aware, through these conventional icons, how deluded the characters are, how tainted by lechery.14

Iconographic detail can also identify specific acts with moral or theological virtues, as, for example, in Massinger and Field's *Fatal Dowry* where a blindfold associates the judge Rochfort with the idea of impartial justice and thus enables the audience to see his condemnation of his daughter in terms other than the personal or psychological.15 Visual detail can also express a character's state of mind. Hamlet's black clothes, book, and skull are only the best known of the many symbolic renderings of melancholy on the Renaissance stage. And the poniard and rope universalize the suicidal man by connecting him to the state of despair in no fewer than six of these tragedies.16

A less well known visual detail, the nightgown, associates the dramatic character who wears it with the idea of human mortality. Repeatedly the costume of stage characters when they face death, the nightshirt seems to be more than merely natural-istic clothing; it resembles a conventional icon of a shirt, re-curring in Renaissance emblem books, and, like that icon, sym-bolizes death which strips man of all possessions except his shirt or shroud.17 In *Antonio's Revenge,* for example, both the aven-ger Antonio and his intended victim Piero appear at a sepulcher in their nightgowns; the language of this scene, rich in references to shrouds and the sleep of death, reinforces the sight of the nightgowned figures. Visual as well as verbal elements thus com-municate man's inevitable loss of life, power, and worldly pos-sessions and bind villain and hero in a common mortality. Similar uses of the nightgown occur in such diverse plays as Barnes' *The Devil's Charter,* Ford's *Love's Sacrifice,* and Suckling's *Aglaura.*18 In all these instances, the actual nightgown serves as a powerful, visual reminder of the impending death of all men and thus places the deaths that follow in a larger, philoso-phical context.

Physical action, too, can visually link the character perform-ing it to an idea he embodies. When Lapirus in Drue's *The Bloodie Banquet* kneels, when the revengers in Marston's *An-tonio's Revenge* shake their fists, when Strotzo in the same play *"lays his finger on his mouth,"* their actions enlarge our under-standing of their stories by associating them with such concepts as penitence, vengeance, and conspiracy.19 Falling is one of the

most common of such emblematic actions. Viewed as merely
literal movement, the physical falling of characters seems curious.
Viewed as an iconographically significant stage picture, however, the action makes thematic sense, for it resembles traditional
depictions of men flung to the bottom of fortune's wheel and
thus links the individual with the concept of fortune ruling him.
Certainly the physical fall of the Viceroy in *The Spanish
Tragedy* works emblematically; after he *"falls to the ground,"*
the Viceroy complains: "Fortune is blinde and sees not my desserts." Likewise, the stage picture of Antonio lying on his back
in *Antonio's Revenge* visually expresses the hero's words, "I
am . . . the wrack of splitted fortune," and the image of Bussy
prone on the ground in Chapman's *Bussy D'Ambois* communi-
cates to the eye Bussy's assumption that "Fortune, not Reason,
rules the state of things." Through these and other stage falls[20]
the image of fortune's wheel enlarges the audience's understanding of the particular and specific circumstances of the
characters.

The stage pictures created by these characters' falls, like
such visual details as costumes, properties, and disguises, suggest to a viewing audience how an individual may embody a
universal. In no way does such a technique undercut a character's psychological dimension or deny a character's unique
personality. Rather, psychological and symbolic, particular and
universal coexist, complement, and inform each other in these
dramatic characters much as the real woman Elizabeth I and
the ideal of monarchy she personified were always fused in the
minds of her subjects. In these plays, as in so much of Renaissance art and culture, visual icons provide a key to understanding the way a specific individual partakes of an ideal form. The
tragedians' frequent use of these icons is another illustration of
the pervasive Renaissance belief that "men are more led by the
eye, then eare."[21]

NOTES

1 "Elizabethan Action," *Studies in Philology*, 63 (1966), 154; *Jacobean Tragedy* (New York: Barnes & Noble, 1962), p. 11; see also Madeleine Doran, *Endeavors of Art* (Madison: Univ. of Wisconsin Press, 1954), who cites humanistic critical theory to illustrate the Renaissance interest in type but insists that *in practice* the Tudor and Stuart dramatists favored the individual over the particular, p. 256, and Alan C. Dessen, *Elizabethan Drama and the Viewer's Eye* (Chapel Hill: Univ. of North Carolina Press, 1977), who emphasizes the medieval origins and symbolic nature of Renaissance dramatic characterization, pp. 155-56.

2 See informative discussions of this portrait by Frances Yates, "Queen Elizabeth as Astraea," *Journal of the Warburg and Courtauld Institutes*, 10 (1947), 73-82, and René Graziani, "The 'Rainbow Portrait' of Queen Elizabeth I and Its Religious Symbolism," *Journal of the Warburg and Courtauld Institutes*, 35 (1973), 247-59.

3 Ed. Albert S. Cook (Boston: Ginn, 1890), p. 16.

4 For a discussion of Neo-Platonic interest in the visual, see E. H. Gombrich, "Icones Symbolicae," *Journal of the Warburg and Courtauld Institutes*, 11 (1948), 163-92; Samuel Daniel in his introduction to *The Worthy Tract of Paulus Jovius* (London, 1585), quotes Aristotle as saying "we love the sense of seeing, for that by it we are taught and made to learne more then by any other of our senses, whereby we see that all men naturally take delight in pictures."

5 *Sir Thomas Overbury His Wife*, ed. W. J. Paylor (Oxford: Basil Blackwell, 1936), p. 77; *Resolves* (London, 1628), p. 65.

6 *Antonio's Revenge*, ed. G. K. Hunter (Lincoln: Univ. of Nebraska Press, 1965), I.ii.96-98; *Edward II*, II.ii.11-46 (*The Complete Works of Christopher Marlowe*, ed. Fredson Bowers [Cambridge: Cambridge Univ. Press, 1973], Vol. II); see also the ways *impreses* reveal character in John Marston, *The Insatiate Countess*, II.i.52-58 (*The Works of John Marston*, ed. A. H. Bullen [London, 1887], Vol. III); and John Webster, *The White Devil*, ed. John Russell Brown (Cambridge: Harvard Univ. Press, 1960), II.i.323-31.

7 Cyril Tourneur, *The Atheist's Tragedy*, ed. Irving Ribner (Cambridge: Harvard Univ. Press, 1964), IV.i; John Fletcher, *The Maid's Tragedy*, ed. Howard B. Norland (Lincoln: Univ. of Nebraska Press, 1968), II.ii.39-78; see also Henry Chettle, *The Tragedy of Hoffman* (London, 1631), IV.i.1440-45.

8 *Alphonsus* (London, 1654), II; *Women Beware Women*, ed. Charles Barber (Berkeley: Univ. of California Press, 1969), V.i.176-79. I discuss in more detail the iconography of the masque scene in *Women Beware Women* in my article, "The Thematic Juxtaposition of the Representational and the Sensational in Middleton's *Women Beware Women*," *Studies in Iconography*, 2 (1976), 66-84.

9 *The Duchess of Malfi*, ed. F. L. Lucas (London: Chatto & Windus, 1958), IV.ii.114-233. For other discussions of this disguise see M. C. Bradbrook, *Themes and Conventions of Elizabethan Tragedy* (Cambridge: Cambridge Univ. Press, 1957), p. 17; Ribner, *Jacobean Tragedy*, p. 113; and Inga-Stina Ekeblad, "The 'Impure Art' of John Webster," *Review of English Studies*, 9 (1958), 262-63.

10 See, for examples, George Wither, *A Collection of Emblemes* (London, 1635), no. 3, book IV, where the picture of a fool is accompanied by the motto, "By seeming other than thou art, thou dost performe a foolish part," and Francis Quarles, *Emblemes* (London, 1634) where the picture of a fool playing with toys is accompanied by the motto "O Lord thou knowst my Foolishnesse, and my Sins are not hid from Thee."

11 *Antonio's Revenge*, IV.i.7-8; *The Changeling*, ed. N. W. Bawcutt (London: Methuen, 1958), III.iii.138-46; *Love's Sacrifice*, III.ii (*The Works of John Ford*, ed. William Gifford, rev. Alexander Dyce [London; 1869], Vol. II).

12 *Edward II,* IV.vii.

13 Cesare Ripa depicts Avarice with a moneybag in his *Iconologia* (Rome, 1603), p. 31; *The Jew of Malta,* I.i.25-37 and II.i.47-54; *The Atheist's Tragedy,* ed. Irving Ribner (Cambridge: Harvard Univ. Press, 1964), V.i.1-31.

14 *The Maid's Tragedy,* V.i.52-63; *The Devil's Charter,* ed. R. B. McKerrow (London: David Nutt, 1904), IV.iii.2016-65; *The Bloodie Banquet* (1639; rpt. Oxford: Oxford Univ. Press, 1961), III.i.976-1011.

15 *The Fatal Dowry,* ed. T. A. Dunn (Berkeley: Univ. of California Press, 1969), IV.iv.105-12.

16 For additional icons of melancholy, see *Antonio's Revenge,* II.ii; *The Second Maid's Tragedy* (Oxford: Oxford Univ. Press, 1909), IV.iv.1886-87; Cyril Tourneur, *The Revenger's Tragedy,* ed. R. A. Foakes (Cambridge: Harvard Univ. Press, 1966), I.i. For examples of the use of a poniard and/or rope to symbolize despair, see Thomas Kyd, *The Spanish Tragedy,* ed. Frederick S. Boas (Oxford: Clarendon Press, 1901), III.xii. 6-14; Christopher Marlowe, *Doctor Faustus,* V.i.1724-33 *(Complete Works,* Vol. II); *Antonio's Revenge,* IV.i.; William Rowley, *All's Lost by Lust,* V.iii.1-9 *(William Rowley,* ed. Charles Wharton Stork [Philadelphia: John C. Winston, 1910]); John Webster, *The Duchess of Malfi,* III.ii.70-155.

17 Icons of a shirt are used to express the idea of human mortality in such emblem books as Claude Paradine's *Devises Heroiques* (Lyons, 1557), p. 61; Geoffrey Whitney's *A Choice of Emblemes* (Leyden, 1586), p. 86; and George Wither's *A Collection of Emblemes,* Book IV, No. 8.

18 *Antonio's Revenge,* III.ii.; *The Devil's Charter,* IV.v.2506-19, 2569; *Love's Sacrifice,* V.i; *Aglaura,* V.iii.179-85 *(The Works of Sir John Suckling,* ed. A. Hamilton Thompson [New York: E. P. Dutton, 1910]).

19 *The Bloodie Banquet,* I.iii.314-33; *Antonio's Revenge,* II.ii.212-13 and V.i.1-25.

20 *The Spanish Tragedy,* I.iii.8-30; *Antonio's Revenge,* IV.ii.1-5; George Chapman, *Bussy D'Ambois,* ed. Nicholas Brooke (Cambridge: Harvard Univ. Press, 1964), I.i.1-33; see also the physical actions of falling and rising in John Marston's *The Malcontent,* ed. M. L. Wine (Lincoln: Univ. of Nebraska Press, 1964), V.iv.64-89; George Chapman's *The Revenge of Bussy D'Ambois,* V.v.14-100 *(The Plays and Poems of George Chapman,* ed. Thomas Marc Parrott [London: George Routledge & Sons, 1910], Vol. I); and John Mason's *The Turke,* ed. Joseph Q. Adams, Jr. (Louvain: A. Uystpruyst, 1913), where physical falls occur no fewer than twelve times.

21 Thomas Jenner, *The Soules Solace* (London, 1626), p. 9.

Ritual in Marlowe's Plays

Thomas B. Stroup

Jocelyn Powell has rightfully observed that critics have wrongfully made excuses for Christopher Marlowe's stagecraft in that they have failed to recognize his plays as drama of spectacle. They have failed to realize that in his plays he tried to fuse "the timeless and soul-searching of the morality with the relentless progress of the chronicle."[1] They have failed to realize also that in making such fusion he pays most "careful attention to visual effects made by each scene in action, and contrives that the movement of actors, their properties, costumes and background against which they appear, shall combine to form a picture as representative as words."[2] And only within the last decade have they noted that Marlowe integrates his pageantry with blank verse to set forth his ethical values objectively and not as if they were *exempla* in a sermon.[3] These observations represent a part of the recent defense of Marlowe as an effective and sensitive stage dramatist, not a miscast lyric poet.[4]

Now the spectacle of Marlowe's plays is provided mainly by pageantry, and integral parts of the pageantry are ritualistic and ceremonial actions. It seems that critics have ignored or deprecated the appearance of rites and ceremonies in his plays quite as much as they have generally made excuses for spectacle in them.[5] They have not systematically observed the extent and variety of these phenomena or their dramatic function. I believe such observation may lead to still better understanding of what Marlowe was trying to do as a stage dramatist and therefore make possible a better appreciation of his plays as works to be acted, not merely read as fine poems.

I am not here concerned with the play as ritual in itself, however much one might discover similarities between the structure of certain rites and the structure of certain plays; rather I am concerned with the appearance of recognized rituals and cere-

monies, both ecclesiastical and secular, within the plays: ritualized processions, prayers, oaths, betrothals, blessings, charms,
challenges, catechisms, coronations, curses, the holding of court,
and the like. I shall not try to discover original rites which the
poet may himself devise, only the use he makes of those recognized as such by reader and audience. Formal orations,
though scarcely rites, are ritualistic and were presented formally; so also were the processions, dumb shows, and *tableaux
vivants*.6 Indeed such a play as *Tamburlaine,* in both its parts,
is really little more than a series of pageant-like processions going on and off the stage, stopping only long enough to allow an
episode to be enacted. Although I shall here point out in some
detail the number and variety of the formal processions and
identify the rites and ceremonies which come upon the stage with
them, I am more concerned with their dramatic use, in how
they may provide the recognition of meanings beyond the literal event by which an audience may be moved and satisfied in
both mind and emotion.

Some sixty formal or ceremonial processions bring the characters upon the stage in Marlowe's six plays.7 In *Dido Queen
of Carthage* few of the entrances, perhaps only three, would
normally be presented as processions. But a wise director would
surely make the opening of III.iii a procession. Dido, Aeneas,
Anna, Iarbus, Cupid (as Ascanius), and the whole court appear, splendid in their hunting costumes. The Queen, addressing
Aeneas formally, calls attention to the fact that she has laid aside
her princely dress and has put on Diana's "shrouds." (To refer
to the dress of the goddess of chastity as "shrouds" adumbrates
and calls attention to the irony of what happens later at the hunt
and at the end of the play also.) Similarly near the opening of
IV.iv a ceremonial procession is indicated, where Anna, Aeneas,
Achates, Ilioneus, Sergestus, and followers appear at court and
where Dido gives Aeneas the crown of Lybia. The procession and
the presentation of the crown should constitute a coronation
indeed. As such it heightens the occasion and intensifies Aeneas'
later perfidy and the audience's pity of Dido. In her ecstasy
(agonizingly ironic to the audience) at his acceptance and
promise that "When I leave thee, death be my punishment," she
exclaims in her most poignant and beautiful lines,

> If he forsake me not, I never die,
> For in his looks I see eternity,
> And he'll make me immortal with a kiss. (IV.iv.121-23)

But in this early play Marlowe makes infrequent use of processions as compared with what he does in the two parts of *Tamburlaine*. In it at least twenty-two processions bring the characters onstage, seven in Part I and fifteen in Part II; and most of these processions onstage require similar processions offstage. These do not include the simple coming in of a group without fanfare, such as one finds often in Part I. Evidently the playwright had discovered the dramatic appeal of the device by the time Part II was called for. *I Tamburlaine*, I.ii, for example, opens with a triumphal procession wherein Zenocrate is brought on as a prisoner. Later (V.ii.369) Zenocrate's father is brought on in another triumphal-prisoner procession; and in Part II alone at least four of these triumphal marches with prisoners occur. Tamburlaine took special delight in having himself drawn on in a chariot pulled by conquered kings; in much the same manner he mounted his throne on Bajazeth's back in Part I. The triumphant conqueror with his prisoners became a conventional spectacle of the drama and has continued until recent times, perhaps its grandest example being that in Verdi's *Aïda*.

Just as conventional is another type of ritualized procession in *Tamburlaine:* that of the royal train sweeping into the royal court to determine state actions or to hold state conferences. The king holds court. For example, Bajazeth and the kings of Morocco, Fez, and Angier enter in "great pomp" to settle formally their plans and duties for the coming engagements with Tamburlaine. Six processions of this variety open scenes in Part II. Notable among them is the procession of kings (I.i.) who have come to make treaties. Another group of rulers open the next scene. The occasions are formal and ceremonial; they follow ritualistic patterns; they result in official acts of state.

Perhaps the most elaborate and moving procession in *Tamburlaine* is the funeral procession of Zenocrate (Part II, III.ii). The hearse is carried in by four attendants, drums sound a doleful march; Tamburlaine, his four sons, and Usumcasane follow it; and the town burns in the background. Preceding the procession, Zenocrate has died in state—an elaborate *tableau vivant*. With this *tableau*, the procession marks the dramatic high point of the play; it creates the reversal and subsequent decline of Tamburlaine's character and his fortunes. Among the playwrights who followed Marlowe the funeral procession became almost a fixture in the chronicle and history plays. Other such processions as that into a banquet (Part I, IV.iv) likewise became a common ritual in later plays, and the strange procession of the Governor of Damascus with his citizens and the four virgins with branches in their hands (Part I, V.i) anticipates similar prayerful processions in the works of later dramatists. Indeed *Tamburlaine* furnished prototypes for many of the conventional ceremonial processions for later Elizabethan plays. Part II, the epic story of a world-conqueror, required the elevation of ceremonial style in its presentation. And apparently the audience at the Rose delighted in it.

In *The Jew of Malta,* by contrast, one counts only half a dozen processions. And these are of two sorts only: processions into the room of state to hold court or parley and processions of prisoners or slaves. Act I.ii opens with the formal entrance into the room of State of Ferneze, the Bashaws, and Calymath. There they make their formal international agreement. Similar processions to councils of state open II.ii, III.v, and V.i. As in *Tamburlaine,* such processions are required here, and in dozens of later plays, as a simple matter of realism: if a dramatist is to present the affairs of state, he must present them as stately affairs. Furthermore, affairs of state are by nature dramatic, by which we mean that they are patterned occasions, not the simple events of ordinary life. They are anticipated and planned; upon their outcome depends the fate of men and nations.

The procession of prisoners and slaves furnishes the same kind of dramatic appeal. They provide visible evidence at once of the triumph and of the disgrace of men and states. In II.ii, officers bring into the market place a group of slaves, among them Ithamore whom Barabas buys. But the more spectacular procession is that of the guarded prisoners at the opening of V.ii, in which Calymath and the Turks turn over Ferneze and his knights to Barabas. The visual evidence of what has happened makes the audience more anxious than ever about what next will happen.

The Massacre at Paris dramatizes the St. Bartholomew's Day Massacre, itself an affair of state and an international incident. As one might expect, at least twelve of the twenty-three scenes are opened with formal processions. Of these some five, or almost half, move into the room of state where the ceremonies of the court take place. The first is especially splendid, with two kings, three queens, a prince, a lord admiral, and then the court at-

tendants, all in royal court dress. Here King Charles opens court
with a marriage contract solemnly made between Navarre and
Margaret. As the initial action of the play, this ceremony sets up
the basic dramatic conflict; it is formally, swiftly, and forebod-
ingly executed. Just as fearsome is the next court procession and
ensuing scene: in it the Old Queen is poisoned and the Lord
Admiral is wounded. Each such procession leads to as foreboding
or as violent scene as these two. Scene xi (acts are not marked
in the text) opens with five or six "Protestants" in procession
"with books," who (reminding one of the Virgins in *I Tamburlaine*) kneel together and pray as they are slain. The splendid
opening of the final scene leads to the stabbing of the King. And
(reminding us of the last procession in *Hamlet*) to conclude the
play comes the grand funeral procession, the King's body being
borne offstage on four men's shoulders. In this play splendid
processions are prelude to danger and death. By them the shock
of irony is deliberately created.

Marlowe made good, if not extensive, use of ritualized
pageantry in *Edward II*. Although the courtly procession is ger-
mane to the history or chronicle, here, in contrast to *II Tamburlaine* especially, the poet has become more discriminating in
using processions or other pageantry. Yet at least seven entrances
ask for processions, and most of these, the same kind of exits.
Of these seven, four are court processions; one (III.iii.35) is a
procession of prisoners wherein Edward's soldiers bring in the
captured barons; and one (V.iv) a magnificent prelude to the
challenge of the Champion at the coronation of Edward III.
Another is held at Lambeth (I.iv). In it the Archbishop with
his attendants and the barons make up the splendid entry for the
ceremony of signing the papers requiring Gaveston's banishment.
Later (IV.iv) the Queen opens her court with a grand procession, formal prelude to her official speech and the barons' oath
of allegiance. In every case, the procession, setting the ceremonial tone, serves the ritual which forms the basic action of
the scene. Though quarrels may ensue, they are yet part of the
state ceremony. Directors who disregard such ritualistic entrances, or fail to recognize them for what they are, weaken the
effectiveness of their production of the scene.

Doctor Faustus is no chronicle or history play; hence its
processions are fewer and of a different sort. Many, if not all of
them, are burlesque and satirical. A director may advantageously

require some eight processional entrances and exits if he is to
create what appears to have been Marlowe's intention, or that
of the dramatist who may have added or modified some of the
middle scenes. Notable among these is the procession of the
Seven Deadly Sins (II.ii). Calculated in earlier literature to
make sin repulsive and serve as a warning, this procession produces quite the opposite effect: to Faustus it is an amusing ritual
in which he takes great delight. With proper costuming and acting, the director may easily make it a burlesque of courtly
processions.

If the ritual procession of the Seven Deadly Sins is satirical,
that of the Pope with his pompous entourage of bishops, monks,
and friars (III.i.) is burlesque. It is prelude to the Pope's ascen-
sion of his throne, after Tamburlaine's manner, upon the back of
Bruno. Thus ignorance, tyranny, and bigotry mount to power
upon the back of the enlightenment of the new learning. Then
the papal banquet is brought in, and the invisible Faustus robs
the court of its food. The banquet ironically foreshadows the
procession of devils who with covered dishes (V.i) bring
Faustus his last meal. The final procession is the ritual by which
Lucifer, Beelzebub, and Mephistophilis ascend from Dis to claim
Faustus' soul. There is little difference in tone between this
diabolical ritual or the farcical papal procession and the futility
of the procession into the Emperor's court (IV.ii) to see the
dumb show in which Alexander kills Darius for his crown and
then gives it to his mistress. From the pageant-like processions
of *Tamburlaine* designed to create noble pomp and circumstance,
Marlowe moves in the later play to processions calculated to
ridicule pomp and circumstance. In the former play the mag-
nificence of the processions serves in the end only to intensify the
bitter disillusionment of the Scourge of God; in the latter the
ritualized pageantry, created by necromancy, is itself illusion,
serving no good purpose, in the end signifying nothing even to
him who evokes it.

To turn from ceremonial processions to the self-evident
rituals and ceremonies which the processions so often introduce
is to find varied and numerous such identifiable forms. Approximately eighty-five performances of ceremonies are fairly readily
recognized in the six plays, and probably others are too deeply
embedded in the dialogue to be perceived. I count, moreover,
eighteen kinds, not reckoning among them "set speeches" or

orations or the formal court ritual (already accounted for among the processions), and among them I observe several combinations of kinds.8 For example, a betrothal requires a ritual in which an oath provides a contract, which forms still another ritual; an oath or a curse may be part of a prayer; a blessing may be a curse in disguise; a prayer may be a malediction; and among them all may be liturgical echoes from other rituals. Taken together, they form a very considerable part of the stage activity of the plays.9 By all odds the most numerous of these are the curses, oaths, and prayers (difficult to separate one from another), some of them presented very formally, others bursting out as if spontaneously from the speaker's mouth.

However great the number and variety of ceremonies and rituals, their dramatic use is more important. One recalls that drama, both ancient and medieval, had its origins in ritual and that rite as well as drama is an imitation of an action, or at least the presentation of an often repeated social or religious occasion having its own conventional forms. Betrothals, marriages, prayers, curses, charms, blessings, etc., are repeated symbolic imitations of an original prototype. They formalize repeated happenings in human society. They set aside or celebrate or "dramatize" special occasions. Properly acted and directed they become extremely effective dramatic devices within the larger device of the play as a whole. They give the occasion which they represent its emotional setting and overtone, evoking at once the proper associations and values. They greatly heighten its dramatic qualities. The marriage of Webster's Duchess of Malfi, though it is *per verba presenti* and no sacrament of the Church, so hallows and makes gracious the occasion, so sublimates it, as to lift the hearts of the viewers beyond its tragic implications. It stretches the emotions to the breaking point. Without the ceremony we lose what is dramatic and are given a perversion of the meaning; without it, we have only a lustful widow inviting her steward to her bed. So with other ceremonies: if not so intense, they yet lift the event to an occasion. The examination of the dramatic effectiveness of several of these may reveal something of Marlowe's craftmanship.

The Church's sacrament of marriage would not be allowed upon the Elizabethan stage, but betrothals and affirmations of marriages and troth-plights were allowed—as well sometimes as interrupted church ceremonies, such as that in *Much Ado about Nothing.* Some four such occur in Marlowe's plays. The most notable and effective of these appears in *Dido,* the betrothal of Aeneas and Dido. The two have come into the cave, where Dido, burning with desire, calls upon Aeneas to "quench these flames!" Aeneas, swept off his feet and forgetful of the gods, then bursts out his formal pledge:

> If that your majesty can look so low
> As my despisèd worths that shun all praise,
> With this my hand I give to you my heart
> And vow by all the gods of hospitality,
> By heaven and earth, and my fair brother's bow,
> By Paphos, Capys, and the purple sea
> From whence my radiant mother did descend,
> And by this sword that saved me from the Greeks,
> Never to leave these new-upreared walls,
> Whiles Dido lives and rules in Juno's town,
> Never to like or love any but her.   (III.iv.40-50)

Dido's reply is an ecstatic acceptance, followed by the bestowal of the kingdom upon Aeneas. Giving him golden bracelets (if the scene is properly acted), she slips upon his finger the wedding ring she had from her late husband Sichaeus, and then creates him king of Carthage: "Sichaeus, not Aeneas be thou called,/ The king of Carthage, not Anchises' son." Here two ceremonies are combined, a formal betrothal and the bestowal of a crown, an informal coronation, or what should be presented as one. Aeneas should on bended knee accept the bracelets and the ring. It is a momentous occasion, the turning point of the play, the perepeteia, heightened dramatically by grim irony: it is celebrated by most impassioned, most unequivocal, ceremonial oaths, which are neither presented nor even mentioned in Virgil and which will be most unceremoniously and fatally broken in the play three scenes later. Probably most of the audience were familiar with the original account in the *Aeneid.* In it Virgil quickly draws a curtain over the scene, passing over in a few lines what may have happened in the cave, leaving it to "Rumor" to spread her speculations. Marlowe's presentation, on the other hand, excites and intensifies the emotions of those who see or those who read it, and it creates the irony Virgil's account was not calculated to do. The ceremony makes drama out of narrative.

Likewise the bitter irony of the simple betrothal of Abigail and Lodowick in *The Jew of Malta:*

Lodowick.	Then, gentle Abigail, plight faith to me.
Abigail.	I cannot choose, seeing my father bids.
	Nothing but death shall part my love and me.
Lodowick.	Now I have that for which my soul has longed.
Barabas.	So have not I; but yet I hope I shall. *Aside.*

(II.iii.312-16)

It is a sinister arrangement Barabas has made to serve his own purpose; the anticipated joy of the two lovers will turn to death.

The whole action of *The Massacre of Paris* stems from the marriage of Henry of Navarre and Margaret, sister of Charles IX of France. The ceremony has taken place just before the opening lines of the play are spoken by Charles, whose words are a ceremonial sealing of the contract and marriage and a blessing upon it:

> Prince of Navarre, my honorable brother,
> Prince Condé, and my good Lord Admiral,
> I wish this union and religious league,
> Knit in these hands, thus joined in nuptial rites,
> May not dissolve till death dissolve our lives;
> And that the native sparks of love
> That kindled first this motion in our hearts
> May still be fueled in our progeny. (i.1-8)

As the ceremony ends and the court leaves the room of state, the Queen Mother, the notorious Catherine de Medici, the evil power behind the throne, in an aside threatens to dissolve "with blood and cruelty" the union here just celebrated. Her sinister threat warns the audience, casting its ominous tones ahead even to the end of the play. The joyous ceremony at the opening being marred by this sinister aside foreshadows and balances the tragic ceremony that ends the play: the funeral procession of the king.10

Not so easily recognized are the two perverted catechisms in *Doctor Faustus.* The first is the more extensive. Appearing to Faustus as a Franciscan friar, Mephistophilis asks what he can do for Faustus, whereupon Faustus puts to him a series of questions bearing upon what may be called the theology of hell. He asks Mephistophilis first whether he did not appear at Lucifer's command. After Mephistophilis explains the conditions under which he appears to mortals, and after Faustus in proper catechismal manner explains "So Faustus hath already done," he goes on to further questions:

	Tell me what is that Lucifer thy lord?
Mephistophilis.	Arch-regent and commander of all spirits.
Faustus.	Was not that Lucifer an angel once?
Mephistophilis.	Yes Faustus, and most dearly loved of God.
Faustus.	How comes it then that he is prince of devils?
Mephistophilis.	O, by aspiring pride and insolence,
	For which God threw him from the face of heaven.
Faustus.	And what are you that live with Lucifer?
Mephistophilis.	Unhappy spirits that fell with Lucifer,
	Conspired against our God with Lucifer,
	And are forever damned with Lucifer.
Faustus.	Where are you damned?
Mephistophilis.	In hell.
Faustus.	How comes it then that thou art out of hell?
Mephistophilis.	Why this is hell, nor am I out of it.

(I.iii.62-76)

And so on they go with other questions and the well-known answers. The irony here is created by a two-fold perversion: not only is the Christian purpose of the ritual (to examine the candidate for full admission into the Christian community and prepare him for ultimate salvation) perverted into preparing him for a place in hell, but the catechumen preparing for the new religion does the questioning rather than the catechist, the representative of the cult. Thus the anxious desire of the neophyte to embrace damnation is horrifyingly emphasized.

The second catechism, less obvious in form than the first, follows upon Faustus' delivery of his "deed of gift of body and soul" to Mephistophilis (II.i.112-26). Now that Faustus has become a very member incorporate in and spiritual inheritor of hell, Mephistophilis welcomes more questions. They all concern hell, its place and conditions. The irony again lies in the perversity of Faustus: whereas he has concluded a contract with the agents of hell, he now scoffs at the whole idea of such a place. He refuses to believe Mephistophilis' answers to his questions and says that after death there can be no pain, that the whole concept is an old wives' tale. The substance is simply that hell exists in man's soul, and Faustus rejects as absurd any belief in the soul. (It may be recalled that Falstaff's famous catechism upon honor also ended in denial, in lack of faith, the reverse of its religious purpose.) The formalizing of the occasion into a ritual sharpens by recognition the audience's awareness of just what is happening, and creates, moreover, that fear which is the requisite of tragedy.

A spectacular ritual in *Edward II,* and the only one of its kind in Marlowe's plays, follows the coronation of young Edward III as part of the larger ceremony. It is the traditional Challenge of the Champion to any who would question the new king's right to the throne to trial by combat. The trumpet sounds, and the young Edward appears (crowned and in coronation robes) with the Bishop of Canterbury, the Champion, the Queen Mother, and a train of nobles:

Canterbury.	Long live King Edward by the grace of God,
	King of England and lord of Ireland.
Champion.	If any Christian, Heathen, Turk, or Jew,
	Dares but affirm that Edward's not true king,
	And will avouch his saying with the sword,
	I am the champion that will combat him.
Mortimer Junior.	None comes, sound trumpets.
	[*Trumpets sound*]
King Edward III.	Champion, here's to thee.
	[*He gives a purse*] (V.iv.73-80)

No one comes forward to defend the right of the young king's father, not yet dead, although Mortimer Junior has just sent Lightborn to murder him. The splendor of this ritual is to be directly contrasted with the degradation of the preceding scene in which the abused and wretched Edward II is shaved in puddle water by his tormentors. The tragic pity is even further intensified by the fact that the young king is immediately hustled off by his mother to the evil protectorship of Mortimer Junior. The ritual was not put into the action for its spectacular value alone.

The pronouncing of charms in Elizabethan drama is not uncommon, perhaps the most notable being that of the Weird Sisters in *Macbeth* (IV.i.). Marlowe makes two effective uses of charms, one in *The Jew of Malta,* the other in *Doctor Faustus.* Usually unnoticed, that in the former is Barabas' preparation of a pot of poisoned porridge to be taken by Ithamore to the nunnery to effect the murder of his daughter, upon whom he places a curse within the charm. As he stirs the pot Barabas intones,

> As fatal be it to her as the draught
> Of which great Alexander drank and died,
> And with her let it work like Borgia's wine,

> Whereof his sire, the Pope, was poisoned.
> In few, the blood of Hydra, Lerna's bane,
> The juice of Hebon, and Cocytus' breath,
> And all the poisons of the Stygian pool
> Break from the fiery kingdom, and in this
> Vomit your venom, and envenom her
> That like a fiend hath left her father thus.
>   (III.iv.92-101)

In the next line Ithamore exclaims gleefully, "What a blessing has he given't!" He recognizes the perverted grace before meat: what should have gone as a blessed gift to the holy house, goes instead as accursed bane and with murderous intent.

Likewise in *Doctor Faustus* the gleefully pronounced "charm" by which Mephistophilis makes Faustus invisible so that he may upset the papal banquet is a sacrilegious perversion of the Laying on of Hands. It appears to be a burlesque of the sacrament of Holy Orders, rather than of Confirmation, both of which require that hands be laid upon the head of the initiate. The rite, here derisively and mockingly presented as a diabolical "charm," is appropriate preparation for the farcical tricks of Faustus as magician at the banquet to follow.[11] Faustus having asked to be charmed, Mephistophilis speaks as follows:

>   Then kneel down presently:
> *Whilst on thy head I lay my hand*
> *And charm thee with this magic wand.*
> *First wear this girdle; then appear*
> *Invisible to all are here.*
> *The planets seven, the gloomy air,*
> *Hell and the Furies forked hair,*
> *Pluto's blue fire, and Hecate's tree,*
> *With magic spells so compass thee*
> *That no eye may the body see.*   (III.ii.14-23)

Here as in other cases the Elizabethan dramatist may only suggest by analogy the Christian rite of the Book of Common Prayer; to profane it would be to risk prison. But he may paganize and ironically pervert the rite by mixing it with a witches' charm. The alert theatre-goer would get the fearful implication.

Of all the rites and ceremonies available to the Elizabethan dramatist, none had greater possibility for panoply than the coronation of a monarch. Yet the religious character of the coronation of a Christian king had the same stage restrictions as other Christian rituals. Often the monarch appears only after the ceremony in his coronation robes and crown, as does Richard III following his coronation in Shakespeare's play (IV.ii). Marlowe is not hampered by such restrictions in either *Dido* or the two parts of *Tamburlaine*. I have already discussed the coronation of Aeneas in *Dido* as connected with the betrothal; another follows his first attempt to leave Dido, when he is returned by Anna. The Queen here actually bestows her crown upon him and exclaims over his majesty. Marlowe devotes twenty-six lines to the ceremony—from Dido's "Wear the imperial crown of Libya./ Sway thou the Punic scepter in my stead," to "O, how a crown becomes Aeneas' head," and through Aeneas' formal oath of eternal constancy to Dido (IV.iv.34-60). Although the wavering Aeneas struggles with the gods for three more scenes, the audience knows well the heart-breaking outcome. By the ceremony they are made to realize acutely the bitter irony and the pity of the action. Without it, the tragic value of the occasion would be gravely diminished.

But richest of all in coronations is *I Tamburlaine*. Seven monarchs are crowned in four separate ceremonies. Cosroe in an elaborate ceremony usurps the crown of his cowardly brother Mycetes and by the nobles of the empire is crowned

> monarch of the East,
> Emperor of Asia and of Persia,
> Great lord of Media and Armenia,
> Duke of Africa and Albania,
> Mesopotamia and of Parthia,
> East India and the late discovered isles,
> Chief lord of all the wide, vast Euxine Sea,
> And of the ever-raging Caspian lake.
> Long live Cosroe, mighty emperor!
> (I.i.161-69)

In ironic contrast to this splendid scene comes the short, blunt ceremony in which Tamburlaine achieves "The sweet fruition of an earthly crown." He has captured the wounded Cosroe, upon whose death he takes up the crown, puts it on his own head, and swears that "Not all the curses which the Furies breathe/ Shall make me leave so rich a prize as this." His followers then shout, "Long live Tamburlaine, and reign in Asia!" The ceremony takes place on the battle field and runs to only twelve lines (II.vii.53-64). Thus the uncouth shepherd puts down the mighty emperor from his seat. But at a later time he

will crown, at a banquet, as glitteringly staged as any director
may desire, four kings to rule under him (IV.iv.105-37), while
he throws, as if to a dog, scraps of bread and bones to Bajazeth,
former Emperor of the Turks. It is not alone the pageantry which
makes the dramatic appeal.

Nor is it merely the panoply which furnishes the appeal of
the elaborate coronation of Zenocrate with which Part I ends
(V.ii. 421-66). Tamburlaine has just now overcome Zenocrate's
father, the Soldan of Egypt, and her sometime betrothed, the
King of Arabia, who has died in combat. But it is a generous
conquering, for Tamburlaine makes the Soldan ruler over more
than he had ever ruled before. He will also marry Zenocrate and
make her his queen: "Then sit thou down, divine Zenocrate,/
And here we crown thee Queen of Persia,/ And all the kingdoms and dominions/ That late the power of Tamburlaine sub-
dued." This ceremony, then, effects the proper reconciliation
and the play achieves an Aristotelian conclusion.[12]

Curses, oaths, and prayers are by all odds the most frequently encountered ceremonials in Elizabethan drama. They are,
moreover, difficult to distinguish one from another: a curse is a
kind of prayer, a prayer may be an oath, or an oath a contract
or a curse or both. There are also varying degrees of formality
in all such rites. A curse may involve a formal railing such as
that of the primitive Irish satirists, so caustically spoken by
Thersites in Shakespeare's *Troilus and Cressida* and Malvole in
Marston's *Malcontent;* or it may rise to the formal Catholic malediction by bell, book, and candle. Some of these are simple and
incidental, scarcely lifted above the level of ordinary conversation; others are elaborate rituals. But all of them are to some degree expressions of heightened emotions; all are emphatic statements cast in a recognizable form. And Marlowe used them
effectively.

Barabas rails against the "partial heavens" which would
seem "To make me desperate in my poverty" (I.ii.258-69)
when he learns of the loss of his property. Later he turns upon
his daughter and curses her formally before he prepares the
poisoned porridge to send her:

> And Ithamore, from hence
> Ne'er shall she grieve me more with her disgrace;
> Ne'er shall she live to inherit aught of mine,
> Be blessed of me, nor come within my gates,

> But perish underneath my bitter curse,
> Like Cain by Adam, for his brother's death.
>
>   (III.iv.25-30)

And Faustus curses Mephistophilis in such form when he realizes the terrible imprecation he has, as Mephistophilis ironically reminds him, brought down upon himself:

> When I behold the heavens, then I repent
> And curse thee, wicked Mephistophilis,
> Because thou hast deprived me of those joys.
>
>   (II.ii.1-3)

But by all means the most dramatic and formalized curse of this play, or of any of Marlowe's plays, is the Papal curse by bell, book, and candle following the legerdemain at the Papal banquet in which Faustus has stolen the food from off the table. Faustus sportively welcomes the, to him, ludicrous coming of the friars to pronounce their rite:

> Cursed be he that stole his holiness' meat from the table.
> Maledicat Dominus!
> Cursed by he that struck his holiness a blow on the face.
> Maledicat Dominus!
>
> .   .   .   .
>
> Maledicat Dominus! Et omnes sancti. Amen.
>
>   (III.ii.99-108)

As the friars speak the last line, Faustus and Mephistophilis beat them off the stage. All of this is as amusing to the anti-papist English playgoer as it is to the non-believing Faustus. Unfortunately, it becomes the major irony of the play: Faustus indeed is damned. And Mephistophilis in providing the amusement is actually carrying out the damnation pronounced by the friars.13

The highly sensational banquet scene in *I Tamburlaine* provides a formal curse as a perverted grace before meat, in which the caged Bajazeth and his wife antiphonally curse the food brought in to serve Tamburlaine and his court. Bajazeth begins with these words:

> Fall to, and never may your meat digest!
> Ye Furies, that can mask invisible,
> Dive to the bottom of Avernus' pool,
> And in your hands bring hellish poison up,
> And squeeze it in the cup of Tamburlaine!
> Or winged snakes of Lerna, cast your stings,
> And leave your venoms in this tyrant's dish!

And Zabina continues with these:

> And may this banquet prove as ominous
> As Progne's to th' adulterous Thracian king
> That fed upon the substance of his child.
>
> (IV.iv.16-25)

Similarly Bajazeth had asked that the holy "priests of heavenly Mahomet" "Suck up poison from the moorish fens,/ And pour it in this glorious tyrant's [Tamburlaine's] throat!" (IV.ii.2-7) Later Bajazeth and Zabina rail out, as a primitive Irish satirist might, at Tamburlaine, both praying that his body may be gored with many wounds and that every pore may "let blood come dropping forth,/ That lingering pain may massacre his heart/ And madness send his damned soul to hell" (V.ii.151-66).

In addition to the dozen or more perverted prayers or curses, Marlowe puts into his plays some twenty-odd direct prayers involving petitions. Whether addressed to God or man, they intensify the emotions of the audience just as they create such intensification among the actors on the stage.

In Part II a citizen of Babylon on bended knee prays the Governor to submit to Tamburlaine and "hang up flags of truce" (V.i.24-33). In another, Theridamus, Usumcasane, and two of his sons on bended knee pray Tamburlaine to pardon his cowardly son Calyphas (IV.ii.22-27). In Part I the First Virgin likewise makes an extensive petition to Tamburlaine in formal prayer:

> Most happy king and emperor of the earth,
> Image of honor and nobility
> For whom the powers divine have made the world
> And on whose throne the holy Graces sit,
> In whose sweet person is comprised the sum
> Of nature's skill and heavenly majesty,
> Pity our plights! O, pity poor Damascus!
> Pity old age, within whose silver hairs
> Honor and reverence ever more have reigned.
>
> (V.ii.11-19)

And she goes on for twenty-two more lines asking for pity.

Earlier in this same scene the Second Virgin before the gates of Damascus, instead of making her petition directly to Tamburlaine, speaks in proper and familiar form her prayer to "the majesty of heaven":

> With knees and hearts submissive we entreat

Grace to our words and pity to our looks
That this device may prove propitious,
And through the eyes and ears of Tamburlaine
Convey events of mercy to his heart.
Grant that these signs of victory we yield
May bind the temples of his conquering head
To hide the folded furrows of his brows,
And shadow his displeased countenance
With happy looks of ruth and lenity.
(V.i.50-59)

The form here is that of a collect, and the audience would recognize the fact, just as they would recognize the truncated collect Barabas prays in *The Jew of Malta* asking Jehovah to enable Abigail to retrieve his treasure:

O Thou that with a fiery pillar led'st
The sons of Israel through the dismaľ shades,
Light Abraham's offspring, and direct the hand
Of Abigail this night, or let the day
Turn to eternal darkness after this. (II.i.12-16)

In *Dido* Iarbus' prayer to Jove apparently involves a sacrifice of some sort, with an altar and offering called for in the lines before the formal beginning. It is a lengthy petition for the redress of the wrongs wrought by Aeneas at his coming to Carthage:

Eternal Jove, great master of the clouds,
Father of gladness and all frolic thoughts,
That with thy gloomy hand corrects the heaven
When airy creatures war among themselves,
Hear, hear, O hear Iarbus' plaining prayers.
(IV.ii.4-8)

And then for the next fourteen lines he pours out his lament, grievances, and petition.

Still another kind of prayer occurs. In *The Massacre at Paris* the Admiral as he is about to be murdered asks to be allowed to pray, but his murderer Gonzago says, "Then pray unto our Lady; kiss this cross." But the good Huguenot refuses, managing only to cry out simply, "O God, forgive my sins" (V.v. 28-30). Similarly Edward II is murdered, but as he dies manages to echo in his last words the ritualistic prayer of those trained in the *ars moriendi:* "I am too weak and feeble to resist./ Assist me, sweet God, and receive my soul" (*Edward II*, V.v.107-08). Not so with Faustus as he approaches his end. Frustrated, in the last hour of his life, he cries out in agony, "Stand still, you ever-moving spheres of heaven,/ That time may cease and midnight never come," and continues his futile efforts at prayer for some fifty lines or more (V.ii.138-87). They complete the frustration brought on earlier by Mephistophilis when Faustus, urged by the Good Angel, had cried out, "O Christ, my Savior, my Savior,/ Help to save distressed Faustus' soul" (II.ii.83-84).

These examples are sufficient to indicate the number and suggest the variety of prayers in Marlowe's plays.14 In moments of mental anguish and spiritual distress his characters turn naturally to this means whereby they may double the intensity of their expression and thus double the intensity of the audience's emotion.

Now oaths are often involved in prayers, and they are necessary to formal contracts; and Marlowe did not overlook their dramatic value. He made use of them a dozen or more times. I have already called attention to his highly effective use of Aeneas' betrothal to Dido, as well as to the betrothal at the opening of *The Massacre at Paris,* both involving oaths of contract. So does Theridamas' oath of allegiance to Tamburlaine in Part I of the play:

> I yield myself, my men, and horse to thee,
> To be partaker of thy good or ill,
> As long as life maintains Theridamas.
> *Tamburlaine.*   Theridamas, my friend, here take my hand,
> Which is as much as if I swore by heaven
> And called the gods to witness to my vow.
> Thus shall my heart be still combined with thine,
> Until our bodies turn to elements,
> And both our souls aspire celestial thrones.   (I.ii.228-36)

To make evident the ritual here both Theridamas' surrender and Tamburlaine's oath of acceptance are based on the words and imagery of the marriage ceremony.15

A compact of disagreement comprises the exchange of boasting oaths made by Bajazeth and Tamburlaine before their battle. They resemble medieval flytings. Bajazeth swears "By Mahomet my kinsman's sepulcher,/ And by the holy Alcoran" to make Tamburlaine a eunuch; Tamburlaine, by his sword to rise through Bajazeth's fall (Part I, III.iii.75-86). A still different oath is the compact Edward II makes with himself. It comes as the turning point of the play, forming the reversal in Edward's character, the most moving and effective dramatic device in *Edward II*. When he learns that the barons have captured and killed Gaveston, he kneels and swears,

> By earth, the common mother of us all,
> By heaven, and all the moving orbs thereof,
> By this right hand, and by my father's sword,
> And all the honors 'longing to my crown,
> I will have heads and lives for him as many
> As I have manors, castles, towns, and towers.
>
> (III.ii.128-33)

Having sworn so vehemently, he rails out against the barons and then proceeds in another ceremony immediately to adopt Spencer and create him Earl of Gloucester and Lord Chamberlain. From this time forward Edward elicits the audience's sympathy; however weak he may appear at times, especially at his forced abdication, the right is on his side.

But the formal oath and contract is most effectively used in *Doctor Faustus*. Indeed the whole plot of the play turns upon the fearsome initial contract Faustus formalizes with Mephistophilis in the long ceremonies of its writing and reading (II.i. 48-111). Having called up Mephistophilis by means of a slight incantation, *"Veni, veni, Mephistophile,"* Faustus is asked to "write a deed of gift with my own blood." He stabs his arm and says, "Lo, Mephistophilis, for love of thee/ I cut my arm, and with my proper blood/ Assure my soul to be great Lucifer's." But as he writes, his blood congeals, and fire is brought to warm it before he can complete the writing and then say, "Consummatum est; the bill is ended,/ And Faustus has bequeathed his soul to Lucifer." The perversion of Christ's last words as he hung upon the cross (John xix.30) here foreshadows Faustus' own end and makes terrifying the irony of the words. The audience will remember the context of those words, their associations and implications: *"Cum ergo accepisset Jesus, dixit: Consummatum est. Et inclinato capite tradidit spiritum."* So Faustus unwittingly received the vinegar; so has he capitulated and given up the spirit; so has he crucified himself. A second part of the ceremony is the reading of the deed of gift now writ in blood. In the form of a legal contract, this instrument constitutes ironically a last will and testament.16

But before the diabolical compact can be effected, Faustus must meet and know an agent from Acheron. Such meeting can be accomplished only by yet another ritual, by a sensational magical conjuring and incantation. The conjuring has been prepared for at length. It is Faustus' first attempt at magic. Will it work? The audience is keyed up. Tension is at the breaking point when Faustus appears, draws his circle, names the figures in it, and with thunder in the background calls upon Mephistophilis to appear. The Latin incantation, or invocation, involves a frightening perversion of the liturgy of the Asperges with the making of the sign of the cross (I.iii.1-34). Suddenly Mephistophilis appears in his natural shape as a devil, only to be sent back to hell and ordered to change his shape and reappear as a Franciscan friar. Devils are shape-shifters, deceivers; the implication would not be lost on the audience. The intoning of the *"Sint mihi Dei Acherontis propitii"* by such an actor as Edward Alleyn, the thunder, the appearance of Mephistophilis in flames and smoke from the trapdoor were sensational enough, but the daring blasphemous perversion of rites provided a veritable purgation of emotion, an overwhelming experience.

A few less frequently occurring ceremonies and rites deserve mention for their dramatic effect. King Edward adopted Young Spencer and created him Earl of Gloucester and Lord Chamberlain. Earlier he had in formal ceremony created Old Spencer an earl: "Spencer, I here create thee Earl of Wiltshire,/ And daily will enrich thee with our favor,/ That as the sunshine shall reflect o'er thee" (*Edward II*, [III.ii.49-51]). The words suggest the liturgy of Confirmation. And in the same play, Queen Isabella similarly creates "our well-beloved son/ . . . Lord Warden of the realm" (IV.v.32-35), again echoing liturgical formulary and heightening occasion. Tamburlaine's formal greeting of the triumphant Theridamus is coupled with the latter's formal proffering him "my crown [that of Argier], myself, and all the powers I have" (Part II, I.v.1-16). And immediately following this ritualistic offering in scene vi comes the greeting and the offerings of Usumcasane and Techelles of their crowns of Morocco and Fez with all their power. Indeed the whole scene is made up of these formal offerings and Tamburlaine's acceptances. The most effective ritual of offering, however, is made by the newly crowned Edward III. In the very last lines of *Edward II* he lays the head of Young Mortimer on his father's "hearse" and says, "Sweet father, here unto thy murdered ghost/ I offer up this wicked traitor's head." Thus Edward II is vindicated in death and his bier is borne off in triumph. Finally, Marlowe gives us ritualized murders. Tamburlaine brings out his cowardly son Calyphas and, speaking a lengthy denunciation, asks Jove to "receive this fainting soul [of Calyphas] again," and then swears by Mahomet enmity to Jove for sending him such a son (Part II, IV.ii.28-56). And Guise in *The Massacre at Paris* runs down Loreine, a Huguenot who says he is a "preacher of the word of God," and stabs him. As he does so, he begins the recitation of a formulary from liturgy: " 'Dearly beloved brother'—thus 'tis written." Whereupon Anjou, who is with Guise, cries out gleefully, "Stay, my lord. Let me begin the psalm" (vi.6-9).[17] A ritualized murder, it enhances the brutality as well as the blasphemy and sacrilege of the two murderers.

I have pointed out examples enough and more to indicate the great number, and I have identified a wide variety of rites and ceremonies with which Marlowe enriched the dramatic value of his plays. I hope the evidence has shown that he was very conscious of what he was doing: that he was using them to heighten the emotional tension of an audience. They were ready at the poet's hand as a means for moving from narration to dramatization of his lengthy source materials, from the recitation of events to the presentation of events—more importantly, to the celebration of events. The audiences are not merely told that a conqueror wins a crown, but they see it placed upon his head with the proper, if foreshortened, words pronounced for the occasion; or they see a commoner created an earl according the proper rite; or they actually see a formal papal curse performed with bell, book, and candle. The rites and ceremonial processions furnish the means for action; prescribe what is to be done as well as what is to be said; direct the director, who disobeys at his peril. By their form the audience at once recognizes what they are and what they mean. Recognition brings satisfaction and enriches meaning. By means of rites or ritualized action the timelessness of the morality is in part fused with the "relentless progress of the chronicle," to quote Powell again. And frequently they take upon themselves the mystery of things.

But I believe Marlowe has done more. If he has not sounded a new note in his own peculiar use of ritual, he has at least exploited that use in his plays more than any earlier English dramatist: I speak of the ironic use, the perverted, the scornful and satirical. It occurs in all his plays, even in *Dido,* but more especially in *The Jew, The Massacre,* and *Doctor Faustus.* In these the rite, often perverted, turns unwittingly to ashes in the mouth of the speaker, or the words of the rite are consciously used for the reverse of their ritualistic intent.18 The petitions of prayers turn into curses; the burlesqued curse turns into a true curse; the procession of the Seven Deadly Sins brings, not revulsion, but their joyful welcome; that of the solemn papal court becomes a farce; the grace before meat curses the food; and catechisms are perverted. If not itself the very heart of dramatic action, the irony thus created provides the diastole whereby the pressure of the blood of action is built up powerfully for the systolic release which enables the necessary return for its purification. It is a powerful agent for emotional excitement and release, for the production of dramatic catharsis. And Marlowe has effectively used ceremony and ritual for this purpose. In so doing he has pointed the direction in which later dramatists were to go, especially Shakespeare, Marston, Webster, Beaumont and Fletcher, and Ford.

NOTES

1 "Marlowe's Spectacle," *TDR,* 8, 4 (Summer, 1964), 195.

2 Powell, p. 197.

3 See Robert Kimbrough, *"I Tamburlaine:* A Speaking Picture in a Tragic Glass," *Renaissance Drama,* 7 (1964), 20-34.

4 The usual evaluation of Marlowe's plays until fairly recent years has been that they are great "literary" achievements but poor stage plays. See *CHEL,* V, 169-76; or John Bakeless, *Christopher Marlowe: The Man in His Time* (New York: Washington Square Press, 1964), p. 210 (originally published in 1937); or Philip Henderson, *Christopher Marlowe* (London: Longmans, 1952), pp. 145-57; or Michel Poirier, *Christopher Marlowe* (London: Chatto & Windus, 1951), pp. 203-12; or Frederick S. Boas, *Christopher Marlowe: A Biographical and Critical Study* (Oxford: The Clarendon Press, 1940), pp. 312-13. Among others who, on the other hand, have found in Marlowe an effective writer for the stage, are Leo Kirschbaum, "Marlowe's *Faustus:* A Reconsideration," *RES,* 19 (1943), 225-41; Robert Ornstein, "The Comic Synthesis in *Doctor Faustus,"* *ELH,* 22 (1955), 165-72; A. L. Rowse, *Christopher Marlowe: His Life and Work* (New York: Harper & Rowe, 1964), pp. 67, 74, 139; Eric Rothenstein, "Structure and Meaning in *The Jew of Malta" JEGP,* 65(1966), 260-73; Marion Perret, *"Edward II:* Marlowe's Dramatic Technique," *REL,* 7, no. 4 (1966), 87-91; and James L. Smith, *"The Jew of Malta* in the Theatre," *Christopher Marlowe,* Mermaid Critical Commentaries, ed. Brian Morris (London: Ernest Benn, 1968), pp. 3-23.

5 The rise of realism brought with it a distrust of ritual and ceremony as effective dramatic devices. The realistic dramatists and their adherents seemed to believe that every event put upon the stage should be unique. Hence rite and ceremony, because they are set forms, basically mimetic and non-spontaneous, were said to blunt the

audience's expectation or disappoint their desire for surprise or dull their perceptions, thus weakening dramatic effect. See, for example, William Frost, "Shakespeare's Rituals and the Opening of *King Lear*," *Hudson Review* (Winter, 1957-58), reprinted in *Shakespeare: The Tragedies: A Collection of Critical Essays*, ed. Clifford Leech (Chicago: University of Chicago Press, 1956), pp. 190-200. Such misconceptions have in recent years been answered on the stage by the success of the plays of such dramatists as Dürrenmatt, Beckett, Brecht, Genet, and Christopher Fry, as well as by such historians and critics as O. B. Hardison, E. M. W. Tillyard, J. Dover Wilson, C. L. Barber, and especially Francis Fergusson.

6 Elsewhere I have briefly suggested that Marlowe made extensive use of processions and ceremonies in his plays. See my *Microcosmos: The Shape of the Elizabethan Play* (Lexington: University of Kentucky Press, 1965), pp. 92-93.

7 I accept, with the usual reservations about revisions, the usual canon of Marlowe's plays: *Tamburlaine*, Parts I & II, *The Massacre at Paris, Dido Queen of Carthage, The Jew of Malta, Edward II*, and *Doctor Faustus*. Unless otherwise noted, references are to *The Complete Plays of Christopher Marlowe*, ed. Irving Ribner (New York: Odyssey Press, 1963).

8 I count twenty scenes in Marlowe's plays in which a ruler holds court, a ritual sufficiently treated in my discussion of the processions.

9 Although I cannot claim absolute accuracy for these figures, they are close enough to reveal the extent of ritualistic action in the six plays: Betrothals 4, catechisms 2, challenges 1, charms 2, confessions 2, contracts 2, coronations 9, conferring of noble titles 3, curses 12, funerals (with procession) 3, formal greetings 2, incantations 3, laments 1, murder ritual 1, oaths 2, formal offerings 2, prayers 22. In addition one may consider the *tableau vivant* which opens *Dido* as ceremonial and the liturgical echoes in various places but especially in *Faustus* I.i.41-44 as ritualistic. The greatest number appears in *Tamburlaine*, some 28 in the two parts, 17 in *Doctor Faustus*, 12 in *The Jew of Malta*, 13 in *Edward II*, 9 in *The Massacre at Paris*, and 6 in *Dido*.

10 Another use of the betrothal rite is the reconciliation of Queen Isabella and Edward II. It is a reaffirmation of their betrothal, with its ironic overtones—an oath soon to be broken and with tragic consequences. (*Edward II*, I.iv.333-35.)

11 This charm appears first in the 1616 quarto, not in the 1604. It might, then, have come from the pen of a dramatist other than Marlowe, such as Samuel Rowley. On the other hand, it is quite in keeping with Marlowe's penchant for such devices; it is logically necessary to explain how Faustus could act invisibly at the banquet; and as Sir Walter Greg has argued, the 1604 quarto is a shortened version filled in and made complete in the 1616 quarto, probably from Marlowe's own drafts.

12 In Part II comes a very formal coronation of Callapine (III.i) requiring the whole scene, and at the end of the play comes the formal coronation of Amyras as part of the ceremonially staged death of Tamburlaine.

13 One here recalls that Faustus had (I.i.40-44) scorned the Scriptural caveat, "If we say we have no sin,/ We deceive ourselves, and there's no truth in us," by deliberately omitting the sentence of consolation immediately following, "If we confess our sins, he is faithful and just to forgive us our sins" (1 John 1.8-9). Faustus thus deceives himself. It is worth noting that the verse without the caveat just as Faustus quotes it is one of the prefaces to Morning Prayer in the Book of Common Prayer of Elizabeth. It immediately precedes the invitation to the General Confession.

14 Other varieties include Dido's celebrated immolation (V.i.302-13); Theridamas', Techelles', and Usumcasane's threefold prayer for the life of Tamburlaine (Part II, V.iii.1-41); and Barabas' prayer to the Prime Mover to damn the souls of his enemies to everlasting pain (I.ii.163-69).

15 Other examples of oaths involving compacts are these: the formal treaty sworn to by Sigismund and Orcanes (Part II, I.ii.45-68); another paralleling this sworn to

by Callepine and Almeda (Part II, I.iii.64-73); the formal compact made between Guise, Anjou, Dumaine, Gonzago, and Retes to "Kill all you suspect of heresy" in *The Massacre at Paris* (v.1-8); and that made by Mortimer Junior, Mortimer Senior, Lancaster, Warwick, and Queen Isabella in *Edward II* (I.iv.290-97) to return Gaveston to the court so as to prevent accusations of treason and enlist support of the people.

16 Two other oaths should be noted in *Doctor Faustus:* Having been tempted by the Good Angel to repent, Faustus is required by Lucifer, Beelzebub, and Mephistophilis to swear to keep his agreement; so he "vows never to look to heaven,/ Never to name God, or pray to him,/To burn his Scriptures, slay his ministers,/ And make my spirits pull his churches down" (II.ii.97-100). Later on, his request to see "bright-resplendent Rome" is accompanied by an oath sworn not by heaven but "by the kingdoms of infernal rule,/Of Styx, of Acheron, and the fiery lake/Of ever-burning Phlegethon" (III.i.47-51).

17 It is the customary beginning of invitations and admonitions spoken by the priest. The one here used and appropriate to the occasion derives from the opening of the invitation to the General Confession in the Book of Common Prayer: "Derely beloued Brethren, the Scripture moueth us in sondry places, to acknowledge and confesse our manifolde sinnes and wickednes, . . ."

18 James H. Sims has pointed out the frequent reversals of meaning in Marlowe's use of Biblical allusions, especially in *The Jew of Malta* and *Doctor Faustus.* See his *Dramatic Uses of Biblical Allusions in Marlowe and Shakespeare* (Gainesville: University of Florida Press, 1966), pp. 16ff.

The Changing Faces of Love
In English Renaissance Comedy

Ejner J. Jensen

In this paper I want to explore certain manifestations of love
in English Renaissance comedy, particularly the language of
love and the changing function of love as a theme. My path
will lead from Lyly to Fletcher (with and without Beaumont).
But this chronological disposition of the material ought not to
be taken as a signal that my topic is development. Surely we have
had ample warning in recent years of the latent evolutionist tendencies we all share to keep us from that fallacy. My topic is the
changing faces of love. The forces that brought about the
changes I will describe are varied and complex, and I am little
concerned here with influences outside the drama; my focus will
be on those aspects of love that the drama reveals on the stage.
Chronology will be violated in the case of Shakespeare, for as
usual he takes a way of his own; I will return to him in a final
section of this discussion.

The case of Lyly affords a useful starting point, for Lyly's
plays confront us immediately with many of the issues that sur-
round the comic presentation of love throughout this period. The
first of these is a question about the theme of love itself. (1) How
is love understood in these plays? — i.e., how does it operate
as a force in human affairs, and what do the characters believe
about its origins? (2) How far in these early plays is language
merely conventional, rhetorical patterning rather than an expression of feeling clearly related to the characters to whom it is
assigned? (3) And finally, what are the actors called upon to do
as they attempt to convey these aspects of love to their
audience?

To the first of these questions no easy answer is available,
though G. K. Hunter, in his fine book on Lyly, has provided the

most detailed available context for a discussion of the issue.[1] On
the surface the comedies of Lyly seem to offer, in unassimilated
form, most of the ideas about love in vogue at the time, including generous helpings of the paradoxes so dominant in the sonnet
most detailed available context for a discussion of the issue.[1] On
the surface the comedies of Lyly seem to offer, in unassimilated
tradition and in Shakespeare's early work. Cupid in *Gallathea*
defines love as

> A heate full of coldnesse, a sweete full of bitterness, a pain
> full of pleasantnesse; which maketh thoughts have eyes, and
> harts eares; bred by desire, nursed by delight, weaned by
> ielousie, kild by dissembling, buried by ingratitude; and this
> is love![2]

The nymph to whom he offers this precious commodity can only
conclude that "If it be nothing else, it is but a foolish thing"
(I.ii.14-21).

Foolish thing though it may be, love is nevertheless the
mainspring of dramatic action in Lyly's comedies—as a force
opposed to military and political greatness in *Campaspe,* as a
disruptive element in the lives of both gods and men in *Sapho
and Phao,* as a miraculous transforming power in *Gallathea,* and
as a pervasive and dominant universal influence in *Endimion.*
Most of the stock love themes are taken up in Lyly too. Unre-
quited love drives Tellus to seek revenge and reduces Venus to
a state of powerlessness. Conflicting claims of love and duty bid
for dominance in *Campaspe.* Love as a motion of the mind is
contrasted with love as a prompting of the flesh in *Endimion.*
Yet if we ask what the characters in Lyly believe about the
nature and origins of love, we are thrown directly against the
barrier of convention that surrounds these plays and makes them
to some degree inaccessible to modern readers. As we try to
come to terms with that convention and its particular manifestations in Lyly—allegory, mythological figures, and all the rest—
we can accept the answer given in another context as an explanation of convention's real function. We can try to see, that is,
that "allegory and the conceit do not hide or veil or conceal
meaning. They are rationalizing and analyzing devices without
which Western man could not have illuminated the dark secrets
of his own deepest nature."[3] But we should at the same time
recognize, as Michael R. Best[4] has demonstrated, that in the
sort of static drama created by Lyly the primary concern is

with the pattern itself, with the ideas arranged in the form of a debate, and that the characters function primarily as the servants of this pattern.

Now the language of Lyly's plays, language spoken both by goddesses and pretty pages, is eminently suited, in its extreme reliance on balance, for playing part against part and for presenting an echo to the sense of the play's argument. It so insistently calls attention to itself that were it not that "the word is overworn" we might describe it as Brechtian. And though the word does seem to have exhausted its usefulness, having been applied to everything from the inset fables in Webster to the silence of Gorboduc, the effects it signifies of distancing and of the creation for the spectator of an objective, analytical attitude are not inappropriate in describing Lyly's use of language. Euphuism as a style invites comparisons and contrasts. Put in the service of plots that set antithetical abstractions against one another, it necessarily operates at a remove from character. Thus situations that ought to gain force and immediacy as portrayals of universal human dilemmas emerge as the artful productions of the humanist as courtier. The very language that gives wit and point to the abstract issues insures, by its artificiality, that our concern as spectators will remain on the level of abstractions. But even this level, in most of the plays, seems hopelessly involved in confusion. Our idea that drama is a mirror offers little help when we cannot identify what is being reflected. This, I think, is the ultimate failure of Lyly's comedy. Language, a seemingly perfect instrument for the playwright's intended effects, leads nowhere but to itself again. Choice episodes of linguistic or poetic skill remain in our minds—"Cupid and my Campaspe," Endimion's lament (II.i.146)—but they seem set pieces for an anthology; and we feel in excerpting them none of the compunction that leads us in other instances to remark the effects lost by removing speeches from a dramatic context.

Then too the idea of character in Lyly is at once something distinctive and narrow. Just as plot exists in Lyly as a vehicle for ideas, so characters exist as agents of the plot. R. Warwick Bond, in a rhapsodic effusion found under the rubric "He Discovers Women," declared of Lyly that "first among English writers for the stage did he master a knowledge close enough, a taste fine enough, a hand light enough, to render in her wonted speech and fashion that inconstant gleam, that dancing firefly, the English girl."5 Something more than an awed awareness of the raging powers of Women's Liberation prompts me to suggest that, here at least, Professor Bond missed the mark; and to find in Lyly's women precursors of Beatrice and Rosalind as he does is to confuse hopelessly chronology and causality. For Lyly's comedy requires nothing like the grasp of character such claims suggest. For his purposes, the boy actors —brilliant, as Hunter suggests, as "cheeky pages," trained and disciplined "to make a single, controlled, unified effect"—were wholly satisfactory.

Other plays from this period that treat the theme of love are in short supply. F. P. Wilson remarks the absence, in plays written before 1584, of any anticipation of "comedy based upon the love between the sexes, the settled mode of the great age of Elizabethan comedy."6 Love figures as one of *The Three Ladies of London* in Robert Wilson's morality of 1581 and does no more than can be expected of her within the confines of such a design: she strays. Brought before the judge at the play's conclusion, she is forced to recognize how she has "become a monster/ Bolstering thyself upon the lasciviousness of Lucre."7 In *The Rare Triumphs of Love and Fortune* (1582), we find a mythological drama that turns on the question of what forces exert dominant power in the affairs of men. The play does, however, contain an interesting debate on the relationship between jealousy and love; Hermione provides a familiar catalogue of the symptoms of the malady of Love:

> Father if this be love to lead a life in thrall,
> To think the rankest poyson sweet to feed on hunny gall.
> To be at warre and peace, to be in joy and greefe
> then farthest from the hope of helpe, where neerest is releefe,
> To live and dye, to freeze and sweat, to melt yet not to move,
> if it be this to live in love, father I am in love.8

Such incapacitating contradictions are not, however, the lot of all the figures who are caught up in love's power. At the end of the 1580's two quite strikingly new female characters appeared on the English stage. Witty, self-assured, clear-sighted and tough-minded; more than any characters before them, they look forward to the independent spirit of Viola and the wit of Beatrice and Rosalind. These sprightly ladies are, of course, Margaret, the fair maid of Fressingfield, and Fair Em, the miller's daughter. King Edward is smitten with love of a Margaret whose "front is Beauty's table, where she paints/ The glories of her gorgeous excellence" (i.56-57); and he assigns to Lacy the responsibility of gaining her love for him. Margaret receives his advances and falls, but for Lacy himself, not Edward. Along the way, Greene illustrates Margaret's inherent excellence by contrasting her with some country bumpkins who serve as foils for her charms. But her chief triumph comes when Edward, having discovered all, issues a heavily Marlovian ultimatum: "Edward or none shall conquer Margaret" (viii.52). Her reply is properly courteous but firm, and though we may sense that her allusions are a bit precocious for one whose life has been circumscribed by cornfields and the creamery, it is nevertheless impressive:

> Pardon, my Lord. If Jove's great royalty
> Sent in such presents as to Danaë,
> If Phoebus, 'tired in Latona's weeds,
> Come courting from the beauty of his lodge,
> The dulcet tunes of frolic Mercury,
> Not all the wealth heaven's treasury affords,
> Should make me leave Lord Lacy or his love. (viii.67-73)

Fair Em contains a number of love complications involving William the Conqueror and his journey to Denmark where he falls in love not with Blanch, the original motive of his travels, but with Mariana, the beloved of his friend, Marquis Lubeck. But these entanglements fail to carry the interest commanded by the machinations of the play's brilliant eponym. In some cleverly designed stage fooling she manages to persuade one suitor that she is deaf and another that she is blind. By the play's conclusion she is defined as a remarkable woman indeed, and her graciousness moves the king to accept Blanch with the generous admission, "I see that women are not generall evils."

Despite the strong folklore influence on these two characters, the insistence on their natural goodness and the use of that motif as a vehicle for nationalistic propaganda in Greene, the plays on the whole present something new in the treatment of love. A fundamental change comes in the emphasis on a social setting. For all the stock elements at work here (elements of the Patient Griselda motif in *Friar Bacon,* for example), it is nevertheless true that Meg is seen enjoying herself at the local fair and that Em's father, though formerly Sir Thomas Godard, has in fact been reduced to a humble trade. Such an emphasis has incalculable ramifying effects on the total play; it creates a fundamentally different texture. And our response to this change is on as basic a level as we watch these characters come to terms with their dramatic worlds.

Margaret and Em are not figures in a debate about some love issue; they claim, as characters, some freedom of imagination and response. Their cleverness does not exist on the verbal level alone; it extends to invention and action, giving the spectator a wide range of possible responses and satisfying these responses in ways that are both striking and memorable. To see what this freedom of action means to our perception of comedy, we need only set these plays against one of Lyly's or against such an engaging minor triumph as Peele's *Arraignment of Paris*. In the latter play Oenone hardly figures in our recollection of dramatic effects, but "Cupid's Curse" remains a bright memory. It stays with us like one of the star's solo numbers from a Broadway musical or, to cite a more apposite comparison, like the double sestina spoken by Strephon and Klaius in *The Arcadia*.

The effects of *Fair Em* and *Friar Bacon* do not grow out of a response to that sort of art; they emerge instead from our perception of characters entangled in dramatic complexities. Such effects depend for their success on a certain credibility, and this brings me to a final point about these two plays of the late 1580's. In talking about Lyly's boy actors every fact known to us leads to the sort of judgment that Professor Hunter and others have made—that they were highly trained speakers, brilliant in ensemble, and capable of working together to achieve the intended dramatic ends. But there is little warrant for carrying this point of view over to a discussion of the boys who acted in the adult companies, and there is still less justification for appealing to the "piquancy" to be achieved by an awareness that the heroine's role is in fact being played by a young male actor. This whole question of the boy players and their capacity for sustaining a persuasive dramatic illusion has been discussed at length for many years, and it still seems that no single argument commands assent. What I wish to claim here is only this: that it seems probable that the boys who acted with men were capable, in their roles, of sustaining the dramatic illusion equally with the men of their company. Given this, it is fair to suggest that Lord Strange's Men, in presenting both *Friar Bacon* and *Fair Em* to the theatre public, offered something new in the way of character portrayal and thus gave dramatic force to the theme of love.9

For the next several years, if we except for the moment the early plays of Shakespeare, there is a paucity of love comedies until the emergence of Chapman as a comic dramatist toward the century's end. One is tempted to try to make sense of the season of 1595, which saw the appearance of such plays, now lost, as *The French Comedy, A Toy to Please Chaste Ladies, The Wonder of a Woman,* and *Long Meg of Westminster.* But that way, I fear, lies wasteful ribaldry and little profit. Moving instead to the plays written after 1598, we can discern a new complexity in the worlds of comic drama. Characters not only have identities, they have histories as well. Both young couples in *The Shoemakers' Holiday,* Lacy and Rose and Rafe and Jane, are forced to pursue their interests in the midst of the mad whirling atmosphere created by Simon Eyre; but Dekker succeeds in giving each of the lovers a dramatic life of his or her own. *Jack Drum's Entertainment, Eastward Ho, A Chaste Maid in Cheapside*—indeed most of the comedies written after the revival of the boys' companies—display a density of social texture that necessarily affects the meaning of the theme of love.

Marston surprises his audience by offering in *Jack Drum* a play in which the only requirement for marriage is to choose wisely. Sir Edward Fortune simply will not assume the role of blocking character and instead assures his daughters, "I have land for you both/ You have love for your selves" (pp. 186-87).10 In a play which numbers among its suitors a usurer, a cynical Frenchman, and a devotee of Euphuism, and which features in Camelia a grasping opportunist of a female, Marston explores a variety of attitudes toward love and its social meaning. *A Chaste Maid,* with its cartoon figures (Yellowhammer and Sir Walter Whorehound could find a home with Al Capp) and insistent hyperbole, only gives those meanings their most radically satirical reading. Both plays (and with them one might include *The Shoemakers' Holiday, Englishmen for My Money,* and most of the Beaumont and Fletcher love comedies) illustrate the union of the themes of love and money, a union indispensable to the production of comedy manners. Here then, in their complexly detailed milieux and in the inextricable relation of love's meaning to a social context, these later comedies display a leading characteristic.

A second identifying feature of these plays is a matter of character psychology. Theodore Spencer has pointed out that around the turn of the century one of the most important questions being asked by intelligent men was both simple and profound: "What is natural to man?" Spencer and others have described how this question becomes a focus of dramatic concern in Marston's *Dutch Courtezan,* a play that explores the issue of "the normality of concupiscence."[11] Marston's play, with its rather schematic opposition between Malheureux, the self-assured moralist whose morality evaporates at the sight of Franceschina, and Freevill, the sane and yet passionate lover, outlines the question as love *versus* lust. That opposition is not in every case made so extreme in other plays on this subject, many of which seem concerned only to establish the value of love. But whatever particular arguments they may advance, their real theme is that love *is* natural to man and indeed (often comically, even catastrophically) inevitable. This is the leading theme of Chapman's *The Widow's Tears* and of Fletcher's *The Captain,* where Angelo, drawn against his will to see Lelia, laments,

> I have read Epictetus twice over against the
> Desire of these outward things, and still her face runs in
> My mind.   (V.293)[12]

In *The Coxcomb* Valerio argues that such intellectual hesitations should be avoided, for "love . . . is an extreme desire,/ That's not to be examin'd, but fulfill'd" (VII, 345).

This assertion of love's power and naturalness appears in a delightfully comic way in *The Fair Mind of the Exchange.* Two of the brothers Golding are in love. The third, Franke, is a scoffer at love who denies its power. When Ferdinand describes his symptoms and says that love has caused his distress, he goes on to identify love for Franke as "a little boy that's blind." His brother's derision is boundless:

> And be overcome by him! plagude by him!
> Driven into dumps by him! put downe by a boy!
> Master'd by love! O, I am mad for anger:
> By a Boy! is there no rosemary and bayes in England
> To whip the Ape? by a boy! (11. 299-303)[13]

And when brother Anthony, having revealed his lovesickness, asks Franke to define love, he answers with a disdain possible only to one who has never felt its sweet pangs. It is, he declares, merely

> A voluntary motion of delight,
> Touching the superficies of the soule, . . .
> Which motion as it unbeseemes a man,
> So by the soule and reason which adorne,
> The life of man it is extinguished,
> Even at his pleasure that it does possesse. (11. 351-60)

Such hubris demands a fall, of course, and in short order, Franke, having "dipt his foote . . . in Loves scalding streame," confesses that he is "a poore enamorate, and enforcde with the Poet to say, Love orecomes all" (11.515-17).

That motto, honored we recall in different ways by Chaucer's Prioress and his Wife of Bath, signifies an equal range of meanings in the comedies under discussion. Perhaps the most obvious reflection of their variety comes in the language, where bawdy talk, pervasive sexual puns, and the never-failing jokes on cuckoldry are continually brought before us. *The Dutch Courtezan,* in addition to the contrast described earlier, also employs the opposition between Beatrice, Freevill's love, and Crispinella, her sister. Beatrice is moved by the traditional language of love; she has made of the imagery of Freevill's sugared sonnets a vision of her life in marriage. Crispinella, a tough-minded realist, insists on seeing things as they are. When Beatrice quotes from Freevill's sonnet on a kiss—"Purest lips, soft banks of blisses" (III.i.4)—Crispinella launches an attack on the "unsavory" ceremony and concludes, "for my part, I had as lief they would break wind in my lips" (III.i.23-24).14 What Crispinella advocates is not a rejection of love, but an honest awareness of what it means and a forthright acceptance of that meaning—an ability, in her words, to "consider nature without apparel" (1. 35). Crispinella's function is that of an extreme designed to define by its opposition to another extreme a valid center position. It is a function shared by other characters in these plays and carried out primarily through the instrument of language. This dramatic strategy, described in a persuasive way for Shakespeare by Peter Phialas, often operates in conjunction with a plot-subplot structure, giving a lively dimension of wit to the treatment of the theme of love.

With language playing so important a part in defining love, language which is forthright and bawdy in its physical descriptions, it is not surprising that we find in these plays of the early seventeenth century a far greater emphasis on love displays than we have seen before. In *Love's Cure, or The Martial Maid,* Vitelli is urged to make trial of Clara's lips. He does so, and, begging a second opportunity, pronounces them "The best I ever tasted" (VIII, 214). In the plays of this period we see a greater emphasis on physical affection than ever before. The stage becomes an area for displaying not ideas about love but the experience of love; and spectators are not asked to entertain propositions but to experience vicariously the loves of dramatic characters. One may see in this emphasis, I believe, one aspect of the same audience-play relationship that fostered the vogue for tragi-comedy.

In combination, these aspects of comedy—a detailed social context, an emphasis on character psychology, language adjusted to the demands of character portrayal, and on-stage expressions of love and affection—help to produce the realism that marks these plays in a distinctive way. One other aspect of their design ought to be noted. Plot, most often an intrigue plot of some variety, is limited to the world of the play for its meanings. It is not a vehicle for ideas, nor does it seem determined in any arbitrary way. It appears instead as an unfolding of events determined by the human agencies operating within the play. From one point of view, this is merely another function of realism, but I should like to stress that it is an aspect which affects, in profound ways, the audience response.

It is now time to turn to Shakespeare and his treatment of the theme of love. Our first glance tells us that ideas about love are everywhere in Shakespeare but subject always to the pressure of particular fictional circumstances. Thus Valentine, a new convert to the religion of love, speaking to that false friend and inconstant lover, Proteus, says, "Love's a mighty lord." Don Armado, bemused and babbling, finds that "Love is a familiar; Love is a devil. There is no evil angel but love"; and, resigning himself to the power of this spirit, he rationalizes that "Cupid's butt-shaft is too hard for Hercules' club, and therefore too much odds for a Spaniard's rapier." Iago replies contemptuously to Roderigo that his amorous protestations are silly; love, he assures the gull, is a mere "sect or scion" of lust. In the sonnets, of course, one sees a similar disparity: love in its ideal form is "an ever-fixed mark"; as lust it becomes wholly illusory, "Before, a joy proposed; behind, a dream." These diverse accounts of love may help us to an awareness of the word's meaning in Shakespeare. It is a powerful but inexplicable force, transforming men and altering their relation to the world around them. Thus Berowne, finding for himself and the other academicians an explanation for the failure of their enterprise, comes to understand that "love . . ./ Lives not alone immurèd in the brain," but ". . . adds a precious seeing to the eye." Still, the influence of love has its limits, as both reason and Rosalind tell us: "men have died from time to time, and worms have eaten them, but not for love." Nothing more clearly defines Shakespeare's skill as a dramatic craftsman than his management of these various attitudes toward love. Shakespeare's "comic point of view," Peter Phialas has argued, "qualifies both the Petrarchan hyperboles of romantic lovers . . . and the exclusively physical concerns of anti-romantic characters," a circumstance which makes his outlook perfectly suited to his dramatic designs since, as Phialas declares, "the juxtaposition of extremes was, both early and late in his career, a structural necessity."15

Shakespeare's Romantic Comedies, Professor Phialas' attempt to define "The Development of Their Form and Meaning," is one of the latest in a long series of attempts to get at the essential qualities of Shakespeare's comedies of love. The nearly schematic orderliness he discerns in these plays—their neatly balanced opposites, their delicate attunement of structure and theme—appeals to us in part because emerging from it we catch the outline of the pattern's creator, a Shakespeare who is wise (and serene in his wisdom), who is able "to present the lovers' ideal against the fact of man's physical being" and yet somehow able to rest in the assurance that "love is the supreme value in life, that it gives measure and meaning to all human relationships."16 But however persuasive such a view of Shakespeare may be, the particular arguments that bring it to light may not prove so convincing at every point. This should not surprise us, for most of the attempts to discover a single pattern in Shakespearean comedy have likewise proven unsatisfactory. "Each master-key," says Professor Harbage, "while it may work with some hypothetical master-comedy, sticks in the lock of each of Shakespeare's actual comedies."17

Nevertheless, in considering Shakespeare's love comedies it is important to look first at the function of plot; for plot operates here in a fundamentally different way from anything we see before or after. Shakespeare's plots are not designed either to mirror ideas about love or to treat a realistic love situation within the context of a world of affairs and human limitations. They seem designed rather to illustrate the conditions of lovers and the meaning of being in love, and they work toward this end by focusing not on character development but on character at a particular moment in time. This technique is developed most fully in the final plays, where linear dramatic action is at times ignored altogether in the interest of achieving an insight into a character's state of mind. An attitude of forgiveness is the final goal of many of the characters in the last plays, but Shakespeare expends little dramatic energy in drawing the path to that state; he focuses instead on what it means to the character to have achieved it. This is particularly striking in *Henry VIII,* but it is true of the romances as well. Our chief response is to states of being rather than to the struggles of characters as they contend with parental, or social, or economic opposition.

This focus on character in a particular situation or state of mind appears often enough in the comedies for it to be tempting to adopt Wallace Stevens' shorthand: "Pages of illustrations." Perhaps an example or two will suffice. *The Two Gentlemen of Verona* develops the familiar Renaissance theme of the relative importance of love and friendship. Proteus rejects Julia and steals Silvia from his friend Valentine. At the play's conclusion, Valentine, moved by Proteus' repentance, accepts his apology and in a startling demonstration of forgiveness, says, "All that was mine in Silvia I give thee." This line has been the occasion of much ingenuity, for critics have been reluctant to accept Valentine's action. But his offer, if it is that, stands for only a short while, Julia's swoon and the ensuing revelations bringing us quickly to a resolution of all difficulties and the prospect of a sixteenth-century Veronese commune—"one house, one mutual happiness"—perhaps Valentine's most shocking proposal. Tracing the play's events we discover a number of transformations, with those of Proteus, as befits his name, most pronounced. Of the processes that lead to these transformations we learn very little. They occur, but our attention is focused on their manifestations: Valentine as lover, Proteus as false friend, Julia as rejected love. Similarly, in *Love's Labor's Lost,* the plot constitutes a rather mechanical demonstration of the power of love and the blinding effects of love at first sight. Whatever slight interest the plot possesses seems insignificant when set against the display of the academicians' follies and the wit of the triumphant women.

Twelfth Night is by nearly universal agreement the most brilliant of the love comedies. Yet it is surely remarkable that the lovers in the play are never together on stage in a relationship of man to woman (except for the brief moment when Olivia seizes upon the befuddled Sebastian) until the final scene. We are in the most conventional of worlds, and despite the antics of actresses whose eyes light up at the news of Orsino's continued bachelorhood, we should not be led to think of the play in Professor Draper's terms as a play about "social security" any more than we should worry about Illyria's political stability with such a distracted helmsman as Orsino. Everything about *Twelfth Night* announces its conventionality, from Viola's opening "Perchance he is not drowned" to the wonderfully contrived recognition scene. Shakespeare invites his spectators to relax in the comfort of familiar plot surroundings so that within the secure bounds of convention he can create telling dramatic effects. Many of these effects in *Twelfth Night* are produced by the tension between Viola's attempt to play her role successfully and her desire to declare herself to Orsino, a tension handled with the greatest artistic assurance in II.iv. This whole scene is dominated by melancholy and by a sense that Viola is being infected by the pervasive lovesickness of Orsino's court. Feste's song, which "dallies with the innocence of youth," gives a cue for Viola's account of her father's daughter, who "loved a man." In the Russian film version of *Twelfth Night* this scene is handled brilliantly, with Orsino seated against a tree and Viola a bit forward of him, her elbow on his knee. This posture lets us know how far the forces of love have operated on them and gives a special poignancy to Viola's abrupt departure.

Similar brilliant moments appear throughout Shakespearean comedy, and their invariable effect is the creation of a rush of sympathy that brings the audience into direct contact with this moment in time. One occurs at Portia's aside when Bassanio announces his choice of the leaden casket, a moment again introduced by a song:

> O love, be moderate, allay thy ecstacy,
> In measure rain thy joy, scant this excess!
> I feel too much thy blessing.   (III.ii.111-14)

The unwitting confession of Rosalind's swoon creates the same effect in a nearly-farcical vein:

> Ah, sirrah, a body would
> think this was well counterfeited. I pray you tell your
> brother how well I counterfeited. Heigh-ho! (IV.iii.166-68)

and the overwhelmingly grand appearance of Theseus and Hippolyta in the woods reproduces it on a level of magnificent and mature love.

C. H. Herford once argued that "the 'ways of love' which [Shakespeare] treats as comic material are not plausible or subtle approximations to romantic passion, but ludicrously absurd counterfeits of it."[18] But that is the argument of a scholar making a judgment on Shakespeare's plots. The reader alert to stage effects will carry away a far different impression, an impression shaped by the dramatic power of such moments as I have just described to bring the spectator into the closest possible relation with the character on stage.

This concern for short-range effects has as a corollary the fact that Shakespeare pays little attention to the social milieu in which his characters play out their roles. His typical comic world is reduced to the essentials, making use only of these elements required to establish dramatic conflict. What matters is the pressure brought upon the lovers; the sources of that pressure are of minimal importance. Such an emphasis seems ideal for presenting a distillation of the love experience and avoiding the obstacles to audience involvement set up by particulars of time and place, or by manifestations of a recognizably contemporary society.

The language of love in Shakespeare's comedies is, as I suggested earlier, remarkably varied. Orsino's hyperbolic amorousness is qualified explicitly by Feste—"I would have men of such constancy put to sea, that their business might be everything, and their intent everywhere" (II.iii.74-76)—and by contrast with the earthiness of the subplot, where Maria is "as witty a piece of Eve's flesh as any in Illyria" (I.v.25-26). Bottom, an asinine Orsino with Mustardseed and Cobweb rather than Valentine and Curio attending on his whims, and Touchstone, pressing in "amongst the rest of the country copulatives," function in similar ways to help define Shakespeare's idea of love in their respective plays. Peter Phialas has developed this idea rather extensively, and there is no need here to detail its several manifestations. It might be appropriate, though, simply to point to the continuation of this technique in the love tragedies, where Mercutio, Iago, and Enorbarbus reduce the language of love to realistic and even crude levels and thus reveal something of the misconceptions by which the heroes are misled.

As with everything in Shakespeare, we are likely to feel that his dramatic treatment of the theme of love requires a special brilliance in the presentation if it is to be realized in all its complexity and beauty. Yet we know too that the clarity of his dramatic vision renders such demands superfluous. Shakespeare's idea of love is always in the play itself; actors do not have an obligation to function both as characters and as elements in a significant design whose meaning is extra-dramatic. Love in Shakespeare's comedies springs into life. In all of Renaissance drama it stands as the fullest achievement of the poet's capacity to create a golden world. With Sidney in mind we may say, finally, that Shakespeare's treatment of love is poetical. And if some Audrey, a bit suspicious of our intentions (or Shakespeare's) should say, "I do not know what poetical is. Is it honest in deed and word? Is it a true thing?", our reply must be as simple and as significant as Touchstone's—"No, truly; for the truest poetry is the most faining, and lovers are given to poetry."

NOTES

1 *John Lyly: The Humanist as Courtier* (London, Routledge and Kegan Paul, 1962).

2 All quotations from Lyly are taken from *The Complete Works of John Lyly,* ed. R. Warwick Bond (1902; rpt. Oxford Univ. Press, 1967).

3 From the introduction to the *Amoretti* in *Edmund Spenser, Books I and II of The Faerie Queen, The Mutability Cantos, and Selections from The Minor Poetry,* ed. Robert Kellogg and Oliver Steele (New York: Odyssey Press, 1965), p. 453.

4 "Lyly's Static Drama," *Renaissance Drama,* N. S. 1 (1968), 75-86.

5 Bond, II, 283.

6 *The English Drama, 1485-1585,* ed. G. K. Hunter (Oxford Univ. Press, 1969), p. 115.

7 In *A Select Collection of Old English Plays,* ed. W. C. Hazlitt, 4th ed. (London, 1874), VI, 369.

8 Prepared by W. W. Greg for the Malone Society Reprints (Oxford, 1930), 11. 938-43.

9 This limited claim is all that my present argument requires. In "The Style of the Boy Actors," *Comparative Drama,* 2 (1968), 100-14, I offer a more extended view of this question.

10 References are to the edition of H. Harvey Wood (London, 1934-39).

11 See Spencer's article, "John Marston," in *Criterion,* 13 (1934), 581-99; and see also Paul M. Zall, "John Marston, Moralist," *ELH,* 27 (1960), 30-43.

12 All quotations from Beaumont and Fletcher are taken from the ten-volume edition in *The Cambridge English Classics,* ed. Arnold Glover and A. R. Waller, and will be cited by volume and page numbers.

13 I quote from the Malone Society reprint prepared by Peter H. Davison (Oxford, 1962).

14 These quotations are taken from the edition of M. L. Wine in the Regents Renaissance Drama Series (Lincoln, Nebraska, 1965).

15 *Shakespeare's Romantic Comedies: The Development of Their Form and Meaning* (Chapel Hill: University of North Carolina Press, 1966), pp. 214, 110.

16 Phialas, p. xvi.

17 In the foreword to the comedies in *Shakespeare, The Complete Works* (Baltimore: Penguin Books, 1969), p. 54.

18 *Shakespeare's Treatment of Love and Marriage and Other Essays* (London: T. Fisher Unwin, 1921), p. 36.

The Allegory of Wisdom in Lyly's *Endimion*

Carolyn Ruth Swift

John Lyly's *Endimion: The Man in the Moon* is considered by many scholars to be either an allegory of love or a political allegory.1 While these interpretations provide certain insights into *Endimion,* they do not explain adequately the intriguing references to knowledge that appear throughout the play. I suggest that *Endimion* is an allegory of wisdom.

According to its title-page, *Endimion* was first performed before Queen Elizabeth on Candlemas by the Children of Paul's. Candlemas, the traditional name for the Feast of Purification of St. Mary the Virgin, commemorates the ritual purification of Mary after the birth of Jesus and the presentation of Jesus at the temple in Jerusalem. The holy day became in Protestant England a celebration of human aspiration to purity and to the highest possible knowledge—knowledge of God. The Collect in *The Boke of common praier* of 1559 reads, "Almightie and euerlasting God, we humbly beseche thy maiestie, that as thy onely begotten sonne, was this daye presented in the Temple, in substaunce of our fleshe, so graunte that we maye be presented unto the with pure and cleare myndes. . . ." Donne calls the feast "a day of purification to us" and discusses how to learn the essence of God by exaltation of the five senses, of reason, and of understanding—the sensual and intellectual faculties of the soul or mind as understood in the Renaissance.2

The lessons to be read during the morning and evening services on Candlemas are Chapters 9 and 12 of *The Book of the Wisdome of Salomon.* Not every verse of *Wisdome* corresponds to action or theme in *Endimion;* however, the main events in the plot of the play are all present in that book of *Apocrypha.*3 Just as Endimion loves and desires to serve Cynthia from his youth, Salomon loved and wished to marry the female personification of Wisdom in his youth (8.2). Just as Endimion

61

endures his trance and its visions because of the magic of Dipsas, so Salomon says that the unwise are "scattered abroad in the darke couering of forgetfulnes, . . . troubled with visions" (17.3) and with magical illusions (17.7). Just as Tellus must confess the malice that caused her to seek the aid of Dipsas, so Salomon also says that "malice is condemned by her owne testimonie" (17.10). Just as Endimion gains perpetual youth from Cynthia, Salomon gains immortality through Wisdom (8.13). Just as Cynthia restores the lives of the characters in the play to order, Wisdom "renueth all" (7.27).

These parallels demonstrate the similarity between the action of the play and that of *The Book of Wisdome,* but a more subtle resemblance between the two lies in their presentation of reality. In *Endimion,* plot, character, and scene are deliberately confused so that knowledge of ultimate truth becomes beyond the understanding of any human without divine aid. In *The Book of Wisdome,* Salomon asks, "And hardly can we discerne the things that are vpon earth, and with great labour finde we out the things which are before vs: who can then seke out the things that are in heauen?" (9.16). The answer is that God grants wisdom by sending his holy spirit from above (9.17). Lyly constructed his play to imitate the difficulty of discerning the truth about "the things that are vpon earth." Endimion's actions also show the continual spiritual ascent of the dedicated human mind to knowledge of "the things that are in heauen." Wisdom in the figure of Cynthia who possesses her power "by the eternall Gods" (V.iii.25)[4] expands Endimion's knowledge of the divine mysteries of the universe. The ravishment of the trance aids his faculty of understanding to achieve higher knowledge.

Although previous critics of *Endimion* have not recognized that the play is drawn from the reading and the Collect for Candlemas, Lyly's audience would have immediately recognized the play's relation to the liturgy and would have understood that the subject was the acquisition of a pure and clear mind, capable of understanding God's truth. They would have recognized the play's portrayal of the complexity of discovering the truth about mysterious reality because Lyly chose as a protagonist Endimion, who was well-known to be "a manne, whiche founde the course of the mone." To some mythographers, Endimion's love of the moon symbolized his quest for knowledge. For example, Abraham Fraunce in *The third part of the Countesse of Pem-*

brokes Yuychurch describes Endimion as "a figure of the soule of man, kissed of Diana in the hill, that is, rauished by celestiall contemplation."5

In the first section of this paper, I demonstrate that Lyly stresses paradox and human error in order to depict the problems that occur in attempts to understand reality. I then show that Lyly suggests the possibility of human aspiration to knowledge by the use of parallel love actions that are analogous to the Platonic and Neoplatonic system of corresponding levels of reality and knowledge. In the second and third sections of the paper, I show that Lyly draws upon Renaissance conceptions of the power of words and upon the ideas of Neoplatonists such as Giordano Bruno and scientists such as John Dee and Thomas Digges to distort time and space and thus to imitate the multifarious complexities of reality. In the fourth section, I identify Cynthia and Endimion. My conclusion is that John Lyly's allegory of wisdom is based upon *The Book of the Wisdome of Salomon* and may be one of the "new songs" that John Jewel suggested be written in celebration of England's deliverance from error by God's "handmaid" and "instrument," Queen Elizabeth. In *Certaine Sermons,*6 Jewel urged both the Queen and her people to seek "perfect knowledge" just as it is sought by Cynthia and Endimion.

I

The difficulty of understanding reality is introduced at once in the first scene by the portrayal of intellectual error and by the demonstration of deceptive perceptions. In the opening speeches of the play, Lyly shows that error results when individuals mistake opinion for knowledge of the truth. Eumenides argues that Endimion's love for the moon is irrational and doomed to failure since the moon is not capable of affection. Because the myth of Endimion is both ancient and familiar, we know that Endimion's devotion to Cynthia will in fact be rewarded by her kiss. We recognize that the opinion of Eumenides is wrong. Because logic and natural experience justify the concern of Eumenides for his friend's apparent folly, we see the inadequacy of logic and the unreliability of opinion based upon experience. Although Eumenides is absolutely certain that Endimion is mad, it is Eumenides, not Endimion, who feeds on fancies (I.i.23).

Lyly not only shows that our thought processes err, but he

demonstrates how distorted our perceptions often are. Endimion, the man who found the moon's true course, speaks as an authority when he says, "O fayre *Cynthia,* why doe others terme thee vnconstant, whom I haue euer founde vnmoueable?" (I.i.30-31). To us Cynthia seems inconstant because the moon that we look at each night appears different. We know, however, and Endimion knows, that the moon in reality is unchanging and keeps a steady course. Because Cynthia's changing before our eyes is as factual as is the unchanging moon in its settled course, the description of Cynthia either as constant or as inconstant is partly correct and yet partly wrong. Since our incorrect judgment becomes part of the world that we know, the more we attempt to explain reality, the more our conception of it becomes distorted. Reality itself then becomes more problematic and mysterious.

Questions about reality are raised also by Lyly through his use of the word "love." As different people in *Endimion* claim the name "lover," the audience is forced to see that human love varies and that it is a misconception to believe that the expression "love" has an easily recognizable meaning. Misconceptions about the meaning of the word "love" raise corollary questions about our knowledge of reality. We do not know the true nature of love because it appears to us in varied shapes. We observe that Tellus plots to enchant Endimion because of her agony of love. We also see that while Endimion insists upon his devotion to Cynthia in Scene i, he has given to Tellus "oathes without number, . . . kisses without measure, . . . to deceiue a poore credulous virgin" (I.ii.7-8). What, then, is love if it can be seen as devotion, as feigned affection, and even as hate?

The sub-plot parody of the varieties of love in the main plot raises the question of the relationship between love and knowledge. Tophas' strange, self-deceiving infatuation with Dipsas causes him to imagine that his wit is increased (III.iii.63). He writes sonnets and possesses untamed thoughts. His lovesickness burlesques the rituals of love that earlier generations of lovers and writers had proposed seriously as the stairway to knowledge and that Lyly himself accepts in Endimion's "service" to Cynthia (V.iii.242). Instead of increasing wit and achieving knowledge, do lovers really only write fourth-rate sonnets?

Platonists and Neoplatonists would say that the diverse forms of "love" are but reflections of real Love. In the main plot,

Lyly focuses upon this difference between real and apparent love through Floscula's statement that "Affection that is bred by enchauntment" is only like love "in colour and forme . . . but nothing at all in substance or sauour" (I.ii.70-73). The perplexity caused by varied images of real Love is evinced in the sub-plot by introduction of the frank flirtation of Favilla and Scintilla with the pages and by pretended flirtation with Tophas (II.ii). What is only a reflection of reality is itself reflected; pretended flirtation is a debasement of real flirtation which is a debased image of love.

All the images of love that Lyly presents are ultimately contrasted with Endimion's love of Cynthia, a passion that is impervious to physical desire. Although in Act V Cynthia calls Endimion's devotion by the name of "love," she makes it clear that its nature is "honorable respect" (V.iii.179-80). Since all the characters in the play humble themselves to her, we must conclude that Lyly saw all physical love as secondary to the honoring of an idea, an intellectual process.

By these varied manifestations of love, Lyly demonstrates that all questions about the nature of love ultimately concern the difficulty of knowing anything. Can humans ever find truth if they do not know the real nature of love, the Neoplatonic road to knowledge?

II

The action and characters of the sub-plot show us that Lyly's stress is not upon the nature of love but upon the difficulty of understanding the truth about reality. When we first meet Sir Tophas in Act I, Scene iii, he is not a lover but a self-deceived braggart who sees himself as "all *Mars* and *Ars*" (I.iii.91). His actions parallel the main action, and his foolish boast that he devised war (I.iii.50) parodies Endimion's aspiration to love a goddess. Indeed, the braggart and Cynthia's lover use similar words and phrases as they credit themselves with divinity. Endimion says, "Vaine *Eumenides*, whose thoughts neuer grow higher then the crowne of thy head" (I.i.70-71), while Tophas echoes, "Welcome children, I seldome cast mine eyes so low as to the crownes of your heads" (II.ii.100). When Tophas and Endimion speak of their high thoughts, they echo lines from *Isaiah* 55.8-9: "For my thoughts are not your thoughts, neither are your ways my ways, saith the Lord. For as the heavens are higher than the earth, so are my ways higher than your ways, and my thoughts higher than your thoughts."

These lines are also cited by John Jewel in the sixth sermon preached before Queen Elizabeth at Paul's Cross in 1569 and first printed in 1583 when Lyly was producing plays for the Children of Paul's. Lyly may even have read the sermon while working on *Endimion,* whose composition Bond places between 1584 and 1585 and whose first performance Bond places in 1586. Chambers and Hunter date its performance in 1588. Even if the coincidence of locale did not interest him, a courtier who was struggling for the attention of the Queen, as Lyly was, would hardly ignore the contents of sermons that had pleased her and that were relevant enough to contemporary concerns to be newly printed. The special relevance of Jewel's sermons to Reformation England is demonstrated in the margins of a 1583 edition of the sermons, now at Houghton Library, Harvard University. A hand of the late sixteenth or early seventeenth century has written frequently: "a good note for this time."

Jewel interprets Isaiah to his congregation as warning them to "Think that thou mayest be deceived." Mortals lack the wisdom, he says, to realize that the thoughts which they think to be high may only serve their own fancy.[7] The use by Tophas of words that suggest the same biblical phrase ("high thoughts") that Endimion also uses emphasizes the distinction between fancy and knowledge and at the same time shows the difficulty that people have in recognizing that distinction. Whereas in Scene i, Eumenides thought Endimion to be governed by his own fancies, the vain thoughts of Tophas truly are fanciful.

In *Endimion* the words "high" or "height" and "reach" function not only to suggest the possibility of self-deception; they also constitute *leitmotifs* of aspiration.[8] With Tophas' goal of heroism so closely linked to Endimion's goal of loving the moon, we translate Endimion's goal of love to human aspiration in general. And since humans aspire to reach a goal, just as they love, because of what they know or think they know about the objects they seek, the main plot and its parodic sub-plot both stress the overwhelming importance of discerning the truth.

At the same time that Lyly emphasizes the importance of knowledge of reality, he intensifies the difficulty of understanding the world that he presents. He increases confusion about the nature of the characters and also shows that speech, which should increase understanding, may instead cause confusion.

All of the characters appear to be what they are not. We see that Endimion does not have the sterling qualities of which he boasts—qualities that all of the play's characters attribute to him and that we expect to see rewarded at the end of romances. As the discoverer of the true course of the moon, Endimion typifies the man who, according to another of John Jewel's *Certaine Sermons,* was thought erroneously "to be most perfect" because he "beheld the heavens best" (*Works,* II, 1044). Our expectation of Endimion's perfection is also erroneous. Endimion hides his "darke sinnes" as do the unrighteous and unwise in Salomon's *Book of Wisdome* (17.3), and the devotion of the good Eumenides mutes our condemnation of Endimion's exploitation of Tellus "as a cloake" for his affections for Cynthia (II.i.23). But the bitterly angry response of Tellus to Endimion's frailty shocks us into awareness that vital human relationships are easily altered through misunderstandings of another person's real nature. Unless we acknowledge the importance of Endimion's maintaining correspondence between his inner nature and his appearance, we must accept as a norm none other than Tophas, the braggart-hero of the sub-plot, who is the *reductio ad absurdum* of Endimion's assertion that he is what he is not. Lyly stresses the deceptiveness of appearance in other characters, too. Tellus, who seems soft, is cruel (V.iii.70), and Cynthia appears changeable and cold, although she is really constant (III.iv.157) and merciful (III.i.56). The difference is that Cynthia deceives no one deliberately. Those on earth both deceive each other and misjudge Cynthia.

Lyly further emphasizes the unreliability of knowledge based upon appearance through the comments of Epiton and Eumenides, the companions of Tophas and Endimion. Both of these characters firmly believe that they know their friends to be fools. Epiton knows that fishing is not the chivalric warfare that Tophas thinks it is, just as Eumenides thinks that Endimion's love is not only ridiculous—the result of "peeuish" imagination (I.i.19)—but blasphemous (I.i.66). But Eumenides proves to be wrong in thinking that Endimion's quest is impossible, whereas Epiton is correct in viewing Tophas as absurd, for, in contrast to Endimion, Tophas is a self-deceived braggart whose verbal aspirations are not based on his own inner nature or on the real world about him because he knows neither of these. He may desire to be a hero, but he is not of heroic stock, and his battles are with wrens and larks (II.ii.73-74). Tophas is deluded because what he learns is learned from his disordered senses alone (III.iii.6-14). In contrast, the daring, imaginative love-quest of the deceptive Endimion succeeds. Because of his "true hart" (V.ii.181), Endimion enlarges his understanding through contemplation (V.iii.176), is accepted by Cynthia as her servant, and the impossible union between a mortal and the moon is rendered possible.

Events as improbable as Cynthia's acceptance of Endimion's service, and as similar to the "wonderous marueiles" of God described in *The Book of Wisdome* (19.8) are described by Jewel in *Certaine Sermons* as intended by God to be contrary to "all man's reason" and to all sense of nature in order to heighten awareness of the power of God to bring "all these things to pass."9 Yet Lyly's presentation of this resolution emphasizes paradoxically what Salomon calls the obscurity of "the things that are vpon earth," for if deception resides in a "true hart" and if the impossible is really possible, how can anything have a fixed nature and how can mortals comprehend truth?

As the characters of the play attempt to comprehend the realities of their world, Lyly frequently stresses the mysterious powers of speech to change the world either destructively or constructively. Again it is by means of the sub-plot that Lyly stresses that people may present a false appearance to the external world by their mode of speech and that their speech may also give an important clue to their true nature. Because Tophas is a braggart, he displays the ultimate indifference to truth about the external world and about himself when he tries to change substances by giving them new names. He thinks that if fishing is called "warfare," the fisherman becomes a warrior. He thinks also that he will have a beard if Epiton names his "three or foure little haires" a beard (V.ii.18-20). When Tophas misuses the meanings of words and the devices of grammar and rhetoric, Lyly is utilizing stock devices of Renaissance comedy and romance to focus our attention on attitudes toward language in the main plot. There many actions occur merely because of the correct or incorrect use of words, and we see that speech can affect not only the characters' views of the world but also the world itself. While Tophas in the sub-plot *thinks* that naming his four hairs a beard will magically change his face, Zontes in the main plot points out that words *do* alter reality: "Golde and fayre words are of force to corrupt the strongest men" (V.iii.6-7). And Endimion's effective use of deceitful words causes Tellus to believe his gestures of love (V.iii.110) and ultimately to become cruel.

The power of words is manifested also when the possession of a "long tongue"—that is, talking too much or talking in the wrong way—causes Tellus to be immured in a castle, Bagoa to become an aspen tree, Semele to be in danger of losing her tongue, and Corsites to be pinched for calling fairies "hags." Corsites goes to the lunary bank because Tellus, sphinx-like, uses words with double meanings. In *The Book of Wisdome,* Salomon says that only wisdom teaches people to hold their tongues or to speak righteously (8.12). In the sixteenth century, the power of words was in fact generally accepted, not only by the uneducated who believed in magic charms but by sophisticates as well. Not only did the Neoplatonists and hermeticists study to use the power of words in theurgy, but the Aristotelian Thomas Wilson in his *Arte of Rhetorique,* for example, attributed the creation of world order to proper use of speech. God, he said, granted "the gifte of utteraunce that thei [his appointed ministers] might withe ease winne folke at their will, and frame them to all good order."10

It is the power of words to cause "all good order" that we see in the last scene in *Endimion*. Earlier, in her court on the moon, Cynthia threatened to tame tongues and thoughts so as to make speech answerable to duty (III.i.18). Upon descending to earth, she warns Dipsas that "Breath out thou mayst wordes," words will not change her heart which, like Salomon's wisdom (12.22), was persuaded to mercy by God (V.iii.28-31). When Tellus complains about Endimion's false swearing, she is warned by Cynthia that she should speak briefly, "least taking delight in vttering thy loue, thou offende vs with the length of it" (V.iii. 116-17). Variations of the verb "to speak" run through the scene: "utter," "cleare your selfe," "sounded," "swore," "whisper." The tongue "stingeth" or can speak in silence, and all for the purpose of determining "truth," another word repeated with frequency in the scene. Cynthia asks twice, for example, if Tellus has told the truth (V.iii.135, 156) after Tellus has insisted that her answer is truthful (V.iii.55). Upon Endimion's advice, Cynthia accepts Semele's silence as "true" (V.iii.212) and finally decides to release Bagoa for revealing (that is, "speaking") the truth, "if in my power be the effect of truth" (V.iii.282). In *Endimion* as in *The Book of Wisdome* (16.12, 18.15) the words of divinity have healing power upon the earth. Whereas Cynthia's kiss merely wakens an aged man, her truthful use of speech accomplishes the miracle of restoring Endimion's youth: "Your Highnesse hath blessed mee, and your wordes haue againe restored my youth" (V.iii.188-89).

Only by the truthful use of words, corresponding to the truths of the real world, is order restored in the play. Yet even the liars are redeemed in Act V. Mercy is granted to all of the characters, all of whom were earlier too ignorant to recognize or to confess their deceptions. They are saved not by their good works but, as Jewel says all people are, by the mercy of God through His instruments on earth.[11] His instrument in the play is Cynthia.

But if a daring heart, imagination, and even words can make it possible to achieve the impossible and to change reality, how can we know the reality that words should truthfully express? In *Endimion* none of the characters know even themselves fully. Eumenides overestimates his degree of understanding when he argues that Endimion's love cannot succeed. Endimion does not recognize his own nature, for he is sincere but is also lying to himself in his claim to be a faithful lover. He does not admit that he is a liar until the final act (V.iii.136).

Tellus also is not certain of her own identity. First she appears to be a jealous woman, and she accepts that mortal role by asking that "mischiefe be as well forgiuen in women" as perjury is in men (I.ii.11). But in her next speech she claims her beauty to be divine and places "the sacrifice of the Gods" in her bowels (I.ii.24). Her creatures, she says, are infinite. She must then be the earth goddess Tellus, but in her claim that she is a woman, she also asserts, as Renaissance humanists did, that humanity is a remarkable and goodly piece of work. In claiming power equal to Cynthia's she establishes, as Bruno does, that the moon and earth are similar in nature. Richard Linche in *The Fountaine of Ancient Fiction* unites the earth and moon too when he says that the effects of Luna extend even "to the bowels of Erebus."[12] The identification of Tellus with earth is reinforced in Act V when it is from Tellus' lips that the truth about Endimion's faithlessness in love is established. By making Tellus the source of truth, Lyly enacts line 11 of Psalm 85 "Trueth shal bud out of the earth." The psalm continues with a parallel reference to Cynthia: "and righteousnes shal loke downe from heauen."

Peter Saccio has discussed *Endimion* with relation to another line of Psalm 85.[13] On one level Cynthia is, as Saccio explains, the embodiment of the Four Daughters of God, a favorite Renaissance allegory developed from Psalm 85.10: "Mercie and trueth shal mete; righteousness and peace shal kisse one another." Cynthia seeks truth, is just, and has mercy on Dipsas and Tellus as well as on Endimion; thus she brings peace to the court. When we note that Lyly also intends Tellus to embody the allegorical interpretation of another part of the psalm, we recognize that Tellus, as well as Cynthia, is the means by which Endimion confronts the truth about himself. When she reveals the truth about Endimion, Tellus' truth and the mercy of Cynthia meet, just as truth and mercy meet in Psalm 85.10.

Tellus also has powers that resemble Cynthia's. She gives Endimion a kind of peace by sentencing him to a trance. Her use of the magic of Dipsas is a kind of justice in that it is Endimion's punishment for duplicity. The anger of Tellus at Endimion's faithlessness is an image of righteousness because in fact she has been injured. Because they are the result of anger and of the desire for revenge, the righteousness of Tellus and the justice and peace that her righteousness commands are only appearances of true justice and peace.

Although Cynthia is the source of true justice, mercy, and peace, even she does not know the full truth about herself in *Endimion*. She knows enough to show Pythagoras, a classical figure esteemed in the Renaissance for "his approued truth and incomparable learning,"[14] that he is wrong in his "ridiculous opinions" (IV.iii.42). Yet she must learn from Eumenides that her kiss can awaken Endimion (V.i.10), and she does not know that her words will restore Endimion's youth: "What younge againe?" she asks in amazement (V.iii.192). Although she possesses her power "by the eternall Gods" (V.iii.25), she graces humanity only by the grace of God. Her questions reveal that she does not know the full effect of her power in the sublunary world. Cynthia dominates the sublunary world of the play as much in her mastery of partial truth as in her power to com-

mand. In the last act, as the image which all should copy, she
grows in knowledge of herself and of the truth as does Endimion.

As the figure of Wisdom, however, Cynthia is closer to the
divine in understanding and action than are Tellus and Dipsas.
She is the moon—halfway between earth and heaven; she is also
removed from the sinful desires of Tellus and Dipsas. While
Cynthia as Wisdom is an image of God and His goodness
(Wisdome, 7.6), Tellus and Dipsas are counterimages of the
divine. But all three of these women are used by Lyly to increase
Endimion's understanding and are in that sense united with each
other in the same manner that Luna is identical with Diana on
earth and with Hecate and Proserpina in Erebus according to
Abraham Fraunce in *Yuychurche.* The three women aid Endimion's intellectual advancement by a dialectical movement
similar to that of image and counterimage in Platonism and
Neoplatonism. We see Endimion progress toward the revelation
of truth through the schemes of Tellus and Dipsas. Because the
counterimages of Tellus and Dipsas seem evil in their actions
and yet create a good, they embody the confusing appearances
that reside in the sublunary world. Through the good that Tellus
and Dipsas cause by their intended evil, Lyly demonstrates what
Jewel described as the human inability to understand God's
"higher thoughts" without the gift of Wisdom.

III

Lyly complicates the problems of comprehension of the truth
about reality not only through his deceptive characters and
mirror-image actions but also through his confusing references
to time and space, the coordinates of our world both in history
and in the universe. Although R. W. Bond says that Lyly's
treatment of space is consistent with a Renaissance audience's
reliance upon imagination for the location of dramatic scenes,
we should note that Lyly does not ignore definite location;
within a few lines (III.iv.194ff), he explicitly relocates the
lunary bank. The ease with which Cynthia and her courtiers
reach it confirms Saccio's suggestion that in performances of
Lyly's plays multiple mansions were evident at all times.[15] This
type of staging would, as Bond says, require audiences to exercise imagination and to assume the trip to the lunary bank to be
difficult even though they see it accomplished in a few minutes,
but it would also focus attention on the problematic nature of

understanding reality. The lunary bank, at once so close and so difficult to reach, represents symbolically the puzzling universe presented in the play. A character's ease or difficulty in making the journey to it represents the state of his intellectual soul. In a play whose allegory concerns the difficulty of knowing truth because of uncertainty about the nature of the real world, questions of spatial location are functional.

Problems under discussion by Lyly's contemporaries undoubtedly influenced his interest in location as a symbol of the obscurity of truth. The travel books written by navigators, most easily found in editions of Hakluyt, discuss difficult problems faced by those who tried to locate the New World. We can still view the many inaccurate maps of the world that various cartographers drew.16

Astronomers wrote discourses about the relativity of ideas about space. Thomas Digges, translating the words of Copernicus, wrote in 1576 that "the sense of mortall man [is] abused," for the "Earth resteth not in the Center of the Whole world, but onely in the Center of this our mortall world or Globe of Elements." Giordano Bruno, writing in the 1580's, considered the universe infinite, containing many worlds. He said that a sense of location is dependent upon the world from which the viewer looked.17 In *Endimion*, the lunary bank *is* both a tedious journey (III.iv.194) and "hard by" (IV.ii.67), depending on the position taken by the various actors on the stage.

The ideas of the Neoplatonist Giordano Bruno, who was martyred by the Inquisition in 1600, are of particular interest to us in interpreting *Endimion* because Bruno, a flamboyant lecturer, was in London between 1583 and 1585, and, according to Sears Jayne, was an important source of Neoplatonic thought in England.18 He also became a *cause célèbre* when the scholars at Oxford accused him of plagiarism and cancelled his remaining lectures at the university. According to a 1604 account of that incident, Bruno's idea of an earth that revolves around the sun was the source of some scholarly laughter. Lyly's play *Endimion* may have caused similar delight among courtiers by its depiction of a world in which, as Bruno proposed, space was relative, and time must be also since all motion is within time.19

In addition to creating uncertainty about physical distance, Lyly's contradictory descriptions reflect psychological distance.

To Geron, the journey from the fountain to Cynthia's court is tedious because his long separation from it has increased the difficulty. To Epiton at court, the fountain is "hard by" because he has become used to the difficult and to the absurd in his attempts to separate truth from fiction in his relations with Tophas.

Journeys are also traditionally allegorical symbols for approaches to wisdom. *The Book of Wisdome* says that those who misjudge "the waye of trueth . . . haue gone through dangerous waies: but . . . haue not knowen the way of the Lord" (5.6-7). The page Epiton is more presumptuous than Geron and therefore his trip seems easier. Earlier journeys are both literally and figuratively the origins of our judgment. In Lyly, Bruno's theory of the relativity of place and time is used to indicate the state of a person's intellectual soul.

Bond terms Lyly's use of time in *Endimion* to be as arbitrary as his placement of scenes and suggests that it reflects an indecision as to whether the unities "should or should not be observed" (III, 15). Any error in accounting for the passage of years in *Endimion,* however, is so glaring that it is probably purposeful. Not only does Lyly devise the action on stage to stress the time lapses, but he draws our attention to time by frequent references to it.

The passage of time is noted explicitly. On stage, Eumenides converses at the fountain with Geron, explaining that Endimion has been asleep "these twentie yeeres" (III.iv.19). Eumenides has not spoken of Semele, he says, for seven years (III.iv.54). When Endimion awakes, he thinks he has slept only one night, but we are told that Endimion has slept forty years (V.i.50), and the twig against which he was leaning when he fell asleep has become a tree.

Not only does Lyly note passing time, but he seems also to suggest that it does not pass equally for everyone. In my view, in staging the play, the characters should all stay younger than Endimion, whose makeup would stress his hollow eyes, gray hair, and wrinkled cheeks, the features that Cynthia describes (IV.iii.75-76). Thus the passage of time within the play would be both visually and aurally communicated as perplexing.

Sallie Bond argues that R. W. Bond erred in thinking that all the characters remain young[20] She states that Lyly intends "an irresistible visual compliment to Elizabeth [that] would result from the presence of a youthful, stately Cynthia, surrounded by an entourage of elderly, reedy-voiced courtiers." She supports her argument by interpreting a speech by Floscula as an expression of pity for Endimion's having slept away his youth: "Where others number their yeeres, their houres, their minutes, and steppe to age by staires, thou onely hast thy yeeres and times in a cluster, being olde before thou remembrest thou wast younge" (IV.iii.149-54). While her interpretation is plausible, it is equally possible that Floscula is saying that the others aged more slowly as they "steppe to age by staires" and therefore are young while Endimion is old. Endimion's hesitation in recognizing Eumenides (V.i.65) might be evidence that Eumenides has aged, but it might also be an indication that so many years have passed for Endimion that he has forgotten the appearances of his friends just as he has momentarily forgotten—but permanently abandoned—his earlier erring self (V.i.36).

Cynthia's reference to Tellus as harboring many mischiefs in "few yeres" (V.iii.57) and the continued flirtations and courtships among the courtiers seem to contradict the suggestion that everyone on stage is middle-aged at the end of the play. Although one or two of the youthful actors might have been skilled enough to play the roles of middle-aged lovers in dignity and without the support of the ridicule that helped them to portray Dipsas, it is highly improbable that the entire cast of boys would have had the talent to act the roles of aging lovers successfully. Furthermore, if Endimion were the only young courtier at the end, surely some comment about his astonishing youth would be made by the other characters. Instead they accept his renewed youth as so appropriate that no comment is needed.

It is clear, in any case, that he ages differently from the other mortals and that time is endowed with some mystery in the play. Throughout the play there are frequent allusions to the oddities of passing time; I have counted forty-six such allusions. In the prologue, for example, we hear that "it was forbidden in olde time to dispute of Chymera, because it was a fiction: we hope in our times none will apply pastimes, because they are fancies." The onslaught of age is discussed in the form of a proverb in Act II:

> *Tellus:* Is not her beautie subiect to time?
> *Endimion:* No more than time is to standing still.
> (II.i.85-86)

In the sub-plot, Epiton explains that "the tyde tarieth no man," and then simultaneously gives the lie to the proverb and contradicts himself by stating that two hours passed while he was "tide" (IV.ii.9-11).

A Renaissance commonplace, *veritas filia temporis,* accounts in part for Lyly's concern with time in a play about truth, but the people of Reformation England had learned that the relation between truth and time is more complex than the proverb reveals. As John Jewel reminded his congregation in his *Certaine Sermons,* the fact that time has passed is no guarantee that truth has been found. He instructs his congregation that the primitive Christians were closer to the truth than were the Christians of "the time late past, . . . the night of error and ignorance" in which the teachings of Christ were obscured by learned prelates. He points out that what at first seems true may later appear to be false and that apparent falsity may later appear to be true. The intensity with which the sixteenth-century English were concerned with whether time reveals truth is communicated in Jewel's words: "that was once true, is it now become false? that was once catholic doctrine, is it now at last become heresy? O merciful God! was it thy will that thy truth should be true but for a season . . .?" Jewel urges consideration of these questions so that "many consciences [can be] quieted." He makes it clear that truth is so difficult to comprehend that even when we see it, it may appear to be as clouded as the water in the well of truth that Geron watches.21

Lyly was, of course, no more a philosopher of time than of space, and he did not intend in his play to analyze theories of time or of truth. Rather, to show that time eventually serves truth, he let his fancies roam among the various interesting scientific and moral ideas that courtiers discussed. As Marlowe's Dr. Faustus said, "the double motion of the plannets" were "fresh mens suppositions."22 Such elementary notions are the basis of Elizabethan awareness of the complexity of chronology that Lyly used as a metaphor for human confusion. The length of a year will vary according to the length of time taken by each planet to make a revolution; Faustus' explanation that Saturn takes thirty years to revolve implies that the Saturnine years would be thirty times longer than ours.

The accuracy of chronology was always important in an age when astrology was a respectable science. As Tycho Brahe pointed out, the reliability of astrology depends on whether "the times are determined correctly," but as Agrippa noted neither the course of the stars nor the measure of the year is certain.[23] Furthermore, in the 1580's the need to correct the calendar also raised questions about knowing a person's exact age. John Dee records his presentation of a book on the correction of the calendar to Lord Burghley on 26 February 1583.[24] It was inscribed to Burghley in a verse punning on "tyme untrew," using, just as Lyly did, the commonplace of time's relation to the pursuit of truth. The difference in the "New Style" Gregorian calendar adopted by Catholic countries in 1582 and the "Old Style" Julian calendar maintained in use in Protestant countries gave Lyly further opportunity to use variations in the calculation of time as a meaningful symbol of differences of opinion on the nature of truth.

The fact that Easter falls on different days each year because its celebration is governed by the moon probably made most Christians aware of both solar and lunar times, but scientists also discussed those two bases for calculation of a year. Bruno, for example, mentioned two ways of measuring the year, a lunar year and "a round one from season to season." He pointed out that in the New World, explorers had found "memorials of 10,000 years and more, which years are, as I tell you, whole and round, because their four months are the four seasons and because when the years were divided into fewer months, they were at the same time divided into longer months."[25] Lunar time, with fewer months and shorter years, would naturally be an appropriate measure of the time that the moon's lover lay on the lunary bank. It would explain Endimion's aging differently from other characters.

If we consider time in relation to infinity, another measurement is made. Bruno says that in "infinite duration, the maximum time . . . becomes equivalent to the minimum, since infinite centuries have no greater duration than infinite hours . . . in infinite duration, which is eternity there are not more hours than centuries."[26] In relation to infinity, Endimion's aging would have no beginning and no end, for months and years could be exactly the same. Seven years could equal forty years or could equal four hundred years if Lyly so chose. Such an explanation for the duration of Endimion's trance is supported in the play by Endimion's reference to the eternity of his love: "The time was Madam, and is, and euer shall be, that I honoured your highnesse aboue all the world" (V.iii.162).

While wittily suggesting to his audience these assorted and strange ideas of measuring the passage of time, Lyly also refers to Castiglione's explanation of rational love as the proper love of old men. Endimion's love fulfills the requirements of *The Courtier* for rational love with its emphasis on "bodilesse" beauty. Because Endimion's love for the moon is spiritual, he must be in soul like older men who Castiglione says "whan those youthfull yeeres be gone and past, leave it of cleane, keapinge alouf from this sensuall covetinge as from the lowermost steppe of the stayers, by the whiche a man may ascende to true love."27 Since Endimion's aging on the lunary bank symbolizes his reaching the appropriate "steppe of the stayers" for higher love (the love of Cynthia), once the symbol has functioned Lyly can restore Endimion to his youth—adding, at the same time, a concept that the passage of time is relative to the inner state of the man who experiences it.

For Salomon in *The Book of Wisdome* as for Lyly, possession of wisdom deserves in itself the respect owed to the gray hair of age. Salomon writes: "For the honorable age is not that which is of long time, nether that which is measured by the nomber of yeres. But wisdome is the graye heere . . ." (4.8-9). In addition, just as Endimion experiences both youth and age within moments, *The Book of Wisdome* describes comprehension of the mystery of time's passage as an indication of possession of knowledge: "For he hathe giuen me the true knowledge of . . . The beginning and the end, and the middes of the times: how the times alter, and the change of the seasons, the course of the yere, the situacion of the starres . . ." (7.17-19).

For Endimion, then, time has passed in unique and mysterious ways because he is spiritually older and wiser. Having atoned for his treatment of Tellus and having grown wiser through the experience of earthly love, he is now ready for the higher love to which he earlier aspired. This atonement and growth is indicated in Lyly's choice of forty years as the period of Endimion's sleep rather than the thirty years cited by Boccaccio in *Genealogiae Deorum Gentilium*.28 Forty is continually associated with regeneration in the Bible. After forty days, Noah's ark "was lifte up aboue the earth" (*Gen.* 7.17). Moses fasted forty days and forty nights to atone for Israel's sin against

God (*Deut.* 9.18). After being tested by God for forty years in the wilderness, Israel finally reached the promised land (*Deut.* 8.2). Jesus fasted forty days and forty nights before he faced temptation and conquered it (*Matt.* 4.2). Forty days also pass between Christmas and Candlemas, a feast of purification and the day upon which the play *Endimion* was first performed. That Endimion's sleep lasted forty years is emblematic of his readiness for the reward of his quest because he has obtained the renewed purity and clarity of mind asked for in the Collect of Candlemas.

IV

Lyly's use of the Collect and the Gospel from the Feast of the Purification of St. Mary the Virgin may show the accuracy of Peter Weltner's view that in Cynthia Lyly suggests an analogy to the Virgin Mary,[29] but we should stress that Protestant antipathy to Mariolatry would have limited Lyly expressly to mere suggestion of the analogy. One of John Jewel's sermons published in 1583 specifically calls it blasphemy to refer to Mary as "queen of heaven, lady of the world, the only hope of them that be in misery," and a hand-written marginal note in a volume of the 1583 edition assents to Jewel's judgment by calling these phrases "papist praiers." Some may respond that in Scene i of *Endimion* Eumenides parallels Jewel by calling Endimion's love of Cynthia blasphemous. Eumenides, however, does not object to the application of divine names to Cynthia but rather to the presumption of a mortal to love a goddess.

Insight into whether Cynthia is the Virgin Mary is offered by Abraham Fraunce's Countess of Pembroke writings. Although Fraunce writes warmly of Mary and of the wonder of the virgin birth in *Emanuel,* he does not identify Cynthia with Mary in his retelling of the Endimion myth in *Yuychurche,* nor do other English mythographers. Not only do sermons on Candlemas by Donne not mention the Virgin, but even the nativity homily in *The Second Tome of Homilies,* authorized by Queen Elizabeth in 1595 to be preached in all parishes, only mentions Virgin Mary parenthetically.[30] Furthermore, we should note that the Collect on Candlemas does not mention Mary and stresses instead the presentation of Christ in the temple. We cannot conclude, however, that Endimion's renewal represents the resurrection of Christ or the descent of God into the mortal flesh of Jesus since, even in the final scene, Endimion is subordinate to Cynthia, which he would not be if he were the Son of God and the resurrected Christ. Endimion represents Jesus only as all humans are part of God. Endimion is accused of blasphemy as Jesus was, not because he represents Jesus, but because he represents any person who aspires to the pure and clear mind sought in the Collect. Such people are often despised because, as Salomon says, wisdom is always despised by the unwise (3.11). Like the wise person in *The Book of Wisdome,* Endimion resists temptation and undergoes spiritual renewal because these are also the destined roles of humans who aspire to wisdom.

Although Endimion never displays the supremacy we would expect of Christ, Cynthia in contrast does resemble the Virgin Mary as intermediary between the mortal and the divine. No one can prove that silence about the Virgin in liturgy, in sermons, and in the English tales about Cynthia means that she was also absent from the hearts of a congregation, of a theatre audience, or of a playwright. Religious sentiment does not change by fiat of the crown, even though forms of observance do. We can, however, be sure by internal evidence that Cynthia cannot be exclusively the Virgin Mary even if she does suggest such an analogy. Endimion's "service" to Cynthia is also that of the courtly lover to his mistress, whose "divine" intercession for the lover was recounted by poets in many lyrics. As a figure of Wisdom, Cynthia embodies all inspirational persons and inspiration itself, leading human understanding to achieve perfect knowledge. Cynthia understands and thus unites all "imaginacions of men," as Salomon says of Wisdom (7.20). In Cynthia's presence in Act V of *Endimion,* all discord is transformed into harmony just as Wisdom orders all things in *The Book of Wisdome* (8.1). Cynthia's presence resolves the play's paradoxes of love, of time, and of human nature as Wisdom is "the scholemastres of the knowledge of God" (8.4). Just as Salomon learns of justice and mercy through Wisdom (4.4-6), Cynthia teaches justice and mercy by her example.

Lyly compliments Queen Elizabeth by suggesting that her relationship to her courtiers perfects their virtue and understanding, their mercy and justice. Through her wisdom, she brings God's grace to His people: "Good princes and good rulers are the good instruments by whom God setteth forth His glory."31 Although Endimion's weakness caused him to deceive Tellus and then to fall victim to sorcery, his awakened and rejuvenated intellectual soul, eternally young, has been resurrected by Cynthia. He is capable of new heights of understanding as Lyly and Jewel thought the English people were by the grace of their Queen.

V

Lyly's *Endimion*—where time is timeless, where change is constant, where place is no place, where the moon is on earth, and where Endimion the Man in the Moon exists—depicts the puzzling world at the same time that it confirms the possibility of gaining the wisdom to understand it. Lyly "seasoned" his play for the Children of Paul's "with the honey of God's wisdom" as Jewel urged of all eloquent witnesses for truth. Lyly chose *The Book of the Wisdome of Salomon* as the basis of his allegory because it is the bible reading for Candlemas, the day of the first performance of the play. But he may have also wanted to respond to Jewel's articulation of St. Peter's "call upon them that are of the church of God in all places, that they shew forth the mercies of God, that they witness unto the world what the Lord hath done . . . in filling them with all spiritual knowledge and understanding." Lyly interwove divine and secular learning in *Endimion*, his allegory of wisdom, as Jewel desired of the masters of eloquence and the liberal arts. Just as Jewel urged of them, Lyly used his art to glorify God's "handmaid," Queen Elizabeth, and thus to "serve and wait upon the wisdom of God."32 It is impossible, of course, to state definitely that John Lyly wrote *Endimion* because he read Jewel's sermons. Yet the anxiety expressed in Jewel's sermons about whether God's truth can be known by mortals, his concern that the quest for "perfect knowledge" continue, and his desire for celebration of the role of Queen Elizabeth and the English people in that quest help us to understand the depth of the longing for certainty that inspired Lyly's allegory of wisdom about Cynthia and Endimion.33

NOTES

1 For a discussion of *Endimion* as an allegory of love, see Percy W. Long, "The Purport of Lyly's *Endimion*," *PMLA*, 24 (1909), 164-84; E. C. Pettet, *Shakespeare and the Romance Tradition* (London, 1949), pp. 50-53; Bernard F. Huppé, "The Allegory of Love in Lyly's Court Comedies," *ELH*, 14 (1947), 93-113. For a summary of critics who read *Endimion* as a political allegory, see G. K. Hunter, *John Lyly: The Humanist as Courtier* (Cambridge, Mass., 1962), pp. 186-88.

2 *The Boke of common praier* (1559; facsimile rpt. London, 1844). The same lessons and the same collect are in *The Book of Common Prayer* of 1586. John Donne, *Sermons*, ed. Evelyn M. Simpson and George R. Potter (Berkeley, 1954), VII, 326, 345, Sermon 13, Candlemas day, 1626/7.

3 *The Geneva Bible* (1560; facsimile rpt. Madison: University of Wisconsin Press, 1969). Hereafter, all references to *The Book of the Wisdome of Salomon* will be noted parenthetically in the text.

4 All quotations from *Endimion* are from *The Complete Works of John Lyly*, ed. R. Warwick Bond (Oxford: Clarendon Press, 1902), vol. III; hereafter, references to the play and to the editor's commentary will be noted parenthetically in the text.

5 Sir Thomas Elyot, *Dictionary* (1538; rpt. Menston: Scolar Press, 1970). Abraham Fraunce, *The third part of the Countesse of Pembrokes Yuychurch* (London, 1599), p. 43. See also Natale Conti, *Mythologiae* (Lyons, 1605), IV.viii.

6 John Jewel, *Certaine Sermons Preached before the Queens Maiestie, And at Pauls Crosse* (London, 1583), reprinted in *Works*, ed. John Ayre (Cambridge, 1847), II, 985-86, 973, 1036.

7 Jewel, *Works*, II, 1037-38, Sermon VI. For the date of *Endimion*, see Bond, III, 13; Hunter, p. 187; E. K. Chambers, *The Elizabethan Stage* (Oxford: Clarendon Press, 1923), III, 412-17.

8 See for example, I.iii.2; II.i.2; II.i.91.

9 Jewel, *Works*, II, 1032, Sermon V.

10 Thomas Wilson, *The Arte of Rhetorique* (1560), Preface.

11 Jewel, *Works*, II, 1026, Sermon V.

12 Giordano Bruno, *On the Infinite Universe and Worlds*, trans. Dorothea Waley Singer, in *Giordano Bruno, His Life and Thought* (New York, 1950), pp. 313, 317, 371. Vincenzo Cartari, *The Fountaine of Ancient Fiction*, trans. Richard Linche (London, 1599), sig. H3. Cartari, however, describes the unsteady course of Diana (Sig. H). See Digges (cited below, fn. 18) for a discussion of newly-discovered astronomical similarities of earth and moon.

13 In *The Court Comedies of John Lyly* (Princeton: Princeton University Press, 1969), pp. 175-83, Peter Saccio also summarizes the views of Huppé and Bryant on the Four Daughters of God allegory.

14 Thomas Cooper in *Thesaurus Linguae Romanae et Britannicae* (1565; rpt. Menston. Scolar Press, 1969) adds about Pythagoras that "Plato wondreth at his wisdom." As is appropriate to a play whose theme is the difficulty of knowing the truth, Lyly does not reveal in what respect Pythagoras is wrong—or about what. Conti, III.xx, p. 283, explains that Pythagoras denied that the moon ever descended to the earth. Perhaps Cynthia is correcting Pythagoras for his denial of the ancient myth, and thus saying, in effect, "I am here." A more esoteric interpretation is to be found in Renaissance references to Pythagoras as "magister silentii." According to Edgar Wind in *Pagan Mysteries in the Renaissance* (New York, 1968), p. 53n, "Pythagorean silence became for the Neoplatonists the final consummation of wisdom . . ., ultimate truth being ineffable." Cynthia might then be saying that true wisdom is found through proper use of speech in contrast either to Tophas' volubility or to Pythagorean silence. Such an interpretation would be supported by Endimion's reference to his own whispering (V.iii.175), by corresponding ideas about appropriate speech in *The Book of Wisdome* (8.12), and by Lyly's own concentration on Euphuism.

15 Saccio, p. 23: "The houses are . . . not only realistic representations of the settings of the action; they are also symbolic representations of the cruces of the action."

16 To one traveller included in Hakluyt's *Divers Voyages touching the discovery of America* (London, 1582), North America was a continent, while to Sebastian Cabot it was a group of islands (sigs. K-K3, A3).

17 Thomas Digges, *A Perfit Description of the Caelestiall Orbes according to the most Aunciente doctrine of the Pythagoreans latelye revived by Copernicus and by Geometrical Demon-Strations approued*, in *Huntington Library Bulletin*, No. 5 (April 1934), pp. 79-86. Bruno, *On the Infinite Universe and Worlds*, pp. 254-55.

18 Sears Jayne, "Ficino and the Platonism of the English Renaissance," *Comparative Literature*, 4 (1952), 231n.

19 See Robert McNulty, "Bruno at Oxford," *Renaissance News*, 13 (1960), 300-05. Bruno, *De Immenso*, I. 12, cited by Singer, p. 50.

20 Sallie Bond, "John Lyly's *Endimion*," *SEL*, 14 (1974), 196-97.

21 Jewel, *Works*, II, 1044, Sermon VI; II, 1030-31, Sermon V. For contemporary use of the "well of truth" image, see *Certaine Sermons or Homilies* (London, 1582), sigs, A-A1.

22 Christopher Marlowe, *The Tragicall History of D. Faustus* (London, 1604; facsimile rpt. Menston: Scolar Press, 1970), sig. C3.

23 *Tycho Brahe's Description of his instruments, and scientific work*, tr. Hans Raeder, Elis Strömgren, and Bengt Strömgren (Copenhagen, 1946), p. 117. Agrippa von Nettesheim, *Paradox sur l'incertitude, vanite, abus du Sciences, Traduite en Francais du Latin de Henri Corneille Agrippa* (Paris, 1603), pp. 162-64.

24 *The Private Diary of Dr. John Dee and the Catalogue of his Library of Manuscripts*, ed. James O. Halliwell (London, 1842), p. 19.

25 Giordano Bruno, *The Expulsion of the Triumphant Beast*, tr. Arthur O. Imerti (New Brunswick, 1964), pp. 249-50.

26 *On the Infinite Universe and Worlds*, p. 294.

27 Count Baldassare Castiglione, *The Courtier*, trans. Sir Thomas Hoby (London, 1900), p. 346. We should note that Castiglione's stair imagery of aging is the same as that used by Floscula, IV.iii.149-54.

28 Giovanni Boccaccio, *Genealogie Deorum Gentilium Libri*, ed. Vincenzo Romano (Bari, 1951), IV.xvi, p. 175.

29 Peter Weltner, "The Antinomic Vision of Lyly's *Endymion*," *ELR*, 3 (1973), 22, 28-29.

30 Jewel, *Works*, II, 1044, Sermon VI. The French mythographer deWalleys compares Cynthia with Mary (see Prologue, *La bible des Poetes de Ovide Metamorphose*, ca. 1520), but such a comparison is strikingly absent in English accounts of the myth. See *The Fountaine of Ancient Fiction*, s.v. "Diana," in addition to Abraham Fraunce, *Yuychurche*, p. 43. Fraunce's *The Countess of Pembrokes Emanuel* (London, 1591), sigs. A3-B1 contrasts with the nativity sermon in *The Second Tome of Homilies* (London, 1595), which says only ". . . the same Jesus which was born of the Virgin Mary."

31 Jewel, *Works*, II, 973, Sermon I.

32 Jewel, *Works*, II, 983, 985, Sermon I.

33 Sections of this paper were read to the Northeast Modern Language Association in Boston, April 1973. Its preparation was partially financed by a grant from the Rhode Island College Faculty Research Fund.

Ben Jonson's Social Attitudes:
A Statistical Analysis

Judith K. Gardiner and Susanna S. Epp

By organizing and displaying a large variety of patterns from a set of data, computers help us to see relationships which might otherwise elude us and to draw conclusions based on an entirety of information rather than subjective impressions. Up to now, much valuable computer work in the humanities has been linguistic. In this study, we assay another approach toward computer-aided study of literature, an approach currently more typical of the social sciences. This study seeks to use statistical analysis to describe some characteristics of a certain literary world—the comedies and poems of Ben Jonson—and to infer from them Jonson's attitudes toward people of varying social class and of both sexes. The relationships between these attitudes and the genres of works in which the characters appear are explored, as are the changes of these attitudes over time.

Ben Jonson was a gentleman's grandson and a bricklayer's stepson who saw himself as a child of the Muses and an heir of the great Latin poets.[1] During the "War of the Theaters," Jonson had one of his characters, a hack playwright representing Jonson's enemies, explain that he slandered "Horace," representing Jonson, only because "he keepes gallants company" and "better company (for the most part) then I."[2] Jonson enjoyed the patronage and sometimes even the friendship of aristocracy and royalty, yet he boasted of his independent attitude to the titled class. Drummond of Hawthornden recorded as one of "his Narrations" that Jonson "never esteemed of a man for the name of a Lord."[3]

Jonson has a significant reputation as a realistic social commentator who developed contemporary dramatic satire or "city comedy" in Elizabethan London.4 L. C. Knights' well-known study, *Drama and Society in the Age of Jonson,* documents that Jonson reflects his urban surroundings and posits that Jonson exhibits typically conservative, anti-acquisitive Jacobean attitudes.5 Jonson's poetry, too, is known for its social qualities, though in a different sense from his plays. It too mirrors a distinct social milieu.6 Much of Jonson's non-dramatic poetry was written for specific persons on specific occasions: for example, he wrote epitaphs for tombstones, verse thank-you letters, poems to be inscribed on gifts of silver plate, begging poems, and invectives against personal enemies. The majority of his satiric poetry is vivid and specific, though directed against contemporary types, he claims, rather than against contemporary individuals. For these reasons, Jonson's work has long been used as a major source for Renaissance social attitudes by literary historians, and Jonson's social attitudes have attracted wide critical interest as a subject in themselves.

I

Goals and Methods. The starting point for our study was the belief that Jonson dissociated himself from the class of London citizens with whom he worked, and instead identified himself as a "gentleman." Therefore, we believed that Jonson's attitude toward his characters would prove dependent on their social class and would be more favorable to the gentry than to the commoners. More generally, we wished to describe Jonson's social attitudes more clearly and precisely than had previously been done. For this purpose, we used a computer-aided statistical analysis. We coded 442 characters appearing in Jonson's comedies and poems for their social status and sex. We classified Jonson's attitude toward the characters as "positive" or "negative," and we also coded the characters on the basis of whether they appeared in a comedy or a poem, whether in an earlier or a later work. The computer was used to organize this mass of data—442 characters classified for five characteristics—into coherent tables which could be studied both from a descriptive statistical point of view and, where appropriate, as sample data from which inferences could be drawn. For purposes of inductive statistics we viewed these 442 characters as a sample of the theoretical set of all characters Jonson might have created. We drew conclusions, then, about Jonson's "literary attitudes" toward different classes of people and treated separately the question of to what extent his literary attitudes reflected his own personal prejudices.

An initial computer run was made using the Fastabs subroutine of the *Statistical Package for the Social Sciences*[7] to examine some of the relationships among the variables. The resulting contingency tables were studied and the (automatically computed) chi squares were examined for statistical significance. A final computer run was made for the different combinations of the variables, holding others of the variables fixed, to answer questions and examine subtleties raised by the first run. Altogether 126 tables together with associated statistics were computed. All the raw data for the variables class, genre, time, and attitude can be deduced from Table III as annotated in this paper. Table II is reproduced because of the different light it casts on the data. The variable sex led to only a few statistically significant results. Thus, Table I, while representative, does not show the entire interrelationship of the sex variable with all the others. With this exception, then, all of the actual chi square statistics cited in this study could be computed from Table III.

A word is in order about the method of computation used in the Fastabs subroutine of **SPSS**. All chi square statistics are computed according to the usual formula, $X^2 = \sum \frac{(O-E)^2}{E}$, except when there is only one degree of freedom. In this case, if the sample size exceeds 20, the Yates correction factor is used; otherwise the significance level is computed directly using Fisher's exact formula. In fact, most statisticians do not consider the chi square approximation adequate when the number of degrees of freedom, k, is small if the expected frequencies in enough cells are less than five, and this potential inadequacy is not corrected for the Fastabs subroutine. However, each of the chi square statistics cited in this paper has been checked and is free of that possible defect. For a discussion of the statistics used in this paper, we refer the reader to William L. Hays, *Statistics for the Social Sciences,* 2nd ed. (New York: Holt, Rinehart & Winston, 1973).

Our statistical conclusions are intended to be supplementary to standard subjective methods of criticism. However, a statistical study such as ours may provide a useful framework for more detailed studies. Moreover, it can correct generalizations about

Jonson's attitudes based on a critic's reading of only a few works. For example, William Empson deduced from his reading of *The Alchemist* that Jonson had a "working class point of view" and that he was militantly anti-Puritan and anti-Cavalier, being "spiteful about ladies and gentlemen" in his works.[8] Judd Arnold looked at the same play and instead saw Jonson "applauding . . . the personal triumph of the cavalierly aloof, intellectual aristocrat over the hopeless and helpless mass of fools."[9]

II

The Classifications. We coded as separate "characters" each speaking character from a Jonson comedy from *Every Man in His Humour* through *The Magnetic Lady*.[10] Mutes, members of mob scenes, and neutral walk-ons were omitted. The two tragedies were not used because of their historical Roman settings, their consequently different class structure, and the fact that they constituted a different genre from the comedies. Each specific person to or about whom a poem was written was also coded as a separate "character." In the instances where Jonson wrote several separate poems to the same person, as in the four to Lucy, Countess of Bedford, each was coded as a separate "character." On the other hand, "Charis" and Lady Venetia Digby, the subjects of composite poems made up of short poems, were counted once for each composite poem. All of Jonson's relevant nondramatic poetry was used, including *Epigrammes, The Forrest, Under-wood,* and the uncollected poetry.[11] Such a statistical approach involves simplifications and categorizations that may jar some critical sensibilities. Our designation of a "character" for this study gives an equal weight to characters of hundreds of lines and to those of only a few. The justification for this procedure is that if Jonson held consistent attitudes to members of the different social classes, evidence from both major and minor characters should be equally valid.

The first variable coded for each character was genre, that is, whether the character appeared in a comedy (223 characters) or in a poem (219 characters). The second variable was sex. There are 338 male and 99 female characters. Five poems to characters of both sexes (e.g., Epigram lvii, "On Baudes, and Usurers") were not coded for sex.

The third variable studied was the time at which the char-

acter was created. For this category, two periods were used—
"early," ca 1597-1613 (262 characters), and "late," 1614-1637
(180 characters). Jonson's poetry divides naturally at this boun-
dary since the poetry in his first folio, published in 1616, was
completed by 1613.[12] Thus we have a reliable terminal date for
Epigrammes and *The Forrest*. Most of Jonson's later poetry was
published posthumously in *Under-wood* (1640). Poems in
Under-wood were coded as "late" except for a few datable early
poems. Poems from the uncollected poetry were divided into the
same two periods. Placing the plays in the same categories gave
seven comedies coded as early—*Every Man in His Humour*
(1598), *Every Man Out of His Humour* (1599), *Cynthia's Revels* (1600), *Poetaster* (1601), *Volpone* (1606), *The Silent
Woman* (1609), *The Alchemist* (1610)—and five comedies as
late—*Bartholomew Fair* (1614), *The Devil is An Ass* (1616),
The Staple of News (1626), *The New Inn* (1629), *The Magnetic Lady* (1632). Many critics divide Jonson's comedies into
three periods: early or "humour" comedies, the great comedies,
and "dotages."[13] This triple division is useful for the study of
Jonson's comic structure; however, the binary division used here
allows for the synchronous comparison of the plays with the
poems, and it also works to demonstrate the changes in Jonson's
social attitudes over time.

Jonson's designations of social class, the next variable coded
for this study, are also usually clear. Most of the characters in
his plays and poems are carefully labeled by rank or occupation.
For example, many poems have titles like "On Chev'rill the Lawyer," "To Sir Lucklesse Woo-All," and "To the World: A Farewell for a Gentlewoman, Vertuous and Noble." Poems of praise
are usually addressed directly by name; for example, "To Sir
Henry Goodyere," "To Mary, Lady Wroth," "To the Memory of
my Beloved, the Author Mr. William Shakespeare." Nineteen
poems such as "To Person Guiltie" and "An Ode" to "high spirited friend" could not be coded for social class. Entries in the
casts of characters of the plays are similarly labeled. In *Volpone,*
for instance, the *dramatis personae* include "Volpone, a Magnifi-
co," "Mosca, his Parasite," "Politique Would-Bee, a Knight,"
and "Peregrine, a Gent.-travailer." Of course, additional information about the occupation and status of characters is provided
by the texts of the plays. The only play character not coded for
social class was "Echo" in *Cynthia's Revels*.

Since we wished to draw inferences about Jonson's attitudes to persons of varying social class, we defined the social classes in Renaissance terms rather than in modern terms. Peter Laslett argues for the view that pre-industrial England was a "one-class society"; that is, there was a ruling class consisting of the leisured landowners together with higher members of the learned professions and scholars. This ruling class was distinguished from all the rest of the population. The bourgeoisie were not seen as a unified class, but instead were grouped with workers, peasants, servants, and paupers.14 The ruling class was divided into an upper and a lower gentry. To conform with what seem to be Jonson's own categories and also with such historical groupings as Laslett's, we have used a three-class system of classification: the titled, the gentry, the commons.

All titled persons, their daughters, and persons identified by Jonson specifically as "courtiers" were coded as "titled" class (134 characters).

Characters defined by Jonson as "gentlemen" or "gentlewomen" were listed as "gentry," and also coded as "gentry" were all poets and intellectuals not given another class designation (125 characters). Since this category does not correspond with modern classification, further explanation may be helpful at this point. Gentility was a matter of conscious importance to the Elizabethan Englishman. Supposedly birth, not money, determined it. Jonson describes Sogliardo in *Every Man Out of His Humour* as "an essential Clowne . . . yet so enamoured of the name of a Gentleman, that he will have it, though he buyes it."15 For Jonson, as for his contemporaries, a good education was a sign of gentility. Keith Thomas estimates that only 2½ % of the male population of seventeenth-century England was educated at Oxford, Cambridge, or the Inns of Court.16 In *The Poetaster,* Jonson expressed most fully his views on poetry and its place in the social system. Caesar approvingly cries "Sweet poesies sacred garlands crowne your gentrie" to the poets Gallus and Tibullus, and Horace, though poor, is accepted as the social peer of the other "gentle" poets.17 Education is a personal as well as a class attitude, however, and to avoid introducing bias into the "class" and "attitude" categories, we have categorized as "gentle" all poets and intellectuals, including those Jonson criticizes as ignorant, so long as they are not specifically connected with another social class. Thus Crites, John Donne, "Learned Critick," and "Poet-Ape" are coded as "gentry," but the socially degraded poets like Nightingale the ballad-seller are grouped with members of the "common" class.

Also coded as "common" are the remainder of the population—all untitled citizens from wealthy merchants and usurers down to the underworld of thieves and prostitutes; all servants; and the few lower-class country persons who appear in Jonson's work (163 characters).

The last variable coded was Jonson's attitude to his characters, that is, whether they were presented as good or bad, virtuous or vicious. In a contemporary population of human survey respondents such a classification would be naive or impossible, and it would be risky for most literary characters as well. However, most of Jonson's poems and comedies are written on the basis of a rhetoric of praise and blame.[18] There is little difficulty in dividing the praised characters—both the personified ideals and the "straight" witty-gallants—from the satirized world of knaves and fools, even though Jonson's attitude to them varies from simple vituperation to admiring disapproval.[19] Obviously this classification oversimplifies Jonson's characters, but we believe it is reliable enough to provide a common basis for agreement upon which consistent patterns can be seen. The heading "attitude" thus here refers to the "positive" (192 characters) or "negative" (242 characters) evaluation of Jonson's characters. Eight poems in *Under-wood,* all written by Jonson to or about himself and all taking an ambiguous attitude to himself, were not coded as either positive or negative.

In sum, five variables were coded for each Jonsonian character, with exceptions as noted previously. There are four two-way variables and one three-way variable: genre: comedy/poem; sex: male/female; time: early/late; attitude: positive/negative; and class: titled/gentle/common.

III

Results and Interpretation. We report our results in the following order: first, we look at the distribution of characters by class in Jonson's work and the basic relationships between the variables of attitude and class, attitude and sex, and sex and class. Next, we present these relationships as modified with reference to literary genre and discuss possible explanations for our results. Finally, we discuss the changes in the patterns already surveyed from Jonson's earlier to his later work.

The expected frequency of the three social classes in any literary work is difficult to assess. Renaissance romantic comedies revel in dozens of dukes, whereas Roman comic tradition prescribes lower class models. The real distribution of the classes in the Renaissance English population is more definite. Most historical estimates would place fewer than one percent of the population in what is here called the "titled" class and fewer than five percent more in the "gentry" as here defined.[20] For Jonson's comedies and poems together the class distribution is titled characters 32.4%; gentry 28.3%; common 39.4%. Jonson's overall attitude toward his characters of the three classes differs significantly, being overwhelmingly negative toward the common class (89% negative) and strongly positive toward the gentry (64.1% positive) and titled class (67.9% positive). The probability of such an outcome occurring by pure chance assuming that his attitudes to the three classes were the same is less than one in ten thousand ($X^2 = 121.8$, $k = 2$, $p < .0001$). Jonson's attitude to characters of the two sexes illustrates no such disjunction. His attitude to female characters is slightly, but not statistically significantly, more positive than his attitude toward male characters: 52.5% of his female characters are presented positively, and 42.1% of the male characters ($X^2 = 2.9$, $k = 1$, $p. < .09$). However, male and female characters appear in significantly ($X^2 = 12.5$, $k = 2$, $p < .01$) different proportions of the three social classes in his work. (See Table I).

Table I
CLASS

		Common	Gentry	Titled	Row Total
	Male	126	109	92	327
SEX					
	Female	33	16	41	90
	Column Total	159	125	133	417

Five characters were not coded for sex and 20 were not coded for class.

Males of the three classes appear in roughly equal proportions in his works, whereas females of the titled class appear much more often (45.6%) than females of the gentry (17.8%).

Introducing the variable of genre significantly modifies the patterns in Jonson's work discussed above. The characters of the three social classes appear in very unequal proportions in Jonson's comedies and poems (X^2 = 88.4, k = 2, p < .0001). About 60% of the characters in the plays are "common" class, whereas about half of the poems are to titled characters. The gentry is most stably presented in the two genres. Jonson's comedies show the class distribution: titled 15.8%; gentle 25.7%; common 58.6%; the poems: titled 49.5%; gentle 34%; common 16.5%.

Jonson's attitude to his characters is negative for 74.4% of the play characters and positive for 64% of the poem characters, but with significant variation depending on social class. Table II summarizes the relationships among attitude, genre, and social class in Jonson's work.

Table II

COMMON CLASS

		ATTITUDE		
		Negative	Positive	Row Total
GENRE	Comedy	115	15	130
	Poem	30	3	33
	Column Total	145	18	163

GENTRY

		ATTITUDE		
		Negative	Positive	Row Total
GENRE	Comedy	28	29	57
	Poem	14	46	60
	Column Total	42	75	117

TITLED CLASS

		ATTITUDE		
		Negative	Positive	Row Total
GENRE	Comedy	23	12	35
	Poem	20	79	99
	Column Total	43	91	134

Twenty characters were not coded for class and 8 characters were not coded for attitude.

Several conclusions may be drawn.

1. Jonson is persistently and vehemently negative both in his poems and comedies to the "common" class. The approximately nine to one ratio of negative to positive attitudes toward members of this class is constant through both comedies and poems.

2. The gentry is the social group presented most positively in the plays. About half of the members of this class are presented favorably in the plays, as opposed to about 25% of all classes presented favorably in the plays. In the poems, the gentry are presented considerably more positively than in the plays, at an approximate ratio of three positive to one negative "gentle" character ($X^2 = 7.4$, k = 1, p < .01). This ratio is less positive than for titled figures in the poems but much more so than for common ones.

3. Jonson's portrayal of titled figures shows the greatest disjunction and ambivalence from one genre to the other. His poems were often written to specific patrons; they are weighted toward titled figures, and they take a positive attitude toward them at a ratio of about four to one. In contrast, upper class figures in the plays are presented negatively by a ratio of two to one ($X^2 = 22.5$, k = 1, p < .0001).

These general patterns of attitudes to class in the two genres do not vary significantly for the two sexes.

Thus Jonson's poems and plays show a consistent, very strongly negative attitude to the lower classes. They show a positive attitude to the gentry—more positive in the poems than in the plays. They show an apparently inconsistent attitude to the titled class—strongly negative in the plays and even more strongly positive in the poems.

Several explanations would account for these expressed literary attitudes. They might be explained by Jonson's true attitudes —his private purposes and prejudices. In order to infer that his literary attitudes represent his true attitudes, however, we would have to check other explanations. Our findings might be accounted for by the artist's adaptation to his audiences or to the genres in which he wrote, according to Renaissance ideas of decorum. Particularly in the case of the inconsistent expression of attitude toward the titled class, another explanation in addition to that of Jonson's true attitudes might be necessary to account for our results.

The "two audiences" theory was formerly popular as an explanation of the differences between the public and the private theaters, although it has been under attack for some time.21 Some of Jonson's pronouncements have fostered this theory, as in the induction to *Bartholomew Fair* in which a contract is read between the author and his *"Spectators,* and *Hearers,* as well the curious and envious, as the favouring and judicious" that "it shall bee lawfull for any man to judge his six pen'orth, his twelve pen'orth, so to his eighteene pence, 2.shillings, halfe a crowne, to the value of his place; Provided alwayes his place get not above his wit."22 Jonson's plays were performed for both the public and private stages, with the social composition of the audiences changing over Jonson's long career. The view that Jonson adapted his social attitudes to his audiences would lead to the prediction that Jonson portrayed common class "city" characters positively in his popular plays. This is clearly not the case (despite William Empson's attempt to make Jonson a working-class hero).23 Moreover, Jonson claimed only occasionally a desire to please his audiences. Often he showed them contempt, as in the prologue to *The Staple of News*: "If that not like you, that he send tonight,/ Tis you have left to judge, not hee to write."24

Jonson wrote his poems for a somewhat different audience from his plays. Jonson's plays were performed before predominantly citizen audiences which included some gentlefolk and courtiers. The plays' audiences might also include cutpurses, prostitutes, and other of Jonson's satiric butts. In contrast, the poems were intended to be read primarily by "understanders," as he called them, of the gentry and titled classes. Most of the positive poems are addressed to individual members of these classes, and in Epigram xciv to Lucy, Countess of Bedford, Jonson indicates that the subjects of satires do not read them; therefore, he implies that he did not expect "Baudes and Usurers" or "Alchemists" to read his poems about them and that the audience for the satiric poems was thus conceived to be the same persons who were praised in the positive poems. Epigram xcvi displays Jonson's disdain for authors who were willing to write for "pui'nees, porters, players praise."

The frequency of presentation of persons of the three classes in the two genres corresponds to the different audiences of the two genres. Moreover, the assumed aristocratic class prejudices of the audience for the poems corresponds with the attitudes to the three classes shown in the poems. But the assumed democratic prejudices of the stage audiences are not reflected by Jonson's attitudes to his characters in the comedies.

The overall negative bias of Jonson's comedies, rather than his treatment of individual characters, is perhaps best explained by Jonson's adaptation of classical decorum for the genre of satiric comedy. According to the usual interpretation of Aristotle, classical comedy dealt with morally and socially "inferior" characters, whereas tragedy dealt with morally and socially elevated figures.25 Elizabethan romantic comedy does not share this inevitable association of low class status and ridiculousness, though Sir Philip Sidney censured early Elizabethan drama for its indecorous "mingling Kinges and Clownes."26 Jonson does adhere to a negative view of the common class, but he also presents the upper classes quite negatively in his comedies. Rather a high proportion, about 16%, of his play characters are titled, and 65.7% of those are negatively presented. In his poetry, whatever the specific occasions and patrons that inspired him, Jonson was free to write as many satirical or commendatory poems as he wished. To attribute his attitudes to his genres thus begs the question. Renaissance ideas of genre can explain the negative bias of Jonson's comedies, then, but not the distribution of praise and blame towards the three social classes in either the comedies or the poems.

The third explanation of Jonson's treatment of the social classes in his work is that of his own prejudices and attitudes, which caused him to respond to genre and audience selectively as he did. Jonson persistently tries to defend himself against the imputation of slandering particular persons or whole professions through his satirical poems and dramatic portraits. He included the epigram "To True Souldiers," for example, both in *Poetaster* and in *Epigrammes* as an answer to critics of Captain Tucca and of Captain Hungry. Poets, gentlemen, soldiers, servants, and court ladies may be either virtuous or vicious in his world. Frequently, in the commendatory poems to titled figures, Jonson praises the persons addressed as exceptional within their own spheres of society. In Epigram xciv, for instance, he praises the Countess of Bedford though she lives "where the matter" of satire "is bred," and he admires Sir Robert Wroth in *Forrest* III for his withdrawal from the vanities of city and court. Similarly, the beautiful praise of the Sidneys' feudal-aristocratic life style in "To Penshurst" is shadowed by the contrast with the "proud, ambitious heaps" of other, rack-renting country landlords. However, usurers and prostitutes are always satirized in Jonson's work. None of them have hearts of gold, though Doll Common may be no worse than the gentlewoman Dame Pliant.

Renaissance ideas of decorum account for the satiric cast of Jonson's comedies but not for the distribution of praise and blame to the three social classes in either his comedies or his poems. Jonson's expressed attitudes to the titled class seem to be influenced in the poems by his awareness of them as a patron audience, though ambivalence toward the titled appears even in the poems. It seems reasonable to infer from the consistent attitudes expressed in both his poems and his plays that Jonson's true attitude to the common class was strongly negative and that his true attitude to the gentry was positive.

When we introduce the variable of time into this investigation of Jonson's attitudes to characters of different social class, the general pattern of responses shown above remains the same, but some complexities enter the picture. The hypothesis that the proportions of Jonson's negative to positive attitudes toward people remained unchanged over time cannot be rejected ($X^2 = 1.1$, $k = 1$). However, an analysis taking into account class, sex, and genre indicates some areas in which his attitudes did change significantly.

Table III shows the cross tabulation of attitude by class for each combination of genre and time. Jonson's negative bias for the comedies remains constant at about three negative to one positive character in both the earlier and later work. In contrast, his later poems are considerably more positive than earlier ($X^2 = 14.4$, $k = 1$, $p < .001$), increasing from 55.2% to 83.3% positive.[27]

1. Jonson's attitude to the common class is significantly ($X^2 = 4.2$, $k = 1$, $p < .05$) less negative later than earlier. Only 5.7% of common class characters are presented positively earlier, but 17.1% are later. The later plays include proportionately more lower class characters than the earlier plays, increasing from 50% to 67.9%, and they are treated more positively.[28] Although Jonson continues to exhibit much of his earlier contempt for the city's inhabitants, in some ways his later attitudes seem more tolerant than earlier. Many of the lower class char-

Table III

Earlier Comedy

CLASS

	Common	Gentle	Titled	Row Total
Negative	54	17	16	87
Positive	4	18	7	29
Column Total	58	35	23	116

ATTITUDE

Later Comedy

CLASS

	Common	Gentle	Titled	Row Total
Negative	61	11	7	79
Positive	11	11	5	27
Column Total	72	22	12	106

ATTITUDE

Earlier Poem

CLASS

	Common	Gentle	Titled	Row Total
Negative	28	10	18	56
Positive	1	26	50	77
Column Total	29	36	68	133

ATTITUDE

Later Poem

CLASS

	Common	Gentle	Titled	Row Total
Negative	2	4	2	8
Positive	2	20	29	51
Column Total	4	24	31	59

ATTITUDE

All eight characters not coded in Table III for attitude are gentry appearing in the later poems. Of the twenty characters not coded for social class, one is a positively portrayed character appearing in an early comedy; nine are negatively portrayed characters from early poems; three are negatively portrayed characters from late poems; three are positively portrayed characters from early poems; four are positively portrayed characters from late poems.

acters of his later plays are carelessly created stock types, yet his only servant heroine, the maid Prudence, has a substantial positive role in the late play, *The New Inn*. Good lower class characters comprise over 10% of all classed characters in the later plays but only 3.4% of the earlier ones. The few satiric poems that appear in his later work emphasize the class of the person satirized much less than their earlier counterparts.

2. Jonson's attitude to the gentry remains stable over time, with their earlier presentation 62% positive and their later 67.4% positive. The plays show a constant half and half ratio for good to bad gentry both earlier and later, despite the constant three to one ratio of negative to positive characters in both earlier and later plays. The percentage of gentry in the later plays decreases from 30.2% to 20.8% of comic characters. The later poems to the gentry are more positive than earlier, but this is consistent with the general mellowing of tone of the poems over time.

Jonson's attitudes toward his male and female characters do not change significantly over time, but the frequency of his presentation of women in the three social classes does vary considerably from his earlier to his later work. The earlier distribution is top-heavy with titled patronesses; Jonson's later presentation of women assumes a class distribution pattern more nearly approximating that of his men. The most striking change in the later work is the large increase in the number of female gentry. Earlier women are 35.6% common class, 8.9% gentry, 55.6% titled; later they are 37.9% common, 26.7% gentry, 25.6% titled ($X^2 = 6.0$, $k = 2$, $p < .05$),

3. Jonson's attitude to titled characters is slightly more positive and less ambivalent in his later work than earlier. (62.6% positive earlier to 73.1% positive later.) This increase, however, is not statistically significant at ordinary significance levels. Titled characters in the plays are presented less often and less negatively than earlier. Titled characters decrease from 21.6% earlier to 10.2% later. Negatively portrayed titled characters decrease from 13.7% earlier to 5.5% later.

Jonson's later poetry to King James, King Charles, and their courtiers chastises the judgment of the common people, but it does not portray the court or aristocracy as typically vicious as many of Jonson's earlier poems did. These later poems to titled figures are more positive than the earlier ones, which is consistent with the generally less satiric tone of Jonson's later poetry. Jonson only wrote 31 later poems to titled figures in contrast to 68 poems earlier.

Jonson's very positive later attitude to the titled class does not seem to rest on an increased desire for patronage, especially since he wrote so few later poems to the titled. Instead, Jonson's later social attitudes can perhaps best be traced to a combination of typically conservative old age with a social poise gained over his years of success in aristocratic circles.

As Jonson felt more at home with the upper class world in his later years, he may well have become less nervous about its depravities and more convinced of its attractiveness than he was earlier. Those negatively portrayed titled characters who do appear in his late comedies are often knighted citizens like the usurer Sir Moth Interest or the lawyer Sir Paul Eitherside. Many of Jonson's later poems indicate familiarity and ease with titled figures. His late poems to "Charis," "My Lady Covell," and Lady Venetia Digby are more playful than any earlier poems to good women.

Apparently, in his later years he did not need to prove his distance from the common class so vehemently as earlier by writing a body of satiric poetry aimed at it. Nor did he need to prove his integrity by balancing his eulogies of patrons with satires of titled persons.

IV

Conclusion. Our original belief was that Jonson thought of himself as a gentleman rather than as a commoner. We hypothesized, therefore, that Jonson's attitudes toward his characters would depend on their social class and would be more favorable to the gentry than to commoners. We found that his attitude to the common class was very negative throughout his work and his attitude to the gentry positive. We discovered a marked variation in Jonson's treatment of his characters depending upon the genre in which he was writing. Characters of the three social classes appear in significantly different proportions in the poems than in the comedies. His overall attitude is strongly negative toward his comic characters and strongly positive toward his poem characters, being negative in both genres toward the commoners, relatively positive in both genres to the gentry, and negative toward titled comic characters but strongly positive toward titled poem characters. Of three possible explanations for the above results—adaptation to his audience, Renaissance conventions about genre, and reflection of Jonson's own true attitudes toward the three classes—the first helps explain the inconsistent presentation of the titled class, with Jonson presumably adapting his poems to please the patron-audience for them. The second accounts for Jonson's overall negative bias in the comedies. The third seems the probable explanation of the clear patterns in Jonson's expressed attitudes to the commons and the gentry.

When changes in Jonson's attitude over time are examined, he is seen to mellow somewhat toward the common and titled classes while remaining constant in his relatively positive attitude to the gentry. The proportion of the different classes appearing in his work changed over his life with commoners and gentry increasing their representation later while that of the titled class decreased.

Our statistical, computer-aided study provides some definitive descriptions of Jonson's work and some probable inferences about his attitudes to persons of varying social class. However, we do not maintain, as have many critics, that Jonson's social attitudes are typical for his historical period or for Jacobean drama. We believe it would be of interest to study other Renaissance authors using techniques similar to ours and to compare the results directly. This is one reason we chose to use the "canned" subroutine from SPSS. Comparative study of the effect of literary genre on authors' presentations of the social classes would also be of interest.

Shakespeare's sonnets may tell us as much about the conflicts of upward mobility as about repressed homosexuality, natural imagery, or the ravages of time. Ben Jonson, another social climber writing for the Renaissance stage, turned his back on Shakespeare's kings and clowns. Instead, he reveals to us his personal pecking orders among the Renaissance ranks of aristocrats, gentlemen, and commoners.

NOTES

1 All biographical information and the texts for all plays cited in this study are from the edition of C. H. Herford and Percy and Evelyn Simpson, eds., *Ben Jonson,* 11 vols. (Oxford, 1925-52), hereafter cited as H & S. We have, however, regularized the spelling of *u* and *v, i* and *j* according to modern usage. Jonson's biography is discussed in H & S, I, 1-118 and XI, 571-85.

2 *Poetaster* V.iii.317, 450-51; H & S, IV, 311.

3 *Conversations,* 11. 336-37; H & S, I, 141.

4 The term is used by Brian Gibbons, who calls Jonson the "father" of "city comedy," *Jacobean City Comedy* (London, 1968), p. 18.

5 (London, 1937, 1957).

6 Earl Miner makes the "social mode" a defining characteristic of Jonson's poetry in *The Cavalier Mode from Jonson to Cotton* (Princeton: Princeton Univ. Press, 1971).

7 Computer analysis for this study was performed on a Control Data Corporation 6400 computer at the Vogelback Computer Center, Northwestern University, using the *Statistical Package for the Social Sciences,* version 2.3.

8 William Empson, "The Alchemist," *Hudson Review,* 22 (1969-70), 607.

9 Judd Arnold, "Lovewit's Triumph and Jonsonian Morality: A Reading of 'The Alchemist'," *Criticism,* 11 (1969), 165.

10 That is, we have used all the whole comedies entirely by Jonson from the first comedy that he wished to include in his folio through the last of certain date. This excludes the early *Case is Altered* and the probably early but revised *Tale of a Tub,* H & S, I, 306ff and I, 279ff.

11 All quotations from Jonson's poems are from the edition of William B. Hunter, Jr., *The Complete Poetry of Ben Jonson* (Garden City, N. Y.: Doubleday, 1963).

12 H & S, I, 64.

13 Recently, J. B. Bamborough adopts the traditional three categories for his discussion of the comedies, *Ben Jonson* (London, 1970).

14 Pater Laslett, *The World We Have Lost* (London, 1965), pp. 22-37.

15 *Every Man Out of His Humour,* Characters, 11. 78-80; H & S, III, 425.

16 Keith Thomas, *Religion and the Decline of Magic* (New York, 1971), p. 4.

17 *The Poetaster* V.i.17; H & S, IV, 290. It is interesting in this regard that Jonson introduces the English class term "gentle" into the description of the dabbler poet in his revised translation of Horace's *Art of Poetrie* (Hunter, p. 313).

18 For the rhetoric of praise and blame, see O. B. Hardison, Jr., *The Enduring Monument* (Chapel Hill, 1962).

19 Many critics have noted the extent to which Jonson endows his rogues with some admirable qualities. Jonas Barish, for example, concludes "into all these characters Jonson infuses a heavy current of his own creative energy, which counteracts to some extent the formal disapproval he may think he wishes us to feel." See "Jonson and the Loathed Stage" in *A Celebration of Ben Jonson,* ed. by William Blissett, R. W. Van Fossen, and Julian Patrick (Toronto, 1973), p. 52.

20 Maurice Ashley, *England in the Seventeenth Century* (Baltimore, 1952), pp. 12ff, and Christopher Hill, *The Century of Revolution: 1603-1714* (New York, 1961), pp. 17ff.

21 For criticism of the "two audiences" idea see Alfred Harbage, *Shakespeare's Audience* (New York, 1941), pp. 139ff, and Gibbons, p. 27.

22 H & S, VI, 15.

23 Empson, p. 607.

24 "The Prologue for the Stage," 11. 29-30; H & S, VI, 282. D. F. McKenzie discusses Jonson's antagonism to his audiences in *"The Staple of News* and the Late Plays," *A Celebration of Ben Jonson,* pp. 83-128.

25 For example, George Puttenham discusses "Poets that wrote . . . the common behaviours and maner of life of private persons, and such as were the meaner sort of men, and they were called *Comicall* Poets" (*The Arte of English Poesie* [1589] reprinted in *English Literary Criticsm: The Renaissance,* ed. O. B. Hardison, Jr. [New York,1963], p. 159).

26 *An Apologie for Poetrie* (1583), reprinted in Hardison, *English Literary Criticism,* p. 139.

27 The total population here consists of all poem characters coded for attitude.

28 The total population here consists of all comic characters coded for class.

The Ovids of Ben Jonson in *Poetaster* and in *Epicoene*

Joseph A. Dane

In a seminal article on Jonson's use of classical material in *Epicoene,* Jonas Barish described the play as Jonson's attempt to reconcile the courtly "alien spirit" of Ovid and the "more kindred satiric attitude of Juvenal." The result, according to Barish, is dissonance; *Epicoene* contains "a series of brilliant discords, which . . . fail to fuse into a unified whole."[1] Barish's thesis has since been criticized,[2] and the vulnerability of his argument to such criticism is clear. To begin with, a negative judgment as to the play's unity violates the history of the play's critical reception. Neander, in Dryden's *An Essay of Dramatick Poesie,* described the play as follows: "The action of the Play is intirely one; . . . The Intrigue of it is the greatest and most noble of any pure unmix'd Comedy in any Language."[3] Neander's opinion may not be definitive, nor is it necessarily Dryden's own; but it is one Dryden at least considered legitimate and one Barish's essay cannot account for. Furthermore, to "prove" dissonance is less easy than to "prove" unity—the critic arguing for unity always has two basic facts on which to ground his argument: the text itself, printed and read as a single unit, and any performance of the entire text. A play cannot be "proved" to have no unity without denying the validity of both text and performance. Yet as long as the play continues to be published as a single unit and continues to be read at one sitting, such unity has no particular need of a critical defense. The critical responses to the play, both negative and positive, are not so much attacks and defenses of the aesthetics of the play as explorations into the various facets of the text which reflect or constitute its basic unity—a unity which may be described as constituted by the author who wrote this unit, the text which preserves it, or by the audience that acknowledges this unit and the publishers who transmit the text.

In the following paper, I do not argue for or against such aesthetic unity. I assume that both Barish's criticism and later defenses of the play are essentially "correct" in that they represent competent responses to the same text. Rather, I wish to examine one of the elements in the play that seems to me to lie near the center of this dispute: the recognition in this play of elements which can be named "Ovidian." There is no question that such elements are present. Herford and Simpson's notes catalogue a substantial number of passages translated directly from Ovid and no one to my knowledge has denied the relevance of their citations.[4] In that I and perhaps most twentieth-century readers are more familiar with Latin than with Greek[5] and probably are more comfortable with Ovid's Latin than with the more difficult Latin of Juvenal, the texts of Ovid are somewhat privileged; to a modern reader, they are more closely integrated into the text of *Epicoene* than either those of Libanius or of Juvenal. A failure to resolve the classical allusions in terms of the most familiar texts (those of Ovid) is perhaps a more serious failure as far as the modern audience is concerned than it would have been for Jonson's contemporaries.

The question I will ask here is as follows: "What is it in Jonson's two plays, *Poetaster* and *Epicoene,* we describe under the heading 'Ovid' or its derivative 'Ovidian,' and what indications do we have in *Epicoene* that tell us, as an audience, how this is to be defined in the particular play?" In his 1970 article, Ferns criticizes Barish for confusing Jonson the man with Jonson's text (p. 253), but he does not note that, when dealing with a text that includes direct citations from previous texts, the same difficulty is confronted on another level: who was Ovid? what *are* Ovid's texts? and finally, what sorts of attitudes are traditionally associated with or attributed to those texts? When a playwright includes any one of these features in his play, perhaps by providing a name "Ovid" or by alluding to texts or attitudes we associate with this name, precisely what is being introduced? Do we read into *Epicoene* only those Latin passages cited in the notes of Herford and Simpson, or do we read into the play the whole Ovidian canon as well as the various legends associated with that name?

In the pages that follow, I will argue that the above questions are specifically raised by Jonson, particularly in relation to the elements of his two plays that we must relate to the complex of words and meanings attached to the name "Ovid." The earlier play, *Poetaster* (1601), shows that there are different Ovids available to Jonson and used by him; in *Epicoene* (1609), there are different motifs and themes that all may be labelled "Ovidian." I shall continue critical concerns with the notion of unity, and argue for an understanding of the "Ovidian" whereby this feature can be seen as a unifying force in *Epicoene,* not merely as a pole of the Juvenal-Ovid debate. My choice of Ovid as the focus of discussion may be considered arbitrary; the dialogue between Ovid and Juvenal may be viewed as merely an ancillary theme woven over an "elaborate central conceit" from Libanius,[6] or as merely one element in an essentially baroque structure.[7] However, my choice is an implicit acknowledgement of the central importance of a particular theme in *my* understanding of the play—a theme which for convenience I shall posit as central to the structure of the play itself and to the play as conceived by its author.

Of the various Ovids, I shall distinguish three as follows:

(1) Ovid-*poeta:* the poet himself as described in the *Tristia;* and in various medieval legends of Ovid's life (Ovidian *vitae*);

(2) Ovidian texts: the entire *opera* attributed to Ovid;

(3) Ovidian attitudes: attitudes traditionally associated with Ovid and alluded to by recent critics as "Ovidian"; here, the word "Ovidian" is roughly equivalent to the equally undefinable "courtly."[8]

In the earlier work, *Poetaster,* we are dealing primarily with Ovid-*poeta* as described by the medieval *vitae*. The relation of this Ovid to Ovid's own texts is secondary. Ovid's texts never make clear the cause of his exile, although both the *Tristia* and *Ex Ponto* take that exile as their basic subject matter. Furthermore, even Ovid's brief autobiography in *Tristia* IV.x is contradicted in *Poetaster*. According to Ovid, his father was some ninety years old when he died (taking *lustrum* in line 90 as a five-year period); he died before Ovid's exile (lines 75-80) and some thirty or forty years after his advice that Ovid become a lawyer. Ovid himself was married to his third wife when exiled (lines 69-76) and a rather old man at the time (lines 93-96). He was never acquainted with Tibullus and only saw Virgil (lines 51-52).

Jonson is clearly working within another tradition here, one that does not consider itself bound to the factual constraints imposed by the *Tristia*. By the Renaissance, Ovid's *vita* had been elaborated quite beyond the few details given in the *Tristia* through various conjectures by medieval writers. The earliest reference to the causes of Ovid's exile is by Sidonius in the fifth century; but the principal sources for Ovid's *vita* are the later *accessus,* the earliest of which is from the eleventh century.[9] The *accessus* are short introductions to Ovid's works either appearing in a separate manuscript or in manuscripts of Ovid's texts. Like Jonson's play, they were designed to make a point, not to relay biographical information. They were intended to introduce the beginning student to the work of Ovid by answering specific questions, such as "Who was the author?" "What is the title?" and "To what part of philosophy does the work belong?"[10] They provide a quasi-critical introduction to the work and under the heading "author" such commentary is in the form of a biographical etiology—what sort of historical circumstances are coherent with the details presented in the text? At times, biographical details are supplied to explain mere accidents of textual transmission: the *Amores* had no title in some manuscripts; an eleventh-century *accessus* explains "sine titulo i. sine laude": Ovid gave no title *because* (1) he was not seeking fame, or (2) Augustus had been so enraged by his *Ars Amatoria* that he did not dare supply a title.[11] In *Poetaster,* what we have is a continuation of this rather flexible tradition, that of the quasi-critical *vitae.* Jonson's Ovid-*poeta* is not even an historical poet; rather he is a critical fiction emanating from medieval exegetes of the Ovidian texts.

Now critical response to *Poetaster*'s Ovid varies. Herford and Simpson characterize the Ovid story as "only an episode" and the parting scene between Ovid and Julia as having "no proper place in comedy at all unless the unwitting grotesquerie of their love-making suffice to merit one."[12] Others have taken this Ovid more seriously: Talbert finds Ovid the symbol of a "virtuous man in a barbarous age" and equates his banishment to the poets' banishment from Plato's republic.[13] Campbell analyzes the Ovid story as the "structural center of *Poetaster*" with Ovid representing the "dissolute courtly society."[14] To most recent critics, Campbell's conception of Ovid is essentially correct. Ovid represents the poet with no sense of social responsibility; in this, he is distinguished from his classical counterparts and although his punishment is not presented as a subject of laughter, he is justly banished.15

Despite disagreement as to the importance of Ovid in the play, all these critics acknowledge that Ovid here is a personage, a *motif* with certain symbolic implications. Ovid *stands for* something else, and this "something else" does not depend directly on Ovid's texts. The Ovidian *theme,*16 the complex unit defined by various other motifs associated with the name "Ovid," is derived from the tradition of medieval *vitae.*17 Jonson's most direct allusion to the Ovidian texts in *Poetaster* is the translation in Act I, scene i, of *Amores* I.xv. Ignored are the mythological works *(Fasti, Ars Amatoria, Metamorphoses)*— the only works Ovid himself sees fit to mention consistently in his *Tristia* (see, e.g., *Tristia* I.i.61, I.vii.16-23, II.551-56, III. xiv.17-19, etc.). Yet even here, the allusion is indirect. For the translation in *Poetaster* is not Jonson's own; it is Marlowe's, which Jonson only slightly modifies. Ovid's text is as distant as the Roman Ovid. Just as Ovid-*poeta* must be seen through and defined by the opaque grid of the medieval *vitae,* so must the Ovidian text be seen through and defined by Marlowe's translation—one that pays more attention to fluency and style than (often lexical) substance. And if we take the "Ovidian" in sense 3 listed above, that is, as superficial social manners and courtliness, such "Ovidian" attitudes, which are of a kind that a fragment of Ovid's early work could be (mis)construed to represent, are condemned along with their "author."

Although both Barish and his critics refer to the Ovid of *Poetaster* in discussing what is Ovidian in *Epicoene,*18 "Ovid" and "the Ovidian" are not necessarily equivalent. Earlier in this paper, I spoke of my intention to see the Ovid of *Epicoene* as a unifying force rather than as productive of discordance or as the spokesman for indefensible social attitudes. The key to such an understanding of *Epicoene*'s Ovid lies in the sharp distinction made by Jonson between the Ovid of *Poetaster* and the Ovid in *Epicoene.* A symbolic and quasi-historical Ovid is possible in *Poetaster* because he is named: "Ovid" is a symbolic motif. But he is not a named motif in *Epicoene*: Ovid is a theme, and our determination or identification of "the Ovidian" will depend on the motifs we see as constituting such a theme. These motifs are not those of the Ovidian *vitae* but rather those of the Ovidian texts, texts which are kept virtually present throughout the play through direct prose translation and through the inclusion of extensive mythological allusions.

Poetaster opens with Ovid the hero of the *vitae*. The first allusion to Ovid in *Epicoene,* however, consists of Truewit's prose translations from *Ars Amatoria* III (I.i.103-11, 113-26). The name "Ovid" does not appear here; to supply that name, we must first recognize the texts themselves. Whereas *Poetaster* establishes its Ovid through Ovid-*poeta, Epicoene* does so through Ovid's texts. Furthermore, Ovid's verse is rendered here as prose. Marlowe's rhymed couplets in *Poetaster* retain the formal closed couplet of elegy—a purely stylistic feature. The prose in *Epicoene* does away with this mark of elegiac style. As stated by Ferns: "Ovid's lightness and gentle comedy is diminished to a characteristic Jonsonian bluntness" (p. 249).

In Herford and Simpson's notes, only those passages translated directly from Ovid are quoted. In addition to the lines in Act I, a further reference occurs in the closing lines of the play (V.iv.237-39). The bulk of the Ovid translations occurs in Act IV and all this material is translated from the *Ars Amatoria*.19 This concentration by Herford and Simpson on the single text is in a sense misleading. While the editors identify all the lengthy borrowings from Ovid, the impression that the Ovidian theme in *Epicoene* is determined by this particular text would be a false one. For these passages are not *only* borrowings; they are also signals to an extensive and identifiable body of Ovid's texts. While no audience could be reasonably expected to respond with line references and quotations from the Latin originals (that Jonson has distorted Ovid's phrases and even Ovid's intent might be quite lost on an audience without immediate access to the Latin text), an audience could be expected to know and to recognize the author of these lines. They could also be expected to know that there is no single attitude that one could legitimately name and define as "Ovidian" after reading through the texts of that author. Ovid is not only the sophisticated, urbane poet of the *Amores,* nor is "biting satire" something to be found only in his satiric counterpart of *Epicoene,* Juvenal (see, e.g., the *Ibis*). Ovid is also a mythological encyclopedist; due to the popularity of the *Metamorphoses,* once the Ovidian has been established by Ovidian texts, any mythological references in the play, particularly those dealing with transformation, will serve as reinforcement (see, e.g., the reference to the Gorgon in Act I.iii.2 immediately following Truewit's speech).20 Our theme becomes one under which we can organize a whole series of mythological motifs best known through Ovid's texts.

Acts II and III contain no passages that seem translated directly from Ovid. Yet because Ovidian texts have been introduced in Act I, the "Ovidian" in at least one of the senses outlined above is still potentially involved in our perception of the play. What Jonson does in these two acts, I believe, is not merely to set up Juvenal's Satire VI as a polar opposition to Ovid's elegies, but to clarify the "Ovidian" in such a way that it can emerge as a unifying force in the final resolution of the play.

As far as direct translation is concerned, Act II is dominated by Juvenal's Satire VI, probably the best known and most easily recognizable of his work.21 But Ovid is not entirely forgotten. Act II presents the Ovidian in sense 3—"Ovidian" attitudes and sentiments, based not on the poet, nor on his work, but rather on his reception. Truewit introduces Ovidian matter through his prose translations, but in Act II we are presented with what seems to be an "Ovidian" style, or at least a parody of that style by Daw in his "madrigall of modestie" (II.iii.24-40):

> Modest, and faire, for faire and good are neere,
> Neighbors, how eere.—
> No noble vertue ever was alone,
> But two in one.

Repetition, alliteration, assonance—Daw manages to pack in as much superficial and easy rhetorical ornament as the lines can comfortably hold. The elegiac form itself (absent from Truewit's prose) is also parodied to an extreme: Daw's closed couplets caricature the long line/short line opposition of elegy— the only clear formal structure to emerge from his madrigal despite an apparent attempt to produce Alcaics or Sapphics. But Dauphine and Clermont do not respond to the form or style of the song, only to its *sentence*, which is not Ovidian *sentence* at all. The parallels they suggest are Seneca and Plutarch, which only serve to stress how inadequately Daw has considered matters of genre: he has used a lyric form and elegiac clichés (e.g., *duo in uno*) to cloak the matter of Stoic prose.

Daw, then, represents an improper reception of the classical tradition. And this improper reception of tradition constitutes

the focus of Act II. Daw's catalogue of prose writers and poets
following his madrigal includes nearly the entire canon: Aristotle, Plato, Thucydides, Livy, Tacitus, Pindar, Lycophron,
Anacreon, Catullus, Seneca, Lucan, Propertius, Tibullus, Martial, Juvenal, Ausonius, Statius, Politian, Horace (II.iii.57-71).
It is significant that the only popular classical poet who is omitted from this catalogue and whose work has already been cited
and quoted in the play is Ovid. Even when we are directed
toward a style we might associate with Ovid (superficial
rhetorical ornament) and toward attitudes we might name
"Ovidian," Jonson refuses to give us the name "Ovid." Daw, La
Foole, and the Collegiates, all of whom are objects of Jonson's
satire, never quote Ovid directly as does Truewit, and never are
their sentiments directly associated with the name *Ovid*. What
Jonson is doing, it seems, is to limit his definition of the Ovidian.
To Jonson, courtly attitudes are not properly Ovidian at all, but
are the product of a superficial reading of Ovid's texts or a
superficial understanding of them.

Act II, then, in addition to establishing the texts of Juvenal,
also functions to define what is properly Ovidian. Ovid and
Juvenal are surely in opposition here, but the play is not given
over to Silver Age satire. Just as Daw misuses his tradition, so
does Morose. According to Barish, the function of Morose is
primarily to parody Juvenal: "the spirit of Juvenal is kept at bay
and mocked in the figure of Morose." But Morose is also "striving to be like Ovid," which Barish characterizes as a "lapse . . .
where the Ovidian attitude . . . tends to break down."22 This
shift of Morose's allegiance from Juvenal to Ovid need not suggest that Jonson has nodded. Morose represents improper reception of the Ovidian *opera* as does Daw: "I have ever had my
breeding in court" (II.v.31); "Deare lady, I am courtly" (II.v.
46).23 Courtliness and superficial manners are rejected by association with Morose just as superficial rhetoric is rejected by its
association with Daw. The terminology of modern critics (see
above, note 8) proves that both such sentiment and rhetoric
could be understood by a competent audience as "Ovidian,"
and it is precisely this potential definition of "Ovidian" that
Jonson himself rejects.

Act III presents a different perspective on the Ovidian. The
Ovid of Act III is Ovid the mythographer. "*Iupiter* did turne
himselfe into a—Taurus" (III.i.25-26);"Did not *Pasiphae,* who

was a queene, loue a bull?" (III.iii.126-28); "Calisto, the mother of *Arcas*" (III.iii.126-28). It is possible, of course, to find esoteric sources for these references; they may also have been known through English sources. But Jonson himself names a source in III.iii.132: "ex Ouidij metamorphosi," the first mention of Ovid by name in the play. As critics, we have a right to trace these sources wherever we wish; as an audience, however, we have little choice but to follow the directions given in the play. Furthermore, the manner in which Ovid's name is introduced is significant: earlier, Ovid was omitted from Daw's catalogue of poets; here, his name appears, but because of its Latin form and inflection, it is firmly bound to an Ovidian text. What we are to understand as "Ovidian" in *Epicoene* is neither a poet nor a social sentiment, but a body of poetic works. Further allusions to those works follow: "Why, did you think you had married a statue?" (Pygmalian from *Metamorphoses* X.244ff); "Penthesilea," "Amazonian impudence" (*Ars Amatoria* II.743, III.2; *Heroïdes* XXI.120-21, etc.). Ovid's poetry becomes a basic medium of communication. And if we wish to test the range of that medium, Jonson gives us every opportunity. In scene v, the catalogue of curses makes sense not because of its necessary contribution to the intrigue but because it too relates to an Ovidian work, the *Ibis*, a *locus classicus* for virtuoso invective.24 And finally, in the closing scene of Act III, a familiar face reappears, and in this instance its basis in the *Metamorphoses* is explicit:

Morose: Is that *Gorgon*, that *Medusa* come? Hide me,
        hide me.
Truewit: I warrant you, sir, shee will not transforme you.
                              (III.vii.21-23)

It is this context that sets up the numerous passages in Act IV translated directly from Ovid's *Ars Amatoria* and there is little need to add to the citations in Herford and Simpson's notes. Act IV elaborates on the Ovidian theme established in the first three acts but always within the fixed limits of Ovid's texts. The stark prose translations and the absence of the name "Ovid" limit this theme precisely at the point where it could become equated with stylistic ornament or associated with a legendary romance. In the final act, we begin to see how thoroughly Jonson has incorporated Ovidian texts into his own text. The title of Ovid's *magnum opus*, "Metamorphoses," seems

to constitute the logic and the coherence of the entire action of
the play. Truewit can change styles at will and the logic of
reversal controls his various machinations. His scheme to prevent Morose from marrying backfires in Act II: Morose decides
to marry all the sooner. But the apparently negative result turns
out to be a positive one; Dauphine *wants* the marriage to take
place and Truewit's "failure" becomes a success. By Act V,
such a logic of transformation is clearly established, and the
sexual ambiguities, disguises, as well as the revealing of Epicoene's identity and sex are all in conformity with it. This logic
of transformation, as well as what E. B. Partridge defines as the
central image of *Epicoene,* that of hermaphroditism, both develop through allusions to Ovidian texts.25 Morose states the
theme of sexual metamorphosis directly: "I am no man, ladies"
(V.iv.44) and the importance of such sexual transformation is
underscored in the final act when the audience learns for the
first time that the woman is no woman. Sexual transformation
is of course frequent in the *Metamorphoses* (see, e.g., Caeneus
XII.190ff, Teresias III.316ff). But similar themes also occur in
the love elegies. A striking example is *Amores* III.vii(vi), a
single elegy that coordinates many of the same themes that are
central to *Epicoene:* impotence, wealth, and ambiguity of sexual
roles:

> nec potui cupiens, pariter cupiente puella,
>   inguinis effeti parte iuuante frui.
>   (lines 5-6)
> a, pudet annorum: quo me iuuenemque uirumque?
>   nec iuuenem nec me sensit amica uirum.
>   (lines 19-20)
> quo mihi fortunae tantum? quo regna sine usu?
>   quid, nisi possedi diues auarus opes?
>   (lines 49-50)
>
> (Though both of us performed our true intent,
> Yet could I not cast anchor where I meant. . . .
> I blush, that being youthful, hot and lusty,
> I prove neither youth nor man, but old and rusty. . . .
> Why was I blest? why made king to refuse it?
> Chuff-like had I not gold and could not use it?)26

Again, the specific elegy is less important than the mere fact that
it exists; for it is here, in specific works of Ovid, that we find the
basis for the coherence of various motifs and themes in Jonson's
play, not as in *Poetaster* in biographical conjectures. *Epicoene*

is itself a metamorphosis of Ovid's texts: it contains all the varied tones and ambiguities found in those texts that we can still refer to as a coherent unit under the single name of their author. Ovid's poetry contains a scope hardly to be found in the Ovidian *vitae* or in the notion of "courtliness." The strict opposition between Ovid as "courtly lover" and Juvenal the "biting satirist" dissolves if we define the Ovidian by the body of his work rather than by a single fragment of that work or by the romantic elaboration of his own allusive autobiographical notes. Ovid's poetry itself is a synthesis and compendium of classical traditions and it is difficult to view such an Ovid as alien to Ben Jonson.

That Jonson conceived poetry as ethical is not to be doubted. And neither *Poetaster* nor *Epicoene* can be regarded as indifferent to questions of the relation of poetry to society. If we are to see a change in Jonson's use of Ovid in these two works, it is to be found in his manner of stating those questions. In *Poetaster,* poetry itself is viewed as the product of particular poets, whether those poets are historical, contemporary, or purely fictitious. The ethical dimension of poetry is equivalent to the relation of the poet himself to his actual society. In *Epicoene,* however, the *poeta* is nowhere to be seen. Poetic truth is no longer presented as the product of a knower or of a wilful distorter of that truth; rather, the truth itself is allowed to float free.[27] In *Epicoene,* there is no longer a question of good and bad poets. Rather, a particular body of poetry, that of Ovid, is allowed to act as a mediator of discord and an expression of the multiplicity of tones that must ultimately constitute any truth. By pruning away unwanted features of the "Ovidian," Jonson allows the Ovidian texts to support his own text, both of which, apart from their authors, participate in whatever truth the play itself may be said to present.

NOTES

[1] Jonas A. Barish, "Ovid, Juvenal and the Silent Woman," *PMLA,* 46 (1956), 222, 224; see also *Ben Jonson and the Language of Prose Comedy* (Cambridge: Harvard Univ. Press, 1960), pp. 146-86.

[2] John Ferns, "Ovid, Juvenal, and The Silent Woman: A Reconsideration," *MLR,*

65 (1970), 248; see also Mark A. Anderson, "The Successful Unity of *Epicoene:* A Defense of Ben Jonson," *SEL,* 10 (1970), 349-66, and W. David Kay, "Jonson's Urbane Gallants: Humanistic Contexts for *Epicoene,*" *HLQ,* 39 (1976), 251-66.

3 H. T. Swedenberg, Jr., ed., *The Works of John Dryden,* XVII (Berkeley: Univ. of California Press, 1971), 59.

4 C. H. Herford and Percy Simpson, *Ben Jonson* (Oxford: Clarendon Press, 1925-53), X: *Commentary,* 1-46. References to *Epicoene* and *Poetaster* are to Vols. V and VI.

5 Ibid., X, 8: "Jonson used the 1597 edition of [Libanius'] declamation, issued at Paris with a Latin translation by Morellus; Jonson's text occasionally shows traces of the Latin."

6 Ray L. Heffner, Jr., "Unifying Symbols in the Comedy of Ben Jonson," in *English Stage Comedy,* ed. W. K. Wimsatt, Jr., English Institute Essays (1954), rpt. *Ben Jonson: A Collection of Critical Essays,* ed. Jonas A. Barish (Englewood Cliffs: Prentice-Hall, 1963), pp. 133-46.

7 Freda L. Townsend, *Apologie for Bartholmew Fayre: The Art of Jonson's Comedies* (New York: MLA, 1947), pp. 62-66.

8 Anderson, p. 356: "Ovidian position," p. 359: "Ovidian arguments"; Barish, "Ovid, Juvenal and the Silent Woman," p. 214: "Ovidian statement," p. 222: "Ovidian attitude"; Ferns, p. 248: "Ovidian artifices and Ovidian sentiments."

9 For texts of medieval references to Ovid's exile and its causes, see John C. Thibault, *The Mystery of Ovid's Exile* (Berkeley: Univ. of California Press, 1964), pp. 24-32.

10 For texts and discussion of Ovid's *vitae,* see Fausto Ghisalberti, "Medieval Biographies of Ovid," *Journal of the Warburg and Courtauld Institutes,* 9 (1946), 10-60. On the *accessus* itself, see Edwin A. Quain, "The Medieval *Accessus ad Auctores,*" *Traditio,* 3 (1946), 215-64, and R. B. C. Huygens, *Accessus ad Auctores: Bernard d'Utrecht, Conrad d'Hirsau, Dialogus super Auctores,* revised ed. (Leiden: Brill, 1970). Ovid's *vitae* are considerably later than those of Virgil; see Colinus Hardie, ed., *Vitae Vergilianae antiquae,* Oxford Classical Texts (Oxford: Clarendon Press, 1966), which includes a *vita* by Donatus and an *accessus* by Servius. Both were intended to be joined to commentaries and like the later *vitae* are primarily critical rather than biographical; Domenico Comparetti, *Vergil in the Middle Ages,* tr. E. F. M. Benecke (London: Sonnenchein, 1895), pp. 135-55.

11 Ghisalberti, p. 12, n. 2.

12 Herford and Simpson, I, 430, 440.

13 Ernest William Talbert, "Purpose and Technique of Jonson's *Poetaster,*" *SP,* 42 (1946), 244-45.

14 Oscar James Campbell, *Comicall Satyre and Shakespeare's Troilus and Cressida* (Los Angeles: Adcraft Press, 1938), pp. 113-28; cf. Barish, "Ovid, Juvenal, and the Silent Woman," p. 220, n. 10; following Campbell, Barish sees Ovid as a "symbol for poetic talent debased by worldly affections."

15 Eugene M. Waith, "Poets' Morals in the *Poetaster,*" *MLQ,* 12 (1951), 17; Leonard B. Terr, "Ben Jonson's *Ars Poetica:* A Reinterpretation of *Poetaster,*" *Thoth,* 11 (1971), 3-16; Karl F. Zender, "The Function of Propertius in Jonson's *Poetaster,*" *PLL,* 11 (1975), 308-12. See also the excellent discussion in Gabriele Bernhard Jackson, *Vision and Judgment in Ben Jonson's Drama,* Yale Studies in English, 166 (New Haven: Yale Univ. Press, 1968), pp. 20-30 and J. A. Bryant, Jr., *The Compassionate Satirist: Ben Jonson and his Imperfect World* (Athens: Univ. of Georgia Press, 1972), pp. 44-50.

16 For distinction between "theme" and "motif" see Paul Zumthor, *Essai de poéti-*

que médiévale (Paris: Seuil, 1972), pp. 147-52. A motif is a unit of sense combining various semantic and lexical elements of the text; a theme is a unit composed of various motifs. The relation is hierarchical. For our purposes, the difference can be considered to lie in the fact that a motif can be quoted from a text—it is composed of specific words. A theme must be *named* by the critic; e.g., "Ovid" is a motif; "the Ovidian" in any of the senses outlined above is a theme.

17 The ethical focus of *Poetaster* is also consistent with the medieval tradition. To the medieval commentator, any work dealing with manners *(mores)* was part of ethics. See, e.g., Ghisalberti, quoting Giovanni del Virgilio's 14th century commentary—"nam omnes poete tendunt in mores"—and precedents for Giovanni on p. 23.

18 Barish, "Ovid, Juvenal, and the Silent Woman," p. 220, n. 10; Ferns, p. 252.

19 See Herford and Simpson, X, 28-36, notes to Act IV, scenes i-iv.

20 For Ovid's influence on the Renaissance, see Douglas Bush, *Mythology and the Renaissance Tradition in English Poetry* (New York: Pageant, 1947), *passim* and Henrietta R. Palmer, *List of English Editions and Translations of Greek and Latin Classics Printed before 1641* (London: Blades, 1911), p. 79. Whatever esoteric handbook or text Jonson may have known, most of his audience would have been more familiar with Ovid. Charles Francis Wheeler, *Classical Mythology in the Plays, Masques, and Poems of Ben Jonson* (Port Washington, Kennikat Press, 1970) overstresses esoteric sources, listing for the Gorgon such sources as Apollodorus and Hesiod. More familiar sources would be *Metamorphoses,* IV.498ff; *Ars Amatoria,* III.505, II.309; *Amores,* III.iv.14, III.xii.23, etc.

21 For Jonson's use of Juvenal, see Barish, "Ovid, Juvenal, and the Silent Woman," and Kathryn A. McEuen, "Jonson and Juvenal," *RES,* 21 (1945), 92-104.

22 Barish, "Ovid, Juvenal, and the Silent Woman," p. 222, and *Language of Prose Comedy,* p. 148. See also Ferns, p. 251.

23 In line 64, Morose inadvertently associates himself with Ovid's *Invidia:* "That sorrow doth fill me with gladness"; cf. *Metamorphoses,* II.796: "Vixque tenet lacrimas, quia nil lacrimabile cernit."

24 L. P. Wilkinson, *Ovid Recalled* (Cambridge: Cambridge Univ. Press, 1955), p. 30: "The poet is clearly interested in his own hyperbolic ingenuity, not in the efficacy of his curses or even in verisimilitude. . . . [T]he *Ibis* has the qualities of the winning entry in a competition in invective set by a literary magazine."

25 Edward B. Partridge, *The Broken Compass: A Study of the Major Comedies of Ben Jonson* (New York: Columbia Univ. Press, 1958), pp. 161-78; "The Allusiveness of *Epicoene,*" *ELH,* 22 (1955), 93-107.

26 E. J. Kenney, ed., *P. Ovidi Nasonis Amores, Medicamina Faciei Femineae, Ars Amatoria, Remedia Amoris,* Oxford Classical Texts (Oxford: Clarendon Press, 1965). The translation is by Marlowe; Stephen Orgel, ed., *Christopher Marlowe: The Complete Poems and Translations* (Baltimore: Penguin, 1971), pp. 171-72.

27 See *Ex Ponto,* I.i.29-30.
"Si dubitas de me, laudes admitte deorum,
    et carmen dempto nomine sume meum."

Two Renaissance Views of Carthage:
Trissino's *Sofonisba* and Castellini's *Asdrubale*

Beatrice Corrigan

I

"The *Sofonisba* of Trissino, which belongs to the beginning of the sixteenth century, is generally named as the first regular tragedy. This literary curiosity I cannot boast of having read, but from other sources I know the author to be a spiritless pedant. Those even of the learned, who are most zealous for the imitation of the ancients, pronounce it a dull labored work, without a breath of true poetical spirit; we may, therefore, without further examination, safely appeal to their judgement upon it."[1] Since August Schlegel wrote those words in 1809 a long series of critics have been content to accept his estimate of *Sofonisba,* without his candor, however, in acknowledging their ignorance of the work itself. There has been some degree of revaluation done by modern Italian editors, and I should like here to re-examine the tragedy and Trissino's purpose in writing it, and to compare it with another Carthaginian tragedy written forty-five years later, the *Asdrubale* of Jacopo Castellini.

When Giangiorgio Trissino began to compose *Sofonisba* in 1514, he was twenty-six.[2] A nobleman of Vicenza, wealthy, educated by some of the leading humanists of the day, an enthusiast for Greek literature, he was forced in 1509 to leave his native city when it was captured by Venice from the Emperor, whose party he had supported. For eight years he lived in Ferrara, Mantua, and Rome; he met most of the leading figures of the era, and became the friend and correspondent of Lucrezia Borgia and her sister-in-law, Isabella d'Este, married to Duke Francesco Gonzaga. *Sofonisba* was written at least in part in Rome, and was dedicated to the Medici Pope, Leo X. It was not printed until 1525, though it circulated widely in manuscript from the time of its completion.

The subject was taken from Livy's *History of Rome,* Book XXX, with additions from Appian and Dion Cassius. The time of the play is 201 B.C., at the end of the Second Punic War. Sofonisba, daughter of Hasdrubal, niece of Hannibal, is the wife of Syphax, King of the Massylians. Her father had earlier promised her to Massinissa, King of the Numidians, but the Carthaginians bribed Syphax with her hand to desert the Roman cause for theirs. Massinissa in revenge joined the Romans, and when the play opens has just aided them to defeat Syphax and capture his native city, Cirta. Among the captives is Sofonisba, devoted to Carthage and liberty, who pleads with Massinissa not to deliver her alive into Roman hands. Moved by her beauty and his ancient love he promises, and weds her immediately to strengthen his right to protect her. Though the Roman General, Lelius, and Cato rebuke him, he is adamant; but he cannot withstand the logic and lofty virtue of his friend and model, Scipio. He keeps his promise by sending Sofonisba a cup of poison, and she drinks it intrepidly. Too late he devises a scheme for her escape. She is already dead, and he can only assure safety and freedom for her little son and the women of her household.

The choice of an historical rather than a mythological subject had a profound influence on Italian and on Western European tragedy generally. Important too was the love interest, so contrary in its mood to classical tragic tradition, so congenial to Renaisance taste.

Trissino's tragedy was not the first appearance of Sofonisba in Italian literature. Both Boccaccio and Petrarch had celebrated her, the former in *De Claris Mulieribus,*[3] the second in both his epic poem, *Africa,* and in the *Trionfo d'Amore,* where both style and form (Massinissa tells their story while Sofonisba is silent) suggest an analogy to the episode of Paolo and Francesca. A tragedy on the subject actually was written before Trissino's: the *Sofonisba* of Galeotto Del Carretto, irregular in dramatic form and composed in *ottava rima,* was dedicated in manuscript to Isabella d'Este Gonzaga in 1502, but was not published until 1546.

It has been suggested that Trissino, a belated Ghibelline, found the triumph of Romans over barbarians a congenial topic.

But another reason may have made both Trissino and Del Carretto, certainly no supporter of the Empire, see in the misfortunes of Sofonisba—her land invaded, her kingdom lost, her child in danger—a situation familiar in their own day and among their own friends. Del Carretto, like Trissino, was of a noble Northern Italian family, and he too, though earlier than Trissino, visited Mantua and began a friendship with Isabella d'Este that continued until his death in 1530. Both writers were familiar with the Gonzaga family into which Isabella had married, and Trissino at least visited the court of Urbino, and was kindly received by Elisabetta Gonzaga, wife of Duke Guidobaldo della Rovere. In 1502 Cesare Borgia had seized Urbino, and Guidobaldo was forced to flee to Mantua, where Elisabetta was visiting her brother, Francesco Gonzaga. The following year Urbino was restored to its Duke, but Guidobaldo died in 1508; when Trissino knew Elisabetta Gonzaga she was a widow and her constant companion was Emilia Pia, the widow of the Duke's half-brother. Both ladies are affectionately portrayed in Castiglione's *Il Cortegiano,* and it is possible that Emilia's tender solicitude for her sister-in-law may have suggested to Trissino the figure and the name of Erminia, betrothed to Sofonisba's brother. Isabella d'Este too had known the perils of war; her husband had been taken prisoner by the Venetians, and in 1510 she was forced to surrender her little son to the Pope as a hostage. During this period in Isabella's life, Trissino was a frequent visitor to Mantua, and her misfortunes lent an immediacy to his play which would be evident to its first readers. He may also have met in Mantua Isabella's half-sister, Lucrezia, whose husband, Annibale Bentivoglio, had been driven from Bologna by Pope Julius II with great inhumanity, and who found temporary refuge for herself and her little daughters at the Gonzaga court.

A fellow-citizen of Vicenza, Luigi da Porto, had portrayed the woes of his city and his family in a novella, *Giulietta e Romeo;* Ariosto had drawn a parallel between the Saracen invasion of France and the French invasion of Italy in his *Orlando Furioso,* published in 1516. And in the Orti Oricellari, which Trissino frequented during visits to Florence in 1513-14, he must have met Niccolò Machiavelli, who was then discovering in Livy such profound lessons for Italy's future. The practice, then, of allusions to contemporary events in fictional and allegorical works, or of reading history for parallels to current events, was familiar at the period.

This consciousness of repeated historical patterns may explain why Trissino introduced the character of Sofonisba's little son. As his models for tragedy were Greek, the child whose fate hangs in the balance of war may have been suggested by the figure of Astyanax, son of Hector and Andromache, in *The Trojan Women*. Euripides gives him the fate that was his in classical tradition, and he is cast to his death from the walls of Troy by the conquering Greeks. A Renaissance version of his story, however, depicted him as miraculously saved, and Boiardo makes him the ancestor of Ruggiero, founder of the House of Este and heir to Hector's armor and valor. It may be conjectured that in *Sofonisba* as in the *Orlando Innamorato* the child is a symbol of hope for the future of its family and fatherland.

The character of Erminia is original and, as we have seen, was probably observed from life. In Appian it is the traditional nurse of Greek tragedy who is with Sofonisba at her death; Trissino's substitution for this hackneyed figure of a girl as young as Sofonisba herself, her childhood friend and kinswoman, is felicitous. Erminia is one of the most poetical figures in the play, and Tasso admired her so much that he borrowed her name for his exiled princess of Nicea in the *Gerusalemme*.

Syphax, dethroned and humbled, like Annibale Bentivoglio and so many more, must have had a special significance in Trissino's circle; the situation of Massinissa too paralleled that of many Italian princes. Dependent on a foreigner for the maintenance of his state, fighting against his fellow-countrymen under a foreigner's command, forced to subjugate his affections and his pledged honor to the arbitrary will of a foreign general, his plight is similar to that of Lodovico Sforza, of Francesco Gonzaga, and, as the century advanced, of many other Italian prince-captains in the service of the invaders. Brave, generous, impulsive, he must acknowledge his helplessness before the granite authority of Rome.

Sofonisba's character is more ambiguous. Her tenderness is evidenced by her scenes with Erminia and with her son, and by her dying memories of her parents. Tasso found her concern for the women of her household so touching that he attributed it later to his own doomed heroine, Clorinda. Yet her love for liberty and Carthage is probably her dominant emotion, and her husband's fate distresses her less for his own sake than because his defeat menaces Cirta and the Carthaginian cause as well as her own freedom.

The fifth division of Trissino's *Poetica* which deals with tragedy was composed many years later than *Sofonisba,* and was not completed until 1550. However in it *Sofonisba* is constantly used as an illustration of theories on modern tragedy; thus it provides a valuable commentary on the play by its own author. Setting his images of modern woe in antique dress firmly within the rigid confines of his classical Greek models, Trissino defines *Sofonisba* as a simple rather than a complex tragedy, a *tragedia passionale* like the *Ajax* of Sophocles.4 In both the chief character is moved to voluntary death by a trait of character: in Ajax excessive pride, in Sofonisba love of liberty, in both a lofty conception of honor. The play is not divided into acts, but, as Trissino explains in his *Poetica,* it has basically three parts, the second of which is subdivided. The divisions are marked by choruses, which are skillfully integrated with the action. The women of Cirta who compose the Chorus are devoted to their Queen and conscious that their fate depends on hers. Consequently their anxious questions and their comments on events are those of persons who share the hopes and fears of the protagonist, yet who are aware of some unalterable cosmic plan overruling the conflict of human wills. So important is their role that when the play was re-modelled in the eighteenth century many of their lines were distributed between Erminia and a newly invented character.

The Prologue is in the form of a dialogue between Erminia and Sofonisba, in which the latter recounts the story of Dido. This recalls the prologues of Euripides, in which the audience is told of past offences against the Gods which give significance to the tragic events which are to follow. As is fitting in a historical tragedy, Trissino presents in human terms the origin of the doom about to fall on Carthage. Sofonisba is unaware that Aeneas deserted Dido not through ill faith but by the command of the Gods, and that Juno was powerless to preserve her favorite city, Carthage, by preventing him from completing his voyage and founding Rome. It is the audience, familiar with Virgil, who can understand the significance of that ancient story of misplaced love and suicide, and who, later in the play, when

Sofonisba in her turn invokes the aid of Juno, know that the Goddess will still be powerless to save her from Dido's fate. The Gods, as Trissino says in his *Poetica,* should not appear on the stage, but, invisible, they control man's destiny and so elevate it above the trivial causation of chance or fortune to tragic nobility. He may also with this prologue intend to set Sofonisba's fate as a middle term between mythology and contemporary history.

The tragic irony of man's inability to perceive the divine pattern of events or to avert the divine will is more explicitly stated in the final chorus, one of the most beautiful lyric passages in the play with an exquisitely subtle echo of Dante (*Purg.* I, 117):5

> La fallace speranza de' mortali,
> A guisa d'onda in un superbo fiume,
> Ora si vede, or par che si consume.
> Spesse fiate, quando ha maggior forza,
> E ch'ogn cosa par tranquilla e lieta,
> Il ciel ne manda giù qualche ruina.
> E talor, quando il mar più si rinforza,
> E men si spera, il suo furor s'acqueta,
> E resta in tremolar l'onda marina;
> Chè l'avvenir ne la virtù divina
> È posto, il cui non cognito costume
> Fa 'l nostro antiveder privo di lume.

(The fallacious hope of mortals, like to a wave in a proud river, is visible now, then seems to be consumed. Often when it is strongest, when all seems calm and joyous, Heaven sends down upon us some disaster. And sometimes when the sea most rages, and hope diminishes, its wrath is stilled, the ocean waves resume their trembling ripple; future events within the power divine find their control; its laws inscrutable envelop in darkness all our attempts at foresight.)

Trissino's originality in the extensive use of blank verse, *(endecasillabi sciolti),* mingled with other metres particularly in the choruses, is well known; it determined the metrical form of later tragedies as well as of pastoral plays. He chose it, he says in the Dedication, as rendering the emotions more naturally and powerfully than rhyme.

Though *Sofonisba* observes the three unities, with only one apparent irregularity, Trissino was familiar only with two. The unity of place is not mentioned by Aristotle, and does not appear in the *Poetica.* He states the scene, very generally, to be the city of Cirta. The major part of the action takes place in a large square, on one side of which is the royal palace. In what corresponds to the fourth act there is apparently a shift to the Roman camp, to which the Chorus announces it will go "per la più corta strada," by the shortest way. How Trissino visualized this—for he was interested in stage design and agreed with Aristotle that the author must try to imagine the play as it would be presented (*Poetica,* II, 105)—and how it can be reconciled with the traditional fixed set of the Renaissance stage, is evident from descriptions of a performance of the tragedy in 1562. This took place in the Great Hall of the Palazzo Pubblico in Vicenza, with a modified stage-set which had been designed the previous year by Palladio, Trissino's protégé, for a comedy. The production of *Sofonisba* was splendid, with as many as eighty people on the stage besides the speaking actors, all magnificently costumed.[6]

A prologue was written for the occasion by Giannandrea Dall'Anguillara,[7] and from this and a contemporary account of the spectacle it is evident that the apparent change of scene indicated in the text of the play offered no problem to actors or audience.

> . . . teniate per certo
> Di non esser nel loco, ove Voi siete,
> Ma d'esser dentro alla Città di Cirta,
> La qual è questa, che vedete; e ancora
> D'esser Cirtensi Cittadini e intorno
> Aver l'armi nemiche de' Romani,
> Che intendendo esser rotto il vostro campo
> E preso il vostro Re, sendo costretti
> Di dover cangiar Re, leggi e fortuna,
> Sodisferete meglio al nostro intento,
> Ch'è di commover Voi tutti a pietade.

(Consider yourselves to be not in the place where you really are, but inside the City of Cirta, which is this that you see; and as well to be citizens of Cirta, surrounded by the hostile arms of the Romans, so that hearing that your army is routed, your king captured, and that you are compelled to change King, laws and fortune, you will better satisfy our intention, which is to move you all to pity.)

The scene, then, was considered to represent a large portion of the city, and a contemporary tells us that through the right-hand gate a perspective of houses could be perceived; through the left gate could be seen a landscape with trees (Puppi, p. 35).

This suggests that the Roman army was imagined as encamped in the countryside beyond the left gate, and that the fourth act took place on that side of the stage, with the Roman characters coming through the gate and playing their scene in front of it.

The passage quoted also indicates that the audience was supposed to feel itself in the position of the Chorus and share its emotions. "Dall'altro lato," the Prologue promises, "Noi con ogni sforzo/ Chercherem trasformarci in Lelio e in Scipio/ E nella vostra Sofonisba e in tutti/ Gli altri, che, uniti, la Tragedia fanno" ("For our part we will make every effort to transform ourselves into Lelio, Scipio, into your own dear Sofonisba, and into all the others who, united, make up the Tragedy.")

II

The reference to "your own dear Sofonisba" shows how famous the play had become by 1562, and that it was regarded not as a spiritless pedantic exercise but as a most moving story. Jacopo Castellini, whose tragedy *Asdrubale* was published in that same year,[8] takes it for granted that his readers are familiar with the earlier play, to which his own is in many ways a sequel.

The subject of *Asdrubale* is the final struggle of the Third Punic War in 146 B.C. as described by Appian. The Carthaginians, enraged by the continued encroachments of Massinissa, had rebelled once more against Rome. Forced to take extreme measures, Scipio Africanus the Younger informed them that their city was to be razed, and that they must re-settle ten miles inland so that the sea would no longer provide them with a source of wealth or a temptation to power. When the play opens, the desperate Carthaginians have planned a last attempt to defeat their foes. A duel has been arranged between the traitor Phameas, who had deserted to the Romans, and a Carthaginian challenger, Cartalone, who is to be armed by the Carthaginian King, Hasdrubal (Asdrubale). Scipio however knows Punic faith of old. He does not attend the duel but enters the city from another side. The Carthaginians are defeated, and the city set on fire. Hasdrubal's Queen kills herself and their two children; the King, shamed by her reproaches for his submission to Rome, dies of shock.

Although there is the usual compression of historical time, Castellini invented only the duel, the execution of Phameas,

and the death of Hasdrubal. By this date Giraldi Cinthio and
Lodovico Dolce had made Seneca the favorite model for Italian
tragedy rather than Trissino's beloved Greeks, though it should
be remembered that the only play published by Giraldi before
1562 was *Orbecche*. Castellini introduces moments of Senecan
horror, as when the Queen hacks to pieces an aged Carthaginian
escaping from the burning city because she mistakes him for a
Roman. It is Senecan too to describe the severed head of
Phameas raised on a spear above the city walls as a warning to
traitors. Castellini also follows Seneca and Giraldi in dividing
his play into five acts, and using the Chorus, composed of young
men of Carthage, only at the close of each act.

His principal structural innovation is his strange prologue.
In an appended letter to Giovanbattista Strozzi the Elder, he
explains that he feels tragedy would be embellished by dancing,
and so has composed a suitable prologue. It is chanted by
Erebus, who summons forth from Hell his twelve children—
Envy, Arrogance, Obstinacy, Cruelty, and so on. Each personification corresponds to an event in the play: Arrogance, for instance, to Hasdrubal's presumption and pride, Deceit to the false
duel. In a wild ballet they mime the actions they inspire so
vividly that even the actors, Castellini assures us, could not perform them more intelligibly. He refrains from describing the
music to describe this nightmare dance; for, as he says modestly,
since the play will be performed for many years to come, and
musical instruments will undoubtedly change, he does not wish
to fetter future producers. This fantastic prelude may well have
been suggested to Castellini by Strozzi himself, who had written
one of the interludes for Cosimo de' Medici's wedding festivities
in 1539.9 The elaborate entertainment, which lasted several
days, had made allegorical pageants with accompanying dance
and music popular at the Medici court. At the time when
Asdrubale was written, Strozzi was composing a new set of
madrigals in Cosimo's honor, and it is to Cosimo that the tragedy
is dedicated, since Castellini, like Trissino, chose a Medici
patron for his drama of Carthage. In the dedication he gives an
unusual interpretation of Aristotle's theory of pity and terror.
Tragedy, he says, is the mirror of princes; from it the prince
should learn compassion for his fellow-beings and fear for God.
Then his subjects, seeing by his example the happiness conse-
quent on these virtues, the two most certain roads to heaven,

will strive in their turn to imitate them.

Castellini, too, as he tells Strozzi, agreed with Aristotle's recommendation that the dramatist should visualize his scene, and so he had an illustration designed of the stage setting. This frontispiece is of great interest, for it is among the first records of a set designed by a dramatist.[10] It throws light as well on the scene of *Sofonisba,* for again it is clear that the actual space of the stage is considered only a proportional indication of the space in which the action occurs. Again the set is bilateral: Castellini's design shows a building on the right, whose wide portico forms the entrance to the Senate. Beyond it, still to the right, is the Temple of Apollo. High above the Temple is the sun, a dark globe symbolically beginning to obscure its light. In the background are city walls, above which the severed head of Phameas will be raised; in front of them, in the center of the stage, is a round building with a lighthouse tower. To the left, beyond a square wall with round openings, stands the lofty Temple of Esculapius, from which the Queen will hurl herself into the burning ruins. Far to the back of the hilly perspective appears a fortress with a banner; in the sky above it is a star, the rising star of Rome. In front of the whole scene there are rippling waves, to show that the buildings are at the edge of a harbor. The playing space is between the portico and the fort, as well as on the forestage. It is evident that the stage set represents a panoramic view of the city, as did that of *Sofonisba,* and that when the Queen appeared high aloft on the Temple, her words seemed to come from a great distance to those on the opposite side of the stage. This supposes a wide space between the burning city and the security of the Senate house, where Hasdrubal kneels before Scipio. For both tragedies, then, it is evident that the area *represented* for dramatic purposes is much greater than the actual area of the stage; and that this has nothing to do with the long perspectives in depth, so common at the time, which are not related to the action.

Asdrubale, unlike *Sofonisba,* is not concerned with private affections but exclusively with politics and war. The closest Greek parallel is *The Persians* of Aeschylus. The Queen is nameless; she is devoid of any feminine quality except maternity, and even in that she is ruthless: she refuses to flee by ship with one of her sons, and makes both children share her fiery death. She shows no tenderness to her husband, and says she would have murdered him when he became King if the office had not been forced on him. Her ferocity is consistent with Castellini's portrayal of the Carthaginians, for in this play the author's sympathies are with the Romans, not with the rebels against their rule. Indeed the Carthaginians bring their fate upon themselves by their cruelty and treachery.

In his concern to connect his play with Sofonisba—whose name recurs thoughout *Asdrubale* as an example of noble patriotism—Castellini has committed some strange falsifications of history. Cato appears among the characters, though he had died a few years before his consistent policy, "Carthago delenda est," was carried to its conclusion in this campaign. The Hasdrubal of the Third Punic War was not Sofonisba's father, though he mentions her more than once as his daughter and the Queen's step-daughter. He was an unrelated general, as Castellini was well aware, who had been made Commander-in-Chief, not King, of Carthage. Very confusingly, the earlier Hasdrubal's suicide by poison is referred to in the play. The Queen's death and that of her sons is historical; Hasdrubal however did not die of grief but survived in submission to Rome. Castellini ends his play not on a note of hope for the future, as does Trissino, but with the complete destruction of Carthaginian resistance.

With *Asdrubale,* Castellini had written the final tragedy of a cycle which may be compared to the Greek Theban plays. Indeed this may have been another reason why he made his Hasdrubal Sofonisba's father, for Aristotle had praised such cycles highly. Lodovico Dolce's *Didone,* published in 1545 (Giraldi Cinthio's play on the same subject was not printed until 1585), represents the beginning of the cycle, and Castellini, like Trissino, refers to that first Queen of Carthage, doomed, like its last Queen, to die by her own act in flames. Like the Greek cycles, too, the three Carthaginian plays would illustrate the operations of divine enmity and punishment, eventually using as instruments men's own evil passions. How conscious Castellini was of the implications of his work is uncertain; unfortunately he had neither the poetic nor the dramatic genius to produce a great tragedy; his verse, heavy and convoluted, is in marked contrast to Trissino's simplicity—over-simplicity, as Tasso considered it. But *Asdrubale* may be considered as a forerunner of the chronicle plays which were to reach their highest development in Shakespeare.

Like *Sofonisba, Asdrubale* may be read as a parable of contemporary Italian history. Cosimo I, to whom it was dedicated, had come to power in Florence in 1537, and had spent the subsequent years in consolidating his rule over much of Tuscany. His most difficult task had been to subdue the city of Siena, a struggle in which he was opposed not only by the Sienese but by Florentine exiles. When the city capitulated in 1555, Piero Strozzi, as obstinate as Hasdrubal, continued the fight against Cosimo from Montalcino, but in 1558 he died; the following year the Senate of the little Republic was forced to submit to the will of the Duke, as the Carthaginian Senators submitted to Scipio.11 The course of the war had been marked by episodes of cruelty and treachery, which are undoubtedly mirrored in many of the speeches in *Asdrubale,* even though their models are in Appian. It is reiterated throughout the play that the Carthaginians are meeting just punishment for their crimes, and that pertinacity carried to the point of perfidy is no virtue but a vice. Repeatedly Scipio and Cato refer to Invidia (envy) as the cause of the war, probably with an allusion to the *Inferno,* I, 109-111, where Virgil speaks of Invidia as sending forth from Hell, to which the Veltro will drive it back, the evil force symbolized by the wolf. Invidia appears in the Prologue as the leader of the children of Erebus. The Carthaginian Chorus does not deplore, as do the women in *Sofonisba,* the sufferings of the vanquished, but reflects in general terms on Fortune and Destiny. Its role is consequently much less dramatic and moving.

Many minor situations and speeches in the play seem to have contemporary significance. Cosimo's clemency after the final surrender of Siena in 1559 was widely praised, and Castellini commends Scipio's clemency as a truly Roman virtue. In 1560 Pius IV wished to confer on Cosimo, to whom he owed his elevation to the papacy, the title of King of Tuscany. This was refused by the Duke, and probably accounts for the references in the play to the Roman disdain for kings. The unhistorical plot to assassinate Scipio may have been suggested by a conspiracy to murder Cosimo planned in 1559 by Pandolfo Pucci, who owed as great a debt of gratitude to the Duke as Phameas did to Scipio. Various references in the dedication too support this interpretation of *Asdrubale* as a dramatic parable for the times; even

Castellini's insistence on the justice of the Roman cause recalls that at this period a statue of Justice was erected in Florence by Cosimo as a monument to his victories.

The two Carthaginian tragedies, then, different as they are in subject and treatment, are linked not only by their cyclical relation but by their use of ancient history as relevant to the present. They were written at very different periods in Italy's fortunes: *Sofonisba* at the end of a series of foreign invasions disastrous to local autonomy; *Asdrubale* when Cosimo had successfully constructed that large united Tuscany which in some sense was a fulfillment of Machiavelli's dream. Trissino chose wisely when he adapted a subject already hallowed by poetic tradition. Castellini made a bold experiment in a purely historical play which contains no truly heroic or tragic character; though it must be regarded as an artistic failure, it yet has interest in the development of Renaissance tragedy.

A curious coincidence is a further link between the two plays. In 1554 *Sofonisba* was first performed in a French version by Mellin de Saint Gelais at Blois before Henri II and his wife, Catherine de' Medici.[12] Two years later it was repeated, by the Queen's wish, for a wedding celebration. On that occasion an interlude was written by Jean de Baïf in which the Fury Megera shrieked her delight in bringing disaster upon monarchs. (This may indeed have given Castellini the subject for his own infernal prologue.) In 1559 Henri was killed in a tournament, and subsequently civil and religious war devastated France. Catherine was convinced that *Sofonisba* had brought calamity on her and her realm; never again was a tragedy performed at her court.[13] *Asdrubale,* dedicated like *Sofonisba* to one of Catherine's kinsmen, ends with a prediction by the Chorus to the victorious Scipio that he himself will suffer misfortune. By the end of the year that the play was published, 1552, Cosimo's wife and two of his sons had died of fever contracted during a journey in the Maremma. Whether Cosimo, like Catherine, considered the tragedy an evil omen is not recorded. But though Castellini says in his dedication that if the Duke approves his play he has further plans for publication, no later works by him are known, and there is no evidence that *Asdrubale* was ever performed at Cosimo's court, though that hope too is hinted at by the dramatist. Perhaps the mirror held up to Princes should be contrived to present only a smiling image.

NOTES

1 A. W. Schlegel, *Lectures on Dramatic Art and Literature,* trans. John Black (London, 1876), p. 214.

2 The standard biography of Trissino is Bernardo Morsolin's *Giangiorgio Trissino,* 2nd ed. (Florence, 1894).

3 The story of Sophonisba was probably first known in English in 1554 through the translation by Henry Parker, Lord Morley, of Petrarch's *Triumphs.* In 1566 William Painter included her tragic fate, re-told from Boccaccio, in his *Palace of Pleasure,* vol. II, novel 7. The Italian form of her name (though Trissino actually spelled it Sophonisba) is used throughout this article to avoid confusion.

4 *Tutte le opere di Giovan Giorgio Trissino* (Verona, 1729), II, 103.

5 This is probably the first quotation from Dante in Italian dramatic literature. The lines describe Dante's joy on seeing dawn breaking over the sea as he emerges from the dark terror of Hell; they are thus an image of the rebirth of hope and a new life.

6 Lionello Puppi, *Il Teatro Olimpico* (Vicenza, 1963), pp. 31-37. This description of the set suggests that it represents a transition from an earlier type of scene to the later completely architectural scene of classical Renaissance tragedy. Though the set was magnificent with paintings and many life-size statues, the opening onto the countryside is associated rather with comedy, as shown by an illustration in the Venice 1518 edition of Plautus.

7 *Prologo di Giannandrea Dall'Anguillara alla Sofonisba di Giangiorgio Trissino,* ed. Bernardo Morsolin (Vicenza, 1879), from the manuscript in the archives of the Trissino family (*nozze* Bianchini-Franco).

8 Florence: Lorenzo Torrentino. Copies are in the University of Toronto Library and the Folger Library.

9 *A Renaissance Entertainment: Festivities for the Marriage of Cosimo I, Duke of Florence, in 1539,* ed. Andrew C. Minor and Bonner Mitchell (Columbia: University of Missouri Press, 1968). An account of Strozzi is given, pp. 27-30. The predominance of political allegory in the pageants is analysed *passim.* Of particular relevance to *Asdrubale* (and to *Sofonisba*) is the parallel drawn between an episode of the Carthaginian war as described by Livy (Bk. XXII) and an episode during Cosimo's accession to power, p. 143n.

10 It is reproduced in Louise George Clubb's *Italian plays (1500-1700) in the Folger Library* (Florence, 1968), Fig. 3.

11 Castellini addresses Cosimo as Duke of Florence and Siena.

12 Raymond Lebègue, "Les représentations dramatiques à la cour des Valois," *Les Fêtes de la Renaissance,* ed. Jean Jacquot (Paris, 1956), p. 89.

13 Pierre de Bourdeille, Seigneur de Brantôme, *Oeuvres Complètes* (Paris, 1867-73), VII, 346.

Cecchi and the Reconciliation of
Theatrical Traditions

Douglas Radcliff-Umstead

Giovan Maria Cecchi (1518-1587) proved to be the most prolific playwright of sixteenth-century Italy. A notary by profession, this Florentine author completed twenty-one full-length erudite comedies, numerous secular farces, religious dramas, and intermezzi. The public to whom Cecchi addressed his dramatic works consisted of the professional and semi-professional Florentine classes of lawyers, notaries, merchants, clerics and nuns who all looked to the theatre as a source of entertainment and instruction. In the development of his personal artistry Cecchi fused various learned and popular literary traditions to produce a body of dramatic works which reflect all the facets of Cinquecento comic theatre: emulation of the ancient Roman comedies of Plautus and Terence, the influence of the Italian novellistic tradition with its themes of love as a natural right and fortune as the arbiter of human destiny, the *sacra rappresentazione* with its stress on satirizing the vicious tendencies of everyday life, and the Tuscan dialectal farce with its puns and salacious play of words. Performance of Cecchi's plays by companies of amateur actors would highlight the festivities of carnival seasons, contribute to the gaiety of state weddings by members of the reigning Medici family, and relieve the monotony of life in convents. Through his comic works Giovan Maria Cecchi intended to present his society with a mirror portrait of its daily existence, pointing out the ridiculous excesses and the follies of the morally blind while offering hope of a happy outcome to those who recognize their own foolishness.

Cecchi lived during the period of Florentine history which could be designated as the Medici restoration under the rule of Cosimo I and his wife Eleonora of Toledo. Content to remain an observer rather than a participant in the political and military events which secured for Tuscany the status of an independent grand duchy under Spanish imperial protection, Cecchi shared that "unity of the Florentine cultural and intellectual community" which held together artists and scholars of all classes with the encouragement of the grand duke.1 The author's plays are generally divided into four categories: *commedie osservate* (comedies on the classical model), *commedie morali, commedie spirituali,* and farces. It will be the object of this essay to examine four plays from Cecchi's long creative career: a comedy that closely follows a Plautine source; a play inspired by the amorous intrigues of the *Decameron*; a moral comedy derived from a biblical parable; and a farce that combines folk traditions with novellistic themes. Crossing a time period from Cecchi's earliest to his final dramatic compositions, these four plays illustrate the artistry with which the Florentine writer succeeded in reconciling the major literary antecedents of sixteenth-century Italian theatrical practice.

I

Cecchi's play *La Stiava* belongs to the opening phase of his writing for the theatre. Composed toward 1546,2 *La Stiava* appeared in the first printed edition of Cecchi's dramas by the Venetian publisher Giolito de' Ferrari in 1550 along with the plays *La Dote, La Moglie, Gl'Incantesimi, I Dissimili,* and *l'Assiuolo.* Originally written in prose, all of these early dramas except for *I Dissimili* and *l'Assiuolo* were later recast in hendecasyllable verses and published in 1585 at Venice by the Giunti press. Cecchi was following the example of Ludovico Ariosto, who had also refashioned his first two dramas *La Cassaria* and *I Suppositi* from an original prose draft to a version in hendecasyllables in an identical attempt to create a language for the stage which would combine artistic decorum with an everyday naturalness. But in writing *La Stiava* the author bore in mind not so much the example of earlier Cinquecento theatre but that of ancient Roman comedy since he derived the play's plot from Plautus' *Mercator*. Throughout his writings, usually in the prologues to his dramas, Cecchi acknowledged that he enjoyed an especially warm rapport with Plautus, his "buon compagno" and "amico tanto caro" as asserted in the opening lines of the play *Il Martello* of 1561. One can therefore speak of "friendly bor-rowing" by the Florentine author from the comedies of the ancient Roman playwright. It was Cecchi's avowed intention to render the Plautine comic material a living experience for contemporary Italian audiences. Classical influence immediately reveals itself in the structure of *La Stiava,* which like every Italian erudite comedy after Mantovano's *Formicone* (1503) and Ariosto's *La Cassaria* (1508), is written in five acts. Unity of time prevails in *La Stiava,* where the action runs from morning to early evening; and unity of place is respected as the scene remains outdoors between the homes of the merchants Filippo and Nastagio. As the drama concentrates on the disputed slave-girl of the play's title, it therein displays unity of action in spite of all the entanglements into which the various contending parties become involved. Cecchi's desire to reconcile classical imitation with an attempt to depict his own times leads him to set the play in Genoa and not in ancient Athens. Instead of citing Plautus in the prologue, Cecchi compared himself to Ariosto and Machiavelli. While deriving his plot from an ancient play and accepting the conventions and rules of classical theatre, Cecchi sought to fashion a drama which would reflect the customs and values of his own society.

At first it might appear that Cecchi's eagerness to adapt the Plautine comic materials to a modern setting forced the Florentine author into committing a serious anachronism: introducing the plight of a slave-girl into an environment where slavery was not a recognized institution. In Plautus' *Mercator* there was no problem of an anachronism since slavery was, of course, a widespread practice in the Graeco-Roman world. Cecchi himself acknowledged his boldness with this comment in the prologue: "Nè debbe il nome di Stiava spaventare. . . ."3 A contemporary Florentine playwright Anton Francesco Grazzini (il Lasca) declared in the prologue to his comedy *La Strega* that he was opposed to the servile introduction of comic character types and motives from Plautus and Terence which clashed with actual modern mores: "In Firenze non si vive come si viveva già in Atene e in Roma, non ci sono schiavi e non ci si usano figliuoli adottivi."4 Although the situation of the slave-girl in Cecchi's play could be explained as an expression of the author's devotion to the comic heritage of Plautus, the efforts of the Florentine writer to orient the slave-girl's background to the historical circumstances of his own times demonstrate Cecchi's artistry in fusing classical antecedents with a portrayal of the sixteenth-century Italian scene. Slavery did exist in Renaissance Italy, and most of the slaves were females of Tartar blood who were purchased by Italian merchants sailing to the Black Sea ports. Prior to the stage action in *La Stiava,* the young merchant Alfonso bought Adelfia at the slaves' market in Constantinople. The fact that the slave-girl is not of Tartar extraction but Italian-born has enormous importance for the outcome of the play. Cecchi set this comedy at Genoa, one of the ports through which foreign slaves entered Italy. Even though the general enthusiasm to see classical comedy revived on the Italian stage would have made the anachronism of a slave-girl acceptable to most members of Cecchi's public, the author aimed at historical plausibility.5

Both Cecchi's *La Stiava* and the comedy *Il Vecchio Amoroso* (written ca. 1533-36) by the Florentine Donato Giannotti follow Plautus' *Mercator* in presenting the conflict between an elderly merchant and his young son for possession of a lovely slave-girl that the son acquired on a commercial journey, and each of the Italian dramatizations differs from the Latin model through the use of the classical device of a recovery scene (*agnition*) wherein the slave-girl is discovered to be the long-lost daughter of a close friend of the family, so that she will be re-integrated into society with payment of a dowry to marry the merchant's son. Through their very titles these three dramas indicate the social focus which is the aim of their respective authors. In the *Mercator* a tug-of-war takes place between the aged merchant Demipho and his son Charinus from which the younger generation emerges victorious and the father justly receives the censure merited by his vicious conduct. Giannotti seeks in *Il Vecchio Amoroso* to stress how because of a senile erotic frenzy a father loses his dignity so that he appears as a totally ridiculous figure. Cecchi's title *La Stiava* shifts emphasis away from the pretentious *alazon* figure of the *senex iratus* to the pathetic *eiron* figure of the slave-girl.6 Unlike both the *Mercator* and *Il Vecchio Amoroso,* in *La Stiava* the slave-girl never makes a stage appearance, not even after her identity has been established. For Adelfia is not so much a person in her own right as an object of conflict for possession. As a slave-girl Adelfia figures at the center of the drama, an object of barter and disputed ownership. Alfonso hopes to bring the girl into his home by passing her off a a gift to his mother, but his cunning father Filippo rejects the inauthentic gift. When the son refers to the slave-girl as his own property ("questa mia mercanzia e mia cosa," p. 364) that he can sell to a young acquaintance of his, Filippo asserts his paternal authority by claiming that the son's possessions belong to the father: "quanto a dir, ell'è cosa tua, i' penso che ciò che tu hai, sia mio, siccome ciò che io ho è tuo." Throughout the play Adelfia is no more than a creature, designated by the term "fanciulla,"7 whom others manipulate. Cecchi expresses in this drama of human exploitation a mercantile mentality which equates objects of erotic desire with objects of commercial exchange.

Love, rather than a contest of authority, is the inspiring force of Cecchi's play. For Alfonso his beloved remains a person whose integrity he respected by marrying her before they consummated their erotic relationship. In the prologue the author announced as one of the drama's themes the sufferings of lovers. Toward the center of the play old Nastagio comments (III.5) on the power of Love which can transform a miser like Filippo into an extravagant suitor. What Cecchi has done is to infuse the classical plot material from Plautus' play with a Boccaccian love atmosphere. Although no one particular earlier novella could be cited as an antecedent for *La Stiava,* its spirit is modern since it follows Boccaccian models such as *Decameron* II.10, where the older generation must yield its rights to the demands of young lovers. Similarly in Cecchi's play old Filippo must surrender the slave-girl to his son. To effect that proper transferal the Italian author resorts to the classical dramatic device of *agnition* whereby Adelfia is found to be Nastagio's daughter. Recovery scenes are common to ancient comedies and occur in plays such as Plautus' *Cistellaria* and *Casina* as well as Terence's *Eunuchus.* The long-lost daughter in ancient comedies is usually a victim of abandonment by parents who at first did not want a girl to inherit their estate. Since infant exposure was not practiced in sixteenth-century Italy, dramatists like Cecchi who employed the recognition device depicted the lost child as a victim of warfare or piracy. In *La Stiava* Adelfia's identity is determined by the objects in a box she carries with her containing a chain, pendant, and a notation of the date Moorish pirates seized her in the sea near Ischia. Cecchi thus constructed the background of the recovery scene in terms of contemporary coastal incursions by Turkish corsairs. The recovery makes possible the social transformation of Adelfia from a slave with no rights to a daughter-in-law whom Filippo must respect.

Cecchi's *La Stiava* appears as a markedly original drama instead of a pallid reworking of the *Mercator*. The mood of the play is that of the mercantile world of Cecchi's times and not that of Plautine Rome. As a Florentine author working in the tradition of Boccaccio, Giovan Maria Cecchi stressed the happy outcome to the sufferings of two faithful young lovers and the merited defeat of a senile passion. Even in minor details of characterization, as with Nastagio's maid Nuta and the servant Gorgolio, the Italian writer succeeds in enriching the comic material of the Plautine model: Nuta shows herself to be a compassionate friend of the young, while Gorgolio recalls the well-intentioned but inept servants of Ariosto's comedies who further complicate already deeply entangled plots. A character like the farm steward Meino adds a new note that will be developed in other plays of the author: the *agroikos* devoted to the land and livestock but out of his element in the city. Old Filippo results perhaps as the most outstanding characterization, not as the vitiated Demipho of the *Mercator* nor the domestic tyrant Teodoro in *Il Vecchio Amoroso* but as a crafty merchant who temporarily falls prey to a senescent desire to recapture the erotic joys of his vanished youth. Cecchi breaks with classical tradition by having Filippo, instead of one of the servants, deliver the play's farewell *licenza*:

> Non aspettate voi altri, che questa festa si finisca altrimenti, che voi stareste troppo a disagio. La fanciulla, non vi si essendo lasciata veder oggi che la era Stiava, molto manco vorrà che voi la veggiate ora, che l'è padrona. Queste'altre, siccome è mogliama e quella di Nastagio, ancoraché la sua voi l'avete veduta, non sono così gentil figure, che sopporti la spesa, che voi soprastiate qui punto per vederle. Sicchà siate licenziati, e se la nostra favola v'è piaciuta, fate segno d'allegrezza. (p. 404)

In the spirit of comic reconciliation Cecchi permits the defeated *senex* to enjoy the last words that bring to a close this drama of youthful ardor and ridiculous passion.

II

A novellistic erotic fury prevails in *l'Assiuolo*, the play reputed by most critics to be Cecchi's masterpiece. In the prologue itself Cecchi asserts the independence of this play from classical models: "spettacolo d'una Commedia nuova nuova . . . non cavata né di Terenzio né di Plauto. . . ."8 The subject matter of the drama is adultery, a theme that the ancient Roman dramatists never dared to treat. Among the Romans the family was a sacred institution which authors of comedies were forced to respect. Plautus' *Amphitryon* therefore necessarily presents adultery as unintentional, for it takes place between the unsuspecting Alcmena and Jove disguised as her husband. Among the writers of Italian novelle, however, marriage was not an inviolable institution since Love was considered to be greater than any social institution. Fifteenth-century writers of Latin humanistic comedies (e.g., Antonio Barzizza in his *Cauteriaria*) followed the example of the *Decameron* in defending the new morality of adulterous love; and by the first quarter of the Cinquecento Machiavelli produced the most profound of all erudite comedies with the *Mandragola* proclaiming the right to find erotic pleasure outside the bonds of matrimony. Among the Boccaccian novelle which provided Cecchi with material for his comic plot are *Decameron* VIII.7, for the episode where elderly Ambrogio shivers in the cold all night after he is locked in a courtyard; *Decameron* III.6, for the trap where Ambrogio's wife Madonna Oretta is lured into an assignation with young Giulio in the belief that she has caught her husband in a rendezvous; *Decameron* VIII.4, for the episode where Giulio's friend Rinuccio finds himself in bed with the wrong woman; and *Decameron* VII.8, for the astute ploy by which the adulterous Oretta proves her innocence and humiliates Ambrogio before her brother. Boccaccio, more than Plautus or Terence, has inspired this comedy of revolt against inhibiting social conventions.

Cecchi's *l'Assiuolo* is structured on a series of deceptions and disguises. The device of false letters leads different characters such as Ambrogio and Oretta into situations of entrapment. In ancient comedy false letters are rarely used to advance the plot. Plautus' *Pseudolus* presents the case of an astute slave who intercepts the delivery of a letter and identity-token so that he can rescue a young woman from a procurer and turn her over to his master.9 False letters abound in Cecchi's works, reflecting the novellistic tradition of the *beffa* or trick played on an individual who permits his passion to dominate his intelligence. Vanity causes Ambrogio to accept as authentic a letter supposedly from the widow Anfrosina but truly from her son Rinuccio, inviting the old man to visit her that night while Giulio and Rinuccio are expected to be out of town. To counter Rinuccio's plan Giulio sends Oretta a letter purportedly by Anfrosina urging Ambrogio's wife to come to the widow's house and surprise her husband in adultery. Jealous anger impels Madonna Oretta into believing the letter and going to Anfrosina's house, where Giulio takes Ambrogio's place in bed. The mechanical device of false letters becomes a psychological tool in Cecchi's dramas where characters like Ambrogio and Oretta allow strong emotions rather than reason to guide their actions.

One of the most common motives or devices in comedy is that of disguise since the comic cheat frequently plays the impostor to trick his adversaries. Plautus and Terence delight in building situations of disguise where cruel procurers or miserly fathers are duped by clever slaves in the service of young lovers. In Plautus' *Persa* the slave Sagaristio pretends to be a Persian in order to sell a free girl to the procurer Dordalus, who later has to release the girl; in the *Trinummus* a sycophant is hired to disguise himself in elaborate foreign clothes and to deliver letters and a dowry. Terence's *Eunuchus* features a young lover who actually assumes a disguise, as when Chaerea dresses as a eunuch in order to enter the establishment of the courtesan Thais and ravish the girl Pamphila. In *l'Assiuolo* Ambrogio and his servant Giannella disguise themselves as pages when they set out for the ill-fated rendezvous at Anfrosina's house. Cecchi deliberately fuses the device of disguise with the theme of masquerade, for the play's time of action occurs during carnival season:

Gianella:	. . . i' sto per non mi conoscer da me medesimo; se noi avessimo le maschere, noi parremmo duo mattaccini.
Ambrogio:	O mattaccini, o matti grandi, non importa; a me basta non esser conosciuto; e poi noi siamo per carnovale. (p. 169)

Carnival time was, of course, the season of the year before Lent when persons could indulge themselves by donning masks and costumes, attending balls and performances of comedies such as those of Cecchi. Once again the Florentine author takes a mechanical device like disguise and adapts it to the spirit of carnival and erotic madness of his own times.

Disguise also occurs in *l'Assiuolo* through the figure of the transvestite character. In the Italian novellistic tradition as well as in the early erudite comedy the transvestite figure is an individual who is so much under the sway of love that he or she will go so far as to don the garb of the opposite sex to reach the beloved one. Perhaps the most remarkable example of the transvestite in comedy is Bibbiena's *Calandria* (1513), where several of the major characters willingly take on the appearance of the opposite sex: young Lidio dresses as a female and calls himself Santilla so he can hold assignations with the lady Fulvia; and Calandro's wife Fulvia, worried about the absence of her lover, disguises herself in a man's clothes and goes out on the open street to find him. The law of love is supreme, compelling lovers to risk possible humiliation because of the transvestite disguise.[10] Three cases of the transvestite appear in *l'Assiuolo*. When Giulio lures Ambrogio to the courtyard where the elderly lawyer is to be locked for the night, the youth is waiting there disguised as a maidservant. Jealousy, rather than love, convinces Oretta to dress as a male and seek out her adulterous husband at Anfrosina's home. Cecchi strikes a note of feminism in Oretta's lament (IV.3) that while her husband is permitted by society to deprive her of pleasure, she must place herself in grave peril to surprise him in his lecherous pursuits: "e cosí (povera Oretta! non ti mancava altro) stare in una prigione a vita, avere il marito vecchio, geloso, innamorato, e rimbambito; acciocché i' m'avessi a condurre, per riguardarlo a casa, ad avere in abito d'uomo sulle quattro ore a scalar le mura dell'orto per uscir di casa, andar per Pisa, travestita" (p. 171). Oretta's revenge comes at the play's close when her hypocritical husband attempts to denounce her adulterous conduct to his brother-in-law Uguccione. But the "paramour" whom Oretta introduces to her brother and husband as the youth Fabio turns out to be her sister Violante with a false beard and male attire. Again with the transvestite figure the Florentine dramatist has succeeded in integrating a traditional comic expedient into the psychological motivation of his characters.

Ambrogio belongs to the same comic class as Filippo in *La Stiava*: the old man who strips himself of dignity and authority by foolishly falling in love with a younger woman. The attorney of *l'Assiuolo* appears even more ridiculous than the merchant in *La Stiava* because he has a wife who is young and beautiful. As a character type Ambrogio combines many of the features of the classical *senex* with distinctly Renaissance traits. He bears resemblance to the aged Athenian Euclio in Plautus' *Aulularia* in that both men are misers. When pressed to compensate Madonna Verdiana for her services as a go-between with Anfrosina, the lawyer tries to make the woman accept his old shoes as payment. Cecchi particularly wishes to portray Ambrogio in his professional pretentiousness as a Latin-spouting attorney attempting to conceal his inanity with a false erudition. This blind adoration of Latin in a character-type who displays traits of both the *senex* and the pedant recalls the arch-pedantic attorney Messer Nicia Calfucci in the *Mandragola,* except that Machiavelli's character possesses none of Ambrogio's jealousy or lasciviousness. What Ambrogio holds in common with Messer Nicia and with countless other attorneys all through the later tradition of the Commedia dell'Arte and Italian comic opera is their vanity which causes all of them to believe themselves irresistible in either love or their professional careers. But instead of proving himself a cunning strategist, Ambrogio by the play's end has to turn to his victorious adversary Rinuccio with a pathetic appeal for the youth to restore peace in the attorney's household. The self-styled master mind shows himself a dupe.

In spite of his alleged sexual prowess, the lawyer must enlist the aid of M. Verdiana, the bigot or *pinzochera* who seems to have stepped out of the pages of the *Decameron*. Although ancient comedy provides antecedents for the intermediary in sexual affairs like the procuress (*lena*) in Plautus' *Asinaria,* it is to the exemplary literature of the Christian Middle Ages that one must turn to find that venal combination of sensual merchandising and pretense of holiness which characterizes M. Verdiana. She comes from a long line of gray-cloaked bigots that includes Trotaconventos, Celestina, Alvigia from Aretino's comedy *La Cortigiana* (1534), and especially this character from *Decameron* V.10, where Cecchi derived the name for the procuress: "una vecchia che pareva pur santa Verdiana che dà beccare alle serpi, la quale sempre co' paternostri in mano andava ad ogni personanza, nè mai d'altro che della vita de' santi Padri ragionava e delle piaghe di san Francesco, e quasi da tutti era tenuta una santa. . . ." The very language Cecchi uses to describe the falsely devout Verdiana echoes Boccaccio: "quella pinzochera bigia, che va tuttavia per queste chiese con una filza tanto lunga di paternostri, sempre biasciando pissi pissi" and "madonna Verdiana, che pare il santusse" (p. 137). The author had behind him a novellistic and theatrical tradition where the procuress masks her greed and ruthlessness under an appearance of religious zeal, counting her beads while persuading young women to gratify her clientele. Permitting no one to swear in her presence, Verdiana delights in making lewd insinuations about the sexual activities of monks and nuns. Her major scene takes place in Act II, Scene 2, where the bigot confronts the miserly Ambrogio and must employ all her persuasive powers to squeeze adequate payment out of him for her services. The abiding obsession of Verdiana's life appears here as her determination to be paid in cash; even her usual pious expressions vanish from her speech as she insistently demands what she feels is due for her "honest" efforts at seduction. The hard bargaining between the two recalls *Decameron* VIII.2, where the priest of Varlungo argues with monna Belcolore over the price he must pay to enjoy her graces. Verdiana and Ambrogio both represent an attitude of commercial calculation where eros and cash figure as equivalent exchanges.[11]

Every character in *l'Assiuolo* is continually calculating his profit and advantage. The youths Giulio and Rinuccio, as students at the University of Pisa, do not particularly bring to mind the inept *adulescentuli* in ancient Roman comedies; rather they are Goliards intent on enjoying themselves. Their prototype is to be discovered in humanistic Latin plays such as the *Comedia Bile* and the *Electoral Comedy* that were composed during the Quattrocento by university students who represented the Goliard life as a quest for sensual gratification. In those student plays the chief resources of the Goliards are shown to be charm and intelligence. Although the young lovers in Cecchi's drama belong to the modern tradition of the Italian university world with its amorous students, the servants in the play definitely recall their antecedents in Plautus and Terence. Giannella is the typical bungler, like Tyndarus in Plautus' *Captivi*. A coward by nature, Giannella appears something of a braggart warrior in two scenes where he claims he fought off from 150 to as many as 300 assailants when in reality he fled in terror from only

Rinuccio and Giorgetto during the night of the multiple intrigues. Giannella's ravenous appetite matches that of any parasite in ancient Roman comedy. His stupidity functions as a foil for the intelligence of Giulio's servant Giorgetto, who has masterminded the device of the letter to lure Oretta to Anfrosina's house. Giorgetto's ability to accommodate his master's wishes resembles the cunning of the servant Geta in Terence's *Phormio* in obtaining a music-girl for young Phaedria. Giulio's servant emerges as a highly inventive rogue, to whom falls the honor of delivering the *licenza* admonishing old men for taking young wives and afterward displaying jealousy. All of these satellite characters participate in the comedy's festive spirit, each seeking his utmost enjoyment.

Once again Giovan Maria Cecchi has contained the novellistic subject matter of deception and amorous frenzy within a classical structure. In the prologue to *l'Assiuolo* the author expressly mentioned the unity of time by declaring that the play's action unfolded as "un caso accaduto in dieci ore di tempo, o meno . . ." (p. 129). The unchanging scene is a street in Pisa where the houses of Ambrogio and of Anfrosina as well as a church are located; references are made to scaling walls and climbing out of back windows. Within those restricted confines of time and space there develops a fast-paced drama of intense erotic passion. Rinuccio, Giulio, Oretta, and Violante all enter into a relationship of shared affection which contrasts with Boccaccio's ethic of a loving commitment between two persons since Giulio agrees to Oretta's also taking Rinuccio as a lover while Violante will permit Rinuccio's liaison with her sister. The play *l'Assiuolo* stands at a moment in Cecchi's artistic career when a spontaneous, impetuous, and even insolent spirit of erotic fervor dominated his dramas.

III

Late in his life the Florentine playwright underwent a religious conversion, repenting the licentious language and spirit of his earlier works. Besides rewriting some of the first dramas and purifying their language, Cecchi composed religious plays at the request of monasteries and convents. Under Archbishop Alessandro de' Medici (later Pope Leo XI), the Catholic Reformation in Tuscany concentrated on exalting the piety of

the cloistered life and reducing public worship to the passive enjoyment of religious spectacles.12 As an example of the "reformed" Cecchian comedy, the play *Il Figliuol prodigo* of 1569-
70 represents an aesthetic reconciliation of the Tuscan *sacra
rappresentazione* with the erudite comic form. The Tuscan
sacred plays, as they flourished in the Quattrocento, were usually
verse dramas in octava rima; but other meters could be introduced. There were numerous changes of scene in those religious
plays as the performance area (an open field or the refectory of
a monastery) was divided into several compartments from
which the actors passed with the advancement of the drama.
The audience therefore had the entire series of settings simultaneously standing before them like so many mansions of experience or the sequences in the episodic paintings of the
Renaissance. Not only was there no unity of place, but unity of
time was unknown since the time required for a drama could
run from the Creation to the Last Judgment. Thus in an antecedent of Cecchi's play, the *Figliuol prodigo* by Castellano de'
Castellani, the drama proceeds as a *storia* beginning with a street
brawl and continuing through every important event in the
prodigal's life up to the family's final reconciliation. The scene
constantly shifts from the open street to the family home, then
to a hostelry of ill-fame, later out in the fields, and at last back
to the prodigal's home. One of the most important features of
these sacred plays was the effort of their authors to present to
the public contemporary character-types such as innkeepers,
peasants, students, tavern habitués, priests, and physicians. This
attention to the surrounding world became the chief characteristic of sacred plays which the classicizing dramatists of the
Cinquecento retained in composing their own religious works.

Cecchi's debt to his predecessors in the *sacra rappresentazione* is apparent in the setting of his *Figliuol prodigo,* which is
located in Florence at his own times and not in biblical Pales-
tine. Careful observation of contemporary character-types can
be noted in two scenes (II.3 and III.3) where a group of peasants arrive in town and marvel at the wares in the shops; Cecchi
even refers to the laws of the period which decreed different
kinds of dress for various social classes. The peasant lad Tognarino is reminiscent not only of the country bumpkins in Quattrocento religious plays but of the young man in the preliminary
tale to the *Decameron*'s Fourth Day who stares in wondrous

amazement at the sights of Florence on his first trip to the city. On beholding some masks in a shop window, for example, Tognarino thinks they are flayed faces. The flavor of rustic farce enters into the drama with the comical contrast between the ignorance of the peasants and the sophistication of the urban environment. But even with this play's many ties to earlier religious drama, Cecchi's *Figliuol prodigo* displays a predominantly classical form both in structure and general characterization. This *prose* play in five acts features the usual street scene of erudite comedies. Strict observance of the unity of time is evidenced by this remark of old Argifilo in the second scene of the last act: "egli è quel che stamattina mi portò la lettera."13 Cecchi avoided Castellani's historical approach, preferring the tense concentration of true classical drama by starting his play on the day of the prodigal son's return to his family.

At times *Il Figliuol prodigo* seems to be a reworking of Plautine and Terentian material in a Florentine mercantile setting. The story of the repentant prodigal Panfilo sometimes becomes submerged by the intrigue of young Polibio to obtain funds from his greedy father Argifilo. Here the traditional astute servant Carbone appears to rescue his young master, persuading the parasite Frappa to present a forged letter of credit for one hundred scudi from Argifilo's brother Polidoro. When the parasite assumes a disguise and delivers the false letter, the crafty old merchant declines to accept the document without adequate assurance of its authenticity. This intrigue of a scheming parasite especially recalls the title character of Terence's play *Phormio,* where the parasite assists the youths Antipho and Phaedria in their love affairs and dupes their respective fathers Demipho and Chremes. Eventually in Cecchi's play, Frappa (in another disguise) frightens Argifilo out of one hundred fifty scudi in a scheme devised by Carbone who reports that Polibio has been caught robbing the shop of old Andronico. This successful appeal to Argifilo's paternal concern for his son's welfare has a parallel in a similar ruse by the servant Corbolo in Ariosto's comedy *La Lena* of 1528, where the father Ilario believes a false tale, which asserts that his son has been seized in an adulterous affair, and agrees to pay a bribe for the youth's release. Throughout Cecchi's play there is a contrast between two fathers, the miserly Argifilo and the kindly Andronico. It is the latter of these whose generosity in granting Panfilo a patrimony in advance brought about the young man's prodigal adventures. The symmetrical opposition of the fathers resembles the pair of brothers, the strict Demea and the indulgent Micio, in Terence's *Adelphi* in their respective rearing of the youths Ctesipho and Aeschinus. Andronico's sadness over his son's disappearance and his joy upon Panfilo's return also brings to mind another Terentian father, Menedemus in the *Heautontimorumenos,* with the difference that the father in the ancient Roman comedy drove his son away by being too harsh whereas in Cecchi's drama Panfilo took advantage of Andronico's affectionate nature. Cecchi's play opens in a mood of pathos: in the very first scene Andronico's wife Mona Clemenza expresses her grief over her son's absence of two years. What distinguishes *Il Figliuol prodigo* from comedies such as *La Stiava* and *l'Assiuolo* is the author's inspiration from Terence rather than from Plautus. For a serious religious drama, Cecchi must have felt that the Terentian emphasis on tender sentiments and anguished expectation was more appropriate than Plautine salaciousness and buffoonery. In this play Giovan Maria Cecchi, like Terence before him, evokes the memory of a happy past, the grief of the present moment, and hope for a festive reconciliation.

One of the original, modern character-types that the author introduces into this play is Lisa, the *balia* in Argifilo's household. Frequently the family nurse figures as a go-between in romantic affairs, greatly resembling professional procuresses such as Verdiana. In some of Cecchi's comedies (e.g., *Il Corredo* and *Il Medico*), the *balia* appears as a mercenary character totally lacking in loyalty to the mistress of the household. Lisa, however, displays the same sweetness and warmth as the *balia* in Cecchi's play *l'Ammalata,* since both are self-sacrificing characters. The concluding scene of the first act in *Il Figliuol prodigo* features a soliloquy by Lisa in which she describes the unhappiness that entered her life after the death of Argifilo's wife Laildomine. Now Lisa must suffer the constant scolding of her greedy master. Only her devotion to Polibio prevents Lisa from leaving the household. In his portrait of the good *balia,* Cecchi has created a positive character in striking contrast to the numerous evil servants of Renaissance novellistic and dramatic tradition.14

With its bourgeois realism and Terentian pathos, *Il Figliuol prodigo* might seem more a secular drama than a religious play. But throughout the play Cecchi inserts many religious references, several of which are commonplaces of everyday speech that the author invests with renewed meaning in the context of the drama of the son who was dead to the world and is spiritually reborn upon his return to the shelter of his home. In the first scene of the second act, Panfilo states that he has been led home "per grazia del Signore" (p. 15) in the hope of finding pardon. The play starts with Clemenza scolding her maid for not being ready to go to mass. When Frappa first attempts to swindle funds from Argifilo with the counterfeit letter, the anxious Polibio calls out (II.6): "Oh Dio, aiutami." Mona Clemenza consoles her impatient elder son Vascanio that Heaven will favor them: "Dio ce ne dia la grazia" (p. 30). The opening scenes of the second act in which the ragged Panfilo appears before his father's house only to be chased away by the cook and two servants has a parallel in Castellani's play where a maidservant refuses entrance to the prodigal as if he were a thief. Again and again in the drama phrases such as "Dio lo faccia," "benignità di Dio," "Piaccia a Dio," "Ringraziato sia Dio" keep recurring to form a significant pattern of statements that affirm faith in the power of God to intervene in the world and relieve man's tribulations. It has been Cecchi's role as sacred dramatist to transport the atmosphere of biblical parable into Reformist Florence. The concluding feast, where Andronico welcomes his wayward son back to the fold and persuades Vascanio to accept his brother's return in a spirit of love, is the typical banquet of ritual celebration which closes many comedies. In this aesthetic reconciliation of the classical tradition with the Italian sacred drama it is the parasite Frappa who delivers the *licenza* for Cecchi's *parabola* of the repentant sinner. This moral drama celebrates the triumph of Christian virtue in a modern society whose culture is profoundly classical.15

IV

Cecchi's final drama, *La Romanesca* (1585), represents the utmost crystallization of the Tuscan farce. The origins of farcical drama in Tuscany go back to the *maggio* festivals of rural regions in honor of renascent springtime. A mood of fable prevailed in the *maggi* spectacles whose heroes were not only religious figures but Grecian lords and feudal knights. Working within the tradition of the *maggio,* Cecchi employs the prologue of *La Romanesca* to assert the autonomy and artistic importance of the farce as a dramatic genre:

> La farsa è una terza cosa nuova
> Tra la tragedia e la comedia: gode
> Della larghezza di tutte due loro,
> E fugge la strettezza lor; perchè
> Raccetta in sè li gran signori e principi.
> Il che non fa la comedia: raccetta,
> Come ella fusse o albergo o spedale,
> La gente come sia, vile e plebea;
> Il che non vuol mai far donna tragedia:
> Non è ristretta a' casi: che gli toglie
> E lieti e mesti, profani e di chiesa,
> Civili, rozzi, funesti e piacevoli:
> Non tien conto di luogo: fa il proscenio
> Ed in chiesa ed in piazza e in ogni luogo.
> Non di tempo: onde se ella non entrasse
> In un dì, lo torrebbe in due e in tre.16

For the Florentine author, farce figures as an accommodating peasant girl in contrast to haughty Lady Tragedy. Although Aristotle never acknowledged farce as a valid art form, Cecchi in a typically humanistic effort to find classical authority for contemporary artistic endeavors cites a farce which was performed at Caligula's court, thereby demonstrating the ancient origin of this intermediary genre between comedy and tragedy. Free from observing unities of time and place, farce has one invariable characteristic for Cecchi: it must be in verse. The ideal length for a farce should be three acts.

In plot, subject matter, and characterization, *La Romanesca* fulfills all the expectations expressed in the author's prologue. Although in three acts, it can be considered a full-length drama comparable in extent to Cecchi's erudite comedies. The scene is Rome with a view of the Colosseum. Like tragedy this farce presents characters of exalted social rank such as the English crown princess, the king of France, the Roman governor, English and French nobles, diplomats; and like comedy this play also includes private citizens such as servants, a tailor, beggars, a nurse, and guards. Cecchi, who was always sensitive to subtle nuances of language, differentiates his characters linguistically by contrasting the eloquent (and quite lengthy) speeches of ambassadors and court officials with the crude proverbs of tradesmen and servants. Three major sources provide the romantic background for this farce: Boccaccio's story of two faithful friends from *Decameron* X.8; the folktale of the princess who must flee an incestuous father; and tales of cruel mothers-in-law and persecuted daughters-in-law. Cecchi was not the first author to dramatize these sources. A fifteenth-century Italian Dominican friar created a fairy-tale Latin play known as the *Comoedia sine nomine* about a merciless queen-mother who attempted to poison her daughter-in-law and grandson. Two Italian sacred plays, the fifteenth-century *Rappresentazione di Stella* and the sixteenth-century *Rappresentazione di Santa Uliva*, dealt with the persecution of an innocent princess. Another Florentine dramatist, Jacopo Nardi, also turned to the Boccaccian novella for his *La Commedia di Amicizia* (1502). Not only does Cecchi succeed in harmoniously fusing his diverse sources into a concentrated drama, but he even introduces a new element, Fortune, which becomes the dominating force of the play. It was Fortune which had separated the two close friends Claudio and Sempronio and prevented their reunion at the start of the play. Pitiless Fortune had once caused Sempronio to fall desperately in love with his friend's fiancée. A servant-boy observes (II.1) how insensitive Fortune fashioned the lowly class of servants from the dregs of primeval humanity. Unlike many other Renaissance writers who usually differentiated between Fortune and Destiny, Cecchi in this play tends to equate the two forces. This complicated drama is structured on a series of coincidences which prove to be the workings of that inscrutable Fortune. Poetically the drama's climax arrives in the fourth scene of Act III when the servant Roncola describes a painting which is an emblematic representation of Fortune as a lady sitting atop a tree whose branches are laden with precious items such as jewels and crowns as well as valueless objects like brooms while an infinite number of men and beasts await from below for the lady to shower her gifts upon them. In contrast to Dante, who regarded Fortune as an impartial power necessary to bring about change in the world, Cecchi depicts it as a capricious force and makes it the protagonist of his play.

In order to represent the swift and totally unpredictable might of the sometimes cruel and other times generous Fortune, the author compresses *La Romanesca* within the limits of the unities of time and space. Within a single day Fortune elevates Lady Isabella from the humble status of imperial Roman nurse to her legitimate rank as queen of France and England. *La Romanesca,* interpreted as a *maggio* play, re-enacts comic farce as the eternal myth of spring's renewal of life. On two levels— those of the royal adventure and the private misfortune of two friends—this farce belongs to that idealized phase of comedy which merges with romance.17 Rome appears as the goal for the quest-romance both for the lofty French monarch seeking his lost bride and the pilgrim Claudio hoping to find his true friend. Cecchi integrates the diverse elements of his romantic farce within the unifying theme of that arbitrary Fortune which reigns supreme over life.

Comedy served for Cecchi as the means to represent that *"imago veritatis"* which would permit his audiences to glimpse a redeeming vision of themselves in their moral strengths and weaknesses. The Florentine writer adapted the ancient Roman comedy of manners to the needs and conditions of his own times. With literary resources such as the Plautine and Terentian plays, the Italian novellistic tradition, biblical parables, and romantic folktales, Giovan Maria Cecchi created a varied comic theatre which expressed the fervent aspirations of Italian Renaissance society to reconcile the wit and spontaneity of pagan culture with the Christian view of human existence. In Cecchi's secular comedies there prevails a carnival spirit of revelry and masquerade which precedes the Christian season of sacrifice, while his moral plays offer the promise of restoration and salvation.

NOTES

1 Information about the changes in Florentine society brought about by the rule of Cosimo I and his Spanish wife Eleonora of Toledo can be found in Eric Cochrane, *Florence in the Forgotten Centuries 1527-1800* (Chicago: Univ. of Chicago Press, 1973), pp. 53-87. The quote is from p. 78.

2 A detailed chronology of Cecchi's erudite comedies can be found in Bruno G. R. Ferraro, "Giovanni Maria Cecchi, the *Commedie Osservate* and the *Commedia Erudita* in Sixteenth-century Italy," Diss., Flinders University of South Australia (1974), pp. 28-29. General bibliographical information about the categories of Cecchi's plays is in Giovanni Grazzini, "Giovan Maria Cecchi," *Enciclopedia dello Spettacolo* (Rome: Le Maschere, 1956), III, 299-303.

3 Text of play in *Commedie di Giovan Maria Cecchi,* ed. Luigi Fiacchi (Milan: Silvestri, 1850), I, 351. Subsequent page references will be to this edition.

4 Text in *Commedie del Cinquecento,* ed. Aldo Borlenghi (Milan: Rizzoli, 1959), II, 715.

5 Fortunato Rizzi, *Le Commedie Osservate di Giovan Maria Cecchi e la Commedia Classica del Secolo XVI: Studio Critico* (Rocca S. Casciano: Cappelli, 1904), pp. 66-67, comments on the anachronism of the slave-girl, asserting there was almost no slavery in Renaissance Italy. But a lecture delivered by Professor David Wilkins of the University of Pittsburgh on October 6, 1971, at that institution's Medieval and Renaissance Center under the title "The Black and Oriental in Italian Renaissance Art" points out how there was a large sub-class of domestic slave-girls of Tartar extraction working in the major Italian urban centers.

6 For technical names of character types, see Northrop Frye, *Anatomy of Criticism: Four Essays* (1957; rpt. New York: Atheneum, 1970), pp. 172-73.

7 Ferraro, pp. 312-13, speaks of the word "fanciulla" as a *Leitmotif* in the play.

8 Text in *Commedie del Cinquecento,* ed. Nino Borsellino (Milan: Feltrinelli, 1962), p. 128. All further page references will be to this edition.

9 Rizzi, pp. 45-46, cites the example of the letter in the *Pseudolus.*

10 Robert Melzi, "From Lelia to Viola," *Renaissance Drama,* 9 (1966), 67-81, analyzes the psychological forces at work in the transvestite figure.

11 Ferraro, p. 449, mentions the parallel between money and sex in the play.

12 See Cochrane, p. 138.

13 Text in *Commedie di Giovanmaria Cecchi,* ed. Gaetano Milanesi (Florence: Le Monnier, 1899), I, 49. Subsequent references will be to this edition.

14 Ferraro, pp. 138-39, discusses the figure of the *balia.*

15 F. Rizzi, *Delle Farse e Commedie Morali di G. M. Cecchi* (Rocca S. Casciano: Cappelli, 1907), pp. 97-113, studies the originality of Cecchi's moral plays. I wish to thank my student, Robert Antonelli, for sharing with me his insights on the pattern of religious references in Cecchi's moral plays.

16 Text in *La Romanesca,* ed. Diomede Buonamici (Florence: Cenniniana, 1874), p. 2.

17 Frye, pp. 181-82, would place this farce in comedy's fourth phase of mythic experience. Although some critics might trace the origin of a farce such as *La Romanesca* to traditions such as the *mogliazi* and *mariazi* rather than the highly regularized musical *maggi* dramas with their elaborate choreography, my interpretation of the Cecchian farce rests on the piece's undoubted spirit of May-time's promise of renewal.

"Nothing Undervalued to Cato's Daughter": Plutarch's Porcia in the Shakespeare Canon

John W. Velz

Shakespeare's first mention of Portia in *The Merchant of Venice* makes a pointed comment on her name and its source: she is

> Of wondrous virtues. . . .
>
> . . .
>
> Her name is Portia, nothing undervalued
> To Cato's daughter, Brutus' Portia.[1]

These lines are an explicit invitation to place Bassanio's Portia side by side with the Porcia of Plutarch's "Life of Marcus Brutus"—and, by extension, to place her side by side with the Portia Shakespeare had not yet portrayed when he wrote these lines, Brutus' Portia in *Julius Caesar*. No one, so far as I know, has ever accepted that invitation.[2] If we do accept it we may perceive an extraordinary correlation between Shakespeare's two Portias, a correlation that suggests an interpretation of *The Merchant of Venice*. Furthermore, when we once free ourselves from the assumption that the "Life of Marcus Brutus" was important to Shakespeare only mechanically and immediately, in the composition of *Julius Caesar,* we may enter a path of investigation that will show Shakespeare's continuing interest in Plutarch's Porcia through many years and some five works in the canon. Examining Shakespeare's several responses to the character and situation of Marcus Brutus' wife may throw light on his attitude toward marriage and on his conception of possibility in his sources.

The confrontation of Brutus and Portia in the orchard in *Julius Caesar* 2.1 is anticipated by some striking analogues of situation, characterization, and even language in 3.2 of *The Merchant of Venice,* the scene in which Bassanio wins Portia and immediately afterward is faced with the grim news that

Antonio's ships have all miscarried and that the bond with Shylock is forfeit. In both scenes a woman sees the outside world impinge on, indeed threaten, her marriage. The later Portia gives a vivid account of the way Brutus' preoccupation with public life has disrupted both bed and board (237-56), and the earlier Portia sees Bassanio who has just pledged himself to her turn pale as he reads the letter from Antonio about the forfeiture. Bassanio's Portia, who says she will not consummate her marriage while Bassanio has "an unquiet soul" about Antonio's danger (305-06) prefigures Brutus' Portia, who complains that her husband's mind is so overcharged with "some sick offense" (268) that he has "ungently . . ./ Stole from [her] bed" (237-38). Both women demand to be taken into their husbands' confidences, each woman believing (though the first Portia says nothing about it in Bassanio's presence) that she can bear a man's part in the affairs of the world. Each of the women bases the demand that her husband confide in her on the claim that marriage has metaphysically fused her identity with her husband's. In *Julius Caesar:*

> I charm you, . . .
> By all your vows of love, and that great vow
> Which did incorporate and make us one,
> That you unfold to me, your self, your half,
> Why you are heavy . . . .
>
> (271-75)

In *The Merchant of Venice:*

> With leave, Bassanio—I am half yourself,
> And I must freely have the half of anything
> That this same paper brings you.
>
> (248-50)

In both plays this fusion of husband and wife in mutual confidence is insisted on—Brutus' wife distinguishes between wives and harlots in terms of the fusion:

> Within the bond of marriage, tell me, Brutus,
> Is it excepted I should know no secrets
> That appertain to you? Am I your self
> But, as it were, in sort or limitation?
> To keep with you at meals, comfort your bed,
> And talk to you sometimes? Dwell I but in the suburbs
> Of your good pleasure? If it be no more,
> Portia is Brutus' harlot, not his wife.
>
> (280-87)

As the lines about the "great vow/ Which did incorporate and make us one" clearly show, marriage here is not just a meeting of true minds or a question of fidelity, but a metaphysical relationship with supernatural sanction. In the earlier play Portia, her marriage solemnized, though not yet consummated, speaks to Lorenzo about Antonio, Bassanio, and herself as if she and Bassanio were the same person:

> How little is the cost I have bestowed
> In purchasing the semblance of my soul
> From out the state of hellish cruelty!
>   (3.4.19-21)

The "semblance" of Portia's soul is Antonio, who is (through the sanctity of friendship) the semblance of Bassanio, who is her very soul. The context of this passage is interesting when thought of in light of the events of Act V. Portia, in explaining here to Lorenzo her attitude toward Antonio, promotes friendship to a status below (but not far below) the metaphysical fusion of marriage:

> . . . in companions
>   .   .   .
> Whose souls do bear an equal yoke of love,
> There must be needs a like proportion
> Of lineaments, of manners, and of spirit;
> Which makes me think that this Antonio,
> Being the bosom lover of my lord,
> Must needs be like my lord.[3]

Portia, the stubborn exponent in Act V of the priority of marriage to friendship, is the commentator here in Act III on the nearly metaphysical implications of friendship. It is worth observing that she feels the need in this speech to rationalize the implications of friendship for identity while she feels no such need to comment on the implications of marriage: Bassanio is quite simply and confidently alluded to as "my soul." This same Portia, flustered with love and apprehension before Bassanio made his winning choice among the caskets, had spoken of her self as divided: half hers, half his, and paradoxically wholly his (3.2.14-18). There can be no mistaking the prominence of marriage and its implications for identity in both plays.

The historical Porcia is spoken of in Plutarch's "Life of Marcus Brutus" as an ideal Roman matron, "excellentlie well seene in Philosophie, loving her husbande well, and being of a noble courage, as she was also wise."[4] But there is nothing in Plutarch's "Brutus" about her role as Brutus' *alter ego* and, of course, there is nothing in Plutarch about the Christian doctrine of incorporate marriage. We are faced with the inference that in creating the character of Portia in *Julius Caesar* Shakespeare made use of his own earlier play, even though he was following Plutarch's account of Porcia quite closely in *Julius Caesar*.[5] The revelation should not surprise us; this is just the sort of coalescence of analogues that students of Shakespeare's sources have been pointing to since Kenneth Muir first taught us, thirty years ago, to notice Shakespeare's creative eclecticism.[6] Any account of Porcia Shakespeare knew would be likely to find its way into the character of Portia in *Julius Caesar*: if one account was his own earlier one, no matter.[7]

More puzzling is the question why Plutarch's Porcia should have animated Shakespeare's conception of the heroine of *The Merchant of Venice* in the first place; Plutarch's pathetic suicide seems a most unlikely source for Shakespeare's triumphant bride. Indeed, the disparities are so apparent and so great that scholarship has never responded to Shakespeare's overt request that we think of the two women together. The anomaly may, however, be diminished if we regard Plutarch's Porcia as a tragic foil to the Lady of Belmont.

The comedic ending of *The Merchant of Venice* is brought about by a woman's competence in a male world; the Portia of that play is, finally, what Plutarch's Porcia wishes she could be. But Plutarch's Porcia is left behind at home to faint among her women while Brutus is at the Senate chamber assassinating Caesar (Shakespeare dramatized her faintness in 2.4 of *Julius Caesar*, the brief scene with Lucius and the Soothsayer); Bassanio's Portia by contrast goes into the public world with cool self-possession and rescues her husband and his friend from a hopeless impasse.[8] Indeed, Portia in *The Merchant* is so much a perfected "Cato's daughter" that we must wonder at how unlike Brutus Bassanio is. Curiously enough it is not Bassanio but Antonio who is described in the play in terms that would fit Plutarch's Brutus admirably—and Bassanio is the speaker. Antonio is

> . . . one in whom
> The ancient Roman honor more appears
> Than any that draws breath in Italy.
>
> (3.2.294-96)

We may validly think of Bassanio's Portia as a comedic "Cato's daughter," the converse of Plutarch's tragic Porcia who despaired at her inability to help her husband when things went badly after the assassination and who eventually killed herself.

The link between Plutarch's Porcia and Bassanio's is actually closer than the above contrast might make it seem, because Bassanio's Portia is not *all* competence: she has an obverse side. In 3.2, the same scene that has been examined here, she inconsistently enough speaks of herself as an *ingénue,* an untutored girl, a mere possession, passive under the moral aegis of her husband-to-be:

> . . . the full sum of me
> Is sum of something—which, to term in gross,
> Is an unlessoned girl, unschooled, unpractised;
> Happy in this, she is not yet so old
> But she may learn; happier than this,
> She is not bred so dull but she can learn;
> Happiest of all, is that her gentle spirit
> Commits itself to yours to be directed,
> As from her lord, her governor, her king.
>   (157-65)

The protest of her inadequacy continues in this same vein. Portia's voice here is quite different from the authoritative voice she addresses later to Shylock in the trial scene. To use a metaphor the play insists on,[9] Portia is both the inert golden fleece Jason/Bassanio must achieve and the active, resourceful Medea who seemingly by magic rescues her man when he cannot help himself. Plutarch's Porcia is also a divided character in a roughly analogous way: she is as stoic as any man when it is a question of enduring the pain of her self-inflicted wound but weak and "feminine" and incapable of bearing up under the different pain of enforced passivity at a time of crisis. I think it possible that Shakespeare was attracted to Plutarch's "Life of Marcus Brutus" when he wrote *The Merchant of Venice* because in his heroine he was "exploring the limits of acceptable female assertiveness"[10] and he remembered Plutarch's pathetic account of a woman who tried nobly to play the man and failed.[11]

Whatever the reasons for the appearance of "Cato's daughter" in *The Merchant of Venice,* it was not her first appearance in the Shakespeare canon. Two or three years earlier Shakespeare had introduced a part of her story into *Lucrece.*

None of the accounts of Lucretia's rape contains anything

to correspond to the 215 lines in which Shakespeare's Lucrece gazes upon a painting of the siege of Troy and bitterly moralizes it, drawing an analogy between her case and Troy's. In a memorable passage she compares Sinon to Tarquin: both are hypocrites, enemies posing as friends who, welcomed inside the gates, destroy the citadel from within. The vivid detail with which the painting is described in the poem has rightly reminded scholars of Virgil's graphic account of the fall of Troy in Book II of *The Aeneid* and of the passage in Book I where Aeneas sees the siege of Troy depicted on the wall of Dido's temple at Carthage and weeps for his own fate and for the human condition.12

But Aeneas and Lucrece are not the only Romans who gaze thoughtfully on paintings of the Trojan War. Brutus' Porcia in Plutarch does so also, and it can be argued that though the painting itself in *Lucrece* is out of Virgil (with a Breughelesque overlay), the character and situation of the Roman matron who gazes at it are out of Plutarch. In Plutarch's "Life of Marcus Brutus" Brutus, an exile from Italy and on the long path that led to Philippi, reached the point where he could no longer keep Porcia with him; they were at Elea

> There Porcia being ready to depart from her husband Brutus, and to returne to Rome, did what she could to dissemble the griefe and sorow she felt at her hart: but a certaine paynted table bewrayed her in the ende, although untill that time she always shewed a constant and pacient mind. The devise of the table was taken out of the Greeke stories, howe Andromachè accompanied her husband Hector, when he went out of the citie of Troy, to goe to the warres, and how Hector delivered her his litle sonne, and how her eyes were never of him. Porcia seeing this picture, and likening her selfe to be in the same case, she fell a weeping: and comming thither oftentymes in a day to see it, she wept still. Acilius one of Brutus friendes perceiving that, rehearsed the verses Andromachè speaketh to this purpose in Homer:
>
>> Thou Hector art my father, and my mother, and my brother,
>> And husband eke, and [all] in all: I mind not any other.
>
> Then Brutus smyling aunswered againe: But yet (sayd he) I can not for my part say unto Porcia, as Hector aunswered Andromachè in the same place of the Poet:
>
>> Tush, meddle thou with weying dewly out
>> Thy mayds their task, and pricking on a clowt. [*Iliad,* vi]
>
> For in deede, the weake constitution of her body, doth not suffer her to performe in shew, the valliant acts that we are able

to doe: but for corage and constant minde, she shewed her
selfe as stowt in the defence of her contry, as any of us.
(Bullough, p. 107)

Like Plutarch's Porcia, Lucrece sees herself in another's
picture (Aeneas, of course, sees a painting of himself). Like
Plutarch's Porcia (and, of course, like Andromachè), Lucrece
is separated from her warrior husband in her hour of emotional
crisis; Aeneas, though he has lost his wife in the sack of Troy,
is not in quite their case. Like Plutarch's Porcia, Lucrece is
portrayed as emphatically weaker physically than morally.[13]
Like Plutarch's Porcia, Lucrece eventually commits suicide in
response to the same emotions that grip her as she stares at the
painting. Finally, like Plutarch's Porcia, Lucrece is a Roman
matron desperately anxious for her husband's honor. Indeed,
if Coppélia Kahn's interpretation of the poem is correct, Lucrece
kills herself not to protect *her* honor, but to protect the honor of
Collatine, her husband.[14]

It seems to me likely that Shakespeare conceived the episode
of the painting of Troy in *Lucrece* by analogy with Plutarch's
anecdote of Porcia and the painting of Andromachè[15] and that
once it was conceived he amalgamated with it Virgil's two accounts of the fall of Troy because Lucrece, whose citadel has
been sacked as Troy's is in Virgil, is in this one respect closer
to Aeneas than to Porcia.[16] Moreover, the Trojan War is at
root a story of rape; it is not incidental that Shakespeare should
begin this episode in *Lucrece* with that fact:

> At last she calls to mind where hangs a piece
> Of skillful painting, made for Priam's Troy,
> Before the which is drawn the power of Greece,
> For Helen's rape the city to destroy. . . .
> (1366-69)

Having made use in *Lucrece* of Plutarch's story of Porcia
and the wall painting, Shakespeare elected not to dramatize it
in *Julius Caesar*. Perhaps he felt that such a story is better in
the telling than in the staging.[17] Certainly fastidiousness about
re-using his materials is not likely to have entered into the decision to omit the scene from *Julius Caesar:* we have already
observed his re-use of materials from *The Merchant of Venice*
in *Julius Caesar,* and close students of the Shakespeare canon
have reason to believe that reworking elements from his earlier
days was one of Shakespeare's preferred methods of composition.[18]

Shakespeare's tendency to re-dramatize materials that had once been important to him can be illustrated by still further appearances of "Cato's daughter" in the canon. As Robert Adger Law showed many years ago, Shakespeare made use of Plutarch's account of Porcia's curiosity about her husband's public business in two plays other than *Julius Caesar,* varying the emphasis, but obviously drawing on North's Plutarch in each case. (Law did not see that *The Merchant of Venice* 3.2 is a fourth instance of "Porcia's Curiosity" in the Shakespeare canon.)19

The first of the plays Law pointed to (like *The Merchant of Venice*) precedes *Julius Caesar.* In *The First Part of King Henry IV* 2.3 Shakespeare briefly introduces Hotspur's wife, Kate, who demands to know what public business preoccupies her husband: why she has been banished from his bed and what has caused him to give "my treasures and my rights of thee/ To thick-eyed musing and cursed melancholy" (42-43). It is easy to hear the voice of Portia in *Julius Caesar* in these lines written two years earlier. Like the later Portia, Hotspur's Kate also speaks of her husband's loss of appetite, of his restless slumber, of his absent-mindedness. And, like Bassanio's Portia, Kate asks why her husband has grown pale of face. There is, moreover, a hint of both the Portias' insistence on their identity with their husbands in Kate's

> Do you not love me? do you not indeed?
> Well, do not then; for since you love me not,
> I will not love myself.
>
> (92-94)

Hotspur's Kate, however, unlike the Portias, does not find out what she wants to know from her husband. She has, of course, guessed it, because Hotspur has talked in his sleep of military affairs, but her husband will not take her into his confidence. He rides off to die at Shrewsbury without answering her questions except with banter about the looseness of women's tongues. And for all that banter, Kate is the least comedic of the three, because she neither acts on her husband's behalf as Bassanio's Portia does, nor shares her husband's secret, as both Portias do.

Six or seven years after he wrote *Julius Caesar,* Shakespeare dramatized Plutarch's story of Porcia's confrontation with her husband one last time, in *Macbeth* 3.2, where Lady Macbeth upbraids her husband for his melancholy solitude and tries in vain to find out what his plans are for disposing of Banquo and Fleance. Here sleeplessness and loss of appetite appear as in *First Henry IV* and *Julius Caesar,* though (as Law pointed out) it is Macbeth, not his wife, who describes them. Law heard echoes of Kate's language in Lady Macbeth's reproach to her husband in this scene *(1H4* 2.3.34ff / *Mac.* 3.2.8-11) and of Plutarch's emphasis on covering conspiracy with deception in Macbeth's

> . . . we must . . .
> . . .
> . . . make our faces vizards to our hearts,
> Disguising what they are.
>   (32-35)

Law also pointed out that the theme of a woman's ostensible inability to keep secrets appears here as it does in *First Henry IV, Julius Caesar,* and (ultimately) Plutarch's "Marcus Brutus"; he did not, however, sufficiently stress that Porcia's antifeminism in Plutarch is assigned to the hubands in *First Henry IV* and *Macbeth.* Where Shakespeare retained Plutarch's version of the story, in *Julius Caesar,* he effected a sad irony: Portia, who protests that she is "stronger than my sex" (2.1.296) and capable of keeping a secret like a man, essentially blurts out the fact of the assassination attempt in her nervousness in 2.4.

Like Hotspur's Kate, Plutarch's Porcia, and her counterpart in *Julius Caesar,* Lady Macbeth is pushed into a passive role here at a morally crucial moment. In her case it is a bitter touch, since she has proved in the earlier action that she can play the man perhaps better than her husband. Modern feminist critics have made us increasingly aware of the tragic (or elegiac) possibilities of enforced passivity. The tragic motif of an intelligent and morally aware woman forced to sit by as a powerless spectator of the horrifying events engaged in by men was a great favorite in the Renaissance (one thinks of the laments and curses of the three impotent women in *Richard III* 4.4 and of a number of Jacobean plays in which a sensitive woman's tragedy is her inability to take action on her own behalf or that of others). It may be ultimately Senecan in origin. One of the most interesting exemplars for the critical stance of this article is Robert Garnier's first tragedy, *Porcie* (published 1568) which, inspired by the enforced passivity of the heroine in the pseudo-Senecan *Octavia,* portrays the historical Porcia on the day of Second Philippi lamenting the horrors of civil war and anxiously awaiting news of her husband; we learn from her Nurse in Act V that she has killed herself to join him in death, the only assertive action possible to her.[20] There seems no reason to believe that Shakespeare knew *Porcie* (though he probably knew Garnier's later plays, *Cornélie* and *Marc Antoine,* if only through their English redactions). *Porcie* nonetheless makes a highly instructive analogue to the tragic vignettes Shakespeare introduced in the form of "Porcia scenes" into three plays and a poem.

A concomitant of enforced passivity at the perimeter of vigorous activity is alienation, and alienation of husband from wife is one element common to all the accounts of "Cato's daughter" except *The Merchant of Venice.* There, of course, the alienation of husband from wife in the rings plot is more threatened than real, and the play ends in reconciliation, harmony, and confidence. Certainly the real alienation in all the other tragic versions of the Porcia story is instructive. It is worth noting that in four of them, Plutarch's "Brutus," *First Henry IV, Julius Caesar,* and *Macbeth,* enforced passivity and therefore alienation result from a woman's exclusion from conspiracy. In all of these four accounts the husband dies in a climactic losing battle which underscores both the alienation and the tragic teleology of the story.[21] *The Merchant of Venice* is quite different. That this play should be both so like and so unlike these other accounts of "Cato's daughter" tells us, it may be, something important about Shakespeare's conception of possibility in his sources.

NOTES

1 *MV* 1.1.163-66. Shakespeare quotations in this article are from *The Complete Works* (Pelican Text Revised), General Editor Alfred Harbage. Baltimore: Penguin Books, 1969. In an earlier form this paper was read in Session 134, Renaissance Drama, of the Twelfth Conference on Medieval Studies, The Medieval Institute, Western Michigan University, May 8, 1977.

2 The closest approximation I know to an acceptance is a passing reference to the analogy between *MV* 3.2.248-50 and *JC* 2.1.267-75 in Ch. IV of Patricia Saxon's doctoral dissertation, "The Limits of Assertiveness: Modes of Female Identity in Shakespeare and the Stuart Dramatists" (Univ. of Texas, Austin, 1977). Sigurd Burckhardt ends his article *"The Merchant of Venice:* The Gentle Bond" *(ELH,* 29 [1962], 239-62) with the cryptic statement: "Brutus speaks the tragic epilogue to *The Merchant of Venice:* 'Portia is dead'." I am grateful to Christopher Spencer, Editor of the New Variorum *Merchant of Venice,* who generously shared his knowledge of *MV* scholarship with me. My own research on *JC* has turned up no substantial commentary on Shakespeare's two Portias (see *The Tragedy of Julius Caesar: A Bibliography to Supplement the New Variorum Edition of 1913.* New York: The Modern Language Association of America, 1977).

3 *MV* 3.4.11-18. Cf. Plutarch's "Amatorius" *(Moralia)* 759C-D (see note 5 below), where Cato Major is said to have expressed very much these sentiments about the affinity between friends. (The ultimate source is, most likely, Plato's *Phaedrus.)*

4 Quotations from North's Plutarch are from Geoffrey Bullough, *Narrative and Dramatic Sources of Shakespeare* Vol. 5: *The Roman Plays: Julius Caesar, Antony and Cleopatra, Coriolanus.* London: Routledge and Kegan Paul; New York: Columbia University Press, 1964. This quotation: Bullough, p. 98.

5 Plutarch never showed any interest in Christianity, and he nowhere approximates the theology of incorporate marriage; but he was intensely interested in the validity and indeed in the sanctity of marriage. (See M. W. MacCallum, *Shakespeare's Roman Plays and their Background* [1910]; Rpt. New York: Russell & Russell, 1967, pp. 98, 108, 182-84.) In the *Moralia* are several works in which the morality of marriage figures prominently: for three examples, the "Mulierum Virtutes" (anecdotes of heroic women, many of them wives), the "Consolatio ad Uxorem" (which consoles his wife lovingly on the death of their daughter), and the "Conjugalia Praecepta" (advice to newlyweds). The most interesting work in the *Moralia* for the case of *MV* and *JC* is the "Amatorius," a dialogue on love in which the claims of heterosexual love are weighed against those of pederasty, marriage defended against the claim that friendship is the only true love. It is of interest that the question of female assertiveness in a male world is prominent in this dialogue and that Plutarch comes down firmly on the side of a divine sanction to the bonds of love. The claims of marriage get the last word (766E-771E) in the dialogue. Philemon Holland first translated the *Moralia* into English in 1603; there is some evidence, however, that Shakespeare knew another treatise in the *Moralia,* "De Fortuna Romanorum," perhaps in Guillaume Budé's Latin, perhaps in Jacques Amyot's French. See Michael Lloyd, "Antony and the Game of Chance" *JEGP,* 61 (1962), 548-54; John W. Velz, "Undular Structure in *Julius Caesar" MLR,* 66 (1971), 21-30.

6 See, e.g., "Pyramus and Thisbe: A Study in Shakespeare's Method," *SQ,* 5 (1954), 141-53; "Menenius' Fable," *N&Q,* 198 (1953), 240-42.

7 It is just possible that the Portia *(JC)*/Portia *(MV)* relationship finds an independent analogue in the Cinna the Poet/Shylock relationship. Cinna the Poet, who is reluctant to leave his house because he has dreamed of feasting with Caesar and who nevertheless goes "forth" to disaster is prefigured by Shylock in 2.5 of *MV* who, having dreamed of moneybags, is reluctant to go to feast with Bassanio, but does so and suffers as a result the disaster of Jessica's robbery and elopement. Most of the details in *JC* 3.3 come from Plutarch's two (very similar) accounts of the murder of Cinna the Poet ("Life of Caesar," Bullough, p. 88; "Life of Brutus,"

Bullough, p. 105). It seems probable that one or both of these accounts in Plutarch lies behind the Shylock passage in *MV;* the motif is prominent in Plutarch's accounts of the assassination of Caesar because Caesar himself goes out to meet disaster despite the premonition of a bad dream (Bullough, 83-84, 100, 101). Oddly enough, though the word "forth" appears in all three Shakespearian accounts and is insisted on in both 3.3 and 2.2 of *JC* it appears in none of the four *loci* in Plutarch. Whether Shylock made a small contribution to *JC* or not, it is illuminating to consider that Shakespeare may have drawn for him on the circumstances surrounding the murder of Julius Caesar.

8 The moral issue and the source of strain on the marriage is assassination in both *MV* and "Marcus Brutus," though we ought not to attach much significance to that fact in itself, especially since there is a great difference between Brutus' role as potential assassin and Antonio's as potential victim.

9 See 1.1.169-72; 3.2.241-42; 5.1.12-14.

10 The phrase is Patricia Saxon's in Chapter 4 of her dissertation, cited in fn. 2, above.

11 A student once called my attention in an examination answer to a revealing fact about the two Portias: Portia in *Caesar* has two very brief scenes while Portia in *The Merchant* dominates the play with more than 1/5 of the 2564 lines.

12 See Geoffrey Bullough, *Narrative and Dramatic Sources of Shakespeare.* Vol. 1: *Early Comedies, Poems, Romeo and Juliet* (London: Routledge and Kegan Paul; New York: Columbia University Press, 1957), 181; F. T. Prince, ed., *The Poems* (Arden Edition) (London: Methuen; Cambridge, Mass.: Harvard University Press, 1960), note on 1366-67 and refs. therein.

13 The question of where Porcia's stoic strength lies is answered in contradictory ways in both Plutarch and in Shakespeare's *JC.* Here in this passage from "Brutus" Brutus says of his wife that she had a "weake constitution of her body" though her moral strength ("corage and constant minde") was as great as that of "any of us." (Here cf. *JC* 2.4.8 where Portia speaks of the disparity between her "man's mind" and her "woman's might.") Brutus appears painfully wrong about his wife here: her repeated weeping in the presence of the suggestive painting does not spring from "corage and constant minde"; moreover, her fortitude after gashing herself with a razor would not suggest a "weake constitution of her body." The truth is that in both biography and play she can endure physical pain like a man, but is frail in her "inability to bear suspense," as M. W. MacCallum (note 5 above) put it, p. 274.

14 "The Rape in Shakespeare's *Lucrece,*" *ShakS,* 9 (1976), 45-72.

15 The description of the painting in *Lucr.* contains a vignette reminiscent of what Brutus' Porcia wept to see:

> And from the walls of strong-besiegèd Troy
> When their brave hope, bold Hector, marched to field,
> Stood many Troyan mothers, sharing joy
> To see their youthful sons bright weapons wield;
> And to their hope they such odd action yield
>   That through their light joy seemèd to appear
>   (Like bright things stained) a kind of heavy fear.
>   (1429-35)

Here, however, (if Plutarch is the focus of infection) the grieving wife is replaced with plural mothers who have mixed emotions. Later in the *Lucr.* passage Lucrece identifies herself not with Andromachè but with Hecuba—in a passage (1443-63 et passim) that prefigures the First Player's account of Hecuba in *Ham.* 2.2. Hamlet in his resulting "rogue and peasant slave" soliloquy attacks the Player's artificial identification with Hecuba and implies that he himself might better identify with her, having a better "motive and cue for passion"; that motive and cue for passion is, of course, Claudius—it would perhaps be rewarding to consider Claudius as a Tarquin.

16 Geoffrey Bullough observes that Dido, like Lucrece, is "betrayed by a man" *(Early Comedies. . . ,* p. 181); there is, however, a vast difference between forcible rape and a willing liaison followed by desertion.

17 Paul Stapfer, in *Shakespeare and Classical Antiquity* (trans. Emily J. Carey, London: C. Kegan Paul, 1880), expressed the opinion that Shakespeare fell in *JC* "a little short of" Plutarch's "Brutus" because he had "to leave out some of its beauties, which apparently belong peculiarly to the form of narrative and refuse to be transplanted into dramatic regions. It requires all the wooden inflexibility of a systematic admiration not to regret the absence, in Shakespeare's tragedy, of the beautiful scene in which Brutus and Portia take leave of each other at Elea" (p. 370).

18 As long ago as 1948 Robert Adger Law could regard this perception as "a mere commonplace of criticism" (see note 19).

19 "Porcia's Curiosity: A Tale Thrice Told By Shakespeare," [*University of Texas*] *Studies in English,* 27 (1948), 207-14. I am much indebted to this perceptive article, though I have gone beyond its conclusions in several ways.

20 The best analysis of the play is Maurice Gras' in *Robert Garnier: Son Art et sa Méthode* (Travaux D'Humanisme et Renaissance LXXII), Genève: Librairie Droz, 1965, pp. 24-28 et passim.

21 Lucrece is also tragically alienated, but in a different sense; she feels herself set apart from her world by the violation of her honor and her husband's (see Coppélia Kahn's essay, cited in note 14 above, for a full discussion). *Lucr.* in one sense inverts the prototypical Brutus/Porcia situation: it is Lucrece, not her husband, who has a secret to impart. Shakespeare strongly emphasizes the drama inherent in her revelation late in the poem—she puts her listeners to an oath of faith and only then reveals Tarquin's name. In this poem the revelation *leads to* conspiracy.

"Ower Swete Sokor":
The Role of Ophelia in *Hamlet*

Cherrell Guilfoyle

The virtuous disguise of evil in woman is described most bitterly by Shakespeare in *King Lear* (IV,vi.120-29): "Behold yond simpering dame/ Whose face between her forks presages snow . . ./ But to the girdle do the gods inherit,/ Beneath is all the fiends'." If she can be separated from sexual considerations, for example in royalty or in comedy, woman can appear on a level with, if not equal to, man; but where his feelings are most deeply aroused, in love and veneration, or in lust and frustration, the writer finds her angel or devil, separately or interchangeably. In the opening cantos of *The Faerie Queene*,[1] Spenser presents the two pictures of woman which combine in a potent myth in the literature of all ages: the pure, young, innocent Una, characterized by her name, and her exact physical duplicate, who is, behind the façade, a filthy fiend. This sinister figure is later presented as Fidessa/Duessa, but in her first appearance she usurps the fair form of Una, the one truth. In one of the fragments of Euripidean tragedy, there is the saying "Woman brings to man the greatest possible succour, and the greatest possible harm."[2] The words for "greatest possible succour" are *ophelian . . . megistan.*

Ophelia's name links her to the idea of succor; "ower swete sokor" was a phrase used of Mary Magdalen in the Digby Magdalen play. In different ways, Ophelia and Magdalen embody the "angel/devil" dichotomy of woman, and the figure of Magdalen appears in the imagery of Ophelia's scenes throughout *Hamlet*. Conventions in Shakespeare are often hidden, because in his hands they do not appear conventional, but if the strands of the Magdalen legends are examined, it can be seen that many of them are woven into Ophelia's words and actions. These images reflect Shakespeare's preoccupation, not with the horrific figure described by Lear, but with innocence or good faith mistaken—for example, Desdemona mistaken by Othello, Hermione by Leontes, Imogen by Posthumus, Cordelia by Lear—and Ophelia by Hamlet. The young woman in the Saxo and Belleforest versions of the *Hamlet* story was not virtuous (and not, of course, called Ophelia); Shakespeare changes this into the figure which seems to have haunted him. The tragic mistake is explicit in *The Tragedy of Hoffmann,* a crude revenge play which borrows much from *Hamlet* and may have been commissioned on the heels of *Hamlet's* success. Mathias describes the innocent Lucibella thus: "Shee is as harlots, faire, like guilded tombs/ Goodly without; within all rottenness . . . Angel in show,/ Divell in heart."3

In *The Faerie Queene,* angel and devil are presented in simple allegorical form, as two different figures that look the same. The Red Cross Knight abandons Una, because he assumes that the girl he finds *in flagrante dilectu* is his virgin fallen. In *Hamlet,* the duality is used differently, but basically the same thing happens. Hamlet abandons Ophelia, maligning her in the most brutal terms, because he assumes her to be corrupt or, at the least, on the first step downwards. Archimago creates the false Una; Hamlet, on this occasion as on others, combines the roles of hero and villain in creating for himself his false Ophelia. He, like the Red Cross Knight, is mistaken; but his mistake is not retrieved.

The presentation of the relationship between Hamlet and Ophelia at first seems contradictory. In Act I.iii Polonius and Laertes warn Ophelia that Hamlet's wooing may not be honorable, and she is instructed to avoid his importunities. It should be noted that his wooing is of recent date: "He hath my Lord of late made many tenders/ Of his affection to me." But in Act III.i, she appears as the neglected mistress and reproaches Hamlet for his coldness. This may be an inconsistency, but it may alternatively reflect a major change in Hamlet. Between the picture of the ardent young lover given by Ophelia to her father, and Hamlet's bitter comments to her father (II.ii.181ff) and to herself (III.i.103ff), there is the key encounter of Hamlet and Ophelia in her closet.

Images from the various Magdalen stories appear in all Ophelia's scenes except the "fatal mistake" scene in the closet, recounted in Act II.i. It is therefore entirely appropriate that this scene should be offstage, as an unseen key to the tragic role of Ophelia. For she is not the prostitute, the early Magdalen taunted by Hamlet in the nunnery scene; she is pure, as her name suggests and as her brother repeatedly describes her, "Whose worth . . ./ Stood challenger on mount of all the age/ For her perfections." She is the figure not of the repentant sinner, but of the purity which can atone for the sins of others. She is to intercede, in her "orisons," in the nunnery, as a ministering angel. Her prayers are all for others—"O help him, you sweet heavens!" "O heavenly powers, restore him!" "God dild you!" "God be at your table!" "God ha' mercy on his soul! And of all Christian souls I pray God," "God bye you." Her final utterance (reported) is "snatches of old lauds."4 She opposes truth to Hamlet's feigning and feinting; he pretends to be mad, she is really mad; he meditates on death, she dies. Critics have noted that Ophelia never mentions her love for Hamlet. Her function goes far beyond that of a girl caught up in an unhappy love affair.

The Magdalen imagery serves to illumine on the one hand the succor which the pure Ophelia can offer through atonement; and on the other, the delusion of female wantonness from which Hamlet suffers and which is part of his tragedy.

"O my lord, my lord, I have been so affrighted!" introduces the description of Hamlet face to face with female depravity—depravity that exists only in his imagination, as the scene itself exists only in the imagination of the audience. Hamlet has seen something of the rottenness within in his mother's summary grief and incestuous marriage; he subsequently hears from the ghost the story of the murder, the stain of which, together with the stain of adultery, is added to the defaced image of his mother. Distracted, he runs to Ophelia, to gaze on the pure young face which between her forks presages snow. What he sees is presumably what Fradubio saw when he came upon Duessa bathing herself in origen and thyme, and saw her "in her proper hew." Hamlet leaves Ophelia with his head over his shoulder in the gesture of the damned, that of the runner in Dante's seventh Circle of Hell, and of Trevisan fleeing Despair.5

Hamlet makes no reference to Ophelia in the play until after this encounter. We hear of Hamlet as an ardent young lover and as the author of the exaggerated and very youthful jingle beginning "Doubt thou the stars are fire." But once he has rejected womankind, including Ophelia, he never (until the funeral scene) speaks or refers to her except with the imagery of sexual corruption. He calls Polonius a fishmonger (or brothel keeper) and after what seems to be a passing reference to the sun breeding maggots in a dead dog, he says of the "fishmonger's" daughter: "Let her not walk i' the sun; conception is a blessing, but as your daughter may conceive—friend look to't." Traditionally, the serpent's egg was hatched by the sun; Brutus, resolving on the death of Caesar, decides to "think him as a serpent's egg/ Which hatched, would as his kind grow mischievous" (*Julius Caesar* II.i.32-33). Ophelia's "kind" is now, in Hamlet's thoughts, the progeny of the serpent; and possibly, if we go back to the maggots, the swarming brood of Error, "soon conceiv'd," which will devour its mother.6 With Ophelia in the nunnery scene, Hamlet is still haunted by this image: "Why wouldst thou be a breeder of sinners?"

From the time of his fatal mistake, Hamlet is without the support, the *ophelia,* that he needs. His mother is sunk in adultery, incest and complicity in murder;7 he is forced to reject her, and with her he rejects all women, and Ophelia suffers the same fate as Una.

By Act IV, Ophelia's rejection is total, her brother gone, her father dead, her lover brutally estranged from her having killed her father and treated her as a prostitute. In her rejected state, she rejects reason. In this she is like Lear, and like Lear, she will die, the will to live being annihilated. In her mad scene she can only "play" the tragedy in which she is caught up, like Cassandra helplessly enacting what she can truly see but cannot intervene to prevent.

The mad scene is, at first glance, a jumble of songs, dialogue, and lament. However, characters who go mad in renaissance drama frequently speak more truth, and deeper truth than when sane, and this can be said of Ophelia (who is sadly confused when her wits are about her) as of Lear. It is the order of what she says that is disturbed. "Oh when degree is shak'd . . . the enterprise is sick";8 conversely, in the Elizabethan world picture, when the mind is sick, the divine order by which man can live in harmony is shaken and in chaos. What happens to Ophelia is what she has described as having happened to Hamlet—the sweet bells are jangled, out of tune and harsh, as bells will be if rung out of order. The images of her mad scene show derangement in its literal sense, but they are nonetheless images of the truth—the truth in chaos because of the havoc in her mind. Laertes, who provides a commentary on her madness, sums this up when he says, "This nothing's more than matter." It is "nothing" because evil derangement has taken over the order of a rational mind; but the disordered fragments are of something good and precious, which has been under attack ever since Hamlet's irruption "as if he had been loosed out of hell."

The Magdalen legends bear strongly on the detail of Ophelia's mad scene, and it is therefore appropriate now to consider the outline of the legends. In these, the images of virtue and depravity in woman, as symbolic of the problem of good and evil, provide the emotive power. Little of this power can be gleaned from the New Testament. The legends grew firstly by the identification of various women mentioned in the Gospels as the one Magdalen—including the woman taken in adultery, the "Mary" who was the sister of Lazarus, and the woman of Samaria—and secondly by a process of polarization of her states of sin and repentance. She is made not merely a sinner, but a prostitute, not just a repentant disciple, but a saint. From a practitioner of the oldest profession, she rises to be no less than the "beata dilectrix" of Christ.[9] In medieval literature she and Christ address each other as "love," "true love," and "lover."[10] She is the most important figure at the tomb of Christ (in the Coventry Resurrection play costumes were provided for Magdalen and for "two side Maries"),[11] and was the first witness of the Resurrection. Her tears were symbolic of the purifying waters of baptism. Her hold on dramatists, ballad writers, and artists can be well understood.

One other aspect of her legend bears on the parallel imagery of Ophelia, and that is the threefold interpretation of her relationship with God. God for Magdalen is father, lover and brother—all as manifestations of the same divine love. In the ballad "The Maid and the Palmer" an old man—the figure of the Father—appears to the woman at the well, identified in medieval tradition as Magdalen. She hopes he is "the good old man/ That all the world beleeves vpon." In a Scandinavian version of the ballad, it is Jesus who appears in the pilgrim's

robe.12 Magdalen's Christ/brother is Lazarus, whose raising
from the dead prefigured the Resurrection, and Ophelia's brother
at one stage briefly enacts this. In the deeply symbolic graveyard scene in *Hamlet,* with a setting redolent of the Last Judgment plays in the mystery cycles, Laertes leaps into his sister's
open grave and then emerges from it.

The young woman in the known sources of the *Hamlet* story
has neither father nor brother; the provision of both in Shakespeare's play opens the way for the multiple imagery of the
threefold relationship in Ophelia's mad scene.

Three religious plays—the Digby *Mary Magdalene,* Wager's
morality play *The Life and Repentaunce of Marie Magdalene,*
and the Benediktbeuern Passion play—are convenient texts
from which to trace parallels with Shakespeare's heroine.13
Shakespeare may not have known the plays, but the legends
were common knowledge, and the plays contain many of
them. In the main, the following parallels are traced through
the Digby play, which has been dated late fifteenth or early
sixteenth century. The play begins with an affectionate family
scene between Magdalen, her sister Martha, her father Cyrus
and her brother Lazarus. The family is about to be scattered,
as Cyrus divides his estates between his children. It can be seen
that although the topic of conversation is different from *Hamlet* I.iii, there is some similarity in the characters present and
in the occasion. After leaving her home, Magdalen is led to
an inn by Luxuria, and is seduced by Curiosity, who gets the
better of her, so to speak. Curiosity's conversation with her, in
a tone of mock gallantry mixed with indecency, is reminiscent
of the cruel banter with which Hamlet assails Ophelia in the
play scene. In Wager's play there is a similar conversation
between Magdalen and Infidelitie, the Vice. It is interesting
to see Hamlet so nearly assuming the role of vice, or villain,
in this instance.

The seduction in *Hamlet* is described in Ophelia's "valentine" song. In the Digby play, Magdalen becomes a prostitute
and is seen in her "erbyr" waiting for her "valentynes"—"A!
god be with my valentynes,/ My byrd swetyng, my lovys so
dere!" (ll. 564-65). In the Wager play she decks herself in
elaborate costumes and jewels, and is persuaded to buy cosmetics to paint her face. In the Benediktbeuern play, she visits
a shop with her fellow prostitutes to buy cosmetics. Hamlet in

the nunnery scene adopts the tone of a contemporary preacher rebuking the painted ladies of the town: "I have heard of your paintings too, well enough; God hath given you one face, and you make yourselves another; you jig, you amble, and you lisp, and you nickname God's creatures . . ." (III.i.145-48). The "sweet ladies" to whom Ophelia later bids goodnight, the coach for which she calls, are part of this life *"in gaudio."*14

In the mad scene Ophelia is acting out, among other facets of the tragedy, the role of harlot which Hamlet has foisted on her. To the king she suddenly says, "They say the owl was a baker's daughter." This is perhaps the only direct reference to a legend almost certainly linked with Magdalen. According to a country legend cited by Douce, Jesus asked for bread at a baker's shop, the girl in the shop cheated him, and he punished her by changing her into an owl.15 This is typical of many New Testament apocryphal stories, in which the character of Jesus is made stern and retributive to sinners. The outline of the story is similar to that of the ballad "The Maid and the Palmer." There an old man asked for water at a well. The girl at the well refused him, and he punished her by changing her first to a stepping stone and then to a bell-clapper, and lastly by sending her to hell for seven years. The ballad tells one of the stories af Magdalen and Jesus which grew up after identification of Magdalen with the woman of Samaria. The owl and the baker's daughter may have derived from stories of St. Mary of Egypt, who was always depicted with loaves of bread, and was often confused with Magdalen.16

The Digby Magdalen described herself when a prostitute as "drynchyn" (drowned) "in synne" (1. 754). In her death Ophelia re-enacts this drowning in sin; the "long purples," which some critics have found so incongruous in the Queen's speech describing the drowning, can be seen as the key to this re-enactment.17

The waters that meet over Magdalen's head are those of baptism, and she emerges repentant. In token of her changed condition, she sheds her jewels and dresses in black.18 Later she will assume the appearance of the Donatello Magdalen, her hair dishevelled, her face drawn, her clothing in rags. Early in the nunnery scene, Ophelia returns to Hamlet the "rich gifts," "remembrances of yours," which he had given her.19 There is no reference to her appearance in the mad scene, except for the Q.1 stage direction ("Enter Ofelia playing on a Lute, and her haire downe singing"), but traditionally she assumes the disorder of the penitent's hair and dress, which is equally indicative of mental derangement. It is worth noting, because other similar instances will emerge, that the "nighted colour" of mourning which Hamlet wears is also the outward show of repentance; Hamlet is, in a sense, wearing Magdalen's color when he confronts Ophelia.

The central scene of the Magdalen story is the Resurrection. She first visits the sepulchre with the two "side" Maries, bearing herbs and spices to anoint the dead body of Jesus. They find the tomb empty and are told by an angel that Christ is risen. Left alone, Magdalen is the first person to see the risen Christ. This scene, described in the gospels with some variations, is also the subject of the first recognizably dramatic ceremony in the liturgy—*"Quem quaeritis in sepulchro,"* "whom seek ye in the sepulchre?" to which the angel adds, "He is risen, he is not here" (*"non est hic, surrexit"*).[20] This scene is linked in Magdalen legend with a passage from *The Song of Solomon,* for Magdalen, the *beata dilectrix* of Christ and sister of Lazarus the Christ-figure, was identified with the sister/spouse of the Old Testament: "I will . . . seke him that my soule loueth; I soght him, but I founde him not./ The watchemen that went about the citie founde me; to whome I said, Haue you sene him whome my soule loueth?"[21]

It takes little imagination to see that from this line one could continue directly with the first line of Ophelia's song—"How should I your true love know?"—which like Raleigh's "As you came from the Holy Land," seems to start from an old ballad about a pilgrimage to Walsingham, but finishes in the poet's own idiom.[22] Since Magdalen traditionally calls Jesus her love, the song which (with interruptions) runs through the mad scene can be seen as the negative *Quem quaeritis* of an evil, disordered world. Parts of the song, including the opening lines, are missing; it is jumbled and broken up, and spoken by various persons who are not identified. But the answer to the seeker's question is clear: the true love, or Father, or brother, is dead, not risen; "he will not come again." The lines beginning "And will a not come again?" are full of negative-resounding doom—*not, not, no, no, never*—and give the counsel of despair, "Go to thy death-bed."

The true love is to be recognized "by his cockle hat and staff/ And his sandal shoon"—the pilgrim's dress worn by the risen Christ on the road to Emmaus, and by the man at the well in "The Maid and the Palmer." The pilgrim is buried, "At his heels a stone"—an indication that he is not in a grave, where the stone would be at the head, but in a sepulchre sealed by a stone. The "O, ho!" which follows this line is the mourner's cry of grief, as Magdalen wept over her brother Lazarus and at the sepulchre of Christ. The white shroud of the martyr is "Larded all with sweet flowers," the equivalent of the herbs and spices that Magdalen brought to the tomb. The faulty rhythm of "Which bewept to the grave did not go" points the intrusive *not;* this body was not destined for the grave. The "true love showers" are the tears of the mourner (cf. *Richard II,* V.i.20: "And wash him fresh again with true-love tears"); Magdalen's tears are among the most famous ever shed. But Shakespeare is always alive to a double meaning, and "showers" are also pangs, the bitter pains felt by the "true love." In the Digby play Lazarus exclaims, "A! a! now brystyt myn hertt! þis is a sharp shower!" (1. 822), and the word was in use in this meaning as late as 1637. The first part of the song ends, and Ophelia, after greeting the king, says, "they say the owl was a baker's daughter."

The lament over the dead love begins again with "They bore him barefaced on the bier." The "hey non nonny" line which follows is not in Q.2 and looks like an interpolation.23 The many tears again recall the copious water which flowed from Magdalen's eyes. The figure in the last verse is that of the father—indeed, of the Ancient of Days: "His beard was as white as snow,/ All flaxen was his poll" (cf. *Daniel* 7.9: "the Ancient of daies did sit, whose garment was white as snowe, and the heere of his head like the pure woll"). The earthly father dead, and the earthly brother who has gone away, are mourned by Ophelia in her visionary state as Magdalen mourned Jesus, who was at once the heavenly Father and her "true love," and also Lazarus, her brother who was a type of Christ. Thus it is not, in this strangely haunting scene, a particular death and absence which is lamented; it is the death of Ophelia's whole world, and she symbolizes this also with the flowers which she scatters among the assembled company. They are funeral flowers, handed to those who will shortly die—the King, the Queen, Laertes, and herself.

The legends of Magdalen's later life describe her as a preacher, converting the heathen, and as a hermit in the wilderness, where she is fed by angels until her death and ascent to heaven. In a long poem published at Lyon in 1668,[24] Magdalen is described as preaching to her former fellow-prostitutes and exhorting them to enter nunneries. With no earlier reference, this cannot be directly related to Hamlet's repeated exhortations to Ophelia to "get thee to a nunnery," but it is at least likely that the Magdalen of legend would do this, as the patron saint of reformed prostitutes and as a preacher.[25] If so, Hamlet in the nunnery scene is opposing the repentant Magdalen to the figure of her former self which he sees in Ophelia. He not only wears Magdalen's "nighted colour" but also speaks her words.

In the death of Ophelia, borne down the weeping brook, the main image is of another suffering innocent, the Fair Maid of Astolat, who floated down the Thames. This story from Malory may also have influenced the funeral scene, for it is the King (Arthur) who commands arrangements for the funeral, and the ceremony is attended by the Fair Maid's "true love" (Lancelot) and brother (Lavaine).[26] These images may testify to the "embryology" (to use T. S. Eliot's word[27]) of the episodes of the drowning and of the funeral rather than to their meaning; but it may be worth noting that Claudius's "arrangements" for Ophelia's funeral are the reverse of what they seem. According to the Clowns, Ophelia killed herself, and only by "great command" was she allowed Christian burial; even so, only "maimed rites" were permitted. Yet it is clear from the Queen's description that Ophelia did not deliberately throw herself into the water; it appears that although the Queen knew well enough what happened, different information was given to the "crowner," which deprived her of the benefit of the full funeral service. It is Claudius who has "maimed" the rites, not for the first time, as Polonius her father was interred "hugger-mugger"; and his action aligns Ophelia's funeral with the hasty burial of Christ, leading in turn to Magdalen's visit to the tomb with herbs and spices.

The stage properties which accompany Ophelia are, significantly, specified in the text. The traditional symbol of Magdalen's contempt of the world, the skull, is thrown from

Ophelia's grave early in the funeral scene, and lies nearby as her body is prepared for burial. Earlier, in the nunnery scene, she carried a book, the symbol of Magdalen the contemplative. The flowers in the mad scene may be taken to stand for the funeral herbs and spices which Magdalen carries in her traditional ointment jar. The rue, which she probably hands to the King since it must be worn "with a difference" (that is, with a sign that he is not in the main line of succession)[28] is also the "herb of grace," a phrase as relevant in this context as the "long purples" are to the drowning.

In tracing religious imagery in *Hamlet*, it is instructive to compare it with *Der Bestrafte Brudermord*, a corrupt German version of Shakespeare's play in which all religious reference is omitted. Thus in Ophelia's part, there is no scene with her father and brother; no account of her confrontation by Hamlet in her closet; no book or skull; no drowning (she commits suicide by throwing herself from the top of a hill); her mad scenes are utterly secular nonsense, and there is no graveyard scene.[29] The Magdalen imagery changes all this. As has been noted above, the drowning is parallel to the "drowning in sin" of the early Magdalen, and the water to which Ophelia is as "native and indued" is reminiscent both of the tears shed over the feet of Christ and of the redemptive waters of baptism; water is as much part of Ophelia's story as it is of Magdalen's. Laertes, Ophelia's commentator in this as in the mad scene, evokes the saint-like figure that she is to be, the fair and unpolluted flesh in earth, the "minist'ring angel" in heaven. The idea of *ophelia,* succor, is implicit in "minist'ring."[30]

Like Cassandra, like Iphigenia, Ophelia suffers for the sins of the house. Johnson's famous comment can therefore be seen in an unusual light: "the gratification which would arise from the destruction of an usurper and a murderer is abated by the untimely death of Ophelia, the young, the beautiful, the harmless, and the pious."[31] The devout Johnson would undoubtedly have been shocked at the suggestion that the untimely death of Christ robs us of any gratification arising from the defeat of Satan; but without the idea of atonement, the power of Ophelia's tragedy cannot be fully grasped. In her mad scene she mourns the loss and absence which has doomed the court of Denmark, polluted by lust and murder. "Where," she asks, "is the beauteous majesty of Denmark?" Where, indeed? Her words echo the transferred epithet of Horatio's lines in the first scene of the play, "What art thou, that usurps't this time of night,/ Together with that fair and warlike form/ In which the majesty of buried Denmark/ Did sometimes march?" Ophelia's death is the signal for the retributive action which at last is taken when her beloved brother unwittingly provides the poisoned weapon for Hamlet's hand.

As Ophelia is not the double character of the legendary Magdalen, but only the purer half, the other half being painted in by false accusation, why should Shakespeare choose the image of Magdalen to illumine the role of Ophelia? The popular appeal of Magdalen is that she epitomizes hope. She sins, she repents; she is forgiven, and by grace she is made pure. She is therefore the hope of every sinner. For Hamlet, "all is not well," "how ill all's here about my heart"; but Ophelia says "I hope all will be well." The Magdalen raised from prostitution to sainthood provides a resolution of the Una/Fidessa riddle. The sin in Magdalen could be atoned for, sinner and penitent made one and purified. Ophelia acts this atonement through the scenes of Magdalen's life. Hamlet speaks of the ghost as a hellish resurrection, out of the "ponderous and marble jaws" of his father's sepulchre, "making night hideous"; Ophelia evokes the heavenly resurrection in the search for her "true love."

The idea of atonement (*adunamentum*) brings us back to Spenser's Una, who like Ophelia is the face of true purity. With his "Una," Hamlet might have reached the Castle of Holiness; he rejects the woman who could have been his "swete sokor"—the phrase used of Magdalen by her grateful disciples in the Digby play (1. 1963). Laertes gives the key lines on his sister: "O Rose of May,/ Dear maid, kind sister, sweet Ophelia." The rose of May is probably the white rose, the symbol of both the Virgin and Magdalen, whose tears were supposed to have washed it white. The "dear maid" is a virgin, pure in spite of all Hamlet's suspicions; the "kind sister" is in contrast to the incestuous and therefore unnatural (unkind) sister-in-law of Claudius; and "sweet Ophelia" is a version of "swete sokor."

To go back to woman's nature as described by Euripides, Ophelia could have given to Hamlet the means of salvation, *ophelian megistan;*[32] but he is fatally convinced that she brings him only the greatest harm. Nothing could be more decisive than his rejection; he first abuses her, and then forgets her. Her living image is only fleetingly recalled in the funeral scene, and the last reference to her in the play is Hamlet's half-mocking challenge which brings his rejection of her to its conclusion: "Be buried quick with her, and so will I."33

NOTE ON THE STOBAIC FRAGMENT LXIX.7

The text of the Stobaic fragment referred to in this paper is taken from a lost play by Euripides on *Alcmaeon*. Editions of the fragments of ancient Greek collected by Stobaeus were published, in Greek and in Latin, at various times through the sixteenth century, and it is possible that Shakespeare had some knowledge of them, as F. P. Wilson suggested.34 I propose to examine in another paper the possible link between *Hamlet* and the story of Alcmaeon, but the connection may be noted briefly here. The story of Orestes is often cited as parallel to *Hamlet,* in that a son avenges his father's death, that death being caused by the wickedness of the mother. Alcmaeon has a similar story; his father, Amphiaraus, is killed, having prophesied that his death would be caused by his wife, Eriphyle. Alcmaeon is charged with revenge, and kills Eriphyle. Both Orestes and Alcmaeon are pursued by the Furies once their vengeance is achieved. One feature of the Alcmaeon story is much closer to *Hamlet* than is the story of Orestes. The ghost of Amphiaraus appears, and, moreover, he appears in full armor, dressed as he was when he died on the battlefield. "He rose up again from the chasm of earth, even as he was—the shades had touched his team alone"35—that is, he appeared in battle array, but without his horses and chariot. Alcmaeon may well have been in Shakespeare's mind when he introduced the somber figure on the platform in Act I of *Hamlet*. Collier lists a play on Alcmaeon (now lost) given in the court revels before Elizabeth around 1580.36 Either at second hand from this play, or directly from Stobaeus, Shakespeare might have come across the word which named his heroine.

NOTES

Quotations from *Hamlet* are from the New Shakespeare edition, ed. J. Dover Wilson (2nd ed., Cambridge, 1936). Quotations from the Bible are taken from *The Geneva Bible: A Facsimile of the 1560 Edition,* introd. Lloyd E. Barry (Madison, 1969).

1 Book I.vii.1: note also Book IV.i.17 (the theme runs through much of *The Faerie Queene*). Citations are to *The Works of Edmund Spenser: Variorum Edition*.

2 Augustus Nauck, ed., *Tragicorum Graecorum Fragmenta* (Hildesheim, 1964), p. 384 (Stob. Flor. LXIX.7).

3 Henry Chettle, *The Tragedy of Hoffmann, or A Revenge for a Father*, Malone Soc. Reprints (Oxford, 1950), II. 823ff.

4 Q.2. The emphasis is changed in F.1—"snatches of old tunes."

5 *The Faerie Queene* I.ii.40, I.ix.21.

6 *Julius Caesar* V.iii.69; cf. *The Faerie Queene* I.i.25.

7 In his own eyes, at least; *vide* "As kill a king and marry with his brother" (III.iv.29).

8 *Troilus and Cressida* I.iii.101-03.

9 Louis Réau, *Iconographie de l'art chrétien*, III, Pt. II (Paris, 1958), 848.

10 Cf. the Digby Magdalen play (see note 13 below), 1. 1068 ("I his lover"), 1. 1588 ("mary my lover"); and the version of "Noli me tangere" in the York Wynedrawers' play: "Negh me not, my loue, latte be!" (1. 82).

11 Thomas Sharp, *A Dissertation on the Pageants or Dramatic Mysteries anciently performed at Coventry* (Coventry, 1825), p. 47.

12 Francis James Child, ed., *The English and Scottish Popular Ballads* (1882; rpt. New York, 1957), I, 228.

13 F. J. Furnivall, ed., *The Digby Mysteries* (London, 1882); Lewis Wager, *The Life and Repentaunce of Marie Magdalene*, ed. F. I. Carpenter (Chicago, 1902); *Ludus de Passione*, in Karl Young, *The Drama of the Medieval Church* (Oxford, 1933), I, 518-33.

14 Cf. E. K. Chambers, *The Mediaeval Stage* (Oxford, 1903), II, 90.

15 Horace Howard Furness, ed., *Hamlet* A New Variorum Edition of Shakespeare (Philadelphia, 1877), I, 332.

16 Cf. Edith C. Batho, "The Life of Christ in the Ballads," *Essays and Studies*, 9 (1924), 81: Réau, p. 847.

17 The connotation of "long purples" is most explicit in Q.2 (IV.vii.170), for which most editors substitute the F.1 version: "But our cull-cold maydes doe dead mens fingers call them."

18 Cf. Robert Potter, *The English Morality Play* (London and Boston, 1975), p. 48; Chambers, II, 75-76.

19 Cf. Dover Wilson's stage direction, p. 61: "she takes jewels from her bosom and places them on the table before him."

20 Chambers, II, 9-10.

21 *The Song of Solomon* 4.9, 3.2-4; cf. the sub-title *Soror mea sponsa* of R.-L. Bruckberger's *Marie Madeleine* (Paris, 1952).

22 Cf. *The Poems of Sir Walter Ralegh*, ed. Agnes M. C. Latham (London, 1929), pp. 100, 184.

23 "Hey nonny nonny" and, later, "down-a-down," both common phrases in ballad refrains, may indicate the disorder and parody of her song. Cf. Wager's opening lines, spoken by Infidelitie: "With heigh down down and downe a downe a,/ Saluator mundi Domine, Kyrieleyson,/ Ite, Missa est, With pipe vp Alleluya."

24 Pierre de S. Louys, *La Madeleine au désert de la Sainte Baume en Provence*, Book 4; cited by Françoise Bardon, "Le thème de la Madeleine Pénitente au xviième siècle en France," *Journal of the Warburg and Courtauld Institutes*, 31 (1968), 293.

25 The Order for reformed prostitutes (Pénitentes de Sainte Marie-Madeleine), known as *Dame blanches* or *Weissfrauen* because they were dressed in white, was first set up in the early thirteenth century (see Victor Saxer, *Le Culte de Marie Madeleine en Occident* [Paris, 1959], pp. 222-23).

26 *Le Morte Darthur,* Book XVIII.19-20.

27 In "The Music of Poetry" (*Selected Prose of T. S. Eliot,* ed. Frank Kermode [New York, 1975], p. 111).

28 Cf. *Much Ado about Nothing* I.i.69: "If he have wit enough to keep himself warm, let him bear it for a difference between himself and his horse." Of course the real "difference" between Ophelia and the King is between the pure and impure.

29 Geoffrey Bullough, *Narrative and Dramatic Sources of Shakespeare* (London, 1973), VII, 146-56.

30 Cf. John Ruskin, *Munera Pulveris,* quoted in Furness, *New Variorum Shakespeare: Hamlet,* II, 241.

31 Quoted in Furness, p. 146: from Samuel Johnson, *The Plays of Shakespeare,* VIII, 311.

32 Cf. Richard Helgerson, "What Hamlet remembers" *Shakespeare Studies,* 10 (1977), 91: "his [Hamlet's] misogynism keeps him from discovering the grace that might redeem both him and the natural world."

33 Cf. H. Granville Barker, *Prefaces to Shakespeare* (1930; rpt. London, 1958), I, 254: "he, at heart, is as dead as she. This is indeed, the last pang he is to suffer."

34 In "Shakespeare's Reading," quoted by Emrys Jones, *The Origins of Shakespeare* (Oxford, 1977), p. 91.

35 Statius, *Thebaid,* trans. J. H. Mozley, Loeb Classical Library (London and Cambridge, Mass., 1957), Vol. II, Book X, ll. 202-05.

36 J. P. Collier, *The History of English Dramatic Poetry to the Time of Shakespeare,* III (London, 1831), 24. See also ibid., I. 207.

The Fragile World of *Lear*

Peter S. Anderson

Drama is a form of ritual, and like its "savage" ancestor, it begins in a felt discontinuity—a certain fragility of the human series in the face of temporal and spatial change.[1] Seeking to overcome this deficiency, it enters into dialogue or exchange with what is not human—either divinity or the natural series—to give to the sociomorphic "sacred" or "natural" form. Tragedy tends toward the former, comedy toward the latter. May Day, Midsummer Eve—the seasonal feasts—give Shakespeare, as C. L. Barber has pointed out, the social pattern of his "festive comedy." Tragedy casts its eye through the more readily available natural series toward the unseen: divinity itself. The central form of tragedy is, thus, that ritual we call sacrifice, where the "real" is exchanged for the "unreal." As Claude Lévi-Strauss demonstrates in his structural study of *La Pensée Sauvage,* a representative of the human series (in dramatic terms we would call him the *tragos,* the scapegoat) is sacralized and sacrificed, so that the void caused by his removal (this the actualized discontinuity of the human series) will, hopefully, be filled by the divinity to whom he has been related. Drama thus voices our continuing concern over social structures threatened by discontinuity in time and space. It is this fragility, felt at the level of the human series but having its roots in our very perceptions, that I wish—by the somewhat circuitous route of Montaigne— to explore in Shakespeare's *Lear.*

In that famous chapter in the first book of the *Essais,* "That to Philosophie, Is to Learn How to Die" (which is certainly as large a part of Shakespeare's debt to Montaigne as the "Apologie of Raymond Sebond"), Montaigne, after citing other men's deaths "frequent and ordinary examples, hapning, and being still before our eies,"[2] soon turns to nature as a proper teacher of how to die:

Nature her selfe lends her hand, and gives us courage. If it be
a short and violent death, wee have no leisure to feare it; if
otherwise, I perceive that according as I engage my selfe in
sicknesse, I doe naturally fall into some disdaine and contempt
of life. I finde that I have more adoe to digest this resolution,
that I shall die when I am in health, than I have when I am
troubled with a fever: forsomuch as I have no more such fast
hold on the commodities of life, whereof I begin to lose the
use and pleasure, and view death in the face with a lesse un-
danted looke, which makes me hope, that the further I goe
from that, and am the nearer I approch to this, so much more
easily doe I enter in composition for their exchange. . . . Often
somethings seeme greater, being farre from us, than if they bee
neere at hand: I have found that being in perfect health, I have
much more beene frighted with sicknesse, than when I have felt
it. The jollitie wherein I live, the pleasure and the strength make
the other seeme so disproportionable from that, that by imagination I amplifie these commodities by one moitie, and appre-
hended them much more heavie and burthensome, than I feele
them when I have them upon my shoulders. The same I hope
wille happen to me of death. Consider we by the ordinary
mutations, and daily declinations which we suffer, how Nature
deprives us of the [sight] of our losse and empairing: what hath
an aged man left him of his youths vigor, and of his forepast
life? (I.xix.57)

Our confidence that Shakespeare was familiar with this particular passage in the Florio translation of 1603 is founded not
only on the sense but also on the very language of Edgar's anguish at the sight of blinded Gloucester: "My father, poorly led?
World, world, O world!/ But that thy strange mutations make
us hate thee,/ Life would not yield to age" (IV.i.10-11), and
Gloucester's answer, a few lines later, to the Old Man who is
leading him:

> I have no way, and therefore want no eyes;
> I stumbled when I saw: full oft 'tis seen
> Our means secure us, and our mere defects
> Prove our commodities. (IV.i.19-22)

This last, of course, begins to plunge us immediately into
that centric image for *Lear* of "unaccommodated man," but
Montaigne's method, it seems to me, deserves special comment.
Those qualities which most clearly mark Montaigne's method—
I mean that cultivated humanism which, in Donald Frame's expression, "must rise above the common herd by his readiness
to meet pain and death like a sage" (*Montaigne's Discovery of*

Man [New York: Columbia University Press, 1955], p. 48),
and that realism which the paratactic randomness of his style
images (see Eric Auerbach's chapter on Montaigne in *Mimesis*)
—these qualities of cultivated realism are here. But beneath this
surface there is a primitive at work, ritualizing an "exchange"
with that oldest of enemies to the human series, time. The old
game between the living and the dead, whereby the living,
postulating in advance an asymmetry, as Claude Lévi-Strauss
terms it, between the "profane and sacred, faithful and offici-
ating, dead and living, initiated and uninitiated," make "all the
participants pass to the winning side" (*The Savage Mind* [Chica-
go: The University of Chicago Press, 1966], p. 32)—Montaigne is playing that old game, and no other. "I am not pur-
posed," he says, "to devise you other new sports" (I.xix.60).

Ostensibly Montaigne "humanizes" and internalizes natural
law, that is, figures life and death not as mutually external
moieties, but as two moieties of life: health and sickness. But
this is the stoic's old trick—to win by default—to give death
(or the dead) the appearance of winning so that they threaten
no more; they all pass to the "winning" side, life. The "game"
is thus a true ritual, which seeks equality between contestants
that are initially felt to be unequal. "The being you enjoy,"
he says a few pages later, "is equally shared betweene life and
death" (I.xix.59). Thus so, temporal dissolution, of such threat
to the fragile human series, is stayed: the contingency of event
equated with the necessity of structure. "Nature compels us to
it. . . . *Your death is but a peece of the worlds order*" (I.xix.59).

But if Montaigne ritualizes the "exchange" between "one
moitie" and the other (these are the words he uses), and structures them primitively, there is also a manner of being, a point
of view toward the world, an insertion in time and space, which
implies a phenomenology. The image of *facing death* haunts
the passage: "view death in the face." A few lines earlier he
asked to be informed of dying men "what face they shew at their
death" (I.xix.56). The ritualized exchange which seeks to re-
organize a fragile humanity from the eventful divisions into
which it is prone to fall has its roots in a change in point of
view in time and space: to assume the point of view of the
"other," to see death from its own point of view, to have it "bee
neere at hand" so that what makes the other seem so "disproportionable"—that is, its "being farre from us," its distance—will

be closed. So much "further I goe from that, and the nearer I approch to this," he says, that he is composed "for their exchange." Distance is an amplifier of commodities, which are "much more heavie and burthensome, than I feele them when I have them upon my shoulders." Temporally, this facing it or shouldering the burden of "ordinary mutations, and daily declinations" produces what we call the modification of time; in his homely example, which seems as good now as then, getting sick is the most painful at the beginning—once sick you can live with it. By viewing "death in the face," by adopting death's point of view, Montaigne leaps across the finitude of perspective which declares the "other" is there and I am here, toward a truth which emerges by the very transgressing of finite perspective. Montaigne's negative method accomplishes this transgression; he expresses the onesidedness of his perspective by expressing sides which he does not see. As Paul Ricoeur in his phenomenological reduction of man's fragility says, "As soon as I speak, I speak of things in their absence and in terms of their non-perceived sides" (*Fallible Man* [Chicago: Gateway Editions, 1965], p. 41). By *speaking* of his situation as a point of view on death, Montaigne intentionally trangresses it. The sense of the "other" (other men's deaths, other states of his own health) *is* the point of view in "That to Philosophie, Is to Learn How to Die." The "other" is the modifying occasion by which the narrowness of perspective is recognized as such, for to express one-sidedness, to name it as such, is to recognize other sides in their absence. The "other" of the other is at once the fragile disproportion of the narrow openness of seeing and the transgressional intention of truth. "Make roome for others, as others have done for you," he says shortly. "Equalitie is the chief ground-worke of equitie, who can complaine to be comprehended where all are contained?" (I.xix.61).

Maurice Merleau-Ponty remarked that "Nothing guarantees us that morality is possible. . . . But even less is there any fatal assurance that morality is impossible. We observe it in an experience which is the perception of others. . . . The perception of the other founds morality by realizing the paradox of an *alter-ego*, of a common situation, by placing my perspectives and my incommunicable solitude in the visual field of another and of all others. Here as everywhere else the primacy of perception . . . [is] the realization, at the very heart of our most personal experience, of a fecund contradiction which submits this experience to the regard of others" (*The Primacy of Perception* [Evanston, Ill.: Northwestern University Press], p. 26). In this "tension of an experience which transcends itself" the true is an exchange or a "reversal" which "takes place before our eyes" (p. 27).

The dialogue of exchange converts the certainty of the narrowness-in-the-face-of-the-other ("Our senses are narrow," Montaigne says, quoting Cicero in the "Apologie") into a recursive "truth" about that limit. The "primitive mind," we might observe, is not relegated to a by-gone epoch; the urbane skeptic, no less than the primitive Bororo tribesman, may totalize his world by dialogues of exchange, mediating across fissures in meaning, in an effort to transcend himself. "Dialectical reason," which Lévi-Strauss compares with "the savage mind" itself, "is always constitutive: it is the bridge, forever extended and improved, which analytical reason throws out over an abyss; it is unable to see the further shore, but it knows that it is there, even should it be constantly receding" (*The Savage Mind*, p. 246). In fact, we might term man's fragility the torment of transcendence: that division within himself which he vows to account for *otherwise*.

Montaigne continually trembles at this abyss:

> Hath not God made the wisdome of this world foolishnesse? . . . Yet must I see at last, whether it be in mans power to finde what he seekes for; and if this long search, wherein he hath continued so many ages, hath enriched him with any new strength or solid truth: I am perswaded, if he speake in conscience, he will confesse, that all the benefit he hath gotten by so tedious a persuit, hath been, that he hath learned to know his owne weaknesse. That ignorance which in us was naturall, we have with long study confirmed and averred. . . . So men having tried, and sounded all, and in all this Chaos, and huge heape of learning and provision of so infinite different things, and found nothing that is substantiall firme and steadie, but all vanitie, have renounced their presumption, and too late knowen their naturall condition. . . . My profession is not to know the truth nor to attaine it. I rather open than discover things. *The wisest that ever was being demanded what he knew, answered, he knew that he knew nothing.* He verified what some say, that the greatest part of what we know, is the least part of what we know not: that is, that that which we thinke to know, is but a parcel, yea and a small particle of our ignorance. . . . *Our senses are narrow, our mindes are weake, and the race of our life is short.* (II.xii.446-47)

Fifty pages later, still going strong in the "Apologie," he says we are

> no way capable of knowledge. . . . Truth is engulfed in the deepest Abysses, where mans sight can no way enter. . . . Of so many things as are in the world, at least one should be found, that by an universall consent should be beleeved of all. But . . . no proposition is seene, which is not controversied and debated amongst us. . . . For my judgement cannot make my fellowes judgement to receive the same: which is a signe, that I have seized upon it by some other meane than by a natural power in me or other men. . . . This diversity and infinite division, by reason of the trouble which our owne judgement layeth upon our selves, and the uncertainty which every man findes in him-selfe, it may manifestly be perceived, that this situation is very uncertaine and unstaid. . . . Onely things which come to us from heaven . . . [are] markes of truth: Which we neither see with our eyes, nor receive by our meanes . . . except God . . . reforme and strengthen . . . our fraile and defective condition.
>
> (II.xii.506-8)

As the "Apologie" nears its conclusion (another forty pages later) Montaigne, concentrating on a continuing theme of division, picks up again that embodiment of judgment, judges them-selves. He concludes that the only possible judge, "That were no man. To judge of the apparances that we receive of sub-jects, we had need have a judiciatorie instrument: to verifie this instrument, we should have demonstration; and to approve demonstration, an instrument: thus are we ever turning round" (II.xii.544). The completely recursive relationship of the judg-ing and the judge he treats as another sign of our division: "We have no communication with being; for every human nature is ever in the middle between being borne and dying" (II.xii.545). All is labile; the present threatens to be a bare and radically eroded nothing: "Concerning these words, *Present, Instant, Even now,* by which it seemes, that especially we uphold and principally ground the intelligence of time; reason discovering the same, doth forthwith destroy it: for presently it severeth it a sunder and divideth it into future and past time, as willing to see it necessarily parted in two. As much happeneth unto na-ture, which is measured according unto time, which measureth her" (II.xii.547).

It is perhaps a thankless thought to suggest that the savage thrill we feel as these recursive, self-feeding passages—or at Edgar's "The worst is not/ So long as we can say 'this is the

worst' " (IV.i.28-29)—is indeed that: the torment of transcendence which reminds us that we, too, share the savage mind. So
Montaigne's fragile discourse goes on—"my Comedie" as he
calls it (I.xii.60 and elsewhere); whether it is as risible as all
that is perhaps more a matter of the habitual distance we have
achieved in appreciating him. For as much scornful enjoyment
as Montaigne gets in recounting a tale told on Plato—"But what
dream'd or doted he on, when he defined man to be a creature
with two feet, and without feathers; giving them that were disposed to mocke at him, a pleasant and scopefull occasion to
doe it? For, having plucked-off the feathers of a live capon,
they named him the man of *Plato*" (II.xii.489)—nonetheless
this featherless biped approximates Montaigne's own image of
man: "Truely, when I consider man all naked . . . and view his
defects, his naturall subjection, and manifold imperfections; I
finde we have had much more reason to hide and cover our
nakedness, than any creature else. We may be excused for bor-
rowing those which nature had therein favored more than us,
with their beauties to adorne us, and under their spoiles of wooll,
of haire, of feathers, and of silke to shroude us" (II.xii.430).
Lear, too, trembles hysterically on the brink of this grotesque
laughter, the release of an ever worsening succession of bad
jokes which strip man to his natural condition: "Thou art the
thing itself: unaccommodated man is no more but such a poor,
bare forked animal as thou art" (III.iv.105-6).

   The image is iterative; even in a chapter called "Of Modera-
tion" in the first book of the *Essais,* where Montaigne is clearly
intending the stories of sacrifices with which he ends to be
examples of immoderation, and where he clearly places himself
far from such savage rituals, the same curious image haunts: "In
another province, to welcome the said *Cortez,* they sacrificed
fiftie men at one clap. I will this one story more. . . . Messengers
presented him with three kinds of presents, in this manner: *Lord,
if thou be a fierce God, that lovest to feed on flesh and bloud,
here are five slaves, eat them, and we will bring thee more: if
thou be a gentle mild God, here is incense and feathers; but if
thou be a man, take these birds and fruits, that here we present
and offer unto thee*" (I.xxx.160). "We two alone will sing like
birds i' th' cage," says Lear; "Upon such sacrifices, my Cordelia,/ The Gods themselves throw incense" (V.iii.9, 20). And
it is upon a feather's breathless motion that Lear's chance "to

redeem all sorrows" stirs as he holds the dead Cordelia. Even Edgar, by whose salvific guidance Gloucester's attempt at sacrificing himself fails, asks:

> What are you, sir?
> *Glo.*   Away, and let me die.
> *Edg.* Hadst thou been aught but gossamer, feathers, air,
> So many fathoms down precipitating,
> Thou shiver'd like an egg; but thou dost breathe. . . .
>   (IV.vi.48-51)

The fragile world of *Lear* shares many concerns with the *Essais;* it is a critique of justice, reason, nature, social structure —perhaps Shakespeare's deepest glance into the abyss. Each theme is a compound of disproportion. As a universal moral court, the play is convincing in its proposition that only the guilty can get justice (one must be a criminal in *Lear's* court to be well served). Retributive justice does strike Cornwall, Regan, Goneril, and Edmund; but for the innocent (Cordelia, Kent) and for Lear and Gloucester (each more sinned against than sinning) there can be no justice. Montaigne's treatment of justice as a disproportionate partner of judgment and nature (particularly the chapter "Of Vanitie" in Book Three) clearly informs Shakespeare's—especially the split trial scene, at the end of the first half of which Lear asks a question to which the play as a whole gives a resounding answer of "Yes!": "Is there any cause in nature that makes these hard hearts?" (III.vi.76-77). Montaigne's raw and ironic percept *"We cannot erre in following Nature"* (III.xii.958), is only matched by his earlier observation of what the natural series tells the human series about the game of living and dying:

> That our wisedome should learne of beasts . . . [is] a singular testimonie of mans infirmitie. . . . We must [even] seeke for a testimony of beasts, not subject to favor or corruption. . . . What availeth this curiosity unto us, to preoccupate all humane natures inconveniences. . . . Not onely the blow, but the winde and cracke strikes us . . . for surely it is a kinde of fever, now to cause your self to be whipped, because fortune may one day chance to make you endure it: and at Mid-Sommer to put on your furr'd Gowne, because you shall neede it at Christmas?
>   (III.xii.949-50)

To "cast your selves into the experience of all mischiefes, that may befall you, namely of the extreamest: there try your selfe" is needless: "If you know not how to die, take no care for it, Nature her selfe will fully and sufficiently teach you the nicke, she will exactly discharge that worke for you; trouble not your selfe with it" (III.xii.950-51). The same cluster is in *Lear*: "Allow not nature more than nature needs,/ Man's life is cheap as beast's" (II.iv.265-66); "Blow, winds, and crack your cheeks . . ." (III.ii.1ff); "furr'd gowns hide all" (IV.vi.165). The mixture at the heart of things (Ricoeur's word is *mélange*) is at once man's reason and his nature; it is the occasion for the disproportion which he seeks to justify by ritual exchange. Lear's trial (for that is what it turns out to be) is clearly such an exchange: reason for madness. That there is no loss in this exchange—that is, that madness comes back as reason ("O, matter and impertinency mix'd! Reason in madness!" [IV.vi. 176])—is Shakespeare's comment on how little there is to lose to begin with; everything is precariously close to nothing. Mixture is a sign of division.

Nowhere is the fragility of the world of *Lear* more clearly figured than in the opening scene. "The division of the kingdom" is a formal and light ritual whose "darker purpose" gets unmasked; it is the deadly serious "game" of inheritance which we play to give the dying the appearance of winning. It is a preliminary bout to teach both contestants how to fight the clock which is ever running out on the human series, and it is played out on the same field as "That to Philosophie, Is to Learn How to Die," where the moieties are the living and the dead. The means of instruction, the epistemology of the ritual, is the very structure of the game itself: *division* into sides or parts in such a way that there are *no losers*. Lear's kingdom has already been divided before the play begins; Gloucester tells Kent, "In the division of the kingdom, it appears not which of the Dukes he values most; for equalities are so weigh'd that curiosity in neither can make choice of either's moiety" (I.i.2-6). Lear confirms this: "know that we have divided/ In three our kingdom" (I.i. 36-37). But the undertones of the game of the living and the dead are here: "Meantime we shall express our darker purpose./ Give me the map there. . . ./ 'tis our fast intent/ To shake all cares and business from our age,/ Conferring them on younger strengths, while we/ Unburden'd crawl toward death" (I.i.35-40). The importance of division, even to Cordelia who does little to mend her speech, is caught in her response:

> Haply, when I shall wed,
> That lord whose hand must take my plight shall carry
> Half my love with him, half my care and duty.
> Sure I shall never marry like my sisters,
> To love my father all. (I.i.99-103)

Deprived of further preliminaries, the game is on. Lear disclaims "parental care/ . . . And as a stranger to my heart and me/ Hold thee from this for ever" (I.i.112-15). Cordelia is as good as "dead": Lear says shortly, "Better thou/ Hadst not been born" (I.i.233-34). When Kent tries to intervene—that is, cross the lines being formed—Lear stops him with, "Come not between the dragon and his wrath./ . . . Hence and avoid my sight/ So be my grave my peace as here I give/ Her father's heart from her! . . ./ Call Burgundy. Cornwall and Albany,/ With my two daughters' dowers digest this third. . . ./ This coronet part between you" (I.i.123-38).

"Out of my sight!" shouts Lear, indicating the moiety to which he is sending Cordelia and now Kent. "The true blank of thine eye," is Kent's double-entendre. "Miscreant," screams Lear, "Recreant"—and parodies a world's creation where, by his limit of ten days, the moiety of death takes its blinded shape. "Freedom lives hence, and banishment is here," is Kent's rephrasal. Everything and everyone is divided up. Lear will spend half his time with Goneril, half with Regan. Division equates death with blindness and madness. When the "out" son of Gloucester, the bastard Edmund, must have the land of the legitimate Edgar he counterfeits a letter for Gloucester's unseeing eyes ("Let's see," he says three times; "I shall not need spectacles" [I.i.34, 42]). In the letter itself, death and division are hand in hand: "If our father would sleep till I wak'd him, you should enjoy half his revenue forever" (I.i.49-50). "Brothers divide," laments Gloucester, "the bond crack'd 'twixt son and father . . . there's father against child. We have seen the best of our time" (I.ii.104ff). Edmund, on Edgar's appearance, feigns madness: "Tom O'Bedlam—O, these eclipses do portend these divisions! fa, sol, la, mi" (I.ii.130-31). The pun on musical divisions signs the sound of the spheres; the whole natural series is in eclipse. This little scene also prefigures what form exchange between the moieties will take: disguise (Edgar returns in the guise of madness). Likewise, Kent disguises himself to Albany in order to remain and serve Lear. The blindness attending division is imaged in the Fool's egg game with Lear: "Nuncle, give me an egg, and I'll give thee two crowns./ *Lear.* What two crowns shall they be?/ *Fool.* Why, after I have cut the egg i' th' middle and eat up the meat, the two crowns of the egg. When thou clovest thy crown i' th' middle, and gav'st away both parts, thou bor'st thine ass on thy back o'er the dirt" (I.iv. 155-60). The relationship of the literal to the figural becomes even clearer when a servant goes to fetch "whites of eggs" for Gloucester's bleeding face after he has been blinded (III.vii. 105ff). Though the Fool "would feign learn to lie," he must tell the truth of division: "Thou hast pared thy wit o' both sides, and left nothing i' th' middle. Here comes one o' th' parings. [Enter Goneril]" (I.iv.177-78).

The developing action of the play is the trial of nature, the test of reason—the stretch of judgment in division. The epistemology is surprise: gasps at the judgment called for in response, bolting leaps across unexpected fissures in meaning. At Goneril's first "liberated" words, Lear exclaims, "Are you our daughter? . . . Does any here know me? This is not Lear./ . . . Where are his eyes?/ . . . Who is it that can tell me who I am?/ *Fool.* Lear's shadow" (I.iv.217-30). Fissures in meaning are often accompanied by actual division; Lear finds his retinue cut: "What, fifty of my followers at a clap!" (I.iv.293). One hundred has been divided in two. Regan shortly divides his force again: "Bring but five and twenty" (II.iv.247).

There are at least half a dozen other instances of division, the most interesting of which is the Fool's exchange with Lear in the last scene of Act One: "Thou canst tell me why one's nose stands i' th' middle on's face? *Lear.* No. *Fool.* Why to keep one's eyes of either side's nose, that a man cannot smell out, he may spy into" (I.iv.18-22). This is the very face of unaccommodated man, figuring a fragile and disproportioned sensorium. Vision is divided; smell is mediating. Gloucester's "I stumbled when I saw" points toward the fault, the fracture, which vision faces. Its face to the world and the world it faces are commensorate: fault to fault, division to abyss. "Do you smell a fault?" Gloucester asks Kent of Edmund's illegitimacy at the opening of the play. "Let him smell/ His way to Dover," says Regan after they have blinded him (III.vii.92). The epistemology of vision *is* division; sight in seeing disproportions, divides itself. "If," says Montaigne in the "Apologie," "the senses be our first Judges, it is not ours that must only be called to counsell: For, in this facultie beasts have as much (or more) right, as we. It is most certaine, that some have their hearing more sharpe than man; others their sight; others their smelling" (II.x.540). *"Nothing comes unto us but falsified and altered by our senses"* (II.xii. 544). Montaigne gives that example of visual fragility in the face of great heights which informs the imagined cliffs of Dover in Gloucester's "suicide"—"the sight of . . . exceeding height" which must "dazle . . . [the] sight, and amaze or turne . . . [the] senses" (II.xii.538):

> I could not, without horror to my minde and trembling of leggs and thighes endure to looke on those infinite precipices and steepy downefals. . . . I also noted, that how deep soever the bottome were, if but a tree, a shrub, or any out-butting crag of a Rock presented it selfe unto our eyes, upon those steepie and high Alpes, somewhat to uphold the sight, and divide the same, it doth somewhat ease and assure us from feare, as if it were a thing, which in our fall might either helpe or uphold us: And that we cannot without some dread and giddinesse in the head, so much as abide to looke upon one of those even and downe-right precipes. (II.xii.538-39)

"Come on, sir; here's the place," says Edgar, leading Gloucester to what he thinks are the Cliffs of Dover:

> Stand still.   How fearful
> And dizzy 'tis to cast one's eyes so low!
> The crows and choughs that wing the mid-way air
> Show scarce so gross as beetles. Half-way down
> Hangs one that gathers samphire . . .
>
> I'll look no more;
> Lest my brain turn, and the deficient sight
> Topple down headlong. (IV. vi.10-23)

Shakespeare has Edgar use the same device—to "divide the same" as Montaigne said, "half way down." Even Edgar's characterization of his own late disguise shares the shape of the fragile face:

> As I stand here below, methought his eyes
> Were two full moons; he had a thousand noses . . . .
> (IV.vi.69-70)

Nearly immediately Lear enters "fantastically dressed with

weeds"—and Edgar can't believe his eyes: "The safer sense will
ne'er accommodate/ His master thus" (IV.vi.82-83). We recall
Lear in the storm:

> Why, thou wert better in a grave than to answer with thy un-
> cover'd body this extremity of the skies. Is man no more than
> this? Consider him well. Thou ow'st the worm no silk, the beast
> no hide, the sheep no wool, the cat no perfume. Ha! There's
> on's are sophisticated! Thou art the thing itself: unaccommo-
> dated man is no more but such a poor, bare, forked animal as
> thou art. Off, off, you lendings! Come unbutton here.
>   (III.iv.100-8)

Now Lear, feathered in weeds, holds court on a fantastic vision, where his fractured sight is mediated by an insane odor
compounded of sulphur, burning flesh, civet, and genital fluids.
He spies Gloucester: "Ha! Goneril, with a white beard! . . . I
found 'em, there I smelt 'em out . . ./ Behold yond simp'ring
dame/ Whose face between her forks presages snow" (IV.vi.96-
119). Lear sees in Gloucester's "squiny" face the shape of
woman's genitals. "Down from the waist they are centaurs/
Though woman all above;/ But to the girdle do the gods inherit,/ Beneath is all the fiends';/ There's hell, there's darkness,
there is the sulphurous pit—/ Burning, scalding, stench, con-
sumption./ Fie, fie, fie! pah, pah! Give me an ounce of civet,
good apothecary, to sweeten my imagination. There's money
for thee./ *Glo.* O, let me kiss that hand!/ *Lear.* Let me wipe it
first; it smells of mortality" (IV.vi.124-33). Ixion's "wheel of
fire" has come full circle, the inheritance, but for Cordelia, complete. At the center (we should say *Centaur!*) of one moiety is
Goneril, the sexual sub-contractor; but from the other moiety
Lear is inspired by a different scent: "Upon such sacrifices, my
Cordelia,/ The gods themselves throw incense" (V.iii.20-21).
We are reminded of Job (who also had three daughters): "As
God liveth, who hath taken away my judgment; and the Al-
mighty, who hath vexed my soul; All the while my breath is in
me, and the spirit of God is in my nostrils" (Job 27:2-3).
     And we are reminded, too, of Montaigne's chapter "Of
Smells and Odors": "The most exquisit and sweetest savour of a
woman, it is to smell of nothing" (I.1v.271; see also the "Apologie," p. 501). The smell of incense and, in Montaigne's word, a
woman's "sweate"—the sacred and the profane, the salvific and

the mortal—mingle in one moiety to which the fragile and disproportioned sensorium of "forked" man cleaves.

NOTES

1 This essay was originally read at the Sixth Conference on Medieval Studies at Western Michigan University in May, 1971. I have made only minor changes — in focus, and with respect to the peculiarities of tone and convention which print suggests. Because historiography was not my primary intention — nor contribution except in a most general way to the exactitude of Shakespeare's "debt to Montaigne" — I have not made close use of nor re-read the studies by Robertson, Taylor and others. Rather, I have tried, in looking at the *Essais* again, to bring to light a structure which *King Lear* shares. In the process of doing so, I hope I have made good on a promise to C. L. Barber a few years ago to clarify some observations on the play to which his response was, as I recall, much like the disguised Edgar's: "Fie, foh, and fum. . . ."

2 *The Essayes of Montaigne* (New York: The Modern Library, 1933), p. 52 (Bk. I, Ch. xix). I have used for convenience this edition of Florio's 1603 translation of the *Essais*. Future reference to Book, Chapter, and page follow quotations.

Theodicy, Tragedy, and the Psalmist: Tourneur's *Atheist's Tragedy*

R. J. Kaufmann

> Evil and good stand thick around
> In the fields of charity and sin
> Where we shall lead our harvests in.
>
> Edwin Muir

> What can be said
> Except that suffering is exact, but where
> Desire takes charge, readings will grow erratic.
>
> Philip Larkin

Despite the journalists' banal breviary of daily violence, we know very little about the process and structure of evil. Routine information about daily transgressions, stale registers of corruption and titillating intimations of malevolence accumulate steadily but add up to less than nothing. They are a seawall blocking moral explorations as well as a protective barrier allowing us to harbor unproductive illusions about our relation to the larger, less charted state of things. If we have the courage to cherish the fragile occasions of smaller, domesticated happinesses, we will not undervalue such a seawall. Human beings seem to require fairly calm waters to preserve ordinary equilibrium; those deeps beyond the seawalls threaten, with strange analogies, our own inner turbulence. It is as easy to undervalue reason as it is to overvalue it. The moral area between these two modes of misvaluation is tightly squeezed by their converging claims. There is little room for a poised life which is not at the same time an ignorant one.

Tragic enquiry is easily discussed in terms of its centrifugal movement. Standard critical rhetoric assumes the exclusive initiative of the hero. If all tragic literature were the "matter of Ahab" which sees the tragic hero as a serendipitous being tracking his enemy beyond the edge of all ideological maps, this romantic variant would be as sufficient for tragic theory as it is relieving to our mundane frustrations. The harsh persistence of Oedipus, the intellectual stamina of Hamlet, the uncheckable erotic drives of Phaedra, or the absolute imprudence of Medea would constitute the whole story. But they do not. It is important to take some trouble to discover just why they do not.

I

Let Marlowe stand momentarily as an abbreviated instance. Nineteenth-century romantic critics, when they rediscovered Marlowe, quickly enshrined him and his heroes (whom they saw as unambiguous projections of his thrusting ego) as the archetype of rebellious resistance to all that compromised pure individualism. He became a symbol of daring intellectual defiance and of all those things which swelled *their* connotations for "renaissance man." This position has been canonized by repetition and reinforced by intelligent critics right down to the present moment. This belief in heroic initiative as the prime motor in Marlowe has not gone unchallenged. Since Roy Battenhouse's book on *Tamburlaine* in 1941, there has been an ever more fully documented counter-case drawing Marlowe's plays into the tradition of Medieval Christian Humanism or even more narrowly into an anti-humanistic Christian theological connection. This interpretive posture finds its orthodox fulfillment in Douglas Cole's study of *Suffering and Evil in the Plays of Christopher Marlowe* in 1962, just as the earlier more romanticized reading reached its summit of sophistication in Harry Levin's *The Overreacher* a decade earlier in 1952. This polarization is familiar to students of Renaissance drama. Irving Ribner, in his careful appraisal of the state of Marlowe studies for the *Tulane Drama Review*'s special issue in honor of the 400th anniversary of Marlowe's birth, described this radical division of opinion on Marlowe's attitude towards his materials as

> a state of confusion, with some critics seeing Marlowe in terms so radically different from those in which others view him that it is difficult to believe that all are writing about the same man.[1]

Ribner's point is well made, but it does not get deep enough into the problem, for the conservative, theologically affiliated critics are merely standing the romantic position on its head. Their work is polemic and revisionist; it challenges the adequacy of the romantic reading by exposing its historical naiveté and by demonstrating the presence within Marlowe's texts of elements invisible to romantic

critics blinded by their ideological presuppositions. The conservative critics are, nevertheless, bound by the same axioms about the
hero's absolute centrality. They recast the hero as a minatory example of presumption, and the process of the play as ideologically
repressive rather than subversive, but their method still centers on
judgments of the precise moral import of the hero's initiative. There
is no theoretical enlargement of the aesthetic or modal issues. Both
positions, when developed by their most talented proponents, betray
symptoms of chaffing under theoretical constraint. On both sides
there is concessive talk of "ironic undertones," "modifying ambiguities of tone," etc. These concessions function like the epicycular
hypotheses of late medieval astronomers struggling to preserve the
Ptolemaic cosmology against the slow accumulation of contradictory empirical evidence.

I would like to argue that this problem is eased if we enlarge our
assumptions to include a subset of tragic dramas which are deformed
in a particular way by the inertial demands of reason, as reason has
been defined in any given anterior historical system. In tragic dramas
of this sort the protagonist is both enlarged and belittled by the framing theoretical assumptions. These assumptions are clearly too
narrow to contain his spirit, but, equally, he is not invested with
enough *axiologically independent* initiative to shatter the frame.
Thus the protagonist of such plays is not vindicated by his choices.
At the same time, the "editorial" ideology of the play is not confident
enough to eliminate the subversive effects of the protagonist's non-
traditional selfhood as this is demonstrated within the process of the
play. There are numerous examples of this type of play in English
Renaissance drama, and they are often tonally the most perplexing to
critics. These plays can be differentiated according to their shadings
of sympathy for the protagonist, but hey are radically of a type.
Traditionally they are classified—uneasily—as "dark" comedies or
"imperfect" tragedies. Clearly the standard classificatory system is
so narrow and rigid, that no one is really satisfied. Some examples of
these plays with antinomic protagonists are: *Volpone; The Jew of
Malta; Timon of Athens; Tamburlaine* considered as ten act unit; *The
Atheist's Tragedy;* and *The Dutch Courtesan.* Other plays might be
added, but the list is long enough if the case can be made; if it can not,
then additional examples would be superfluous.

To do justice to the historical register of tragic enquiry, we must
abandon stiff, normative definitions of the tragic. Tragedy as a
category is best seen in terms of a Wittgensteinian "family of resem-
blances," wherein the possession of some combination of the

familial attributes qualifies a play for membership in the class. Individual plays can differ so much from each other that only their restoration to the larger definitional harmony of the "family" can validate their affinity. The Wittgensteinian theory of definition does not stretch the category, "tragedy," into meaningless looseness, since there *are* crucial attributes as in any familial grouping, but it does prevent the tiresome error of arguing from a magisterial (or patriarchal) example to which all aspirants to inclusion must be made narrowly to conform.

Rigid, normative definitions of tragedy can stand in the way of critical clarity. Tragedy is a mode not a format. It is an address toward motive, providing a means of evaluating the consequences of choices which deflect moral responses outside traditional grooves of judgment. The accepted logic of a culture in important ethical matters can become an illusory structure which dupes instinct and makes unwonted forms of energetic initiative automatically repellent. Tragedy is a device for rousing thoughtful attention to novel increments of behavior that have been rejected or classified *thoughtlessly*. A tragedy can function as a critique of passivity; it can also function in a converse manner as a critique of ill-judged activisms which threaten an ideologically anchored passivity. Since the *Book of Job*, the dramatic form has been useful in providing this kind of laboratory for ethical reappraisals. Job is both right and wrong in his view of himself. He is not "wrong" as compared to his shallow, reflexive "comforters," but, structurally, he is "wrong" in supposing he has any means to evaluate God's motives or intentions. We are required to grasp both these qualitative relationships in a new light in order to "understand" the explanatory force of *Job*. Tragedy is a means of *Re-Cognition*, wherein a larger circumference of experience is used as our contextual frame, when we "think" the hero and what his *agon* connotes.

What I am talking about is similar to but still crucially distinct from the problem of "tainted heroes" as this phrase is applied to Shakespeare's later protagonists. In these late plays Macbeth, Antony and Coriolanus purchase our respect through a tenacious truth to self. In their struggle with genuine and often formidable structures of authority, however aberrant their moral vision may be, they obstinately preserve their hold on one rigidly conceived aspect of their life. They are noble *and* fixated, imbued with folly by an irreversible commitment. In each of these plays, their energy steadily subsides, their freedom is progressively cribbed and confined. Each dies having lost his love of self and his love of life. The process of the play is the attrition of antecedent nobility. The plays I'm concerned with are quite different.

These plays display aberrant energy in forms of social activism which bears no general endorsement. The hero is an outcast or intruder, a parvenu, an immoral opportunist, or culturally ineducable. He has more energy than anyone else in the play. In *Tamburlaine*, which is a simplistic paradigm of the mode, the earlier sections of the play are devised to show almost allegorically what a state of "maimed empery" (in Marlowe's phrase) or, in more modern terms, what a power vacuum exists. The typical world confronting the protagonist of these plays is dispirited, slack, cynical or directionless. The feeble Mycetes, whose pathetical simulations of authority in *Tamburlaine* always end with a question, is the satiric embodiment of this state of affairs. Where the normative characters opposing the hero are not ridiculous or faint nullities, they are often committed to an ethic of repression or to a quite abstract idealism. Whichever way the received morality is depicted in these plays there is a sense of exhausted sanctions.

In *Measure for Measure*, which is a comedic variant of the form, Vincentio has failed to embody authority convincingly with the result that disorder reigns; his self-transformation eventually effects a cure, but though he is hygenically admirable, he smacks of moral contrivance; so the process of reëducation and moral rehabilitation of the world of Vienna remains too schoolmarmish to satisfy us that Lucio, for example—so tonically amoral—is wholly to be despised, despite the clearest possible *structural* cues directing that judgment. Chapman's *Bussy D'Ambois* likewise divides our sympathies and our judgment. Bussy is egotistical to the point of silliness, his braggadocio and thin-skinned vanity stand directly in the path of our solicited admiration for his virility and his courageous exposure of the snobbish pretensions of the unsatisfactory courtier world he sets out to conquer. We want to approve of him more than we can. Volpone and Mosca, on the other hand, provoke more admiration than we can readily justify and no amount of careful scholarly reconstruction of their *cupiditas* suffices to annul our gratitude for their sheer joy in activity in a world otherwise as stagnant as the Venetian canals which are the literal and symbolic setting for their enterprise. Marston's *Dutch Courtesan* (unquestionably his most vibrant play) has an infra-structure in which the expression of positive sexual energy seems preferable to any other mode of existence—and this despite the editorial elements of the play which deliberately contradict this sensation.

The common denominator of this group of plays is a final irrecon-
cilability between the activated energies they dramatize and the
playwright's capacities for disciplining this released energy in an
authoritative manner. There is a noticeable hiatus between his *overt*
moral intentions and his *covert* sympathy for these agents whose
activities are ideologically reprehensible. The ethical frame does not
really cage the aberrant protagonist's energies. Hence these plays are
at one and the same time subversive *and* orthodox. They dramatize
points of stress in the ethical system, issues on which the engines of
doubt are being brought to bear. It is in this light that we should look
at Tourneur's *Atheist's Tragedy*. In the end, D'Amville's "voice"
lingers in our minds even though he has been "proved" wrong. Historically speaking, the play is an act of exorcism rather than effective
refutation, and its dramaturgical stress pattern is most readily explained when we operate from these assumptions in interpreting it.

By this definitional procedure, tragic dramas in which the classic
distribution of sympathies is disturbed: by farcical counter-currents,
as in *The Jew of Malta*; or where compassion is extruded and hence
lost, as in *Timon of Athens*; or where theological anxiety leads to
excessive reinforcement of the play's ideology and consequently to a
kind of emblematic literalism as in *The Atheist's Tragedy*, need not
be patronized as false instances of the tragic. They can be seen instead as members of the tragic family under the forms of stress
peculiar to that family. A just apprehension of the distinguishing
traits of that family derives in part from a sense of the family's stress
pattern. Neurotic fears can be manifested in *the structure of* a play as
well as in its content. No slippery depth analysis of Cyril Tourneur is
required to suppose that (if he is the author both of *The Revenger's
Tragedy* and *The Atheist's Tragedy*) the excited fascination he seems
to feel for evil in the former play, might well be countered therapeuti-
cally by the punitive binding of D'Amville's ideologically provocative arguments in the latter play. The excessive weight of these
needed reinforcements in *The Atheist's Tragedy* partially deforms
the tragic *structure*, partially cripples and de-sophisticates his art,
just as obsessions deform the psychic economy of the individual.

We can designate this subset of tragic dramas "Dramas of Ethical
Display" so as to direct critical attention towards the qualitative
frame in which the protagonist is placed, and less towards
"protagonal biography," in its opposing forms of romantic
Prometheanism or disciplinary, negative *exempla*. These "Display"
plays have heroes who, while stimulating fascination with the outre
and larger-than-life, are not fully humanized. But, it is inaccurate to

think of them as allegorical. Allegory does not require such detailed identification of the agent it seeks to reprehend. These "Display" protagonists are specimens whose proper dramatic identification obliges the playwright to draw upon many defining analogues, including evocations of allegorical prototypes from the cultural repertoire accessible to the playwright and his audience. However, these traditional analogues function much like the mutually qualifying metaphors of a good lyric poem, so that we are being historically retrograde if we label as "allegory" these dramatic efforts to identify novel refractions of human energy, and thus to augment an inadequate traditional typology. The drama of ethical display is not a mechanical application of canonized typological similes. They have to do with what is troublingly new.

II

Tourneur's *Atheist's Tragedy* is an explicit dramatical projection of the themes of the 127th Psalm, "*Nisi Dominus*, nothing can be done without God's grace," and a Calvinist reading at that. The correlation is detailed, so that the imagery and governing ideas of *The Atheist's Tragedy* are brought into intimate dramatic conjunction.

In his *Third Ennead*, writing of Providence, Plotinus reminds us:

> All is just and good in the Universe in which every actor is set in his own quite appropriate place. . . . What is evil in the single soul will stand a good thing in the universal system; what in the unit offends nature will serve nature in the total event—and still remain the weak and wrong tone it is, though its sounding takes nothing from the worth of the whole, just as, in another order of image, the executioner's ugly office does not mar the well-governed state: such an officer is a civic necessity; and the corresponding moral type is often serviceable; thus, even as things are, all is well.[2]

These calm, reliant words sum up well the substance of Tourneur's hopes. Some of the images are even specifically appropriate to his play. They put us firmly in touch with that theodiciacal tradition of high Christian thought running from Augustine, who imbibed here, through Calvin and Milton, to come seasonably to rest in Pope. Though the terms, being simple and essential, remain the same, the ease with which they are believed varies. The tone in Tourneur is urgent and to a degree fearful. His play is a careful construct to bind up and intensify conviction. That he partly fails in this is a direct outcome of his excessive concentration on making his case.

Tourneur evidently shared with Calvin a liking for one of the latter's favorite Psalms, the *Auxilium Domini* (No. 127, or No. 126 in the *Vulgate*). Its repertoire of subjects appeals to those devoted to a life of aggressive political stewardship under an authoritarian God:

> Except the Lord build the house, they labour in vain that build it: except the Lord keep the city, the watchman waketh but in vain.

What precisely Calvin has to say of this psalm could almost be inferred by a student of his theological position, but we will seek detailed evidence of his comment later.

Meanwhile let it be stated that this is a short psalm of only five verses, but in its brief compass it neatly incorporates: 1) a text for the doctrine of work; 2) a clear image of God's overlordship and Providence; 3) an assertion of the primary value of children; while 4) stressing their contingent derivation. Moreover, since among the central drives of post-Reformation life were the establishment of a *house*, the building of a *family*, and the fathering of a business *house*, and since all of these are readily fused in standard English usage, so that in the context of provident familial ambition, "house" and "family" mean the same thing, Psalm 127 provides a side-by-side association of two things that become one—the desire to build and the desire to have children, to found a house and to have a family. The theme of the Psalm in Elizabethan terms is "building a family," and "Happy is the man," the Psalmist assures us, "that hath his quiver full of them." Tourneur's play it will be remembered is about the naturalist D'Amville who seeks to "found a house." First, then, pertinent excerpts from Calvin's commentary on the 127th Psalm:

1. The initial precis made by Calvin:

The Conteyntes of the CXXVII Psalme

> It sheweth that the order of the world, as well in publicke affaires as in household matters, standeth not by the pollicie, diligence, and forcast of men, but by the only blissing of God, and that issew of mankind is his singular gift. (p. 204, column 1)

2. The significance of *house*:

> By the woord house hee not onely betokeneth a building of timber or stone: but also coprehendeth the whole order of householding: like as a little after, by the woorde citie hee betokeneth, not onely the building or compasse of the walles, but the general state of the whole comon weale. And in the words [builder and keeper,] there is the figure Sinecdoche. (p. 204, columns 1 & 2)

3. On the Fathering of Children:

> The most part of men dreameth, that after God had once ordeyned it
> at the beginning, from thence foorth children are bred and borne by the
> secret instinct of nature, and God dooth nothing unto it: yea and even
> they that be indewed with some feeling of godliness: although they
> denye not that God is the father and fownder of mankynd: yit
> acknowledge they not that his providence descendeth too this
> peculiare charge, but rather thinke that men are begotten by a certeyne
> universall motion. (p. 205, column 4)[3]

These bear with exact particularity on the tightly related themes of
the play; a further passage on the "Suffering of Believers" will be
adduced later when it is time to show its bearing on *The Atheist's
Tragedy*'s longest and most peculiar scene, the churchyard scene
(IV.iii).

This special exegetical comment should be related to the more
philosophical theology of the relevant portion of Calvin's *Institutes*.
I refer to chapter xv of Book I, where we have Calvin on Providence,
entitled, "God's Preservation and Support of the World by His
Power and His Government of Every Part of it by His Providence."

Calvin's chapter gives a galaxy of arguments for believing that
nothing happens which is not a part of God's perfectly detailed
design for the universe—nothing is fortuitous, nothing may be
ascribed to chance or fortune whose reified philosophical utility
Calvin specifically refutes, while doing scholastic cartwheels to distinguish his perfectly resolved and totally non-permissive God from
he pagan Fate. The distinction Calvin makes has considerable
historical validity but no philosophical force, since there is no reason
why Fate as the source of Necessity should not have acted just like
the necessitarian God had it been so imagined; that it did not do so is
an historical accident. The most relevant passage in Calvin's argument shows how the sun serves as God's instrument to promote
natural growth. Calvin waxes as near lyrical as his severe lawyer's
mind will permit him to do (these botanical ramifications of God's
efficacy through the "sun" are usurped, along with much else, by
D'Amville, as we will see shortly):

> trees likewise and vines, by his genial warmth, first put forth leaves,
> then blossoms, and from the blossoms produce their fruit![4]

Intermixed with this rhapsodic strain there is a darker, more tragic
element, as subsequent degeneration of puritan doctrine has dramatized. The *agon* of the Calvinist nature defines itself as a struggle for
authentic status, which easily devolves into a self-circumscribing,
swelling of the Will. For the Calvinist, God's *essence* is remote and

inviolate, but functionally the need for spiritual confirmation is so great that Godhead is expropriated lest one be forced to confess, "God knows, man does not know." Calvinism loves the scriptures and wants to use them as a means to certain knowledge of God's aims, but since God's nature is radically unknowable beyond his empirical functions as predestinate and omniscient shaper of a total pattern, man's use of the scripture is philosophically irrelevant. Hence, the unmistakeable fear that man's activity is compulsive and unintelligible to any but the unknown God grows. Calvinism is a brand of self-subverted Socratism. It loves the search for knowledge but it can't believe in its righteousness or its efficacy. It sees life as a threatening game of reading the signs aright, a game in which disaster is equivalent to sin and possesses the same shaming force. The prudent man, being in harmony with God, reads the signs aright or, like Charlemont in *The Atheist's Tragedy*, waits patiently (if somewhat priggishly) until matters are clarified. The depraved man (the fool) is wrong and lost—a pragmatic tautology. The fool is condemned because he is the kind of man to whom such things are permitted to happen. The objectively "tragic space" in Calvin's worldview is marked out by the ethical contradictions inherent in their conception of prudence (or, in Tourneur's terms, in being provident). Not to be prudent advertises folly; to be prudent invites arrogation of divine privilege. Tourneur's *Atheist's Tragedy* is a dramatic meditation on this meta-ethical quandry. Calvinists need one set of statements about God and another set of notions about human responsibility; their doctrine is metaphysically schizoid, but this metaphysical no-man's land of doubt creates the situation for a peculiar kind of tragedy. One must choose definitively but without confidence in the act's meaning; this moves us close to the absurd, and *The Atheist's Tragedy* teeters on the brink of black comedy or "gallows humor" much of the time.

The Atheist's Tragedy is a theological play. This does not mean, as Ornstein in his otherwise excellent study strangely assumes,[5] that the aim of the playwright should have been to have his heroine, Castabella, systematically refute the evil, naturalistic doctrines of her would-be seducer, the play's hero and her father-in-law, the atheist D'Amville. There can be no water-tight, philosophical refutation of total atheism, since the atheist and the theist reside in different communities of discourse. Tourneur was perhaps wise enough not to send his gentle heroine on such an errand. To refute atheism before a community disturbed in the year 1610 by some nearly unformulatable doubts about the ways of providence could only be done through that mode of pragmatic ritual we call drama. The dramatist could employ emblematic means to show that as a course of action atheism does not work. At its most philosophical, drama, as an imitation of an action, is truest to itself when it is pragmatic. It operates through actions which are brought to meaning by the playwright's provision of motive and by the audience's imaginative concurrence in this plastic diagnosis.

The Atheist's Tragedy is thus a concrete reanimation of a distinctively pictorial variant of the traditional Christian view. In an iconographic fashion it composes a complete specific action, the life-choices of D'Amville against an architectonically intelligible world order. It is a dogmatic celebration of the agency by which life is ordered. The ideas that Tourneur sets to work are commonplaces, though they are less prevalent in the drama of the time than one would suppose from reading the routine criticism of the play. The language of the play is not so original and exciting as the nervous and impatient idiom of *The Revenger's Tragedy*, but the deliberately managed mutual interplay of concept and rendering image is more consistently sustained than in any other play of its general kind outside of Shakespeare.

Though the play is explicitly homiletical in its dramatization of the 127th Psalm, H. H. Adas excluded it from his book on Homiletic Tragedy. The Psalm establishes an economical format of relationship between: the play's iterative imagery; its informing concepts; and its ground theme. The theme of the Psalm is the extent and nature of God's providence. Tourneur has thickened the texture of his study of Christian *hybris* by punning on the seminally divergent meanings of one word, "Providence." It means both God's benevolent and interested participation in men's affairs *and* man's prudent and carefully considered superintendence of his own affairs. In Geoffrey Whitney's *A Choice of Emblemes* (1586), the crocodile's alleged ability to anticipate the rise of the Nile is used as an emblem of Providence; this image and his commentary on it indicate that prudent foresight is one of the primary meanings of the term: "When anie one doth take in hande a cause . . . longe thereon to ponder" (p. 3). This second meaning of "providence" is just emerging historically as the play is written. Though Tourneur opposes the two readings of providence in a too relentless manner, the play is composed with great care. Tourneur has succeeded better than most dramatists do in discovering adequate objective correlatives for his moral prevision. When *The Atheist's Tragedy* is classified with plays of the same mode, what I have called "Dramas of Ethical Display" or Neo-parabolical dramas—like *The Jew of Malta, Measure for Measure, Volpone, Timon of Athens,* and *A New Way to Pay Old Debts*—Tourneur's borderline interplay between realism and emblematic dramatization does not seem so crude as the rigid, illusionistic presuppositions of earlier critics of Tourneur caused them to believe.

III

> Unless the Lord build the house they labour in vain that build it

and

> Behold the inheritance of the Lord are children: the reward, the fruit of the womb.

These two verses express in brief the two important constituents of the short 127th Psalm; they equally clearly state the central themes of *The Atheist's Tragedy* as well as accounting most economically and exactly for the imagery in which Tourneur expresses the atheist's desire to supersede God in his creative dominion over object and person. Stated most concisely *The Atheist's Tragedy* presents the didactically rationalized account of one who questioned God's providential power, arrogated to himself in specific terms the traditional operations of that Providence, tried to *build* a monument for *himself* and for *his* posterity through that posterity and thereby achieve through the sons whom *he* had generated the secularized immortality which *he* had a need for. The play is then a dramatization of man in his finitude contesting the rights of time and death and losing ignominiously. The contest, it turns out, isn't even close.

D'Amville's projected relationship to his real antagonist, who is not the "Christian-Stoic-Pure one," Charlemont, but rather the Deity Himself, reflects in its neat working out the pattern of the whole play. There are two clear and divergent usages of the word "Providence": 1) God as the supervising author of all things creates not only man but also the "plot" that man acts out. All creatures are part of the cast who wait on His will and occasionally move forward on the stage to become intelligible enough parts of the great design to be called "instruments." God's universe is His work, and He may be said to have *built* it in fact, or to seem to be *building* it from our limited viewpoint in time. Furthermore, if God oversees our lives He has to *watch* us. To express this men's fancy has adopted two standard and iconographically related emblems: a) the *eye* functions as the symbol for the all-knowing and ever-present God; and b) the *stars* which in Sir John Davies' simple but eloquent lines, are seen as

> The lights of heav'n (which are the World's fair eies)
> Looke downe into the World, the World to see.[6]

God as the author, director, hovering over the world-stage of man's action and seeing all is contrasted to 2) the simulation of this providence in the activities of D'Amville, the modern provident man (i.e., foresighted and carefully planning). The language of the play is most explicit in its reflection of Tourneur's attempt to show D'Amville as the very usurper of God—His ape and His intended supersessor.

In the first scene D'Amville is already speaking of himself in the terms we are directed to recognize as an especially Christian kind of *hybris*. He is characteristically engaged in the familiar ritual of the ambitious man, discussing *his* "plans" and *his* reasons for them:

> A man has reason to *provide* and add
> For what is he hath such a present *eye*,
> And so prepar'd a strength that can *forsee*,
> And *fortify* his substance and himself
> Against those accidents, the least whereof
> May rob him of an age's husbandry?
>
> > (I.i.47–52; *italics mine*)[7]

He adds that as my children multiply, "so should *my providence.*" Notice not only that he begins to pile up the words denoting specifically providential activity but that with the phrase "*fortify* my substance" the imagery of building the structure of one's strong, lasting house is already under way.[8] The marriage of *hybris* to this Elizabethan desire to found a house and to live on in it is accented by the exaggerated frequency with which D'Amville is made to use the pronoun *my, mine,* etc. In this same thematic first scene, Borachio, D'Amville's creature, uses the word "providence" to signify schemes to defraud the good nephew Charlemont of his inheritance. Then D'Amville's two sons enter almost as if in dumb show for choral exegesis by their father. The dramatic device underscores the sons' contingent role in their father's ambitious schematization of human relationships,

> Here are *my* sons. . . .
> There's *my* eternity. *My* life in them
> And their succession shall for ever live,

And in *my* reason dwells the *providence*
To add to life as much of happiness.
(I.i.123–127; *italics mine*)

To make D'Amville's abuse of this word even more overt Tourneur has him make light of his brother's fears for his son, Charlemont's death in war by affirming his own belief in Fate which makes death a matter

so certainly unalterable,
What can the use of providence prevail?
(I.ii.50-51)

Here only the fact of his own egocentricity prevents him falling into a contradiction.

There is a much more elaborate analogy to convince one that D'Amville (damned villain?) is developed in the play as the tragically absurd one who seeks to usurp the governing role of the providential God, but before coming to that let us speak about the ethical quality of his proceedings as these are evaluated in the play. One of the aspects of a belief in providence is that God has to *use* people to effect his plans. They are His instruments. D'Amville uses all other human beings to effect his ends. He has an instant genius for the main chance which makes him constantly able to convert the routine follies of men to prudent advantage. After D'Amville's creature Borachio has several times gloried in his self-identification as

Your instrument shall make your project proud
(I.ii.241 and e.g., I.ii.223)

D'Amville, viewing the drunkness of his brother's servants, and deciding to murder his brother says,

Their drunkenness . . .
Shall be a serious instrument to bring
Our sober purposes to their success. (II.ii.19–21)

This notion of making instruments of any and everyone is brought to a species of emotional climax, when immediately after the treacherous and stealthily executed murder of his ailing brother, D'Amville in an ecstasy of self-congratulation speaks a hectic duet with his creature, Borachio. At this point in the play, the notions of plotting, of building, of planning, of scheming so coalesce as to become indistinguishable. Since the legitimate definition of providence includes not only the dimension of planning and foreseeing but of benevolent intent, D'Amville's parody of the divine power grows more appallingly grotesque. Calvin is very specific on this point. A key remark in the *Institutes* provides a virtual epigraph for Tourneur's play:

> For how does it happen that a prudent man, consulting his own welfare, averts from himself impending evils, and a fool is ruined by his inconsiderate temerity, unless folly and prudence are in both cases *instruments* of the Divine dispensation? (*op. cit.*, p. 195)

Flourishing the rock with which his brother was brained, D'Amville in a speech of black-comic burlesque on Christ's words proclaims,

> Upon this ground I'll build my manor house
> And this shall be the chiefest corner-stone.
> (II.iv.99–100)

And then, intoxicated by his own boldness, he refutes all other claims to a part in the design of events,

> Not any circumstance
> That stood within the reach of the *design*
> Of persons, dispositions, matter, time,
> Or, place, but by this brain of mine was *made*
> An *instrumental* help. . . .
> (II.iv.103–107; *italics mine*)

Then in operatic duet, the two conspirators gleefully catalogue the steps of the scheme, in which friendly conviviality between members of the family, D'Amville announces, was economically

> . . . us'd by me to make the servants drunk,
> An *instrument* the *plot* could not have miss'd.
> (II.iv.125–126; *italics mine*)

The servants and friends walking with them were made unwitting accessories ("The *instruments*, yet knew not what they did" [II.iv.135]). And then lest we miss the extent of D'Amville's claim, Tourneur in the undaunted pedantical fashion that differentiates him from all his contemporaries has D'Amville explicitly generalize it:

> That power of rule, philosophers ascribe
> To him they call the supreme of the stars.
> (II.iv.136–137)

In short, what the supposedly wise call Providence ("that power of rule"), I have just embodied by "creating" and "executing" this scheme through a series of instruments. The play's precise flavor cannot be tasted unless we see that D'Amville, unlike the usual subphilosophical villain, is more interested *in the meaning of his own actions* than in the acts themselves. He is not seeking power in any ordinary sense; his challenge is to the Deity. In the same fashion that Marlowe's *Tamburlaine* is a dramatized critique of the concept called *Nemesis*, so *The Atheist's Tragedy* is an emblematic critique of the arguments for the primacy of *human* providence. Another constituent of the play echoes D'Amville's argument but in a more ceremonial mode.

At the opening of Act IV there is a little inset scene which bears the same relationship to the whole play as the porter's speech to *Macbeth* or to a dream interlude in a modern novel, i.e., it condenses the thematic content, or to put it another way, it is the inert meaning of the play divorced from the action. Here, moreover, as in the case of *Macbeth*, it is the "meaning" of the play seen *sub specie* unmediated by human intention or concern. Macbeth's actions transform any world he can know into Hell; the "porter scene" helps us to modulate from the fairly objective world of the early scenes to the subjectified latter scenes, where Macbeth actively tries to recreate the world in his own image. Similarly in *The Atheist's Tragedy*, Tourneur's inset scene involves a minor, thematic character, the Bawd, Cataplasma (i.e., "poultice," or one who applies something warm and soothing to swollen members) and her maid. They are doing needlework. The prior scene has just closed on Rousard, D'Amville's sickly son, who has been married to Castabella as part of D'Amville's master plan to raise his posterity to wealth and dignity, where the sickly Rousard (indeed he is dying) is made to say,

> A gen'ral weakness did surprise my health
> The very day I marry'd Castabella,
> As if my sickness were a punishment
> That did arrest me for some injury
> I then committed.
>
> (III.iv.63–67)

The sins of the father are not only visited upon the son, they are symbolically figured in his physical condition. That there is a direct connection between D'Amville's scheming and botanical iconography is shown in D'Amville's hypocritical remarks to Charlemont whose father he has murdered just preceding the inset scene itself:

> I will supply your father's vacant place,
> To guide your *green improvidence* of youth
> And make you *ripe* for your inheritance.
> (III.iv.51–53; *italics mine*)

The scene that follows this with the two sub-plot females (Cataplasma and her maid) is pointless in itself, i.e., we have no reason to be interested in their opinions for their own sake. The two are examining a piece of needlework:

> What's here? a medlar with a plum tree growing hard by it; the leaves o' the plum tree falling off; the gum issuing out o' the perished joints; and the branches some of 'em dead, and some rotten; and yet but a young plum tree. . . . The plum tree, forsooth, grows so near the medlar that the medlar sucks and draws all the sap from it and the natural strength o' the ground, so that it cannot prosper (IV.i.2–9)

and then immediately following a slightly varied repetition of the scene's point:

> But here th'ast made a tree to bear no fruit. Why's that?

and the answer:

> There grows a savin tree next it.
> (IV.i.10–12)

Savin is an irritant poison used to cause women to abort. The point is somewhat subtler and more functional than might readily appear. The medlar's symbolic force isn't limited to its familiar application to the prostitute, though, of course, the scene is heavily charged with sexual puns in keeping with the lust-ridden atmosphere of the play's quasi-comic subplot. The medlar also symbolizes the wisdom that supposedly accompanies the natural decline of physical strength—that is it betokens a certain kind of maturity. Under "Mespilus" in Philippo Picinello's *Mundus Symbolicus* we find that its famous property "non maturum prius, quam putridum" is to be understood "in Plato's words" to mean:

> Mentis oculus tunc acute incipi cernere, cum primum corporis oculus deflorescit.[9]

We then are to understand that a *natural* process of growth would produce wisdom and spiritual insight in D'Amville and that by this means he should be able to nurture and promote the ready growth of his children towards the independent strength which the plum tree conventionally symbolizes. In the very first scene D'Amville has linked his specious "providence" with the image of a tree:

> And as for my children, they are as near to me
> As *branches* of a *tree* whereon they *grow*,
> And may as numerously be *multiply'd*.
> As they *increase*, so should my *providence*,
> For from my *substance* they receive the *sap*.
> Whereby they live and *flourish*.
> (I.i.53–58; *italics mine*)[10]

But we see both in the play and in the thematic iconography of this little scene that this is not so. His age being wisdomless simply draws off the independent life of the child, since his roots are deeper, which is to say that his power to gratify his own needs is greater. The savin (i.e., the juniper) image emphasizes that, while all the time talking of his concern for his posterity, he is actually aborting natural growth through usurpation of his children's independent status as souls.

From this inset, emblematic scene onwards, the play's tempo picks up as D'Amville's elaborate, self-serving schemes begin to fall apart. Since the crucial indicators of the play's tone as well as of its consciously composed referential system reach a point where the action is virtually swamped under the burden of the preconceived meanings it must bear, it is time to stand back a moment, so that we can see the contours of the play more clearly.

The basic or main plot of the play is very simple by Jacobean standards. D'Amville wishes to seize the wealth of his baronial neighbor, Montferrers, and to raise higher the fabric of his own house. His drives are less from greed than to magnify his posterity and so to secure his name against eclipse by death which he fears to an unnatural extent. Hence he has the double aim of murdering Montferrers and replacing with his own son Montferrer's son, Charlemont—the play's exemplar of goodness—as the husband-to be of Castabella, daughter of D'Amville's brother, Belforest, who is also a baron. By this design, D'Amville can arrogate to himself all three large estates: his own, his brother's and his neighbor's. The treacherous cupidity which serves this aim, and his self-lauding way of premeditating and executing it, make him into a kind of parodic trinity. With Charlemont out of the way at the wars in the Low

Countries, his father murdered and Castabella married to
D'Amville's son, Rousard, D'Amville will have achieved a puny
version of omnipotence over both the present substance and the
potential for the future of his "world." The first two acts of the play in
an almost diagrammatic fashion exposit this scheme and trace its
swift and adroit accomplishment. The real substance of the play, to
which the first two acts are a circumstantial premise, follows in the
last three acts which open with the lyric hypocrisy of D'Amville's
funeral eulogies over the body of the murdered Montferrers and
before the empty monument of Charlemont whose pretended death at
the seige of Ostend D'Amville has contrived to promulgate, so as to
speed the marriage of his son to Castabella now left bereft by this
specious death.

The action from this point is one immense peripety, multiplying
evidence of the foundationless nature of D'Amville's apparent
"providential" design. Modern critical discussions of the play are
faithful enough to its obvious structural movement, but they diverge
in the most misleading way from its tone as a felt experience when
reading it.[11] If these modern readings are permitted to become
surrogates for the experience of the play, we conclude that the play is
intellectually relentless, sombre in tone and almost dirge-like in
tempo. It isn't at all. Much of the action has the pace and intricacy of
bedroom comedy; a large percentage of the dialogue is allocated to
Sebastian, D'Amville's reckless, sexually rampageous but still
rather decent younger son; to the garrulous puritanical imposter,
Languebeau Snuffe, and his sneaky if inept lechery; to the ever
hopeful intrigues of Castabella's lusty step-mother, Levidulcia; and
the trivial clownish antics of Soquette and Fresco, the would-be
sexual objects of these hustling lechers.

Moreover, the play has a double plot structure reminiscent more of
The Changeling or *The Dutch Courtesan* than of the standard
revenge or heroic plays to which it is conventionally compared.[12]
The sub-plot roughly parallels the main action: Cataplasma "founds
a house" of ill-fame where women can meet secretly with their
lovers. This part of the play is a fairly spirited, saturnalian parallel to
the main plot. Its hallmark is a licentious and "free" thinking, sexual
naturalism which is the grosser physical analogue to D'Amville's
philosophical licentiousness. Just as D'Amville's older son Rousard
is spiritually sick and wholly impotent as scion of that godless
foundation, his father's house; so is Sebastian, the younger son, a
kind of moral castrate who is all cheerful, unabashed, headlong
libido. Both die appropriately; Rousard just gutters out like a feeble

flame—snuffed out by the miasmic atmosphere of his father's ethos; Sebastian dies in a bawdy house quarrel, striving in his not ignoble but thoughtless fashion to protect the non-existent honor of his uncle's wife, Levidulca, with whom he had meant to copulate. He kills his uncle and dies himself in the encounter. His death is almost wordless. He is snuffed out too in darkness and confusion, with shouts of the converging nightwatch as his death's noisy *continuo*. The hysterical penitence of Levidulcia when she discovers his bloody corpse seconds later, culminating in her stagy, implausible and unregarded suicide, offers suitably minute recompense for his genial imprudence. The point here is the almost negligible quality of these unilluminated lives. The impact of the play is meager if we view it too solemnly; but if we sense its partial affinities to the theater of the absurd, then Tourneur's play, no longer the awkward product of humorless ineptitude, takes on new vitality.

D'Amville's manipulative and egocentric talents presumptuously claim immense foresight, whereas the latter part of the action is conducted in almost surrealistic confusion. D'Amville is perpetually surprised by the turn of events. As personified in his two sons, he has neither staying power nor circumspection, rather poor credentials for a would-be providential deity. D'Amville, largely through his high spirited and conscienceless "instrument," Borachio, *does* some evil things. He murders a guiltless man, and with gleeful hypocrisy he publicly mourns him; he "uses" others constantly in direct contradiction to Kant's updating formulation of the central imperative of Christian charity: that "No man should ever be treated as a means to anything but always as an end in himself"; he incestuously propositions his virtuous daughter-in-law, Castabella; he vainly plots the murder of the guiltless Charlemont. But, in the frame of the play these acts are not so much horrible as pretentious. No one he actually succeeds in harming is a fully realized character; his designs are like the false pregnancy which forms one of the images of the play, "a tympany" (i.e., a swelling or tumor) which "turns but to a certain kind of phlegmatic windy disease" (IV.iii.38–40)—in short, a gigantic fart, the noisy evidence of false claims.

D'Amville and Borachio, a physically lazy but ingenious master and his utterly amoral and frisky instrument, are more like Volpone and Mosca than threatening presences from the world of tragic revenge. And, this is not because of lamentable artistic incapacity on the part of Tourneur; it is because the premises of D'Amville's providential schemes make him seem more foolish than terrible. The magnitude of his possible accomplishment is so trivial and vain when held up against the theoretically posited God who is omniscient stage-manager of Tourneur's world, that everything he does to invite direct comparison to providential sovereignty shrinks him smaller. In the end, D'Amville is sleepless—as far from the peace of self-contentment as Faustus or Macbeth. His insomniac condition has been prefigured, by contrast, in the play's longest and most overtly symbolic scene, that in the churchyard when Borachio is killed by Charlemont and D'Amville's hopes are thereby irretrievably lost. In this dark setting replete with charnel house, gravestones, skulls and numerous ghostly shenanigans, the "good ones," Charlemont and Castabella, surrounded by foes and apparently lost, "*lie down with either of them a death's head for a pillow*" and sleep (IV.ii.190–204). Here let us recall a further section of Calvin's commentary on the 127th Psalm which the play dramatizes:

On the Suffering of Believers:

If any man obiect ageyne, that the faythfull doo often broyle in sore cares, and thoughfull [sic] for the morrow when they be pinched with want of all things and destitute of all meanes to come by any thing. I answere that if there were perfect faith & devotion in the woorshippers of god, the blissing of God which the prophet mencioneth should bee apparant. Therefore as oft as they be tormented without measure: that happeneth through their own default, bycause they rest not throughly upon Gods providence. And this I say further, that they be more streightly punished than the unbeleevers, because it is necessarie for them to bee haryed hither and thither with unquietnesse for a tyme, *that they maye come too thys sleepe in the ende*. But yet in the meane whyle Gods grace preuayleth, and shyneth foorth alwaye in the middes of dark nesse, *bycause the Lorde cherisheth hys children as it were by sleepe*. (p. 205, col. 2; *italics mine*)

If we can accept the vantage point which makes undue thinking foolish (and Hamlet, who has superior credentials for making such a judgment, supplies a classic text in his "I defy augury" speech), then it is readily possible to see not only why D'Amville proceeds towards absurdity as a limit but also to catch hold of the comedic force of his unintentional self-execution at the end of the play. This episode has been, and possibly will remain, an embarrassment to Tourneur's admirers. D'Amville, before a court of judgment which is charged with the trial and sentencing of the virtuous young couple, Charlemont and Castabella—and here again the trial scene invokes for us not the tragic courtroom of Webster's *The White Devil* but the plight of the equally idealistic and misused Celia and Bonario in another "Drama of Ethical Display," *Volpone*—breaks with all decorum in characteristic display of impatience. At no point in the play's action has he been content to let the initiative reside with God or with any other man. Hamlet's "Readiness is all" is utterly beyond his absurdly restricted moral capacities. Typically, then, he usurps the court's function, and proceeds to play judge, jury and, though not intentionally, executioner to himself. When he leaps to the platform, seizes the executioner's axe and *"As he raise up the axe strikes out his own brains*," we are not to see this as God's hand reaching down as in a crude 15th century woodcut, but as a further example of the cosmic silliness of D'Amville's usurping role. When the dying D'Amville says, "The lust of death commits a rape on me" (V.ii.267), the flamboyant figure is quite precise. As the latter part of the play makes clear, D'Amville's basic drive has been to cheat death of its fearfulness, thus the overweening impulse to arrogate initiative to himself in his swollen efforts to simulate Providence which assigns death's moment as it closes each life account. We have seen in the "churchyard" scene, with its explicit commentary by Calvin, that patience (which is thus a by-product of faith) is most perfectly manifest in an untroubled disregard of death and its unpredictable coming as symbolized by the childlike sleep of the virtuous. D'Amville's insomniac restiveness is the polar opposite to this and is implicitly a form of self-destruction, of suicide. Still more, when married to such relentless self-advertisement as D'Amville's, to such sterile misuse of all other lives, it becomes grotesque—repellent yes, but absurd too. His silly expropriation of the instrument of death, the axe, symbolically recapitulates his misconceived life style. Like Agamemnon's treading on the scarlet carpet in the *Oresteia*, the final act of D'Amville is not the cause of his death in itself, it is the emblematic summation of the process of his life.

The Atheist's Tragedy is unusually self-consistent as, indeed, a play of Calvinistic inspiration should be. There are many plays in the Tudor-Stuart period which have a strong religious orientation. Tragedy often stems from a sense of the problematic nature of providence. In Tourneur's play, however, an extra step towards theodicy is taken. He believes God's intentions are explicit and demonstrable, so that for him God's justice literally vindicates itself. Whenever an artist operates from a convinced sense of God's express availability as a *deus ex machina* of unlimited prerogative, there is bound to be a comedic infusion, since divine judgment is full, irresistible and provides a context for the action so much more embracing than any dramatizable alternative, that human ambition is transposed into the cosmic silliness of unfounded presumption. Dramas of Ethical Display have a special competence for molding philosophical ironies into dramatic structures which invite a disjunction of response. This special inflection of the tragic may be summed up in the figure oxymoron: D'Amville is "displayed" as a "tiny monster," or as a "dangerous trifler," or as "vigilant blind man," or as a "life-hoarding suicide." What seem to be contradictions in the play's tonal stresses are resolved, when we see that Calvinism places a low valuation upon human *life qua life*: its stress is on *innocence* and *theoretic virtue*. Hence, we are unfaithful to the theological imperatives of the play, when we permit a few deaths (or life annulments) to darken our sense of the sovereign concerns of the play as a symbolic action. *The Atheist's Tragedy* possesses considerable energy when we accept all its elements and do not diagram it according to some magisterially fixed notion of the tragic. As a dramatization of the 127th Psalm, it takes a very high point of vantage in measuring human capacity. From such heights our plannings seem like scurryings, our deflections are returns, and our selfish escapades, as in Chaucer's *Pardoner's Tale* of which *The Atheist's Tragedy* is a remote descendent, lead to surprising, yet obvious retributions.

NOTES

[1]*Tulane Drama Review*, 8 (1964), 215–16.

[2]*Plotinus: The Enneads*, trans. Stephen MacKenna (London, 1956), p. 177.

[3]*The Psalmes of David and Others with J. Calvins Commentaries*, trans. Arthur Golding (London, 1571): STC 4395.

[4]Jean Calvin, *Institutes of the Christian Religion*, trans. John Allen (Philadelphia, 1930), II, 184.

[5]Robert Ornstein, "*The Atheist's Tragedy* and Renaissance Naturalism," *SP*, 51 (1954), 194–207.

[6]Cf. innumerable scriptural references and a standard handbook such as George Ferguson, *Signs and Symbols in Christian Art* (New York: Oxford Univ. Press, 1954), p. 64. For Davies, see his "Nosce Teipsum," in *The Poems*, ed. Grosart, p. 25.

[7]All quotations from *The Atheist's Tragedy* are from Irving Ribner's edition for *The Revels Plays* (London and Cambridge, Mass.: Methuen, 1964).

[8]M. C. Bradbrook, *Themes and Conventions of Elizabethan Tragedy* (Cambridge: Cambridge Univ. Press, 1935), pp. 175–80, notes the pattern of building imagery as does Una Ellis-Fermor in "The Imagery of *The Revenger's Tragedy* and *The Atheist's Tragedy*," *MLR*, 30 (1935), 296 *et passim*. Indeed, the building imagery is so functional and explicit that one supposes all readers must in some sense note its presence.

[9]Philippo Picinello, *Mundus Symbolicus* (Rome, 1729), I, 576.

[10]As suggested by my earlier comment on Calvin's rhapsodic passage on the fertilizing and nurturing power of God's seminal instrument the sun, D'Amville tries to usurp the *natura naturans* aspect of Godhead as well as God's more administrative functions. His sterile efforts in this sphere act as an ironic doubling of his groundless presumption. The play's deepest image stratum has to do with the negation of growth, the abortion of natural process.

[11]Irving Ribner in the introduction to his useful edition of *The Atheist's Tragedy* which I have already cited as my own text for quotation, supplies a good review of

critical discussion of the play over the past thirty years or so. Essays by L. G. Salingar (1938), Harold Jenkins (1941), Michael Higgens (1943), John Peter (1956), and Inga-Stina Ekeblad (1959) may be joined to those of Ornstein, Bradbrook and Ellis-Fermor already cited to get a sense of the tradition. Ribner's own commentary is also valuable.

[12]After completing this essay, I read Richard Levin's useful essay, "The Subplot of *The Atheist's Tragedy*," *HLQ*, 29 (1965), 17–33. This carefully schematized study supplies welcome confirmation of my general claim of the deliberate reflections of the main-plot issues in the secondary plot. It is full and particularized in establishing the conscious artistry with which the parallels are developed. Since Professor Levin's perceptions of the tone, movement and intellectual *tendenz* of the main action are wholly in tune with the conventional critical commentary, his interpretation of Tourneur's use of his subplot and my own are healthily complimentary rather than in competition.

Coriolanus: History and the Crisis of Semantic Order

Leonard Tennenhouse

The dramatic structure of *Coriolanus* is in many respects unique among those tragedies of Shakespeare which are based on English and Roman history. This uniqueness derives, I believe, not only from the moment of Roman history which Shakespeare chose to consider, but also from that point in the unfolding of the political process at which Shakespeare begins the play. With the exception of *Coriolanus,* all of the English and Roman tragedies center upon the transitional period in an historical process during which the political order of the state permanently changes at the moment when the protagonist is destroyed. The deaths of Richard II, Richard III, Caesar, and Antony are part of such processes, and their deaths involve the appearance of new political alignments in England and Rome. The political structure which emerges at the end of each play marks a new stage in the history of the state because adherents to the new order possess the kingdom and have established new political eras. No new political alignment or structure comes into being with the destruction of Coriolanus. When he dies, there is no vision of the destruction of evil, no revelation of God's control of history, no mourning for an old order destroyed, no sense of loss, no sense of regret that the world could not contain so noble a hero.

No new political structure comes into being with the death of Coriolanus because at the opening of the play a new political structure has already been established. The creation of the tribunes, which has taken place just moments before the play begins, has introduced a new political force into the state. It has also displaced Coriolanus from his position in society. The presence of the tribunes signifies the presence in the state of a

217

populace with a political voice. Words have been let loose among
the people, and there is a new basis for both political and
semantic authority.1 In effect this crisis of semantic order is
reflected in the displacement of Coriolanus. In structuralist
terms, Coriolanus as the representative of the old order organizes
the play, grounds the oppositions, and characterizes the relation between language and violence that produces the tragedy.2
He is the center of both the play and the historical narrative
which the play dramatizes.3 While his presence governs the
structure of the historical narrative and the dramatic work, it
generates as well the thematic issues of language and politics.
These two issues must be seen in their Jacobean contexts if
we are to understand the particular urgency the play reflects
and the specific anxiety its structure tries to control. The crisis
of semantic order in *Coriolanus* involves political, historical,
cultural, and psychological consequences, and it is in political,
historical, cultural, and psychological terms that the play has
to be read.

I

Shakespeare's treatment of the Coriolanus material differs
from that of historical traditions in the mode of delineating the
character of the hero and in the degree of importance assigned
to the tribunes. Plutarch presents Coriolanus as a man who
suffered from his mother's failure to provide a proper education. He reports that Coriolanus was eloquent, politic at times,
and, of course, the very model of *virtus,* but finally so uncivil
that he was destroyed. Shakespeare removes any hint of a
politic Coriolanus, and in place of eloquence, he gives us a
man who suffers, when speaking to the plebians, from logorhea.4
Shakespeare's most significant variation from the traditions related by Plutarch, Livy, and Florus, however, is his decision to
highlight the creation of the *tribuni plebis* and emphasize their
prominence in the political affairs of Rome.5 The Roman historians note the creation of the tribunes only in passing and
with approval. For Shakespeare and his audience, the importance of the creation of the tribunes, the first time in history
that an aristocracy was forced to share authority with representatives of the citizenry, lay precisely in the emergence of a
new balance of power within the state and in the complications
that arose from this new alignment. Unlike the Roman his-

torians, sixteenth-century writers tend to be critical of the creation of the tribunes, seeing in this act the consequences of the failure of monarchy. Sir Thomas Elyot, for instance, sees the audacity and the power of the tribunes as dangerous to political authority:

> The communalitie more and more encroached a licence, and at the last compelled the Senate to suffre them to chose yerely amonge them gouernours of theyr own astate and condition, whom they called Tribunes: under whom they resceyued suche audacitie and power that they finally optained the higheste authoritie in the publike weale, in so moche that often tymes they dyd repele the actes of the Senate. . . .6

To be sure not every writer shared Elyot's view, but the term "tribune" did carry pejorative connotations especially for those who believed in an absolute monarchy. At the time of Shakespeare's writing of *Coriolanus,* however, the term "tribune" had particular currency, for James and Parliament were divided precisely upon the issue of royal power and the increasing claims of the House of Commons.

The first Parliament that James called was contestual about its rights to speak and anxious to debate matters on which Elizabeth had been largely successful in suppressing controversy.7 In the Parliament of 1604, the business of the assembly was no longer run by a court-controlled coterie, as had been the case under Elizabeth; there was strong parliamentary demand to debate matters of money and religion.8 At the opening session of 1605, James singled out for attack "some tribunes of the people whose mouths could not be stopped either from matters of the Puritans or of purveyance."9 The royal statement suggests the political and cultural issues expressed by the word "tribune" in the period in which Shakespeare was writing the play. Because of the growing power of the House of Commons, there was serious concern in England with the political consequences of rhetorical manipulation and with language as an instrument of political power.

Throughout his reign, the difficulty James had with "tribunes," verbal opposition, and uncontrolled debate stemmed in part from what he perceived as a challenge to his semantic authority. To James, "Rex est lex loquens."10 It was typical of James to say, as he did to the Spanish Ambassador following the dissolution of Parliament in 1614, "The House of Commons is a body without a head. The members give their opinions in a disorderly manner. I am surprised that my ancestors should ever have permitted such an institution to come into existence . . . ."11 The image is a familiar one, reminiscent of Menenius's parable of the body, and in its very familiarity we should recognize the persistence of this topos as a sign of a recurring political anxiety.

James's belief that the king is "lex loquens" and his frustrations with Parliament have as much to do with the history of that body as they have to do with James's own personality (that history was by the way only imperfectly grasped by James and his contemporaries). From the time of the Reformation Parliament to the death of Elizabeth, the House of Commons had become "the body which makes laws overriding all laws."12 With the rise of Parliament as the legislative body of government and the growth of a complicated procedural mechanism, the question of the voice which had legitimate semantic authority was at the heart of a series of long and complex arguments between monarchs and certain members of Commons. Sir John Neale writes that during Elizabeth's reign a consuming interest in parliamentary affairs "caused some members to keep diaries; and it was the erection of speaking into an art, calling for wit, phrase and quotation that led many to write out their more deliberate speeches." In the reign of James the subject matter and the rhetorical style of parliamentary debates was of such interest that "Stationers sold copies of speeches . . . and 'true relations' of the House of Commons proceedings."13 Not only had the private business of Parliament become public entertainment by the time of James, but also the art of rhetoric had become a self-conscious medium of the contest.

II

An understanding of the Jacobean context allows the reader of the play to hear the cultural resonances struck by Shakespeare in his presentation of the creation of the tribunes, his suggestion of the political forces they represent, and his exploration of the linguistic concerns their creation implies. Within the play itself the tribunes are used to express the relation between language and power; they are linked poetically with the major image complexes that run through the play. The tribunes provide a mouth for the plebeians and as such they are

associated with all forms of oral power; images link them to
speech, to voices, to feeding. Against the tribunes stands Coriolanus, the exemplum of the old patrician order. He is associated
with images of the physical body, wounds, blood, martial
power, as well as with devouring war, verbal rage, and rhetorical
impotence. Moreover, while the establishment of the *tribuni
plebis* is described initially as a minor concession by the patri-
cians, an expedient solution to a passing problem, it is in fact,
as only Coriolanus recognizes, the end of the old Roman state
and of an historical period.

Plutarch explains that the internal chaos which threatened
Rome was the consequence of an irresponsible patrician authority which permitted usurious practices to enslave the plebeians.
To the starving citizens in the play, however, the particular
cause of their misery is neither the structure of the state nor
usury: it is quite specifically Caius Marcius. When the play
opens, the citizens cry out for the death of Marcius which they
see as the means of getting corn at their own price:[14]

> 1. Cit.   First, you know Caius Marcius is the chief enemy
> to the people.
> All.   We know't, we know't!
> 1. Cit.   Let us kill him, and we'll get corn at our own
> price.
> All.   No more talking on't! Let it be done! Away,
> Away. (I.i.5-10)[15]

As the citizens speak, the issue does not become any clearer:

> We are accounted poor citizens, the patricians good. What
> authority surfeits on would relieve us. If they would
> yield us but the superfluity while it were wholesome,
> we might guess they relieved us humanely; but they think
> we are too dear. The leanness that afflicts us, the object
> of our misery, is as an inventory to particularize their
> abundance; our sufferance is a gain to them. (I.i.12-20)

One is not sure in this speech that the citizens are simply speaking of corn, for authority surfeits on power as well as corn, and
it is power which controls the distribution of corn. The deliberate opacity in these opening lines allows the concepts of food,
power, authority, and Marcius to merge in such a way as to
suggest that Marcius's death will somehow relieve their hunger,
literal and metaphoric. There is something profoundly disturbing in the mob's language here; it presents the cannibalization
of Marcius as the single solution to multiple problems.

For all the characteristics this discordant, savage, irrational mob shares with those in his other tragedies, Shakespeare complicates our moral response to them by the specific depiction of their hunger.16 In so doing, he makes it as difficult to sympathize with the furious attack by Marcius on the plebeians as it is impossible to approve the mob's murderous desires. At no point in the play, however, does Shakespeare show why the citizens perceive Marcius as responsible for withholding corn.

To Marcius the citizens are "scavengers," "cowards," "curs," and "rats." As he comes on stage launching his first scurrilous attack, he speaks out of disgust with the plebeians and dismay with the senators. To him the strange petition granted to the plebeians made "bold power look pale," and it is power, not the demand for food, that concerns him. His own response to the threat ("The rabble should have first unroof'd the city/ Ere so prevailed with me" [I.i.204-05]) would have meant perpetual chaos. It is a telling point that he alone sees the creation of the tribunes as a fundamental assault on the basic reality that lies behind the appearance of patrician power. Nevertheless his counsel, had it been followed, would have resulted in the destruction of the state.17

Whatever else one may say about Coriolanus, regardless of the way in which one chooses to view him, one must concede that he is correct in his belief that the creation of the tribunes directly undermines patrician power in Rome (I.i.190-207). By the same token, whatever may be said about the tribunes and their politic behavior, one must concede that they are correct in their belief that Marcius is the most serious threat to their newly acquired power, for Coriolanus is the ultimate conservative.18 He is so not simply because of his family line, but because the patrician values which marked the old political order provide the very terms of his identity. By the time the play begins, however, that old Roman order, dating back in its purest form to Junius Brutus, has passed. Coriolanus, the definitive product of that order, was born one generation too late, and thus from the moment he enters on stage he is the victim of history.

This moment of history, marked by the creation of a public tongue for the plebeians, is one in which the state is newly defined; therefore the actions which constitute public service, and the means by which power is exercised must also be newly defined. The battle to control Rome, which constitutes the action of the play, in the new order is to be waged with language. It is this new medium of power which Coriolanus most distrusts. His abhorrence of public speech and his distrust of words are functions of his obsessive quest for a personal integrity which can only be concretely realized in physical action. Language to him is a private faculty which at best serves to speak his anger. It is an inadequate vehicle to mediate between feeling and action; for Coriolanus, action is the only public expression that has significance. He strives to fulfill in himself the martial ideals of that world which fathered him, taught as they were by the mother who nurtured him. So completely has he incorporated her ideals that he judges all else against the standards of the mythical Roman warrior he wishes to be. To understand his perception of those ideals is to understand the radical separation between language and action which is reflected in the presentation of the relations between Coriolanus and the mob, the tribunes, Aufidius and Virgilia. All of these are a function of the relation between Coriolanus and Volumnia.

III

Shakespeare presents Volumnia as the chief spokesman for patrician values. It is she who idealizes them; it is she who articulates them; it is she who has made a mother's love conditional upon her son's ability to act on them. Her language is central to his linguistic solipsism. The ground for meaning is in the relation between mother and son, and it is by means of this relation that Shakespeare delineates the primary crisis of semantic order which the play as a whole works out. In the third scene of the play, which presents an incident not found in the sources, Volumnia says to Virgilia, "If my son were my husband, I should freelier rejoice in that absence wherein he won honour than in the embracements of his bed where he would show most love" (1.iii.2-4). It is important to note here that this is no incest fantasy; it is a statement about the conditions of love. Absence is preferred to presence, and action in pursuit of honor is preferred to the gestures of love. As she goes on, she speaks of her willingness, even her desire when Coriolanus was a child to break off his attachment to her, rupturing the mirror relationship of mutual gazing between mother and child. At a time when a child is most beautiful, "when for a day of king's entreaties a mother should not sell him an hour from her beholding, I . . . was pleas'd to let him seek danger where he was like to find fame" (5-10). She says as well that if she had a dozen sons each as dear as Marcius, "I had rather had eleven die nobly for their country than one voluptuously surfeit out of action" (21-23). Being in action is preferable to being out of action; noble death is preferable to voluptuous feeding; the quest for honor and fame please more than the son's presence. It would be wrong to say she does not love her son, for she obviously does. As Shakespeare presents her, however, she has suppressed all maternal qualities, notably those of nurture and tenderness. Virgilia, her own son beside her, is dismayed at Volumnia's lecture; the contrast between the two mothers is distinct. Volumnia excitedly imagines her son wiping his bloody brow and then moving through enemy forces like a harvestman who must mow down all or lose his hire. The image shocks Virgilia: "O Jupiter, no blood!" Volumnia silences her with a description that links the imagery of blood and death to motherhood and nurture:

> The breasts of Hecuba
> When she did suckle Hector, look'd not lovelier
> Than Hector's forehead when it spit forth blood
> At Grecian sword, contemning. (37-40)

Like the superimposition of the pastoral metaphor on a scene of military carnage, her language speaks her ideals while it signals a complete suppression of any feelings we might want to associate with the maternal. Her personal style involves denying all maternal qualities in herself, and she has reared her son to deny to himself any expression of tenderness or love.[19]

It is a point of pride with her that she has trained her son to competition, seriousness, and ambition; that she has encouraged him to deny, to suppress, and to withhold whatever is associated with the feminine and the maternal. In the play we see that Coriolanus, the child denied love in the service of patrician ideals, is perceived by the mob as the one who denies. The mysterious source of the cannibalistic rage directed against him is the recognition by the plebeians that he would withhold from them what the patrician mother would withhold from her son—nurturance and thus life itself. The mob correctly perceives the link between his fanatical pursuit of patrician ideals and their own hunger. They thus believe that his death will miraculously release corn, open to them the sources of nurturance.

What is most disturbing about Volumnia and the language she speaks is precisely that while her speech consistently echoes with public phrases, martial ideals, and her own version of patrician values, her voice is a mother's voice and she speaks in a private context. It is as though her idealized version of herself, at least as Shakespeare presents it, is that of Roma, the mother city. Thus to her, words of praise for her son are what she possesses as a mother, as if she were the state itself. She says to Virgilia, for instance, that if Marcius had died in battle while still a man-child, "Then his good report should have been my son; I therein would have found issue" (I.iii.18-19). She is, however, neither the state nor its public spokesman, and her private vocabulary must always ring false because it always has private signification.

A use of language by a public speaker who for a social purpose considers the occasion and the context of his words contrasts sharply with Volumnia's use of a public vocabulary in a private context. Such a social use of language serves to verify ideals, provide continuity, and mediate differences. When Menenius speaks to the crowd to quell their anger, he is operating in this wide social context. His rhetorical style, his use of parable, his choice of a commonly shared political vocabulary are typical of the socially cohesive potential of language. When Cominius insists that a report be made of Coriolanus's deeds, he is applying language to social concerns. A good report must be made, not because it serves the private needs of Coriolanus, but because it serves the social needs of the state. Cominius says, "you shall not be/ The grave of your deservings. Rome must know/ The value of her own" (I.ix.19-21). Because Coriolanus distrusts words, even words of praise, feeling that words are not deeds, he will not countenance a description of his actions. He flees Cominius's words so that he will not hear his "nothings monster'd" (II.ii.74).

Coriolanus's refusal to hear his actions reported and his general discomfort in linguistic settings are symptomatic of the crisis he precipitates when he must stand for consul. To ask for the plebian "voice" is to acknowledge that the *vox populi* has a power to authorize him. The word "voice" both in the play and in the Elizabethan and Jacobean contexts has specific as-

sociations with political authority. Sir Thomas Smith, for instance, describing in *De Republica Anglorum* (1565) the constituent elements of English society, says of laborers, retailers,
and artificers: "These have no voice nor authority in our com-
monwealth and no account is made of them."[20] To have voice
is to have vote is to have authority. Moreover, to ask for the
voice is to acknowledge that speech is a legitimate political
action.

The terms by which Shakespeare develops the election to the
consulship point to a source of anxiety between *logos* and *praxis*
within the play and point as well to a related concern for the
Jacobean audience of the play. D. J. Gordon has discussed the
particular associations between the election ritual which Coriolanus must endure and the way in which it echoes election pro-
cedures for the House of Commons. Election to Parliament
was determined by voice vote; when several men stood for the
same seat the sheriff had to decide from among the shouts who
had more voices.[21] Thus in reality, political authority was seen
as a function of vocal power and the act of giving voice to a
candidate. Within the play Coriolanus finds it intolerable to beg
the voice of the plebeians because in Gordon's words:

> they are voices that are acts: acts of uttering that are
> acts of decision. Voice is deed and not deed in the same
> moment. Coriolanus' deeds, which must be named, fall
> into this nexus, the relationship between name and thing
> is disrupted: deed must be honour, its name, its voice.
> Deed being named, passes into its opposite: voice.[22]

In the process of the plebeians' naming of the deed, the tribunes
insist on the literal numbering of voices, and in so doing they
literalize the symbolic power of the plebeians and signal the
existence of a new Rome.

As long as the form of what constitutes the public self-image
—its representation as the structure of the state—remains static,
there is no conflict between the state which celebrates social
ideals and the individual who pursues them. One of the most
interesting aspects of *Coriolanus* is the slow and disarming
discovery by the Romans, and it is surprising to them, that
indeed the world of Rome has somehow changed. The testing
point of that change is to be seen in the treatment of Coriolanus.
Thus Cominius delivers his speech on Coriolanus before the
senate, and the senate responds with the customary offer of a

consulship. Similarly the plebeians understand that Coriolanus ought to get their voice if he requests it, for custom dictates how their power must be used in such cases:

> We have power in ourselves to do it, but it is a power that we have no power to do; for if he show us his wounds and tell us his deeds, we are to put our tongues into those wounds and speak for them. So, if he tell us his noble deeds, we must tell him our noble acceptance of them. Ingratitude is monstrous. . . . (II.iii.4-9)

The custom, when it functioned ideally—that is, when it functioned in the past—consisted in a mutuality whereby the wounds of a hero acquired the tongues of the populace and became mouths to speak the honor of the hero and the glory of Rome. Not to grant Coriolanus the honor is to give the lie to Rome, but not to tell of his deeds is to give the lie to Coriolanus.

In every respect Coriolanus by his very nature puts to the test the public values which he has made into his private ideals. However, while the coherence of the society depends on the ritual having meaning, the historical moment itself signals the departure of meaning from the ritual. Capitalizing on the power of the public tongue and seeking to protect their newly acquired power, the tribunes reverse public opinion by insisting on the literal interpretation of the custom, and the ritual is rendered meaningless.[23] The issue, as the tribunes present it, is not whether Coriolanus performed valiantly nor whether Rome knows of his valor, but whether his private actions were and will continue to be located in the service of a public duty. Because Coriolanus cannot be politic as Volumnia and Menenius urge, because his personal integrity is maladaptive in the new world, he threatens the social integrity of the new Rome when public duty is redefined to encompass service to the *vox populi*. Coriolanus has become a source of disorder in the new state precisely because he is the impractical and impolitic ideal of the old state. He exists in a world of private signification; his universe of discourse is so fully grounded in a primary narcissism that he can say "I banish you" when he is banished because he has become in his perversely moral world an autonomous body politic.

There is little difference between the Roman society Coriolanus leaves and the Volscian society to which he goes. Moreover, Coriolanus by his example has made it impossible for anyone in the world to be honorable according to the old, private, martial ideals that both Roman and Volscian aristocracy had valued. Aufidius is the only person whom Coriolanus recognizes as his equal, and yet Aufidius abandons the old ideals of honor through combat in favor of revenge through deceit. When he discovers for the fifth time that he cannot defeat Coriolanus in battle, he says:

> By the elements,
> If e'er again I meet him beard to beard
> He's mine, or I am his. Mine emulation
> Hath not that honour in't it had; for where
> I thought to crush him in an equal force,
> True sword to sword, I'll potch at him some way,
> Or wrath or craft may get him. (I.x.10-16)

The honor of emulation is gone because Coriolanus is so good at the business of war that rivalry with him or emulation of him is foolish. And so Aufidius will resort to a "potch." The tenor of Aufidius's feelings seems to be complicated by his knowledge of his own limitations. There is a politic mean-spiritedness in his desire for revenge which places him on a moral par with the tribunes at Rome. Aufidius reminds one of a Laertes seeking revenge wherever he can find it. Just as Laertes tells Claudius that he would cut Hamlet's throat in a church to show that revenge has no bounds, so Aufidius would commit an equal sacrilege:

> Where I find him, were it
> At home, upon my brother's guard, even there,
> Against the hospitable canon, would I
> Wash my fierce hand in's heart. (I.x.24-27)

Aufidius, however, lacks Laertes' cause, and the language that speaks of revenge by a potch instead of a sword stroke implies the emotional and moral distance between the two revengers.

Aufidius cannot rival Coriolanus on the battlefield where action is its own eloquence. When Coriolanus joins the Volscian army, he grows in stature from the soldierly ideal, to an Achilles, and finally to a god in relation to the other combatants who shrink from soldiers to men and then to mere boys. Aufidius, like the tribunes, knows that the inherent frailty of Coriolanus lies precisely in his moral rigidity and in the linguistic solipsism which make him invulnerable as a warrior and impotent as a political man. Coriolanus dies because of this incapacity to be a political man, this inability to use language rhetorically.

IV

In the tragedies of *King Lear, Macbeth, Antony and Cleopatra,* and even *Othello* Shakespeare explored the experience of the public man whose quest for the satisfactions of private desires led him into a world where only tragic possibilities existed. It was in the history plays that Shakespeare examined the satisfaction of political needs placed on the public man. In the history plays the only fully successful public man whose career is dramatized is Henry V. Regardless of how one views him as a character in the *Henriad,* it must be admitted that he is a man who, for the sake of his political responsibilities, must deny all that is private and human. In *Coriolanus* Shakespeare explores the destruction of a man who is in pursuit of a totally autonomous self which is privately grounded in the public language of the state.[24] Shakespeare has come, as it were, to re-examine one of the persistent themes of the history plays in the mode of the great tragedies. Moreover, the structure of relations in *Coriolanus* and the force behind these relations are variations of a psychological and social configuration found in all of Shakespeare's work.

A model that describes the force and configurations of relations in Shakespeare's work differs from that which could be used to describe another drama in a later time. Roland Barthes, for instance, has suggested in *On Racine* that Freud's model of the primal horde is especially applicable to Racinian tragedy and perhaps to French Neoclassical drama as a whole.[25] There is evidence that this model might be applicable to Dryden's drama as well.[26] By contrast the primal horde is inapplicable to Shakespeare's work and quite possibly to Elizabethan and Jacobean drama and culture. As I have argued elsewhere, the primary network of relations in Shakespearean drama is based on fraternal rivalries.[27] While there is an oedipal pattern to these relations, since by definition the existence of a rival signals the oedipal element, the rivalry is not driven by incest fantasies but by preoedipal fantasies.[28] In the tragedies the issue is not incest even in *Hamlet, pace* Ernest Jones, but it is a configuration of psychological material involving fratricidal rivalries and maternal betrayal. *Othello, Lear, Caesar, Antony and Cleopatra, Hamlet,* and *Macbeth* all reflect different and complex versions of this configuration. The great psychological theme that runs through all of the plays and poems is betrayal, and the anger that accompanies displacement by a rival is the significant emotion. This configuration is clearly at the heart of the sonnets as well both in the relation between the poet, the dark lady, and the rival, and more interestingly between the poet and the young man with whom he identifies and to whom he offers mothering. It is the young man's betrayal which most shocks and pains the poet.29

In *Coriolanus* it is Volumnia who unwittingly betrays her son and makes him vulnerable to his rival Aufidius who is angry that he has been displaced by Coriolanus in the affections of the Volscian army. Coriolanus has already been displaced from Rome by the tribunes, and Volumnia's loyalty to the state, with whom she continues to identify, leads her to make her plea. Even at the approach of the women, Coriolanus struggles to repress his feelings, to drive out affection, and to will himself to obstinacy. Their bows and curtsies, however, touch him at his vulnerable point, and make him only too conscious of his emotional frailty and his childlike inferiority in the one relationship which he can neither ignore nor control: "My mother,/ As if Olympus to a molehill should/ In supplication nod" (V.iii.29-31). His fear of tender feelings forces him to wish for a posture the situation patently forbids: "I'll never/ Be such a gosling to obey instinct, but stand/ As if a man were author of himself/ And know no other kin (V.iii. 34-37). Volumnia, however, courts her son to emphasize the parent-child relationship, and she draws attention to her kneeling before him as an improper show of duty between a mother and a son. While the kneeling emphasizes the appearance of submission to authority, her words emphasize the true relationship: "Thou art my warrior;/ I holp to frame thee" (64-65). Despite his request to her not to bid, ask, tell, desire, or urge him to allay his revenge, she presents herself in the role of mediator between her son and her country. Her rhetorical strategy involves picturing herself as the one who has reared a warrior that now wars on her state. His attack is "fatal" to his mother, wife, and son, because they are caught between their feelings for him and their feelings for the state. As her speech progresses, however, she attributes a maternal quality to the state: "Alack, or we must lose/ The country, our dear nurse,/ or else thy person,/ Our comfort in the country" (ii.109-11). She then completes the identification by shifting from her role as mediator to a role as victim with Rome. She thus makes personal his attack on Rome: "Thou shalt no sooner/ March to assault thy country than to tread/ . . . on thy mother's womb/ That brought thee into this world" (ii.123-25). Like the other transformations in the play, the terms of her argument invert the traditional relationships between public and private. Consequently, what had been public, the war on Rome, is now the private assault on the mother. By the same token, what had been private, the conditions of a mother's love which require a warrior son's denial of anything feminine, is now public in the form of the mother's request for the extending of mercy toward Rome, an act which will bring honor and fame.

In effect her strategy places him in her position as mediator. He must now take on the burden of successful mediation between Roman and Volscian forces as the condition by which he continues to earn honor and in turn love. As Coriolanus tries to turn away one last time, Volumnia enforces her demand with the order: "Down, ladies! Let us shame him with our knees" (169). The threat of shame not only re-emphasizes the parent-child relationship, but stresses as well the threatened rebuke that he is failing to live up to her ideals of honor and *virtus* which are available now only in the new context of mercy, forgiveness, and inaction.

Coriolanus knows full well that he must capitulate to his mother, and that he must succumb to her contradictions. The burden of mediation is in fact a defeat for him and a victory for Rome, and by accepting this burden it is he, not Rome, who will be the victim of a sadistic rage:

> O my mother, mother! O!
> You have won a happy victory to Rome;
> But for your son—believe it, O believe it!—
> Most dangerously you have with him prevail'd,
> If not most mortal to him. (185-89)

Honor is now mercy. Honor is not to be earned in making true war but in framing convenient peace. Words have changed meaning, and to Coriolanus the radical change in the signification of words now that the context has changed threatens his life. Aufidius too sees the linguistic trap which ensnares Coriolanus and recognizes that if mercy now has the positive valence that honor had for Coriolanus, then the rival has become feminized by feelings of tenderness. Aufidius sees that Coriolanus is now vulnerable:

> (Aside) I am glad thou hast set thy mercy and thy honour
> At difference in thee. Out of that I'll work
> Myself a former fortune. (199-201)

Coriolanus has become the figure in which differences clash. In terms of the ideals and values to which his life was directed and by which he earned the name Coriolanus, he has become an empty name, a title with no present signification.

In the final scene of the play we see something of the poverty of the new world where rhetoric is power and language serves the politic man to gain a tarnished revenge. Aufidius destroys Coriolanus by stripping him of his Roman title and accusing him in public of

> Breaking his oath and resolution like
> A twist or rotten silk; never admitting
> A counsel o' th' war; but at his nurse's tears
> He whin'd and roar'd away your victory. . . .
> (V.vi.94-97)

The charge of treason is now familiar, since it is the same accusation the tribunes lodged against Coriolanus when he stood for the counselship. It is, of course, not simply the charge of treason but the epithet which follows ("thou boy of tears") which renders Coriolanus impotent with rage. He had always been vulnerable in his mouth, and now when he must not only defend his political actions, but also deny that he played boy to Volumnia's "mothering," he falls into an apoplexy.

To put the lie to Aufidius, Coriolanus can only insist on the public record, literally on history. In so doing he returns signification to his title and becomes, in the context of history, the hated enemy who earned the name "Coriolanus" by killing Volscian husbands, fathers, and sons. His is an outraged, helpless, self-destructive act of language:

> Cut me to pieces, Volces. Men and lads.
> Stain all your edges on me. Boy? False hound!
> If you have writ your annals true, 'tis there,
> That, like an eagle in a dovecote, I
> Flutter'd your Volscians in Corioles.
> Alone I did it. Boy? (V.vi.111-16)

His cry is answered by the mob crying, "Tear him to pieces," and the conspirators chanting, "Kill, kill, kill, kill, kill him!" In the instant of signification language turns to violence.

In this last scene the Volscians have done what the plebeians in Rome had wanted to do in the first scene of the play. They, like the plebeians, see Coriolanus as the cause of their anger, grief, and frustration. They differ from the plebeians, however, in that they are not projecting onto Coriolanus symbolic associations of maternal deprivation and patrician authority. Rather they see the literal relation between the man and the deeds he performed. Coriolanus is killed precisely at the moment when the words of the mob and the conspirators become the deed itself in the murder of the hero.

At the end of the play there are no heroes left, and Coriolanus has become history. I for one, however, feel neither release nor resolution in the ending. His death does not bring understanding or insight to the other characters, nor does it bring closure to the historical narrative. The structure of the historical narrative has become decentered with the death of Coriolanus; the boundaries separating ancient Rome from Jacobean England have become blurred.30 Unlike any of the other tragedies based on English or Roman history, there is here no historical period clearly defined by the emergence of a coherent political structure that can mark the center of a new historical narrative. The world we find at the end of *Coriolanus* is one in which the mob has become a political entity. There is less coherence in this world and little structure. In such a world, language does not mediate between thought and action, nor does language substitute for action, but rather language turns to violence in a crisis of meaning.31

NOTES

1 There have been several critics who have discussed language as a thematic concern in the play. Among the more fruitful studies are Carol M. Sicherman, *"Coriolanus:* The Failure of Words," *ELH,* 39 (1972), 189-207; James L. Calderwood, *"Coriolanus:* Wordless Meanings and Meaningless Words," *SEL,* 6 (1966), 211-24; Maurice Charney, *Shakespeare's Roman Plays: The Function of Imagery in the Drama* (Cambridge: Harvard Univ. Press, 1963), pp. 34-36, 176-96; Kenneth Burke, *"Coriolanus* and the Delights of Faction," *Hudson Review,* 19 (1966), 185-202.

2 Cf. Roland Barthes, *On Racine,* trans. Richard Howard (New York: Hill and Wang, 1964), pp. 57-59.

3 The choice of a center raises the critique Jacques Derrida has made of the

structuralist project in *L'Ectiture et La Différence* (Paris: Editions du Seuil, 1967); see especially "Force et Signification," pp. 9-49, and "Le Structure, le Signe et Jeu dans le Descours des Sciences Humaines," pp. 409-28. He argues that to choose a center is to impose a limit on the analysis. Derrida's critique is valid if the goal is to discover boundless signification. Context, however, proposes meaning and determines a center. Jonathan Culler has made the following point with regard to Derrida: "The analysis of cultural phenomena must always take place in some context, and at any one time the production of meaning in a culture is governed by conventions" *(Structuralist Poetics: Structuralism, Linguistics and the Study of Literature* [Ithaca: Cornell University Press, 1975], p. 249). "Le Structure, Le Signe et Jeu dans le Descours des Sciences Humaines" has been reprinted in *The Structuralist Controversy: the Languages of Criticism and the Science of Man,* ed. Richard Macksey and Eugenia Donato (Baltimore: The Johns Hopkins Univ. Press, 1972), pp. 247-64.

4 Sicherman, 198.

5 For a discussion of the sources see Geoffrey Bullough, *Narrative and Dramatic Sources of Shakespeare,* V (New York: Columbia Univ. Press, 1966), 453-95.

6 *The Boke Named the Gouernour,* ed. Foster Watson (New York: E. P. Dutton, 1926), p. 12.

7 G. R. Elton, *The Tudor Constitution: Documents and Commentary* (Cambridge: Cambridge Univ. Press, 1968), pp. 228-317. For a detailed study of the development of Parliament under Elizabeth, see J. E. Neale, *Elizabeth I and Her Parliaments,* 2 vols. (London: Jonathan Cape, 1953-57).

8 Williams M. Mitchell, *The Rise of the Revolutionary Party in the English House of Commons 1603-1629* (New York: Columbia Univ. Press, 1957), p. 36.

9 Cited in W. Gordon Zeeveld, " 'Coriolanus' and Jacobean Politics," *MLR,* 57 (1962), 321-34. Zeeveld is especially perceptive with regard to parliamentary echoes in *Coriolanus* although I disagree with his reading of the play. The quote is found on p. 327.

10 Zeeveld, p. 327.

11 Conrad Russell, *The Crisis of Parliaments: English History 1509-1660* (London: Oxford Univ. Press, 1971), p. 253. The disorder of speaking was a feature in later Elizabethan Parliaments as well. See Elton, pp. 245-52.

12 Elton, p. 230.

13 *The Elizabethan House of Commons* (New Haven: Yale Univ. Press, 1950), pp. 408-09.

14 E. C. Pettet, in "Coriolanus and the Midlands Insurrection of 1607," *Shakespeare Survey,* 3 (1950), 34-42, explains that Shakespeare changes the cause of citizen discontent from usurious practices to that of the price of corn because of the Midlands uprising of 1607.

15 All references to the text are to *The Complete Works of Shakespeare,* ed. Irving Ribner and George Lyman Kittredge (Waltham, Mass.: Ginn, 1971).

16 See J. L. Simmons, *"Antony and Cleopatra* and *Coriolanus,* Shakespeare's Heroic Tragedies: A Jacobean Adjustment," *Shakespeare Survey,* 26 (1973), 95-101.

17 Norman Rabkin in *Shakespeare and the Common Understanding* (New York: Free Press, 1967) writes, "Shakespeare offers us two alternatives, the idea of the state as unbending moral imperative and the idea of the state as a community organized for the benefit of its members. . . . Neither of these notions of the state will work" (p. 139).

18 The question how do we judge and whom do we believe in this play has been discussed by Dean Frye, "Commentary in Shakespeare: The Case of *Coriolanus,"*

Shakespeare Studies, 1 (1964), 105-17, and Clifford Davidson, *"Coriolanus:* A Study in Political Dislocation," *Shakespeare Studies,* 4 (1969), 263-74.

19 Ruth Nevo, in *Tragic Form in Shakespeare* (Princeton: Princeton Univ. Press, 1972), pp. 364-68, discusses the deflection of feeling in terms of the taboo on tenderness. She draws on Ian Suttie's *The Origins of Love and Hate* (London: Kegan Paul, 1939) for the concept of a taboo on tenderness.

20 Cited in Joel Hustfield, *Freedom, Corruption and Government in Elizabethan England* (London: Jonathan Cape, 1973), p. 41.

21 D. J. Gordon, "Name and Fame: Shakespeare's *Coriolanus," Papers Mainly Shakespearian,* ed. G. I. Duthie (Edinburgh: Oliver and Boyd, 1964), pp. 42-43.

22 Gordon, p. 50.

23 Calderwood, p. 212; H. H. Oliver, "Coriolanus as Tragic Hero," *SQ,* 10 (1959), 58.

24 Cyrus Hoy, "Jacobean Tragedy and the Mannerist Style," *Shakespeare Survey,* 26 (1973), 61.

25 *On Racine,* pp. 8-17.

26 David Tarbet, "By Reason Dazzled: Perspective and Language in Dryden's *Aureng-Zebe," Criticism,* 18 (1976), 256-72.

27 "Shakespeare's Cain in Eden: Fraternal Rivalry and Maternal Denial in Shakespeare," read at the Symposium on the Tradition of Biblical Brothers, Detroit, 1975. An expanded version of this paper is being readied for publication.

28 In the comedies and romances the desire is to drive out the rival brother and possess the nurturant—not the sexual—mother. The wish to enjoy love in the form of tenderness and nurture is countered by the anger at being supplanted by the rival and hence betrayed by the mother. One of the fantasies frequently employed to ward off such separation and resolve the rivalry is that of becoming one's own mother. In several of the comedies and romances, for instance, a fraternal rival has supplanted a brother and the comedic resolution turns on the re-establishment of a social hierarchy based on a paternal order. This brother, who was once betrayed, assumes not only paternal authority but also maternal qualities of nurture, forgiveness, and love. Prospero, Orlando, and Duke Senior are obvious cases in point. Professor Jim Swan has kindly allowed me to read his forthcoming article on *As You Like It* in which he discusses the pregenital material in that play. For a discussion of fraternal rivalry accompanying pregenital concerns in *The Winter's Tale,* see Murray M. Schwartz, "Leontes' Jealousy in *The Winter's Tale," American Imago,* 30 (1973), 250-73, and his *"The Winter's Tale:* Loss and Transformation," *American Imago,* 32 (1975), 145-99.

29 I am indebted to my colleague Professor Arthur Marotti for this insight on the sonnets.

30 For a discussion of decentering, see Derrida's essay in *The Structuralist Controversy.*

31 The research and writing of this article were aided by a Summer Research Grant from Wayne State University.

The Democritean Universe In Webster's
The White Devil

Norma Kroll

Ha, Ha, ô *Democritus* thy Gods
That governe the whole world![1]

The allusion to Democritus in the opening lines of John Webster's *White Devil,* like much else in the play, has long puzzled his critics; yet it provides us with the cornerstone of his aesthetic theory and practice.[2] Attempts to deal critically with Webster's drama have failed principally because of a predisposition to search for structural unity in terms of Christian humanism. But in Christian or even anti-Christian terms none of the events and characters are consistent. Once we realize that the philosophy of Democritus serves as Webster's unifying principle, however, we have the key to resolving the apparent paradoxes in the play. Basing his metaphors on Democritean materialism, Webster creates a universe where events are caused, not by cosmic intention, but by an indifferent chain of random action and reaction. Thus Webster's imagery reflects a vision of human behavior motivated neither by ethical precept nor enlightened self-interest, but by an inherent, irrational tendency toward self-destruction.

I

In effect, *The White Devil* derives its life and art from a world view shaped about five centuries before Christ. Although this view had been obscured for about twenty-two centuries by prevailing belief in a rational God and ordered cosmos, Democritus' physical theories had been adopted by Epicurus (341-270 BC) as the material basis of his ethical philosophy. During the Latin Middle Ages, these Democritean principles were preserved in manuscripts of *De Rerum Natura,* Lucretius' synthesis of Epicurean thought. Medieval scholars occasionally studied

Lucretius, but solely for his poetry; his atomistic, materialistic theories were either ignored or refuted. Not until the Renaissance did good editions of Lucretius become generally available, but even then, discussions of his philosophic principles consisted largely of attempts to disprove them.3 Montaigne, for example, quoted and discussed Lucretius' Epicurean system only to deride its basic concepts.4 Yet, Montaigne might well have sparked Webster's imagination and sent him to seek further, for Webster borrowed widely from the *Essays,* although they do not treat atomism fully or accurately enough for us to consider them Webster's only source.5 As it happens, Webster's careful use of Epicurean-Democritean physics suggests that he derived the philosophy of his play either from an accurate account of Lucretius or from the *De Rerum Natura* itself. In fact, the elemental stuff of literature, the letters of the alphabet, provided Lucretius with an apt analogy for his basic vital substance, the atoms. Just as a limited number of letters could be artificially combined into innumerable words, so a limited number of elemental atomic forms could combine and recombine into an apparently infinite number of natural forms.6 The crucial principle for both organic and architectonic constructs is that of arrangement.

We need but look at the imagery of the play's opening lines to discover how aptly the Democritean principle of creation applies to the way Webster worked:

Lod.   Banisht!
Anto. It greev'd me much to heare the sentence.
Lod.   Ha, Ha, ô *Democritus* thy Gods
         That governe the whole world!   Courtly reward
         And punishment. Fortun's a right whore.
         If she give ought, she deales it in smal percels,
         That she may take away all at one swope.
         This tis to have great enemies, God quite them:
         Your woolfe no longer seemes to be a woolfe
         Then when shees hungry.

Webster begins by having Lodovico invoke, with more truth than the bitterly mocking tone of the speech indicates, the "Gods" of Democritus. But Lodovico does not proclaim them to be the principles of reward and punishment or link them to the problem of justice, as is mistakenly done in Guevara's *Diall of Princes,* the probable source of the play's image.7 Instead, Webster makes the phrase, "Courtly reward and punishment," an unpredicated, strongly ironic exclamation implying that justice is just what these Democritean gods do not supply. Next, Lodovico indicates that Websterian Fortune works exactly as Democritean matter behaves, for he characterizes her as "a right whore," a commonplace which vividly evokes her precise function, random contact and combination. To this he adds the singular image of Fortune dealing out her infrequent gifts "in small percels"—in atoms, to be exact. But she can also "take away all at one swope."

In the world of the play, this falconry image of "one swope" anticipates all of Fortune's subsequent turnings and blows. It epitomizes Webster's intensification of Lucretius' principle of atomic swerve without which "no clashing . . . nor blow" of matter against matter would occur and "nature never would have produced aught."[8] Like a bird of prey, Websterian Fortune swoops down on her unsuspecting victims to kill as much by dint of impact as by the agonizing clasp of hooked beak and claws. Lodovico, moreover, insists on the capacity of even one such swoop to destroy all if it is struck with the force of "great enemies." Again, according to Lucretius, "what more can we suppose the infliction of a blow can do, than shake from their place and break up the union of the several elements."[9] Total disruption of a body's structure is death, in which, as Lucretius puts it, "nature dissolves everything back into its first bodies [atoms] and does not annihilate things"; these bodies then swerve downward through the void until they re-enter and feed other ongoing material processes.[10] Metaphorically, everything sooner or later becomes a kind of food for everything else, and only physical, not moral, significance can be attached to this fact in a Democritean universe. This principle is directly reflected in Lodovico's commonplace about the wolf, who shows her true nature only "when shees hungry."

The swoop and contact pattern that governs Webster's development of the play's imagery rules his reworking of the play's historical sources. For example, the real Brachiano died naturally; the real Francisco did not participate personally in any of the murders and was not killed as punishment for them.[11] In the play Webster not only increases the number and violence of the deaths—Brachiano is gruesomely murdered and Francisco is to be imprisoned, physically tortured, and killed—but he makes some kind of bodily contact the decisive cause of each, no matter what other destructive machinery is involved. Camillo's neck is not twisted and broken by his jump over the vaulting horse but by Flamineo's hand; Brachiano is not killed by the poisoned mask but must be strangled by Lodovico. In sum, Webster fashions his play's plot, characterization, and imagery according to a design determined by his use of Democritean physics.

II

In Montaigne's "Apologie of Raymond Sebond," Webster would have found highlighted not only the central principles of Democritean atomism but the Epicurean-Democritean structure of the universe as a whole and the dominant metaphor governing the world view of his play: "Even as the preheminence in beautie, which Platoe ascribeth unto the Sphericall figure, the Epicureans refer the same unto the Piramidall or Square; and say they cannot swallow a God made round like a bowle."[12] The "Piramidall" image serves as a version of the cone-shaped form created by the spiraling atomic movement basic to all matter and inherent in every aspect of Democritean and Websterian reality.

The metaphoric processes governing the world view of the play are epitomized in Victoria's prophetic dream (I.ii.220-45). To her, Brachiano is represented by the "goodly *Eu* Tree," a cone-bearing evergreen whose "large roote" draws nourishment from the church-yard ground and thus from the disintegrating matter of other bodies. So we are not surprised to find that the substance of Brachiano's relationship with Victoria depends on the deaths of his wife and her husband. For a single moment of vision, Victoria's dream focuses directly on the bare geometric bones underlying the four characters' destinies. As she "sat sadly leaning on a grave," she saw it "Checkered with crosse-sticks." These wooden crosses are the play's most ironic image. The cross is, after all, the consummate sign of Christianity. Here, however, it becomes the completed symbol of Democritean reality. We need but lean, sit somewhat aslant, as Victoria explicitly says she does, and contemplate the overlapping images from an oblique perspective to see that each marks off four cone-shaped or "Piramidall" forms—Montaigne's emblem of the Democritean gods. In this scene, a slanted cross becomes a kind of diagram of the four characters and their interaction: Victoria and Brachiano are congruent triangles directly opposed by Camillo and Isabella. Thus, Victoria's vision of the crosses is immediately displaced by Camillo and Isabella who, "with picax" and "Rusty spade" in hand, "challenge" Victoria over the *"Eu"* tree. It is a metaphoric challenge directed against Victoria's body but also involving Brachiano's: They threaten to bury her alive as soon as they empty out the "earths scattered bones," symbolically an attempt to substitute her body for theirs because she intends to replace the "withered blacke-thorne," her impotent husband Camillo, with the "well-growne Eu." In turn, the challengers themselves face opposition, in the form of a "whirlewind," the most dynamic of all possible images for Democritean activity. This whirlwind merges with the *"Eu"* tree, a symbolic merging of Victoria with Brachiano; the tree then "let fall a massy arme" upon Isabella and Camillo and "both were strucke dead by that sacred Eu/ In that base shallow grave that was their due," a symbolic anticipation of the juxtaposition of their murders in the two dumb shows. Metaphorically as well as thematically, Webster shapes his characters' fates and the ways they inter- and counter-act according to the dynamic workings of this spiraling or cone-shaped image.

Perhaps because Webster was aware of the difficulties his audience would have in accepting the full significance of his radical departure from the conventional Ptolemaic order, he deliberately pits characters who put their trust in the symbolic or ritual efficacy of circles against the whirling, spiraling forces of reality. Thus, when Isabella invokes the "preservative Circle" to protect her way of life, the attempt is futile (II.i.14-18). Ironically, Brachiano's subsequent invocation of a circle succeeds, but only because his vow, "never" again to "lye with her—by this,/ This wedding-ring," inverts the traditional function of the ring as a Christian symbol of eternal harmony and union (II.i.197-98). His oath is potent enough, in fact, to compel the unwilling Isabella to reverse her position and repeat his words: "Hence-forth I'le never lye with you, by this,/ This wedding-ring" (II.i.256-57).

Not the circle but the whirl governs Isabella's life. Accordingly, the image of an "amorous whirlewind," ironically describing her trip to Rome to find Brachiano, manifests actual reality; imagery of circles, although reflecting the dominant world view held in the thought and literature of Webster's time, embodies only the illusory beliefs of the fearful, the naive, and the weak in the world of *The White Devil.* Webster clearly cannot accept the idea of a universe, a god, the times, or the beautiful as having a spherical form. Thus, he not only differs philosophically from Montaigne, but philosophically and aesthetically from his contemporaries. They were generally familiar with Lucretius, Epicurus, and Democritus, but refused what Webster fully accepted—Lucretius' supposed "atheism," his philosophic materialism and correlative denial of divine creation and providence.13 It is the nonrational physical universe, not a rational god, that informs the unique moral or, more precisely, amoral world of Webster's hero-'villains' and their victims.

III

We can see just how deeply Democritean atomism affected Webster's creative processes by investigating the image patterns in the play. These patterns fall into four interrelated and often overlapping categories—namely, human fortune, personality and behavior, integration, and disintegration—and each consists of a range of images embodying one aspect of what Webster sees as the symbolic significance of the human body. The ruling forces in Democritus' universe are inherent in matter, and in a play, matter is primarily a function of the characters' costumes, actions, and, particularly in *The White Devil,* their bodily substance and form. So, for example, the plethora of sexual imagery is not mere ribaldry, but a metaphoric manifestation of the corporeal Democritean world. For Flamineo, then, the essence of womanhood is embodied in his exclamation that, "Women are caught as you take Tortoises,/ Shee must bee turn'd on her backe" (IV.ii.153-55).

This concern with material form may be first examined in terms of the imagery Webster uses to describe the workings of fate or fortune. Perhaps the best example is a curious image of Camillo's impotence that has puzzled Webster's critics and can only be explained satisfactorily in terms of the world view of the play. As Victoria's husband, Camillo is in the precarious position of an "Irish gamster that will play himselfe naked, and then wage all downeward, at hazard" (I.ii.29-30). In a Democritean universe, once a body is stripped of its defenses, it becomes wholly vulnerable to every disintegrating blow, and, like all atomic particles by virtue of their weight, it is then forfeited downward according to chance.14 As the use of the reflexive, "play himselfe naked," indicates, Camillo is the cause of his own bad fortune, primarily because he is "So un-able to please a woman that like a dutch doublet all his backe is shrunke into his breeches" (I.ii.31-32). Camillo's body is not sexually congruent with any woman's, let alone Victoria's. Thus, his relationship with her generates the kinds of fateful effects we usually attribute to solely extrinsic, natural forces: Whenever they "lay together," "Their grew a flaw between" them (I.ii.55-56). The word "flaw" then denoted a breach or rift as well as a sudden violent squall of wind, and both meanings are pertinent here. As Lucretius explains, speaking of physical matter, "bodies are in many ways mutually hostile and poisonous; and therefore they will either perish when they have met, or will fly asunder just as we see, when a storm has gathered, lightnings and rains and winds fly asunder."15 Camillo and Victoria show precisely this kind of mutual hostility. Although their marriage is religiously and morally sanctioned, their bodies are materially and formally antagonistic. They touch, but only to recoil, a reaction having the force of a localized but driving storm, creating a gap between them, and ultimately sending Camillo off to his death. Thus, for Webster, Camillo's body is equivalent to his fate.

The image patterns in the second category embody Webster's use of Democritean physics as the basis for his characters' personality and behavior. Images of venereal disease, of whores and cuckolds, and even of candlesticks and tilting staffs function causally, not just in the psychology of physical confrontations, but also in that of every dimension of human experience. In the spiritual realm, for example, a sexual image—his "flax soone kindles, soone is out againe" (IV.i.44)—aptly characterizes Cardinal Monticelso. Because his body somehow lacks enduring strength and integrity, Monticelso can at one moment be so intent on revenge that he would willingly "stake a brother's life" (II.i.386-88) and, at the next, forget that revenge in order to realize his desire to be Pope. Thus, his disappearance from the play, with his conflict left wholly unresolved, is not due to Webster's carelessness with structure, but to the careful fusion of structure and character.16

Since people's minds and bodies are, in essence, atomic, people move as Lucretius repeatedly maintains atoms and, consequently, men must do; they swerve obliquely toward each other and touch. Webster deftly delineates this swerving and touching in the imagery of Brachiano's adulterous pursuit of Victoria: Like "an earnest bowler/ Hee very passionatelie leanes that way,/ He should have his boule run" (I.ii.63-64). English bowls do not roll in a straight line, but swerve. Webster also extends the metaphor to reflect the fundamental fact that a body's inner structure determines its course; thus, he identifies Brachiano's "cheeke" with the bowl's "most excellent Bias" or inwardly weighted side which shapes its curving path. Ultimately, of course, the bowl "would faine/ Jump with" the "mistris." Mistress is the game's technical term for the small white ball at which the bowls are aimed, a fitting image for Victoria as the *White Devil* toward whom all courses converge.

In the third category, the image patterns highlight the nature of man's social and sexual integration with others. The underlying processes are again based in Lucretian materialism. When physically congruent, atoms or men can become entangled and join to form larger, more complex structures, as we see in the symbolic encounter between Lodovico and Flamineo. The two come into conjunction solely because of the shape shifting images of Flamineo's pretended madness: "Would I had rotted in some Surgeons house at Venice" and "In this a Politician imitates the devill, as the devill imitates a Canon. Wheresoever he comes to doe mischiefe, he comes with his backside towardes you." These seemingly incoherent but actually Democritean images of changes in Flamineo's body make possible his and Lodovico's otherwise incomprehensible decision to "joyne housekeeping," a relationship paradoxically described as "unsociably sociable." This agreement between the two becomes understandable only when we realize that, for them, "sociable" means physically congruent for just so long as they are both legally obstructed from pursuing their proper courses and thus stand together at the point of despair, and that "unsociably" refers to the inherent opposition of their respective courses, were they free to pursue them. Webster highlights the paradoxical nature of their union in an extended series of singularly cryptic images:

Lod. Sit some three daies together, and discourse.
Fla. Onely with making faces; lie in our clothes.
Lod. With faggots for our pillowes.   *Fla.* And bee lowsie.
Lod. In taffeta lininges; . . . .

(III.iii.74-77)

In this stychomythic duel, the two oppose each other not by repetition and antithesis but by building and completing a congruent image out of essentially antithetical lines.

As we should expect, their congruence is but momentary; it turns to collision and recoil the instant Lodovico receives his pardon and laughs, thereby changing his form. Flamineo objects to the laughter: "There was no such condition in our covenant." According to him, if one "will be merry," he must be so "i'th like [melancholy] posture, as if some great man/ Sate while his enemy were executed" (III.iii.100-02). Consequently, Lodovico does "breake," both in the conventional sense of being bankrupt, here, lacking the proper form of a fellow's face and in the Democritean sense of violating proper form and bringing about a violent physical division. Flamineo then strikes Lodovico, causing the immediate disintegration of their relationship and the delayed wholesale disintegration brought about by Lodovico's counterblows in the fifth act. Fittingly, Lodovico warns Flamineo that he "had bene as good met with his fist a thunderbolt" (III.iii.125), perhaps the very "thunder" Flamineo himself calls to "strike lowde to" his "farewell" to life in the play's final scene (V.vi.276).

The fourth category consists of image patterns of death, ultimate disintegration in Democritean terms. Since the main thrust of the play's plot and characterization, like that of all Democritean matter, moves toward such destruction, these patterns are also more pervasive and still more explicitly Democritean than imagery of integrity and integration. Webster has Flamineo openly proclaim the materialist doctrine of death as total disintegration of the body's structure, even as he mocks traditional beliefs in an afterlife and integrates the conventional elements of the four humors theory with the many kinds of atoms described in Democritean physics:

> Whither shall I go now? O *Lucian* thy ridiculous
> Purgatory—to finde *Alexander* the great cobling shooes,
> *Pompey* tagging points, and *Julius Caesar* making haire
> buttons, *Haniball* selling blacking, and *Augustus* cry-
> ing garlike, *Charlemaigne* selling lists by the dozen. . . .
> Whether I resolve to Fire, Earth, water, Aire,
> Or all the Elements by scruples; I know not
> Nor greatly care,—Shoote, shoote,
> Of all deaths the violent death is best,
> For from our selves it steales our selves so fast,
>   (V.vi.108-18)

Image patterns reflecting the various forms of bodily disintegration into elemental matter characterize each of the play's
many conflicts. Throughout we have imagery of spiraling pre-
dators such as the "yong hawkes" that "fetch a course about" as
their "game flies faire" before them (II.i.47-48). The Democritean influence is perhaps most explicit in Brachiano's stormy
threat against Victoria: "Udsdeath, Ile cut her into Atomies/
And let th'irregular Northe-winde sweepe her up/ And blow her
int' his nosthrils (IV.ii.43-45).17 Thus every character must
face the possibility of enjoying "that miserable curtesie of
Polyphemus to *Ulisses*," of being "reserve[d]" by someone "to be
devour'd last," and of having "turves" dug from one's "grave to
feed" an enemy's "Larkes" (IV.ii.65-67). Clearly, at moments
of greatest tension, the Democritean forces shaping the world
of the play surge closest to the surface of the characters' consciousness. Thus, Webster's imagery embodies the essence of
Democritean action within each succeeding event, intensifying
the significance of each in relation to the whole.

IV

As I pointed out in discussing Webster's imagery, the material and formal nature of each character's body defines and mod-
ulates his personal and "moral" qualities. In the rubrics, for
example, Webster deliberately characterizes Lodovico as "decay'd." This designation is true both of Lodovico's bodily state
and his character as a whole. More truly than they realize, his
two companions metaphorically equate the dissolution of his
fortune and the downward course of his position in the world
with that of his body. He ruined the "noblest Earldome" by making himself food for his followers, who "swallowed" him "like
Mummia"—the ground-up, almost atomized, matter of a dead
body. In addition, he wasted "two faire Manors" for the sake of
"Caviare." Against this background, Webster stresses that it is
as if Lodovico's nature were "begotten in an Earthquake," when
according to Lucretius, the earth itself is eaten away from within and everything, the ground and whatever stands in the vicinity,
is resolved back into its elemental parts.18

Because such cataclysmic processes also dominate the whole
world of the play, Lodovico's bitter praise of Democritean reality
not only opens the drama but closes it. Except for Giovanni's

command to clear away the dead bodies, the play ends with
Lodovico's exaltation of bodily disintegration:

> . . . I do glory yet,
> That I can call this act mine owne: For my part,
> the racke, the gallowes, and the torturing wheele
> Shall bee but sound sleepes to me, here's my rest—
> "I limb'd this night-peece and it was my best.
>   (V.vi.295-99)

This last act is undeniably Lodovico's. He commits three of the
four murders with his own hands and achieves the only kind of
inner peace he can know. Ironically, he finds "rest" in the agonizing disintegration and reduction of his body back into its in-
sentient elements. The word "limb'd" functions as a bitter pun,
for it signifies both to sketch or draw in and to dismember, and
what is still more terrible, it applies not only to Lodovico's
person but to "this night-peece," to the whole world envisioned
in the play.

Webster characterizes Flamineo as both Lodovico's counterpart and his antithesis. Flamineo functions amorally as both a
tool-villain and a close agent of touch and the whirl. Yet his
course directly opposes Lodovico's because, like the flames
symbolically suggested in his name, Flamineo aspires upward.
It is in this difference in their directions that we find the respective meaning and value of their lives within the scope of Websterian morality. Flamineo's way generates the play's positive life
processes, for, in moving upward, he does not seek disintegration (although he just as inevitably causes it), but his own and
others' bodily integration. To serve his purpose, he pursues and
engages Zanche sexually (if less than steadfastly, since change-
ability is also an inherent attribute of his flame-like nature)
and offers to move "prompt/ As lightning" in his lord Brachiano's service and to bring his master into sexual conjunction
with his sister Victoria.

Flamineo differs from Lodovico in yet another vital way
because of his flame-like substance. In Democritean-Lucretian
physics, the small, spherical atoms of fire are closely akin if not
identical to those of mind.[19] Thus, he alone has a mind complex
and motile enough to speculate cynically on the manifold appearances of reality:

> Wee are ingag'd to mischiefe and must on.
> As Rivers to finde out the Ocean

Flow with crooke bendings beneath forced bankes,
Or as wee see to aspire some mountaines top,
The way ascends not straight, but Imitates
The suttle fouldings of a Winters snake,
So who knowes policy and her true aspect,
Shall finde her waies winding and indirect.

(I.ii.341-48)

This image serves both to herald Flamineo's upward course and to affirm the spiraling pattern linking the human, animal, and natural realms. The image is also highly ironic, although Flamineo perhaps chooses at this point to seem unaware of the irony, for the mountain and the snake reflect both his aspirations and their inevitable downward turn. If only because atoms have weight, all Democritean matter, including flame and lightning, ultimately falls. By the end of the play, the dying Flamineo openly acknowledges that to be "gonne" in death is to be "so neare the bottome" (V.vi.254-55), and that every man's essential upward and downward course, his life and death, are inseparably interwound, that from birth we "cease to dye by dying" (V.vi.253).

Because Flamineo's mind and body have identical flame-like qualities, he serves as a vehicle for introducing the central problem in any totally material conception of human nature—the crucial relationship between the atomic substance of the body and the atoms of the mind. In the conflict between Flamineo and Marcello that opens the third act, Webster rejects Lucretius' trust in the morally transforming power of human reason and instead tranforms the underlying physical principles into the moral center of his play.[20] For Webster, it is inconceivable that abstract reason can manifest right and truth when both mind and body are material substances; human wisdom depends on the material quality of both as well as on the material integrity of their relationship. Flamineo, whose "wit" is undeniably "close prisoner" with his body (both because he is under guard for Camillo's murder and because of his Democritean nature), possesses a far deeper and more intelligent grasp of reality than Marcello, who espouses a rational, moral approach. Thus, Flamineo argues that Marcello, too, follows a "great Duke," although as a soldier, and, without considering ethics, "feedest his victories" just "As witches do their serviceable spirits" with his own "prodigall bloud" (III.i.39-41). Flamineo knows that every man, willingly or not, participates physically and thus morally in the relative processes making up the unchanging sum of waxing and waning things. Marcello, however, responds only with a flat Epicurean *non sequitur:* "For love of vertue beare an honest heart,/ And stride over every polliticke respect,/ Which where they most advance they most infect" (III.i.60-63). In sum, Marcello's conventional moral attitudes dull whatever sensitivity to reality he might otherwise have developed and his behavior becomes more, rather than less, irrational. By the fifth act, he feels so morally outraged at his brother's doings that he strikes out bodily, violently kicking Zanche. With such cause, Flamineo finally wonders aloud whether their "mother plaid foule play" at Marcello's conception, a suspicion that, philosophically speaking, is justified: They are very different men, born literally of the same mother and begotten metaphorically by contradictory levels of the same philosophy. It is perhaps significant that this comment of Flamineo's mortally offends Marcello's rigid and humorless sense of morality and that, like "a boy, a foole," he challenges Flamineo to a duel. Flamineo merely takes the proferred sword and quietly runs his brother through with the almost philosophical objectivity of a man puncturing a stupid argument.

Webster resolves the play's moral, intellectual, and physical problems in his heroic characterization of Victoria, the "white divell" herself. As is always the case the question of guilt remains ambiguous, and, apparently by virtue of her being human, the crimes she stands accused of "are but faigned shadowes" of her "evels" (III.ii.150). Victoria's moral qualities depend wholly on the strength she marshals against her own ambiguities and her enemies' attacks, and her strength depends entirely on the physical integrity of her mind and her body. This she fully realizes, for she openly challenges Monticelso to do as he so passionately desires and destroy her integrity by the only means possible—by dividing her mind and body physically: "To the point!/ Find mee but guilty, sever head from body: Weele parte good frindes: I scorn to hould my life/ At yours or any mans intreaty, Sir" (III.ii.140-43).

Victoria's physical beauty, implicitly reflected in the sexually ambiguous jewel imagery of the first act, is matched exactly by the brilliance and hardness of her mind. Thus, she counters Monticelso's reluctantly admiring, "Well, well, such counterfet

Jewels/ Make trew ones oft suspected," with:

> . . . You are deceaved,
> For know that all your strickt-combined heads,
> Which strike against this mine of diamondes,
> Shall prove but glassen hammers, they shall breake—
> (III.ii.146-49)

Webster fashions a significant motif from jewel images because, according to Lucretius, jewels, particularly diamonds, "must consist of particles more hooked together, and be held in union because welded all through with branch-like elements. In this class first of all diamond stones stand in foremost line inured to despise blows."[21] Brachiano and Victoria, we must remember, begin their relationship with a mutual exchange of her "Jewell" for his "Jewell," a jewel which "she must weare," as Brachiano suggestively remarks and Flamineo approvingly repeats, "lower." By stressing the sexual ambiguity of the exchange, Webster indicates the singular structural coherence and consonance of their bodies and, consequently, of their relationship. Victoria and Brachiano alone form a union that possesses any enduring inner integrity. But only Victoria is to demonstrate the integrity characteristic of diamonds, despite her enemies' blow which separates her from Brachiano and reduces her to the ignominy of a house for adulterous women:

> It shal not be a house of convertites—
> My minde shall make it honester to mee
> Then the Popes Pallace, and more peaceable
> Then thy soule, though thou art a Cardinall—
> Know this, and let it somewhat raise your spight,
> Through darkenesse Diamonds spred their ritchest light.
> (III.ii.300-05)

Victoria's integrity makes a "house of convertites" a totally inappropriate setting for her; ironically, she is the only major character who does not experience a radical conversion. In fact, she emerges from her trial with her integrity not only intact but strengthened. Her diamond-like mind matches Flamineo's flame-like character in intelligence even as it enables her to surpass him in courage and strength. Flamineo uses his wit to change his shape in the face of opposition, not to maintain it. For example, in a quarrel with Brachiano, the rubrics tellingly explain that Flamineo *"retreats backwards before"* the angry Duke, exclaiming "I would not go before a Pollitique enemie with my

backe towards him, though there were behind mee a whirle-
poole" (IV.ii.70-71). This metaphoric shape-shifting involves
both his body and his mind:

> It may appeare to some ridiculous
> Thus to talke knave and madman; and sometimes
> Come in with a dried sentence, stuft with sage.
> But this allowes my varying of shapes,
> *Knaves do grow great by being great mens apes.*
>
> (IV.ii.242-46)

Unlike Victoria, who faces Brachiano like one of "two whirle-
windes" and who would not hesitate to cut him off "like a limbe
corrupted to an ulcer" or to return "all" his "giftes," Flamineo
must be continuously fueled, so to speak, by a greater person
whom he "apes," that is, whom he both imitates and is chained
to for sustenance.

Brachiano is greater than Flamineo not only in wealth and
position but, as the jewel imagery indicates, in bodily nature as
well. Like Victoria, therefore, Brachiano is able to sustain the
integrity of his mind and body against Monticelso's and Francisco's psychological blows. Yet, Brachiano is not diamond-like
and unlike Victoria he cannot maintain his integrity to the very
point of death. When poisoned, he withstands the forces of disintegration only long enough to celebrate Victoria's limitless
value in an eminently Democritean universe—"Where's this
good woman? had I infinite worlds/ They were too little for
thee." Then the venom so strongly touches his "braine and heart"
that he changes diametrically, raving with increasing inco-
herence about her lack of integrity, but reflecting the progressive
deterioration of his own (V.iii.13, 82-126).

Webster also uses Flamineo and Francisco as foils for Victoria's heroic qualities by dramatizing the moral, psychological,
and physical ramifications of their susceptibility to disintegration. For the two characters themselves, the problem is psychological. Francisco's mind is so stricken by the sight of his dead
sister Isabella that henceforth he becomes "nothing but her
grave," keeping "her blessed memorie,/ Longer then thousand
Epitaphs" (III.ii.350-52). He has suddenly become like Lodovico; his psyche is wholly permeated with disintegration. Similarly, Flamineo changes because of the piteous sight of his
mother Cornelia mourning Marcello's murder. Although Flamineo had killed his brother without a qualm, he now suffers

the inevitable reaction of his blow, albeit at one remove, and feels "a strange thing" which he "cannot give a name, without it bee/ Compassion" (V.iv.107-09). The psychological change in Flamineo replaces his overriding reckless confidence with a wholly uncharacteristic, if just as reckless, fearfulness. He impulsively begins to worry about what Victoria, the inheriting Duchess, "meanes/ T' assigne" him for his "service," experiences a somewhat maudlin regret that he had "liv'd/ Riotously ill," and, most uncharacteristically of all, admits to having felt the undermining "mase of conscience in" his "brest" (V.iv.110-15).22 Flamineo not only loses his earlier daring and resiliency but, as we will see, becomes like Francisco, imbued with the same disintegrative force that characterized Lodovico from the first.

For Webster, the physical processes involved in Flaminco's and Francisco's disorders are still more crucial than the psychological. To stress their nature and importance, he makes singular use of the device of a Senecan ghost (used conventionally by other Jacobean dramatists to impart a sense of cosmic significance to an otherwise godless Machiavellian world) to display the physical basis for the workings of man's imaginative psychology. The physical processes which occur in Francisco and Flamineo are most vividly manifested in the latter. Perhaps because of the singularly protean quality of his flame-like nature, Flamineo perceives an unexpectedly bizarre ghost-like figure. He sees Brachiano's form dressed in *"his leather Cassock & breeche, bootes, a coule; [in his hand] a pot of lilly flowers with a scull in't,"* a ghost which actually *"throwes earth upon him and shewes him the scull."* This fantastic vision is as physically real as Francisco's vision of the dead Isabella. As Lucretius explains, when for some reason we strain our minds sufficiently, we "see centaurs and limbs of Scylla and Cerberus-like faces of dogs and idols of those who are dead . . . since idols [material films] of every kind are everywhere borne about, partly those which are spontaneously produced within the air, partly all those which withdraw from various things and those which are formed by compounding the shape of these. For assuredly no image of centaur is formed out of a live one, since no such nature of living creature ever existed; but when images of a horse and a man have by chance come together, they readily adhere at once . . . on account of their fine nature and thin texture."23 According to Lucretius' physics, the ghost-like but material form of Brachiano strikes bodily against Flamineo's eyes, penetrates to his brain, and further aggravates the disordered mind that called it forth. After this experience Flamineo is disturbed to such a degree that he, like Francisco, seeks only disintegration. He violently threatens his own suicide and Victoria's and Zanche's deaths. His state of mind is rightly identified by the two women, who think him mad, even though he is merely staging a mocking test of their loyalty to him.

Victoria, by contrast, is able to withstand the disintegrating effects of both psychological and physical blows. When facing Lodovico's knife in the last act, Victoria does not, as he expects, so "tremble" with "feare" that its force "should dissolve" her body "into ayre" or, more precisely, into invisible elemental particles. Instead, she proclaims that she is "too true a woman," one whom "Conceit can never kill" (V.vi.226-28). By accepting herself fully for what her bodily form and substance make her, Victoria achieves the highest degree of integrity possible in a Democritean world, and thereby reinspires courage in the despairing and regretful Flamineo, whose integrity was initially dissolved in fear for no more substantive cause than a sudden "Conceit." As Flamineo now commends her,

> . . . Th' art a noble sister,
> I love thee now; if woeman doe breed man,
> Shee ought to teach him manhood: Fare thee well.
> Know many glorious woeman that are fam'd
> For masculine vertue, have bin vitious,
> Onely a happier silence did betyde them.
> She hath no faults, who hath the art to hide them.
> (V.vi.241-47)

Paradoxically, Victoria's self acceptance makes her as much a man as a woman. In terms of a universal model for human nature, she manifests the play's ideal. She has become "Vittoria Corombona," victory crowned.

V

But Webster is not yet done with the spiraling turns of his plot, for Giovanni emerges in Act V to swoop down not only upon Lodovico but upon his own uncle Francisco. He unhesitatingly condemns both "to torture" and death and thus to the completion of the bodily disintegration they had so actively sought. The fact is that nothing can exist without the force of opposition, for the sum of things in a Democritean world is maintained neither through a Platonic plenitude of forms nor a Christian hierarchy of values but through the reciprocal interchange of force and counter-force. Thus, spiraling conflicts are not only inevitable but necessary for continuance.

Whether or not Webster structured Giovanni's character and behavior to imply that each succeeding generation swoops against its predecessor, Giovanni's characterization does reveal that spiraling opposition is essential and inevitable within the nature of things. Implicitly, we can expect him to be faced with such opposition in his turn. Giovanni thus functions from within the plot to extend the plot beyond itself, beyond the play. Webster's dramatic vision, like the play's structure, is significantly open-ended. The world of *The White Devil* imparts a sense of the infinite possibilities inherent in Democritus' conception of an infinite number of worlds whirling in a void.

NOTES

1 *The Complete Works of John Webster,* ed. F. L. Lucas (New York: Gordian Press, 1966), I, 111. Unless otherwise noted, subsequent quotations from *The White Devil* are taken from this edition.

2 Two strains are evident in Webster criticism: one analyzes his borrowings, the other his imagery. The former school maintains that Webster's sources influenced his work enough to prevent him from achieving anything but a loose and somewhat flawed chronicle structure; see Gunnar Boklund, *The Sources of The White Devil* (Cambridge, Mass.: Harvard University Press, 1957); E. E. Stoll, *John Webster* (Boston, 1905), pp. 119-32; and R. W. Dent, *John Webster's Borrowings* (Berkeley: University of California Press, 1960), pp. 6-12. The latter approach yields little more in terms of architectonic unity: Una Ellis-Fermer, *The Jacobean Drama* (New York: Vintage, 1964), concludes that the play's design is "referable to no canons of dramatic structure but his [Webster's] own" (p. 174) and yet confesses herself baffled by what that design might be (p. 4).

3 George Depue Hadzits, *Lucretius and His Influence* (New York: Longman's Green, 1935), pp. 203-47, 268-71.

4 See *The Essays of Montaigne, Done into English by John Florio, Anno 1603* (New York: AMS Press 1967), 3 vols. Montaigne explicitly states that he "cannot easily be perswaded, that Epicurus, Plato, or Pythagoras have sold us their Atomes, their Ideas, and their Numbers for ready payment. They were over wise to establish their articles of faith upon things so uncertaine and disputable" (II. 218).

5 For example, II, 259; Montaigne mockingly ignores the difference between the natural and the artificial and inquires, "If Atomes have by chance formed so many sorts of figures, why did they never meet together to frame a house, or

make a shooe? Why should we not likewise beleeve that an infinit number of Greek Letters confusedly scattred in some open place, might one day meet and joyne together to the contexture of th' Iliads?"

6 Lucretius, *On the Nature of Things,* tr. H.A.J. Munro (New York: Washington Square Press, 1965), p. 23.

7 Dent, p. 74. Dent also briefly discusses the proverbial and commonplace basis for Webster's images of the whore and the wolf.

8 Lucretius, p. 36.

9 Lucretius, p. 53.

10 Lucretius, p. 8.

11 Boklund, pp. 90, 115.

12 Montaigne, II, 183.

13 Hadzits, pp. 284-87. Even seventeenth-century scientists, beginning with Francis Bacon (1560/61-1626), gradually adopted and promulgated atomism but did not deny the idea of divine creation and providence.

14 Lucretius, pp. 35-36.

15 Lucretius, p. 20.

16 For another example of the way Webster made a seemingly extraneous bit of characterization integral to the architectonics of his play, we have his treatment of Victoria's Moorish maid Zanche who serves as a foil to Victoria. In the first and last acts, Zanche's blackness offers a contrast to Victoria's character as the "white devill," although in substance the two are nearly alike. As Zanche exclaims, "I have blood/ As red as either of theirs; wilt drinke some?/ 'Tis good for the falling sickness: I am proud/ Death cannot alter my complexion,/ For I shall neere looke pale" (V.vi.228-32).

17 Imagery of disintegrating blows also pervades the play. See, for example, I.ii.26-27; II.i.63-78; III.iii.125-32; and IV.ii.84.

18 Lucretius, p. 174.

19 Lucretius, pp. 64-65.

20 Lucretius is a disciple of both Democritus and Epicurus. From the perspective of Democritean physics and perhaps of his own observations, Lucretius maintains that "however much teaching renders some [men] equally refined, it yet leaves behind the earliest traces of the nature of each mind; and we are not to suppose that evil habits can be so thoroughly plucked up by the roots, that one man shall not be more prone than another to keen anger. . . ." From the viewpoint of Epicurean ethics, however, he argues that "traces of the different natures left behind, which reason is unable to expel from us, are so exceedingly slight that there is nothing to hinder us from living a life worthy of gods [a life totally divorced from all worldly concerns]" (p. 68).

21 Lucretius, p. 41.

22 Samuel M. Pratt ("Webster's The White Devil, V.iv.1.115," *Explicator*, 29, Item 11) provides evidence that the word "mase" may signify the weapon "mace." This possibility becomes still more interesting, and indicative of Webster's skill with language, if we keep in mind the fact that the word also means a winding, twisting way.

23 Lucretius, pp. 106-107.

Wives, Courtesans, and the Economics of Love in Jacobean City Comedy

Richard Horwich

Several writers of Jacobean city comedy[1] seem to have anticipated the 19th-century axiom that marriage and money are the only subjects worth writing about, for many of these plays deal with little else, and in such a way as to make the pursuit of love and the pursuit of wealth virtually indistinguishable from one another.

There is, of course, nothing startling about the coupling of love and money on the stage. Marriage-seekers in dramatic comedy have always sought wealth as well—the dowries of Glycerie in Terence's *The Woman of Andros,* of Millamant in Congreve's *The Way of the World,* and of Barbara Undershaft in Shaw's *Major Barbara,* for example, all figure prominently in the action of those plays, and are part of the conventions of the form. But the persistence with which certain Stuart playwrights dwelt upon economic theory and practice transcends those conventions, and makes their plays unique commentaries upon the economic life of the society which produced them.

It is not necessary to believe, as some scholars do, that such writers as Marston, Dekker, Heywood, Jonson, and Middleton intended to depict, or did in fact depict, anything so majestic as The Rise of Capitalism itself. We need only acknowledge that many of the participants in that vast and ponderous upheaval—substantial merchants, small shopkeepers, impoverished gentlemen, adventurers and entrepreneurs—are portrayed with some realism in city comedies, and almost nowhere else. And though Brian Gibbons is correct in maintaining that these works "do not present in any useful sense 'a keen analysis in economic terms' . . . of the actual conditions of the times,"[2] it is well to keep in mind the fact that, if the plays do not analyze economic conditions, they certainly display them, filled as they are with the sights and sounds of mercantile practice.

So much is generally agreed upon. What has not been as clearly recognized is that, in addition to dealing explicitly with the world of commerce (usually in the subplots), these plays also, albeit implicitly and metaphorically, concern themselves with economics in the main, or marriage plots as well; in fact, they employ the institution of marriage itself as a testing ground for many of the new economic ideas which were surfacing at the time. The marital relationship is often seen through an economic prism, so that human transactions, as well as mercantile ones, come to seem matters of debit and credit, profit and loss.

The potential for forming this connection has long existed, and still exists, embedded in the English language itself; certainly the discourse of our own time is, to use an economic metaphor, rich in economic metaphors. We "win" or "lose" at love; an eligible bachelor is a "prize," and a beautiful girl a "treasure"; popular psychologists tell us in newspaper columns that mature and well-adjusted love is the province of those who are capable of "giving" and "sharing." Matters differed little in the sixteenth and seventeenth centuries, to judge from the frequency with which figures of speech like "the riches of the soul" or "the goods of the mind" were employed by writers of expository prose. Indeed, for some moralists of the time, one's attitude toward love literally determined one's attitude toward money: "O let matrimoniall love bee as able to command liberality, as whorish and adulterous affections to procure prodigalitie,"[3] wrote the widely-read William Whateley.

It was probably Shakespeare, more than any other dramatist, who organized such metaphors into a coherent system of values and established them as a characteristic feature of Jacobean theater, from which the authors of city comedies could (and did) freely borrow. John Russell Brown, in an excellent treatment of the subject, has shown that Shakespeare conceived of love "as a kind of wealth." It was, for him, quite distinct from, and even opposed to, "the wealth of commerce," which is "controlled by gain and rights of possession"; the wealth of love, on the contrary, is associated with "giving, generously and of a free will."[4]

Thus, according to Brown, *The Taming of the Shrew* is really about generosity: Petruchio, far from being the fortune-hunter he appears at first, really wants a wife wealthy in spirit, not in substance; and in teaching Kate to give freely of herself, he demonstrates and articulates the basis of successful marriage as the play conceives it. *The Merchant of Venice* goes farther; in his willingness to "give and hazard all he hath,"[5] Bassanio voluntarily renounces the evils of economic calculation embodied in Shylock, as C. L. Barber implies by titling his account of the play "Transcending Reckoning at Belmont."[6] To risk everything for love is prodigal, and prodigality is usually thought of as an economic sin, less serious than avarice but more foolish. In love, however, wealth which can be reckoned, weighed, or calculated, is base and to be rejected, as Bassanio says:

> Look on beauty,
> And you shall see 'tis purchas'd by the weight,
> Which therein works a miracle in nature,
> Making them lightest that wear most of it.
> (III.ii.88-91)

As Antony proclaims to Cleopatra, "There's beggary in the love that can be reckon'd."[7] And it follows that a prodigal refusal to reckon in love leads to the only true wealth.

In the city comedies which are the subject of this paper, the economic aspects of human relationships were similarly investigated, and that investigation soon became associated with a particular structure: the plays are often organized around the contrast between licit and illicit love. During the first years of the seventeenth century it became increasingly common for playwrights to transform one of the traditional motifs of Plautine comedy, a young man's choice between *virgo* and *meretrix,* innocent maiden and wily courtesan, into a model of the economic pressures at work in Jacobean society as a whole. It is just such a contrast which animates hundreds of Tudor and Stuart domestic handbooks, marital treatises, and sermons; thus, when John Marston announced in the Argument to *The Dutch Courtesan* that "the difference betwixt the love of a courtesan and a wife is the full scope of the play,"[8] there was nothing in such a presentation to strike his audience as unfamiliar. Since the middle of the previous century, Englishmen had listened to a swelling chorus of indignant voices protesting the increase and commercialization of extramarital sexual conduct and the concomitant waning of public respect for marriage.

Most of these treatises were essentially amplifications of the official position of the Church of England, as recorded in the

Book of Homilies. Homily 11, *Against Whoredom and Adultery,*
makes a point of noting an increase in the practice of these vices
to the point where "among many it is counted no sin at all, but
rather a pastime, a dalliance, and but a touch of youth,"9 to
be laughed at rather than punished. Philip Stubbes, in *The
Anatomie of Abuses,* called attention to the rising number of
illegitimate children thus produced, and the changing attitude
toward them: ". . . until every one hath two or three bastards
a peece, they esteeme him no man,"10 he complained. And
Thomas Nashe, in *Christs Teares Ouer Ierusalem,* knew where
to lay the blame:

> It is a sinne that nowe serueth in London in steade of an
> after-noones recreation. It is a trade that heeretofore thriued in
> hugger-mugger, but of late dayes walketh openly by day light,
> like a substantiall Merchant. . . . Into the hart of the Citty is
> vncleannesse crept. Great Patrons it hath gotte: almost none are
> punisht for it that haue a good purse. Euery queane vaunts her-
> selfe of some or other man of Nobility.11

A dramatic representation of the distasteful ambience associated with sexual corruption is to be found in Shakespeare's
Measure for Measure, set in a Vienna whose sole industry is
prostitution, and whose citizens' sole preoccupation seems to be
a diseased, venal, joyless sensuality. The constant joking about
venereal disease, the almost Metaphysical hyperbole of the sexual metaphors ("Groping for trouts in a peculiar river,"12 e.g.),
Lucio's sniggering slanders of the Duke (". . . he could mouth
with a beggar, though she smelt brown bread and garlic"
[III.ii.171-72])—all underscore the squalor and degradation of
Vienna's sexuality, in contrast to the funnier and less acerbic
sexual joking of the more romantic plays. The Duke's ultimate
solution is to oppose this sorry state of affairs by decreeing marriage for everybody (including himself), whether they will or
no.

Thus, when Marston explained that *The Dutch Courtesan*
turns about the contrast between connubial and promiscuous
love, we may presume the existence of an audience interested
in the dramatic expression of a contemporary issue, expressed
in what had by the time become its traditional form. However,
the promiscuity of the passionate courtesan Franceschina and
the chastity of the modest Beatrice, fiancée of young Freevill,
have economic, as well as moral, implications. The sanctity of

the marriage bed is seen as being directly in opposition to the
hustle of the marketplace, and when, at the end of the play,
Freevill predictably renounces courtesan for wife, his actions
must be understood as signifying his renunciation of an unsavory
economic milieu as well.

Though the Argument suggests that the play's concern is
with sexual conduct, it is the economic corruption of London,
not its sensuality, which Freevill himself sees as the more profound. Condemning the ways of courtesans, he exclaims,

> —O justus justa justum! They sell their bodies;
> do not better men sell their souls? Nay, since all
> things have been sold—honor, justice, faith, nay,
> even God Himself—
> Ay me, what base ignobleness is it
> To sell the pleasure of a wanton bed?
> Why do men scrape, why heap to full heaps join?
> But for his mistress, who would care for coin?
>
> (I.i.118-24)

It is avarice which is at the root of this world's degeneracy, and
it is Franceschina's covetousness, rather than her lust, which
makes her, in Anthony Caputi's words, the play's "touch-stone
to moral character."13

The connection between these two concerns, sexual and
economic, is mirrored in the relationship between the main plot,
which concerns Freevill's eschewal of Franceschina and the
reformation of his friend Malheureux, and the subplot, which
is the play's repository of most of the direct satire of sharp
economic practices. The gulling of the cheating vintner Mulligrub by the witty knave Cocledemoy closely parallels the main
action in both plot and theme. Mulligrub, the economic hypocrite, is, as M. L. Wine points out, "a farcical version"14 of
Malheureux, the sexual hypocrite who preaches abstinence but
schemes to obtain Franceschina's favors. Mulligrub, too, professes honesty, while he and his wife cheat their customers, and,
after Cocledemoy has robbed *them*, Mistress Mulligrub com-
forts her husband by reminding him that making up the loss
"is but a week's cutting in the term"15 (II.iii.106-07). Water-
ing wine and selling a maidenhead over and over—Franceschina's particular specialty—are the same practice, the same
vice, and Freevill is correct in perceiving not merely cause and
effect between illicit sexuality and economic abuse, but identity.

Marriage to Beatrice represents, for him, an avenue of escape from the sordid world of thieves and confidence men. When he alludes to his impending nuptials as "the unfeigned embrace of sober ignorance" (V.i.72), he is referring to Beatrice's ignorance both of the consuming passions which drive Franceschina mad, and of the grasping and duplicitous world which the courtesan inhabits. Wit, cleverness, and sophistication are highly suspect qualities in this play, for they make possible the deceptions of Franceschina and Cocledemoy. Thus, wit becomes almost synonymous with thievery, and Beatrice's ignorance and simplicity function as the only possible guarantee that she is free of the corruption which surrounds her. Innocent though she may be, she understands well enough the sources of Freevill's attraction to her, and she constantly refers to her possession of these qualities:

> I cannot with a mistress' compliment,
> Forced discourses, or nice art of wit
> Give entertain to your dear wished presence;
> But safely thus, what hearty gratefulness,
> Unsullen silence, unaffected modesty,
> And an unignorant shamefastness can express,
> Receive as your protested due. . . .
> Oh, let not my secure simplicity
> Breed your mislike, as one quite void of skill. . . .
> Do not, then, sweet, wrong sober ignorance.
> (II.i.12-24)

In fact, Franceschina has none of the verbal wit which Beatrice presumes in her; most of her speech is nothing but rant. The guiding spirit of her trickery is the bawd Mary Faugh, who expounds with great facility throughout the play on the ease with which men may be duped. She is seen, ironically, not as a member of the underworld, but as a profitable and reputable businesswoman, as Cocledemoy explains:

> Her shop has the best ware . . . she sells divine
> virtues as virginity, modesty, and such rare gems,
> and those not like a petty chapman, by retail, but like
> a great merchant, by wholesale.   (I.ii.35-39)

This connection is Marston's satiric focus. Upon such metaphors, which equate moral attributes with products for sale and distribution, Marston builds the ethical substructure of his play, using the imagery of the shops, banks, markets, and exchanges of London as a device for commenting upon the lives and characters of men and women, and the ways in which they come together, much as Shakespeare did in some of his plays, as we have noted. But where Shakespeare's economic characters and vocabulary have a timeless and universal quality, Marston's are localized and particular: Shylock is more an incarnation of wealth's power to corrupt and destroy than a portrait of a contemporary usurer, but Cocledemoy must have seemed to Marston's audience a typical, almost a recognizable denizen of the London in which they lived, for all his affinities with the Vice of the medieval morality plays.

The use of economics as a metaphor for human interaction is almost as pronounced in the works of Thomas Dekker, particularly *1 The Honest Whore*. Like Marston, Dekker makes full use of the symbolic possibilities of courtesans. Bellafront, the play's title character, is, like Franceschina, a paradigm of economic corruption, as are her clients. She is perfectly adjusted to what she calls "the falling trade,"16 and delights in gulling her customers—not by promising them a maidenhead she no longer possesses, like Franceschina, but by feigning sensations and emotions she no longer feels.

Like *The Dutch Courtesan,* Dekker's play is structured around the contrast between the love of courtesans and that of wives, or at least wives-to-be; Infelice, the fiancée of Hippolito, is presented as the very archetype of that quality which is here most identified with marriage: fidelity. Marriage throughout the play is seen as the bond of constancy; whoredom thus comes to symbolize the randomness of things shared or held in common, like money or property. It is with commonness, in the literal sense, that Hippolito, a moralist masquerading as a frequenter of brothels, reproaches Bellafront:

> *Bell.* I am in bondes to no man syr.
> *Hip.*   Why then,
>   Y'are free for any man; if any, me.
>   But I must tell you Lady, were you mine,
>   You should be all mine: I could brooke no sharers,
>   I should be couetous, and sweepe vp all.
>   I should be pleasures usurer: faith I should.
>   (II.i.258-63)

Rather surprisingly, Bellafront agrees with his conception of her, and with his system of values; she laments the fact that she has never found a constant lover:

Had I but met with one kind gentleman,
That would haue purchacde sin alone, to himselfe,
For his owne priuate vse. . . .   (II.i.268-70)

And she determines to mend her ways by becoming "an honest
whore,/ In being true to one and to no more" (II.i.310-11).

As in *The Dutch Courtesan,* the metaphoric connection
between the worlds of marriage and of trade is used to criticize
the latter. Commonness is the property of money, which circu-
lates; the moral idealism of marriage has to do with the constancy it demands, and thus the two worlds cannot coexist. William Whateley, as we mentioned, distinguished between licit
and illicit love by identifying the former with liberality and the
latter with prodigality, but the love of a mistress according to
Hippolito is not prodigal, but covetous, even usurious; constancy is perverted into possessiveness. That is why Bellafront is
contemptuous of those who pay for her favors: they, like
usurers, covet her, but she foils them by denying them her feelings as they possess her body. She nevertheless concedes the
commercial aspects of the relationship, conceiving of herself as
a piece of property in search of a buyer, and it is this commer-
cialism which Hippolito most condemns.

When, finally, she decides to reform completely, it is only
natural that she should turn to marriage as an alternative to
whoring. But though marriage can rescue her from a life of
sexual corruption, it is clear from her imagery that she approaches it in the same businesslike spirit: ". . . for all your
wrongs/ Will you vouchsafe me but due recompence,/ To
marry with me?" (III.iii.113-15), she asks Matheo, her first
seducer. Again, at the end of the play, when she sues to the Duke
for redress of her grievance, she does so in economic terms:
"I had a fine iewell once, a very fine iewell and that naughty man
stoale it away from me, a very fine iewell" (V.ii.406-08), she
complains. Of course, the metaphor of maidenhead as jewel
is a traditional one, but it is clear that Bellafront is proposing
a financial arrangement, reimbursement for an injury, and that
her marriage is thus very different in spirit from that of Hippolito, who is simultaneously united with Infelice. Matheo is not in
love with Bellafront, and she herself is preoccupied not with her
husband but with the state of marriage itself, which, she supposes, will retroactively confer upon her the mantle of honesty.

As with the multiple marriages of Shakespearean comedy, these marriages may mean different things, and while Bellafront is not to be condemned (what choice has she, after all?), still, it is quite clear that whatever makes marriage practical and necessary is precisely what keeps it from being romantic in this play. That of Hippolito and Infelice *is* romantic; it is rooted in an idealism that detests all compromise, and in fact, Hippolito is one of the play's most unyielding characters, a man who insists that no whore is capable of reforming. But commerce, like other practical and worldly endeavors, thrives on compromise; indeed, the assumption upon which capitalism rests is that men can always strike some sort of bargain through mutual give and take. As Norman O. Brown says, "Christian mysticism and poetic mysticism have always protested against the economizing principle as a violation of Eros,"17 and Bellafront manifests, in her decision to wed Matheo, Brown's criteria for economic thinking: she is "abstract, impersonal, objective and quantitative"18 all at once. Although she undertakes it to be rehabilitated, Bellafront's is a worldly marriage, where Infelice's is not.

It is in the sequel, *2 The Honest Whore,* that the explicitly economic side of marriage is explored. Matheo, it turns out, is a prodigal who gambles away the household money, and Bellafront becomes a Patient Griselda, long-suffering but loyal. Even her father, the mysterious Orlando Friscobaldo, professes to hate her for her past life; in reality, however, he is arranging an elaborate test of the sincerity of her repentance. He becomes, in a sense, the author of the action, a force for moral stability as he passes, disguised, through a vicious and apparently chaotic world. The terms of his test are to reveal whether her need for money can force her to break her marriage vows and return to the lucrative life of a courtesan. To compound her misery and confusion, her tempter is Hippolito, who, by the force of his moral idealism converted her to honesty in Part One, but who now, inexplicably, attempts to seduce her by offering her money and jewels.

The ordeal which Bellafront undergoes, and the testing of the marital ethic itself, have little to do with lust; the temptations are entirely financial. Her deprivation is a penance for the decadent splendor of her former life, and she herself sees the poverty of her present state as proof of her moral reform:

> She that's a Whore,
> Liues gallant, fares well, is not (like me) poore.
> I ha now as small acquaintance with that sinne,
> As if I had neuer knowne it; that, neuer bin.[19]

Bellafront thus balances her moral books, wiping out her former luxury by her present want. By focusing upon the financial aspects of her earlier life, and not its sensuality, she ensures that a full redemption is possible for her; virginity may be irreplaceable, but if the sin is in living "gallant," it may be nicely adjusted by a salutary period of honest poverty. Finally, having served its purpose, calculation is replaced by a stoic, almost saintly acceptance of self-denial, and Bellafront at the last emerges as a kind of latter-day Mary Magdalene.[20] Like Marston's Freevill, she has found at last a way to escape the marketplace.

The success of *The Honest Whore* on the London stage established certain features of its action as conventions, which were repeated over and over in subsequent city comedies, often with no real logic or moral conviction. The frank and sometimes ranting speeches of Bellafront, her pride in gulling her clients, her self-loathing and subsequent desire to reform after hearing a sermon from an honest man, her conviction that marriage can make her honest and rehabilitate her socially, and, finally, her husband's realization that marrying a whore is really a blessing in disguise—all these motifs are common to many plays of the period. Not all originated with Dekker, but it was he who gave to them the shape which they retained for several years.

A convenient example of the cut-and-dried results of their employment (as well as of an author's tendency toward self-parody) is *Northward Ho* by Webster and Dekker himself. Doll, the mistress of Philip Bellamont but a practicing prostitute on the side, exhibits every one of the features mentioned above, until she finally marries a man who is at the end moved to accept her as his wife because "it's better to shoote in a Bow that has been shot in before."[21] But where these motifs were unified by both a moral and an intellectual logic in Dekker's earlier play, here they fail to cohere. Once having proclaimed her guilt and self-hatred, Doll never refers to them again, and the only sense in which her marriage makes her honest is that her husband, who is not her original seducer Bellamont but a stranger tricked into the match, reimburses her gulled clientele. Indeed, her marriage could easily be seen as a continuation of her original gullery, since she has, in effect, tricked one more unsuspecting suitor into supplying her material needs, but the play does not invite us to reach that conclusion; we are in no sense led to disapprove of her on the grounds that she has not renounced her earlier venality. Nor are we induced to treat the spectacle as comic, and to laugh at and applaud the wittiness of her deception; that sort of comedy, as we shall see, belongs almost exclusively to Middleton. Thus, *Northward Ho* is almost meaningless, a stringing together of conventional scenes with little to connect or support them except their own wooden rigidity.

A more interesting use of these preoccupations and motifs is to be found in Thomas Heywood's *1 The Fair Maid of the West,* in which the apotheosis of the maligned heroine is carried even farther than in *2 The Honest Whore.* The difference is that Bess Bridges, the title character of Heywood's play, is in fact not guilty of whoring, and the action of the play is devoted to an elaborate testing of Bess in order to demonstrate her honesty and the falseness of the charges made against her. Throughout, the tests put upon her are designed to determine whether or not she is covetous, though she has been accused only of sexual misconduct, and that only upon the presumptive evidence that she works in a tavern, and is thus exposed to temptation. So close is the connection between lust and acquisitiveness in this work that it depends entirely upon the unspoken assumption that freedom from one denotes freedom from the other.

Finally, Bess is proven honest by being subjected to various economic traps, all of which she easily evades. Spencer, whose love for her is clouded at first by his suspicions about her character, offers to let her keep a hundred pounds which she is holding for him; she refuses, countering with an offer of her own, which demonstrates, far from her venality, her great generosity:

> *Bess.* Is it coyne you want?
> Here is the hundred pound you gave me late,
> Vse that, beside what I have stor'd and sav'de
> Which makes it fifty more: were it ten thousand
> Nay, a whole million, *Spencer,* it were thine.[22]

As she resists assault after assault on her virginity, and as she continues to display her generous and open nature, her fame begins to spread; where, at the beginning of the play, she resembled somewhat the Bellafront of *2 The Honest Whore,* a Patient Griselda subjected to the scorn and calumny of the world, eventually, like Bellafront, she becomes a celebrated figure, a romantic and economic paragon. Believing Spencer dead, she wills her money to her needy servants and dedicates her life to his memory, saying, "I am resolv'd/ To be a patterne to all Maides hereafter/ Of constancy in love" (p. 305).

In her final test, Mullisheg, the King of Fez, offers her half his domain for her favors. When she refuses, he too marvels at her constancy, and identifies her virtue with that of another Bess, "The Virgin Queene so famous through the world" (p. 323). What distinguishes *The Fair Maid of the West,* then, from *The Honest Whore,* is the clear implication that it is only Bess' innocence that enables her to rise; were she in fact guilty of the charges leveled at her, no reform or rehabilitation would have been possible, since it is her virginity, strictly interpreted, which is being celebrated. Finally, for all the implicit identification of sexual and commercial conduct, Heywood's conception of virtue is not one which can be rendered in economic terms.

Such a morality, so expressed, has rather a sententious ring to it, which may explain why Dekker and Heywood are so little read now. In some of Middleton's works, however, we are dealing with another sort of play altogether: tough, clever comedies in which standards of morality are replaced by those of hedonistic pleasure and creative wit. Not by accident, the attitudes which his plays reflect are very different from those found in the works we have already studied. Middleton's courtesans are indeed courtesans, not innocent girls mistaken for fallen women, and they marry to be reclaimed, but these cheerful and mettlesome women are never reformed by marriage, only enriched, and remain throughout superior in every respect to the fools who marry them.

Thus, though romantic and idealistic marriages are made in Middleton's comedies, they are subordinated in interest and importance to the financial trickery and double-dealing which now occupy the main plot, and are themselves relegated to the subplot—exactly the reverse of *The Dutch Courtesan.* In *Your Five Gallants,* for example, the chaste and idealistic Katherine, seeking a husband, announces, "I shall sooner err through love than wealth,"[23] and systematically rejects all suitors who covet her fortune—but the main action has to do, as the title suggests, with the portrayal of various social and economic vices through the semi-allegorical figures who exemplify them: Frippery, the broker-gallant; Primero, the bawd-gallant; Goldstone, the cheating-gallant; Pursenet, the pocket-gallant; and Tailby, the whore-gallant.

This world of gulls and gullers is fraught with both acquisitiveness and inconstancy; the promiscuity of women and the passing of currency are its main preoccupations and, once again, are so closely related to each other as to amount to the same thing. As one of the gallants puts it, "Gold presents at dice/ Your harlot, in one hour won and lost trice;/ Every man has a fling at her" (II.iii.123-25). The harlots, however, in the persons of the three courtesans from whom Tailby, the whore-gallant, makes his living, are more attractive and less corrupt than the gallants; it is they who prevent Tailby from wooing Katherine. Where Bellafront was eager to marry her seducer, these courtesans at first refuse to be made "honest" by marriage; as one of them exclaims:

> Rather confine us to strict chastity,
> A mere impossible task, than to wed these,
> Whom we do loathe worse than the foul'st disease.
> (V.ii.65-67)

In *The Honest Whore,* the state of marriage itself is rehabilitative, and indeed its very strictures encourage Bellafront to mend her ways. Here, since the courtesans, corrupt though they profess themselves to be, are less so than their prospective husbands, the marital bonds can have no power to amend their lives, even if they wished it. When they finally consent, it is to a business partnership in which they clearly have the upper hand: ". . . when we have husbands we are under covert-baron, and may lie with whom we list" (V.ii.85-86), as one puts it. They are, like Bellafront, honest whores in the sense that they give full value for payment received to their customers, and that they know their place; they do not attempt to invade Katherine's world, and they prevent the gallants from doing so. But for all their honesty, they are still whores; marriage to them is seen as a form of disgrace, and their gallant-husbands are soon to be cuckolded, and thus brought to a fitting, if hardly poetic, justice.

Similarly, in *A Trick to Catch the Old One,* the question of moral redemption for the Courtesan (she has no name, only her title) is disposed of at the start: it is out of the question. Though Witgood blames her for his financial collapse, she is presented as a sympathetic victim, in contrast to the self-sufficient professionals of *Your Five Gallants,* and she defends herself creditably:

> *Witgood.*   My loathing! hast thou been the secret consumption of my purse, and now comest to undo my last means, my wits? wilt leave no virtue in me, and yet thou ne'er the better? Hence, courtesan, round-webb'd tarantula, That dry'st the roses in the cheeks of youth!
>
> *Courtesan.*   I've been true unto your pleasure; and all your lands Thrice rack'd was never worth the jewel which I prodigally gave you, my virginity: Lands mortgaged may return, and more esteem'd But honesty once pawn'd, is ne'er redeem'd.[24]

Thus she abjures Bellafront's easy equation of her lost virginity with stolen goods, for which restitution can be made. The Courtesan is here calling attention to the *difference* between sexual relationships and commercial ones; honesty is not like lands or money. Far from being avaricious, she is a prodigal, like Witgood, and sensuality has been her pleasure, not her trade. Nevertheless, it is tacitly assumed by all concerned, including herself, that Witgood will not and should not be expected to marry her. Her only redemption is to be material, after all, and it is brought about by cleverly tricking a nasty and unattractive, but rich, old man into wedlock.

Curiously, by the end of the play, she seems positively to revel in the pleasures of deception, as Middleton abruptly exchanges one set of conventions for another, and the audience is forced to shift its emotional gears if it wants to stay in the spirit of the play. Though the Courtesan argues that whores make the best wives ("She that knows sin, knows best how to hate sin" [V.ii.154]), Hoard accepts her not as a prize, but as a punishment. Having lived by craft himself, he is justly hoist with his own petard when he is maneuvered into marriage; he is past sixty, and she will, as she puts it with a craftsman's pride, "challenge the utmost power of any old man's love" (V.ii.146-47). However, Hoard's dismay upon discovering that he is married to a whore has nothing to do with her sexual proclivities or reputation, but only with the fact that she is not the wealthy widow she has represented herself to be. That she is penniless is what makes her Hoard's just desserts, a continuing reproach and scourge which he has merited by his own avarice and trickery.

It might reasonably be supposed that the attitudes encountered in the comedies of Ben Jonson should approximate those we have been discussing in Middleton's work, since Jonson's toughness and wittiness are of a piece with Middleton's own. In particular, Doll Common of *The Alchemist* seems a Middletonian character. Like the Courtesan in *A Trick to Catch the Old One* she is more actress than prostitute, a clever impersonator of noblewomen and other desirable commodities, and she is certainly a more attractive and sympathetic figure than Subtle or Face, her partners in crime, or, for the matter, than that "good dull innocent,"25 Dame Pliant, who ends up respectably married. But for Doll, unlike Middleton's courtesans, there is to be no recovery. She and Subtle will remain, together but unmarried, outside the world of moral and social legitimacy. Face, though he is sorry for her, never suggests that she find a rich husband, only a lucrative job with a madam of his acquaintance.

Thus, the sexual morality of this play, and others like it by Jonson, is quite conventional, approaching that of Heywood. Though we may enjoy Doll's wit, inventiveness, and good sense throughout, she never profits by them. What is more, the sin of tricking a man into marriage with a whore is so grave that no one, whatever his own corruption, deserves such a fate—as witness this exchange from *The Magnetic Lady,* in which the servile and dishonest Bias rejects Pleasance, whom he was on the point of marrying for profit, when he discovers she has borne an illegitimate child to another man:

> *Polish.*   Will you leave her then?
> *Bias.*   Yes, and the summe, twice told, ere take a wife,
>   To pick out Monsieur *Needles* basting threds.
> *Compass.*   Gossip, you are paid: though he be a fit nature,
>   Worthy to have a Whore justly put on him;
>   He is not bad enough to take your Daughter,
>   On such a cheat.26

So the unfortunate girl marries the pauper Needle, the two of them to subsist upon the charity of their betters for the rest of their lives.

In complete contrast is the brand of justice to be found in

Middleton's *A Mad World, My Masters,* in which Frank Gull-
man, subtlest and cleverest of all city comedy's courtesans, is
at last tricked herself into a marriage with Richard Follywit, a
bumbling amateur thief. Each has married the other under false
pretenses—she to being a virgin, he to being his uncle's heir.
The newlyweds are conceived as both a blessing to each other,
and a mutual penance for their sins: "Tricks are repaid, I see,"27
exclaims Follywit, echoing Hoard, and he is consoled at last
not by Frank's promise to reform, but by the prospect that his
uncle will make him his heir after all. "Tut, give me gold, it
makes amends for vice" (V.ii.267) is his expression of the play's
ethical vision. That their choice of each other seems more a kind
of poetic justice than the workings of mere chance is emphasized
by his uncle's remark at the conclusion: "Who lives by cunning,
mark it, his fate's cast;/ When he has gull'd all, then is himself
the last" (V.ii.271-72). The thrust of this speech seems a moral
one, but in fact clever deception is to be applauded throughout,
and we judge Follywit, as Standish Henning puts it, "by the
brilliance of his inventive tricks . . . rather than by the more
sober standards of right and wrong."28 The same is even more
true of Frank, and together she and Follywit exemplify to perfection what R. H. Tawney called the new spirit of "experiment and innovation"29 which was fast becoming characteristic of business dealing in the earlier seventeenth century.

This new spirit, as it is reflected and approbated in the city
comedies of Middleton, is largely what distinguishes his plays
from those of his contemporaries. He portrays a world in which
wit is prized above all else, no matter what sops are thrown to
conventional morality at the end. It follows that the romantic
ideal of marriage must be subordinated in these plays to one
which involves some form of competition; two people, each attempting to extract from marriage more than he or she puts into
it, embody the very essence of profit-seeking, and wit is as firmly
bound up with profit-seeking here as in the works of Marston or
Dekker. Thus marriage in Middleton's works becomes not an
alternative to or an escape from the predatory marketplace, but
a marketplace itself. The marriage of Hoard and his Courtesan,
of the five gallants and theirs, and of Frank and Follywit are all
characterized by a sort of regulated warfare which leaves little
room for affection or cooperation, not to speak of love, but much

for the operation of those wiles and deceptions which constitute the plays' appeal.

It may be said of them that they reflect the spirit of sexual promiscuity which Jacobean moralists abhorred with such vehemence and at such length, a spirit which made of sex an idle pastime and of marriage a joke. Yet these plays are, in this respect, very much in the great and ancient tradition of such comic writers as Aristophanes, Plautus, Ovid, Boccaccio, and Chaucer, who, though they usually celebrated the union of lovers at the conclusion, often treated marriage in an irreverent and cynical fashion.

By contrast, the plays of Dekker, Heywood, and Marston derive from a different tradition, for their spirit is not that of comedy; to begin with the presumption that wit and cleverness are to be judged and condemned in moral terms is destructive of the comic impulse, which invariably invokes some other mode of judgment—in Renaissance comedy, it is more often a matter of health replacing sickness, of truth and freedom overcoming delusion and bondage, of nature triumphing over artifice, than of good at war with evil. The forbears of Bellafront, in particular, are characters out of romance and domestic tragedy, and anticipate in spirit such sentimental eighteenth-century works as *The Fair Penitent* and *The Conscious Lovers*.

Admittedly, the plays studied here constitute a relatively small sample of the literally hundreds of English comedies written during the first quarter of the seventeenth century. Such masters as Chapman, Fletcher, and Massinger have not been mentioned, since courtesans do not figure with any prominence in their works. Still, the eleven plays we have examined seem sufficiently representative to suggest that economics provides to the form as a whole an important metaphor and a dominant concern. It is the theme of the economics of love, and the figures of the wives and courtesans in whose polar opposition that theme is embodied, which give to city comedy what uniqueness it possesses.

NOTES

1 That is, realistic comedies of London life, which made up the staple fare of the Jacobean stage.

2 *Jacobean City Comedy* (Cambridge, Mass.: Harvard Univ. Press, 1968), p. 29. Gibbons is refuting L. C. Knights.

3 *A Bride-Bush,* 2nd ed. (London, 1625), p. 184.

4 *Shakespeare and His Comedies,* rev. ed. (London: Methuen & Co., 1962), p. 50.

5 *The Merchant of Venice,* ed. J. R. Brown (Cambridge, Mass.: Harvard Univ. Press, 1959), II.ix.21.

6 *Shakespeare's Festive Comedy* (1959; rpt. Cleveland: Meridian Books, 1963), p. 174.

7 *Antony and Cleopatra,* ed. M. R. Ridley (Cambridge, Mass.: Harvard Univ. Press, 1954), I.i.15.

8 *The Dutch Courtesan,* ed. M. L. Wine (Lincoln, Neb.: Bison Books, 1965), p. 3. I have dealt with this play first, and not Dekker's *1 The Honest Whore,* which preceded it, because *The Dutch Courtesan* is a sort of encyclopedia of popular attitudes toward courtesans, to the point where it takes on, in R. K. Presson's words, "the pattern of a morality play" ("Marston's *Dutch Courtesan:* The Study of an Attitude in Adaptation," *JEGP,* 55 [1956], 407). For Dekker's influence on Marston, see Harry Keyishian, "Dekker's *Whore* and Marston's *Courtesan,*" *ELN,* 4 (June, 1967), 261-66.

9 *Sermons, or Homilies, Appointed to be Read in Churches in the Time of Queen Elizabeth, of Famous Memory* (New York, 1815), p. 98.

10 *The Anatomie of Abuses* (London, 1583), p. 96.

11 *Christs Teares ouer Ierusalem,* in *Works of Thomas Nashe,* ed. R. B. McKerrow, II (Oxford, Eng.: Sidgwick & Jackson, 1910), p. 148. First published in 1593.

12 *Measure for Measure,* ed. R. C. Bald (Baltimore: Penguin Books), I.ii.86.

13 *John Marston, Satirist* (Ithaca: Cornell Univ. Press, 1961), p. 227.

14 Introduction to *The Dutch Courtesan,* p. xxiii.

15 I.e., they will only have to dilute their wine for a week during the current term in order to make up their loss.

16 *The Honest Whore, Part One* in *The Dramatic Works of Thomas Dekker,* ed. Fredson Bowers, II (Cambridge, Eng.: Cambridge Univ. Press, 1965), II.i.30.

17 *Life Against Death: the Psychoanalytic Meaning of History* (Middletown, Conn.: Wesleyan Univ. Press, 1959), p. 257.

18 Ibid., p. 234.

19 *The Honest Whore, Part Two* in *Dramatic Works,* II (IV.i.58-61).

20 Fernando Henriques mentions several early Christian legends and hagiographies in which whores are not only reformed but apotheosized: "By some strange transformation," he writes, "the courtesan-temptress is transformed into the courtesan-saint . . . " (*Prostitution in Europe and the Americas* [New York: Grove Press, 1963], p. 74). An example of such a story is the tenth-century play *Paphnutius,* by Hroswitha of Gandersheim.

21 *Northward Ho,* in *Dramatic Works,* II (V.i.506).

22 *The Fair Maid of the West, Part One,* in *Dramatic Works of Thomas Heywood,* ed. R. H. Shepherd, II (London: John Pearson, 1874), 273.

23 *Your Five Gallants,* in *The Works of Thomas Middleton,* ed. A. H. Bullen, III (London: J. C. Nimmo, 1885), I.ii.50.

24 *A Trick to Catch the Old One* in *Works,* II (I.i.30-40).

25 *The Alchemist,* in *Works of Ben Jonson,* ed. C. H. Herford and Percy and Evelyn Simpson, V (Oxford, Eng.: The Clarendon Press, 1938), V.iv.67.

26 *The Magnetic Lady* in *Works,* VI (V.x.114-20).

27 *A Mad World, My Masters,* ed. Standish Henning (Lincoln, Neb.: Bison Books, 1965), V.ii.261.

28 Introduction to *A Mad World, My Masters,* p. xi.

29 "The Rise of the Gentry, 1558-1640," *EHR,* 11 (1941), 16.

The Changeling:
Notes on Mannerism in Dramatic Form

Raymond J. Pentzell

In the first act of *The Changeling* Beatrice-Joanna enters the stage a light-comic ingenue, as transparent and inconsequential as a spoiled Molière *fille,* and just as self-centered. Near the end of the fifth act she dies, guilty of murder and betrayal, her *amour-propre* having grown to fruition as a selfishness which grotesquely perverts her zeal for her own honor. She lies next to the catalyst of her ripening, the hideous De Flores, her lover and her murderer, now a suicide. Her death brings her as close as she ever comes to an *anagnorisis;* self-satisfaction ebbs from her enough that, finally, she can beg pathetically of her surviving victims, "Forgive me . . . all forgive."

No one does. Her father bemoans his own disgrace. Her traduced husband is attentive only to him, comforting him with the observation, "Justice hath so right/ The guilty hit, that innocence is quit/ By proclamation, and may joy again." Suddenly there is set in motion a finale which may be the most insane ever written for a play respected as a tragedy: when Alsemero, the aggrieved husband, begins to retail all the "changes" he has gone through, his catalogue of puns must surely have reminded the playgoers of 1622 no less than ourselves of the kind of drawn-out wordplay used in comedy as early as the prologue to Gascoigne's *Supposes.* Upon finishing his list, he calls, "Are there any more on's?" And up pops Antonio, a comedian from the subplot, who volunteers his "changes." He is followed in turn by other contributors out of the comic subplot, Franciscus, Isabella, and Alibius. Each patters out more "changes" until the "tragic" Alsemero regains his turn with a moralizing speech which slips promptly into rhymed couplets as the "epilogue." Music up. All bow. Exeunt.

There are two dead bodies left on stage. No provision has been made to carry them off. They have been lying there all through the punning changes rung on "change." Now what? Either they lie in place until the whole audience files out chuckling (a bit of the macabre worthy of *Monsieur Verdoux*), or else they also get up, bow, and walk off, no doubt reminding us of Leslie at the end of Behan's *The Hostage*.[1] Either way, our "tragedy" has ended in a double-take of grisly comedy. Nowhere in the canon of tragedy can there be found another example of such an ending.[2] This scene, in its preternatural absurdity, embodies none of the thematic ironies of, say, a Euripidean epilogue. Its ironies lie almost totally in the sharp clap of suddenly juxtaposed tones—juxtaposed, as it were, for the hell of it.

But if the irony of the finale is, strictly speaking, uninterpretable, it is neither meaningless nor unprepared-for. Its meaning lies in the fact that it *is* prepared for, the culmination of a structural pattern which has been at work throughout the play. Many critics have avoided trying to track down an overall structure in *The Changeling*, for to do so is to risk bringing discussion to a halt by admitting the play is a botch. Everyone's first indigestible question is this: What is the subplot, the madhouse farce, doing there?

At the outset we must chew on a paradox. *The Changeling* was written by two men, each writing in a manifestly different set of styles and each (most would say) possessing a different measure of talent. Modern critics typically think of the play as if it were written by Thomas Middleton "with additions by" William Rowley. Though the nucleus of the Beatrice-De Flores plot is Middleton's most obvious contribution and the farcical subplot Rowley's, it was Rowley who wrote the longish first scene and all or most of the final scene. However unmistakably different in style they are from Middleton's scenes, they are of course part of the main plot.[3]

We can imagine, perhaps, the two writers briefly discussing the subject of the play, outlining its progression only roughly, and then going off to separate garrets each to write his own assigned scenes in his own way, never to meet again until their manuscript pages were collated. But this notion will scarcely do. William Empson, M. C. Bradbrook, and Karl Holzknecht have plotted the many correspondences in imagery, situation, and phrasing between the two lines of action; even the most casual reader or spectator will notice the larger movements of this distorting-mirror game.4 The most likely hypothesis, then, has Rowley and Middleton working in rather close collaboration: checking up on each other periodically, discussing their plans and progress, and mutually assimilating their separate products *en route*. No other conjecture about their collaborative arrangement fits the evidence nearly so well.5

Then why did one man wield flexible, crackling dialogue to thrust his characters into scenes of mordant psychological irony while the other man dawdled his way around them: beginning a Fletcherian tragicomedy (largely in neat, old-fashioned verse at times reminiscent of Spenser and even Lyly); hacking together an unoriginal and difficult-to-follow farce which leads nowhere; constructing a formalized denouement which seems almost a prank?

This is our paradox, and even when (as here) we overstate it, it makes a good question. Unless we can find some sort of satisfactory answer, we will not only (in the good company of T. S. Eliot, Una Ellis-Fermor, and Robert Brustein) have to "ignore the silly subplot contributed by Rowley,"6 but also, and with greater difficulty, have to conquer our dizziness as we stand at the finale of the play looking back on what went before and trying to suppress an uncomfortable giggle.

Empson, noting parallels between the two stories, leads us to think of their relationship in terms of parody—the irony that comes of viewing the same basic action alternately as serious and funny. The first alternate (riding on the main plot) entails empathy: to the extent that we can regard Beatrice, De Flores, and Alsemero as creatures like ourselves, their version of the story will appear threatening and pitiful, or at least morbidly fascinating. The subplot provokes the second response, which assumes that we will feel superior to its characters in intelligence, or regard them as somehow unreal, or feel that the outcome of their intrigues will not cause them much harm (or all three attitudes together). For Empson the design of such a play lies in the "double view" of a dramatic action which is essentially single, a view made possible by an artfully closed system of figurative check and thematic balance which (like many forms of irony) allows the playwrights to become as hyperbolic as they wish in either direction without altogether losing the audience's trust in the play's ultimate "sensibleness"—its pertinence to reality as the audience is accustomed to perceiving it.

However helpful Empson's reading, his interpretation is not totally successful in accounting for the subplot's function. The madhouse story is just not similar enough in plot and character to the major plot for us to regard it merely as a comic version of the same action; it is certainly no *gracioso-graciosa* parody taking place belowstairs in a serious Spanish *comedia,* but a tale independent enough to go its own way. (Indeed, it wanders far enough afield that the authors evidently believed the developments necessary to resolve it on its own premises would have delayed unforgivably the climax of the main plot.) If Isabella suggests a Beatrice with better moral balance, it is not so clear whether her elderly husband Alibius can be matched parodically with either Vermandero or Alsemero. Likewise, the fool Lollio may buzz around her as De Flores around Beatrice, but the real threat of bloodshed comes ultimately from Antonio and Franciscus, who, as lovestruck outsiders, could logically be expected to correspond in their rivalry to Alsemero and Alonzo—whom Beatrice keeps from fighting. And the ongoing vaudeville relationship of Lollio with Alibius has no parallel in Vermandero's castle. Although the subplot develops comically some themes which appear also in the main action, and despite the ubiquitous re-echoes of imagery and situation, it is hard to believe that a spectator could feel he was witnessing the progression of an integral dramatic action on which he was invited to hold differing viewpoints in alternation. Further, if we look beyond simple parody for a more variegated system of irony arising from juxtaposed lines of action which coherently mirror a single theme, we will probably be equally disappointed. *The Changeling* behaves neither like *A Midsummer Night's Dream* nor like *I Henry IV,* still less like *Lear.* Even so thorough and sympathetic a reader as N. W. Bawcutt, the editor of the Revels edition of the play, finds "a very real difference in tone and intention between the two plots," and concludes that "The total effect of all these kinds of relationship between the two halves of the play is not easily assessed."[7]

Let us put aside for the moment our Empson-inspired concern with the play's characters, plots, and themes, and pick up as clues Bawcutt's words "tone" and "effect." Perhaps the determinant structure of *The Changeling* can be traced not so much in the order of meaning as in the stylistic flux itself. If so, this might suggest that an audience is more likely to "put the play together" (progressively in retrospect) through its organization of affective "tones" than through any counterpoint of plot or character. Metaphorically, we could imagine that the play's structure is more musical than architectonic, and musically post- rather than pre-Wagnerian.

"Tone," though one of the least precise of critical terms, denotes a most important aspect of style. It can be discussed generally only by way of a style's presumable effect on an audience, since it so often depends on a subtle pattern of stylistic predictability and unpredictability. To perceive any point of style (in dramatic structure no less than in dialogue) as predictable or unpredictable is to predicate a shared consciousness of what is and is not conventionally "appropriate" (plausible or familiar) in language and action. Normally, we call tone the effect of those stylistic "notes" or data (provided by author and actor alike) by which we judge *how* a dramatic action is to be regarded. "How we take" any single theatrical incident, of course, is hugely affected by whatever sense of satisfaction or surprise we can derive from its relation to a previous incident and from our recall of data we previously received. But *within* any single step in a dramatic action tone operates most obviously by causing us to locate our response somewhere on a broad continuum which ranges across many varieties of "funny" and "serious," the ultimate pole of seriousness comprising that "arousal of pity and terror" by which we signify our recognition of high tragedy. Often our very notion of "genre" is, at bottom, simply a recognition of general categories of tone. It is well known that any translator or any actor can, with a minimum of effort, make *Oedipus the King* hilarious.[8]

The tone of a scene can also place it for us on a different but not unrelated scale, that by which we perceive (through our relative "engagement" or "estrangement") a dramatic event as varying from "credible" to "artificial." The former defines the nearest we can come to ignoring our ever-present knowledge that the event and characters are fictitious; the latter, our most pronounced awareness of the playwright or actor as a conscious manipulator of words and actions.[9]

Examined in this light, *The Changeling* is a tonal thrill-show, a roller-coaster ride on hills of many heights and many angles of steepness. As our initial look at its final scene has made clear, far more is involved than the main-plot-serious/subplot-funny coefficient implied in the parody idea. We must notice at once that the Beatrice-De Flores plot, taken *in toto,* progresses on two distinct planes of reality. Surely Robert Brustein (echoing Eliot *et al.*) was not deluding himself when he praised it as "the closest thing to a realistic tragedy in the Stuart canon" and "the most subtle psychological tragedy in English outside of Shakespeare."10 The twisting development of the relationship between the two principals warms the cockles of any Freudian heart. Yet Robert Jordan is equally on the mark in demonstrating how the anecdote cleverly and consistently follows, while inverting, the normative incidents of a stereotypical courtly-love romance on a "Beauty and the Beast" pattern: surely a dimension that would have been promptly appreciated in the early seventeenth century and one that certainly must complicate the tone of even the "unified" central sections.11 We must see Middleton's "psychological tragedy" (as Shakespeare's Hermia says upon waking) "with parted eye."

Moreover, whatever psychological credibility Beatrice and De Flores ultimately have for us can hardly be said to emerge until II.i. Rowley's introduction of the characters of the main plot in I.i is handled unremittingly up near the "artificial" end of our tonal scale. The rather old-fashioned verse with its symmetrical turns of antithetical images (72-85, 119-29) and rhetorical or stanzaic "builds" (1-12, 66-72), the dance-like implied movement (139-57), and a technique of character-motivation that veers from bluntly explicit (6, 160-61) to totally veiled (112-18, 243-44) give the opening of the play an opaque sheen not at all promissory of "psychological tragedy." Indeed, it may be observed that the first farcical scene, I.ii, comes not as a sharp tonal shift but as a tonal narrowing: the notes of sexual punning and badinage running through I.i are here focused upon exclusively, picked up and carried further into a scene which is thereby structured like a vaudeville act.

Middleton himself, when he enters with Act II, does not blast the audience out of its seats with a "whole new play"; on the contrary, he preserves a couple of Rowley's stylistic hallmarks until De Flores opens his mouth to speak. Though we cannot mistake Middleton's own style in these opening speeches, the formality of Jasperino's "The joy I shall return rewards my service" and the reversion not only to Beatrice's "eyes vs. judgment" conceit but also to such verse construction as "A true deserver like a diamond sparkles,/ In darkness you may see him, that's in absence" (15-16) bespeak an intention to keep the tonal transition from becoming too abrupt. With De Flores, of course, there is no turning back stylistically, and the play moves to new levels of both credibility and seriousness. The "comic" and "tragic" halves of the play have completely separated.

Nevertheless, the new tone of "psychological realism" buoyed up by Middleton's taut, truncated verses does not by any means continue through the rest of the main plot, nor does the vaudevillian atmosphere persist at the madhouse. In preparation for her dreaded wedding night, Beatrice gets elbow-deep in potions right out of Jonson's *Alchemist*. Unless we frankly accept IV.i (Diaphanta used as guinea pig) as essentially farcical, we will never understand why Middleton chose "gaping," "sneezing," and "laughing" as the required "virginity" reactions; when Beatrice herself feigns them (IV.ii) she can resemble nothing so much as the gawking Antonio and the giggling Franciscus rolled into one. (Does "glass M" stand for "maidenhead," "murder," or "madness"?) Yet in the Diaphanta scene itself, any such ironic connections must appear remote; they show up superimposed on the straightforward funniness only when they become significant by Beatrice's *feigning*. Immediately following, in IV.iii, Rowley's subplot itself turns sour; the note of violence introduced in III.iii. 247-48 (when Isabella warns Lollio that unless he keeps silent she will have Antonio cut his throat) begins to infect the "farce" with explicit threat. Lollio grows ugly in his direct echoing (38) of De Flores (II.ii.61); Isabella reacts to abuse by an ostensibly prankish charade (106-39) that may hint as much at genuine hysteria (133, 139) as at revulsion; and before the scene ends a dual murder is plotted.

As late as 1622 that old warhorse of romance, the substitution-in-bed trick, could hardly have been taken as the stuff of realistic psychology. Yet not only is it planned (IV.i), Alsemero actually falls for it (V.i). To that extent, the brilliant character revelations in the latter scene (Beatrice: "I'm forced to love thee now,/ 'Cause thou provid'st so carefully for my honor," 47-48) take place against a background of pasteboard plotting conventions. The action becomes generally more pasteboard as Act V proceeds, though not always in ways we can identify as conventional. What is immediately necessary, of course, is that the mare's nest of plot be untangled in the portion that remains of a single act. In order to do so the authors often resort to a kind of dramaturgic shorthand, in which incident itself is detachable from expectations engendered by characterization and preceding events. In IV.ii Tomazo Piracquo saw eye-to-eye with his "honest De Flores"; in V.ii, without preparation, he remarks upon seeing the villain,

> Oh, the fellow that some call honest De Flores;
> But methinks honesty was hard bestead
> To come there for a lodging.   (9-11)

Finding simply "a contrariety in nature/ Betwixt that face and me" (12-13), he promptly strikes him, draws his sword, and is prevented from precipitate murder only by De Flores' equally precipitate attack of conscience, which causes the latter to back off:

> I cannot strike, I see his brother's wounds
> Fresh bleeding in his eye, as in a crystal. (32-33)

De Flores has already seen Alonzo's ghost glide past him twice, once in the dumbshow preceding Act IV and again just before the house-afire ruse in V.i, but even an outright ghost had not kept him from his villainy before. As with the Cardinal in *The Duchess of Malfi*, this sudden, illogical, and vivid burst of "conscience" functions chiefly as a signal to the audience that they should expect him to have no further successes. Both character-reversals in this scene (but particularly Tomazo's) are radical enough to remind one of Fletcher's techniques, whereby a desired twist of event or a theatrical "passion" takes complete precedence over any logic of human motivation and interrelation.12

Before V.ii has run its course Alibius, in company with his wife and Vermandero, arrives to reveal the presence in his madhouse of Antonio and Franciscus (on whom suspicion for Alonzo's murder falls), thus short-circuiting once and for all the subplot, which was just beginning to "thicken" when we last looked in on it. As V.iii begins, Jasperino and Alsemero come from spying on De Flores and Beatrice in the "garden"; Alsemero's once-allayed suspicions have been rekindled to the point at which they need only an admission of guilt to become certainties. We must leap over dramaturgic oddities here: we are not told exactly what De Flores was doing in this secret meeting occurring so soon after his attack of "conscience." More importantly, we must forego the presumable treat of watching Alsemero's *anagnorisis* actually take place on stage. One cannot imagine a playwright concerned chiefly with revealing and developing his characters declining to dramatize such a spying-scene. But we have made it to the final scene with no more plot left to accomplish than a confrontation, an admission of guilt, and the disposal of Alibius's red herring.

Here, apparently, Rowley takes over, although possibly in tandem with Middleton, and the tone of the dialogue quickly catches up with that of the events. A gauze of formality gradually lowers between the audience and the figures on stage, lifted only briefly for Beatrice's death-speech. We become conscious of the increase of epigrammatic rhythms, the virtual disappearance of colloquial contractions, and the propensity of the characters to use concise if extravagant metaphors such as "The bed itself's a charnal, the sheets shrouds/ For murdered carcasses" (83-84). The incidence of people being addressed as "sir" increases. The dialogue is punctuated with exclamations at each revelation: "Ha!"; "oh cunning devils!"; "Diaphanta!"; "Ha! My brother's murderer!"; "Horrid villain!" When Alsemero presses his questioning, Beatrice smiles, then personifies her "innocence" as the smiler in a short, sentimental speech ending in a rhetorical question (24-27). We at once recognize the diction of I.i. Alsemero's response crouches, springs, and pounces ("You are a whore!" 31) in exactly the same pattern as his first announcement of love (I.i.69-72).

The tone veers from merely formal to an overt suggestion of the comic. De Flores bandies words with his accuser (" 'twas quite through him, sure," 104) and readily owns up to both murder and adultery. When both criminals are locked in Alsemero's closet (along with, presumably, all his virginity-test bottles), Vermandero enters with Alibius, Isabella, Tomazo, Antonio, and Franciscus in tow. Vermandero and Alsemero play Cox and Box:

> Ver.: Oh, Alsemero, I have a wonder for you.
> Als.: No sir, 'tis I, I have a wonder for you.
> Ver.: I have suspicion near as proof itself
> For Piracquo's murder.
> Als.:   Sir, I have proof
> Beyond suspicion for Piracquo's murder.

Ver.:   Beseech you hear me, these two have been disguised
         E'er since the deed was done.
Als.:   I have two other
         That were more close disguised than your two could be,
         E'er since the deed was done.
Ver.:   You'll hear me! These two mine own servants—
Als.:   Hear me! Those nearer than your servants,
         That shall acquit them and prove them guiltless.

(121-32)

At length even Tomazo objects: "How is my cause bandied through your delays!"13 This is the kind of unraveling we expect to find in *The Importance of Being Earnest,* and though it is interrupted by the murder-suicide of the captured pair and by Beatrice's affecting plea for forgiveness, one can see that the scene's tone, while it careens madly, is drifting directly toward the farce-style resolution with which we began our questioning. Our brief examination should, I think, make it clear that the finale is in some odd way merely the capstone of a pile of artificialities, distancing (or "estrangement") effects, sudden comic turns, and parodic notes, which has been a-building during much of the seemingly serious play.14

On the hypothesis that *The Changeling's* runaway tonal variety was to some degree intended by its authors and not simply the result of their ineptitude, we must then ask if their intentions were directed to an overall effect of anarchy (a Marx Brothers' "Night at the Castle" or a random burlesque of tragedy itself), or whether there can be found some control on mere variety by which we might perceive a tonal structure or design. Here Empson's reading helps us. Although the many mainplot-subplot correspondences do not add up to coherent parody, we may see them as effective counterbalances to the centrifugal effects of the tone itself. Operatively, these unmistakable hints of correspondence serve to keep the audience in a state of expectation that "real" (plot, character, theme) connections will eventually be made. The fact that many of these expectations are aroused only to be frustrated throws off balance our ordinary way of discerning dramatic structure (as a recognizable pattern of expectations and recollections moving through time)15 but at the same time keeps us unwilling to throw in the towel and turn from the play as a gabble of unrelated data. We keep waiting, perhaps puzzling, and find our attention skillfully mocked.

The best indication that this *trompe l'oeil* effect is deliberate is, of course, the clear pattern that emerges from the variation in tone itself. The play begins in a never-never land of pure theatricality, no more to be predicted as serious than as funny.16 As it divides into two plots, it flies apart rapidly to the farthest poles of both the funny-to-tragic scale and the artificial-to-credible scale. Then, as the main plot gets progressively less serious and more conventional, the subplot begins to sprout growths of psychological believability and threatened bloodshed—potentially serious in effect. As the subplot evaporates and its characters join the main plot as hangers-on, the tone of the action returns to the artificiality of I.i and begins to oscillate quickly between the tragedy-of-blood seriousness of, say, III.ii and the vaudeville of I.ii, ultimately withdrawing behind the decorative theatrical frame out of which the play first stepped. If the final image with which we are left is that of a comic tableau, it is there, perhaps, to call our attention to the fun we have been having in trying unsuccessfully to "nail the play down" in terms of a recognizable overall effect.

We may imagine a three-dimensional graph of *The Changeling*'s tonal pattern: tracking the progression of the play down a vertical scale marked off scene by scene, we would localize the overall tone of each scene at the intersection of a horizontal scale marking degrees from "farcical" to "tragic" and a scale-in-depth designating degrees from "artificial" to "credible." If such a model could be made, we would, I believe, end up with an uneven but recognizable spiral, wide at the top, snaking downward in a tightening gyre to a point near the edge where "artificial" crosses "black comic." But a relatively straight line could join the three scenes of the subplot, and another straight line could link the four most memorable scenes of the main plot. Such "straight lines" are what we normally expect of a play; these scenes are the ones concentrated on by most critics, who correspondingly despair of the unity of the "double plot."

Finding our clearest sense of *The Changeling*'s overall design in an aspect of its style—moreover in a quality which stresses the reactions of a hypothetical audience—imputes to the play an essentially "theatrical" or aesthetic mode of composition, but it certainly does not imply that the play is finally meaningless *except* as a device for patterning audience emotions. This can be said of Fletcher's plays, but not of *The Changeling*.17 Similarly, the fact that the play's action is bracketed (even "matrixed") by scenes inviting complete detachment from the serious implication of the content does not mean that we have witnessed a "camp" on tragedy or a send-up of the play's own material. There may be a suppressed note of truth in this interpretation; still, if it were taken as the summary perception a reader or spectator must have of the play, then we would not, once let in on the joke at the finale, continue to find the play tentative and shifting in its focus at all. On the contrary, the psychological and moral implications of the Beatrice-De Flores story are indeed there. Appraisals such as those of Eliot and Miss Ellis-Fermor, although based on only part of the play, cannot be dismissed as misinterpretations in themselves.

By the same token, we can note that the madhouse scenes are not mere hackwork or filler, but that, as Isabella's character begins to develop, they exhibit in their own way a series of effective comic strokes on some of the moral and psychological themes suggested by the main plot. Though neither an integral action in itself nor a sustained parody of the main plot, the madhouse plot is far from meaningless. We should see in Middleton and Rowley's work, I think, not the intention of mystifying the spectators nor solely of exciting them, but rather a refusal (or inability) to force their commitment to a single kind of stage reality. The play *is* a psychologically believable moral tragedy; it is also a courtly-love parody; it is also a laugh-grabbing farce and a black-comic "revue" on certain themes.

The patterned juxtaposition of one kind of stage reality with another and one range of mood with another is constantly in flux, continuously unpredictable, yet by means of those very qualities the primary unifying dynamic of the play as it is experienced in time. On the basis of this conclusion, its compositional similarities with many early-seventeenth-century plays should become apparent, not least of which are *Measure for Measure* and *All's Well That Ends Well*, "problem plays" not in the Ibsenite sense so much as in their notorious inability to be read by any two critics in anything like the same way.[18]

By the evidence of collaboration it yields, *The Changeling* gives us no warrant for interpretations rooted in the idea that Middleton and Rowley wrote at loggerheads with each other. But it is possible to speculate that both men occasionally found themselves at loggerheads with the story and the themes they had agreed on. If so, the sense of tentativeness and irresolution we derive from the patterned but unsettled tone might reflect the authors' indecision in striving to entertain their audience with enjoyable and comfortably familiar kinds of dramatic action, while simultaneously feeling a conflicting commitment to the unique meanings embodied in the material. Or we might suspect a personal tension between confident and forthright communication of the story, including its thematic stresses, and self-consciousness about the demands of theatrical form itself—a self-consciousness perhaps made all the more acute in a day when Marstonian cynicism and Fletcherian virtuosity had exploited the private-theatre spectator's delight in stylish contrivance and *bizarrerie*. However such a polarity is phrased, it may be no more than a peculiar example of the uneasy relation of style, tone, and content which Jacobean literature, poised on the brink of Eliot's "dissociation of sensibility" since the Metaphysicals, often exhibited. This critical moment in the history of taste has been explored under the rubric "Mannerism" by pan-generic historians of art, such as Wylie Sypher.

At the risk of leading a snipe-hunt, I suggest it may be worthwhile to expand our inquiry in that general direction. An attempt to describe the kind of precarious success which *The Changeling* is capable of achieving in performance calls up echoes of several plays which can unsettle a modern reader or audience in ways which seem similar. Shakespeare's "problem plays" have already been mentioned as examples of seemingly intentional tonal irresolution. To them we might add *Pericles, Cymbeline, The Winter's Tale,* Fletcher's plays, and perhaps even Marlowe's *The Jew of Malta*—drama which invites, and refuses to answer, the question, "How am I to take this?" We can have no hope of making "Mannerism" or any other label serve as an answer— arguments still break out about its usefulness in discourse about the visual arts—but some collective term can prove helpful in marking notes on the problem. "Mannerism" strikes me as preferable to any other available generality; its usefulness will, I hope, emerge as we proceed.

Historians have taken three fundamentally distinct approaches in trying to isolate Mannerism as a late-renaissance phenomenon. Walter Friedlaender's pioneer treatment of Mannerist painting stressed its dialectic relationship with its predecessor, the accomplished "classicism" of Italian painters from Da Vinci to Raphael, and with its successor, the early-Baroque paintings of the Carracci family.19 Thus Mannerist art began as "anti-classicism" and finally vanished in the 1590s under a wave of "anti-mannerism." Examining the paintings of Pontormo, Rosso, and Parmigianino, Friedlaender saw the style's initial impetus as the upwelling of an essentially medieval taste for intensity and variety—multiple focus, unrealistic or puzzling juxtapositions of scale, acknowledgement of the spectator, heightened or distorted movement—in a context in which the high-renaissance masterworks, with their balanced calmness, organized realism, and mastery of visual rhythm, were regarded as oppressively limiting despite the impressive technical sophistication which inescapably made them models of artistic accomplishment. Northern artists like Dürer, who were still in the process of assimilating the lessons of late-quattrocento Italian painting into a consciousness not entirely cut off from medieval habits of perception and composition, were themselves much admired by the "younger generation" of Italian artists. The result was often an oddly unsettling blend of the pseudo-naive and the highly polished, all evidently governed by a high degree of self-awareness and a corresponding interest in the effect to be had on the spectator.

Certain later art historians have abandoned Friedlaender's emphasis on a historical dialectic of action and reaction as too schematic and not sufficiently applicable to the work of many sixteenth-century artists who clearly share some of the stylistic features of Pontormo, Rosso, and Parmigianino. A recent, thorough survey of Mannerism by John Shearman uses a much wider historical compass and a no-nonsense historical approach to defining the fundamental predilections of the style.20 Shearman finds the common denominator of all sixteenth-century Mannersim in the contemporary importance attached to its root-term, *maniera*—"style," implying both the elegance stressed in Castiglione's descriptive term, *sprezzatura* ("seemingly offhand virtuosity"), and the extreme consciousness of technique evidenced by the importance given to theories of *disegno*. That the painting, sculpture, architecture, and literature which Shearman regards as Manneristic found its patrons, practitioners, and audiences in highly sophisticated—usually courtly—circles is self-explanatory. By emphasizing *maniera* Shearman manages to clarify the stylistic connections between the Italian artists of Pontormo's generation and those following Bronzino (whom Friedlaender considered merely "mannered" in comparison with his earlier anti-classical Mannerists), as well as between the Florentine-Roman schools and late-sixteenth-century artists elsewhere in Europe. Yet he strictly avoids diluting the term to a mere synonym for "sixteenth-century." Thus Bruegel, Tintoretto, and El Greco, who manifest artistic premises essentially unconditioned by admiration of *maniera,* are ruled out, while literary artists of any nationality who exploited styles of elaborate, elegant "conceit" are included: Bembo, Gongora, Lyly. Far from simply compiling a list, however, Shearman stresses more strongly than Friedlaender the fluidity of the borders between Mannerist style and its predecessors, heirs, and contemporary alternatives. He employs "Mannerism" descriptively in a purely historical context (thus subject to the shadings and partial applicability of any historical phenomenon), locking neither the style nor history itself into any idealized critical framework.

Almost at the opposite extreme to the approach represented by Shearman is that first put forward by Max Dvořák in 1920 and developed in various ways by pan-artistic critical historians such as Arnold Hauser and Wylie Sypher.[21] If Shearman attached little importance *per se* to the "subjective," "speculative," and "unearthly" qualities which Friedlaender discerned in Manneristic form, the followers of Dvořák have tended to place their major stress on such psychological determinants. Dvořák saw in Mannerism manifestations of a general "spiritual crisis" in the sixteenth century. Whether one investigates its roots in the crisis itself, in the sociological vein of Hauser, or its stylistic evidences of mental unease, with Sypher, Mannerism emerges principally as an expressive phenomenon rather than as a phase of artistic technique. Close attention is paid to the Mannerists' presentation of "high nervous tension" and their apparent need for incongruity, irresolution, and basic questioning (or abandonment) of the possibility of meaning. Friedlaender's anti-classicists are wedded to El Greco, Cervantes, Shakespeare, and Donne with little intervening but the basilisk stares of Bronzino's portrait figures. The juxtapositions of sunlit classical order with "neo-Gothic" distortion and arbitrariness become a kind of sixteenth-century Surrealism, with much that is thereby implied about twentieth-century-style *Angst,* loss of conviction, and artist-as-ironic-public-performer. Such perceptions of Mannerism have had a lasting effect on criticism and have often proved invaluable in bringing late-renaissance art in focus for twentieth-century eyes.

Though I have not given anything like justice to Friedlaender, Shearman, Dvořák, Hauser, or Sypher in these capsule descriptions, I have tried to isolate three chief areas of emphasis which may allow us to consider Mannerism in more particular senses. Each point of attack is distinct, even in part contradictory, but each can offer help providing we do not make our chief question, "Which is most true historically?" We intend to use the category "Mannerism" critically, as an aid in discussing certain kinds of dramatic structure and effect. If we pick and choose among the salient points of each approach, we may surface with some useful and flexible concepts.

We confront, of course, a historical barrier at the outset in trying to make Mannerism a term for distinguishing kinds of drama *within* the Elizabethan-Jacobean corpus; as a "period" tag "Mannerism" may be used to label all or none of the drama written between 1560 and 1625. If we approach Mannerism as anti-classicism, we must acknowledge that the English dramatic tradition contained no established classicism to be "anti." If we concentrate on *maniera,* we find that Lyly's theatricalist fantasy and costume-jewelry verse at the beginning of the period's crest are at least as stylized as Fletcher's enameled, unmotivated "conversation of gentlemen" at the period's end, as Shearman himself has noted. If we search for a sense of historical crisis, an ambiguity of stage reality, or an attraction to mental anguish, we may choose to find the first as early as *Gorboduc,* the second in *Cambyses,* and the third in *The Spanish Tragedy.* Thus Sypher and Hauser treat Elizabethan drama as *characteristically* Manneristic. Clearly, we must appropriate the art historians' guidelines with some freedom.

From Friedlaender we can derive the idea that, whatever we end up calling "Mannerism" in this context, we should expect it to occur as an aftermath of—if not a reaction to—an artistic synthesis in which evident formal order combines with representational credibility to evoke a sense of "meaningfulness." That is, artistic form in such a synthesis (or "classic" phase) will seem to express the assurance that it is adequate to the artist's and perceiver's common grasp of reality. Any "classic" grasp of reality includes not only observable phenomena but also a fairly clear-cut set of shared values and ideals. Mannerism, then, represents a "decadence" of such a synthesis, the beginnings of an acknowledgement that one's perceptual and conceptual field ("reality") can no longer be adequately expressed by the received norms of formal organization.22 Friedlaender saw Pontormo and his contemporaries rebelling against an art of focal clarity, idealized proportion, and calm orderliness; *prima facie,* we may suppose that these norms seemed inadequate as well to their felt need for "speculative" risk-taking and heightened, "subjective" spirituality. But if Friedlaender's dialectic is viewed more abstractly, "Mannerism" need not apply only to the particular forms distinguishing his anti-classical painters from their high-renaissance teachers. By the same token, "classic" can be used to define any art which similarly integrates form, meaning, clarity, and a sense of finality, no matter how. Indeed, such a "trans-historical" approach to Manneristic form has been used by German scholars and their pupils: E. R. Curtius, G. R. Hocke, G. Weise. If wrenching Mannerism loose from its anchor in mid-sixteenth-century painting thus subjects the definition to historical criticism, the historical problem of Elizabethan and Jacobean drama, noted above, makes such a step necessary if these concepts are to be helpful to the present discussion.

At least since Una Ellis-Fermor, "Jacobean" (post-1600) drama has been thought of as a decadence of the Elizabethan in precisely the sense used here. Bert O. States, in his wide-ranging, Burkean treatment of irony in drama, explores the underlying notion of decadence succinctly.23 Unfortunately, "decadence" is an inexact and loaded word (which is one of the reasons why I have chosen to work with "Mannerism" as a term, though it is scarcely more exact). It is to Friedlaender's credit that by rigorous attention to form he freed Mannerism from being thought of as only an entropic corruption of high-renaissance style. An ostensibly decadent phase of artistic form, as Friedlaender saw, can be a period in which artistic frustration, reassessment, and experimentation result in tense but strongly affecting art.

In a decadence thus defined, artists may take one of two postures to cope with the breakdown of formal and perceptual coherence. If their received classic forms, through familiarity and increasing hints of irrelevancy, seem no longer to touch the bedrock of a reality which thereby threatens to become inarticulable, one strategy is to burrow feverishly toward the shock of naked experience. Sometimes extreme, detailed verisimilitude can be prized above any norms of composition, as in some fifteenth-century Northern (decadent Gothic) art. Surface realism aside, the artist may attempt to force the perceiver's engagement (and perhaps his own) by serving up "raw" a teeming, disordered world. The Mannerist painters' "medieval" abandonment of scale and symmetry may partially embody such an attitude. Certainly the Jacobean satirical impulse, whether manifest in the loosely organized "town comedy," Websterian *grand-guignol,* or the widespread attention paid to psychological extremes, suggests at least a touch of this "super-realistic" strategy. It is not important in this context what *kind* of intensified reality the artist and his audience prefer to the ordered vision already fixed in classic form: the violent, counterthrusting movement of Rosso; the neon colors of Pontormo; the naked, elemental landscapes of *Macbeth* and *Lear;* the seething stage-Italian "court"; the brothels of *Measure for Measure* and *Pericles;* the grotesque dream-life of the modern surrealist tradition; or the amoral and protean pantheon of Euripides. What is important is that "form" itself, insofar as it is still conceptualized in classic terms, is now seen as an obstacle to genuine involvement in the artwork, so that an experience of relative "chaos" becomes necessary as a breakthrough.24 The magnifying mirror is replaced by the X-ray machine, the microscope, and the kaleidoscope.

Nor is it essential that the artist presume that the discrepancy between received form and perceived experience is in fact a discrepancy within reality itself: we need not go all the way with Dvořák, Hauser, and Sypher. Our emphasis here is not on the concept that "the time is out of joint" but on a situation in which an artist's available way of expressing such a concept seems itself out of joint. For such a situation to occur, it is obvious that received classic conceptions of form must exert powerful influences as models by virtue of their erstwhile "perfection"; they cannot be regarded by the artist as easily improved-upon, no matter how lacking he subliminally suspects they have become. No Mannerist painter was a premature Frondist intent upon junking the Renaissance; quite the contrary, his conscious models were normally the very high-renaissance masterpieces Friedlaender sees him rebelling against.

At the opposite pole an artist may altogether avoid trying to force empathic or emotional engagement. He may even refuse to allow his audience (or himself) any presupposition of a connection between "art" and "life." Here is a part *maniera* can play. The "stylized style" seems exaggerated when compared to its classical origins, because to some extent the artist expects it to be noticed in and for itself. Style, more than content, becomes the artist's preoccupation irrespective of how egotistic, "mannered," or self-conscious he is, since the possibilities of content, recognizable to him only through the medium of his received forms, have all been "used up." "Content," here, is not the fundamental connection with experience dug for by the super-realists, but the already-formed conceptual possibilities perfected by the classic predecessors through their own developed techniques: the explicit subject-matter of a painting (together with its intended spectator-response), or the plot, characters, themes, and *milieu* of a play.

It must be recognized that *maniera,* with all that it implies about a manipulation of fantasy and artifice, can in fact be a dominant concert of an artist prior to a recognized period of classic synthesis. Botticelli is *manieroso*; he accepts the technical conventions of his predecessors (outlines, frieze-like composition) as given, and proceeds from there to an individual ideal of pure elegance and grace. Lyly, even more than Spenser and Sidney, was usually content to mine the same kind of romance material (whether medieval or "classical" in explicit subject) as the journeyman authors of romantic drama from the Digby *Mary Magdalene* to *Mucedorus,* without developing it significantly toward greater inclusiveness of theme, character-psychology, or composition. In the context of the choirboys' courtly "entertainment," he put his energy almost totally into stylistic elaboration ("decoration") and in so doing learned to exploit some of the possibilities of disengagement which the naive material would naturally suggest to a clever and ambitious hanger-on at court.25

However, when stylistic virtuosity becomes a preoccupation of a post-classical artist, quite different results occur, for "high style" seems somehow to have been "imposed" on a content already made familiar by complex, fully realized classical models. That is, such work often has the effect of seeming to treat its material *as if* it were naive, in the face of the audience's conditioned expectation of the contrary. *The Changeling*'s putative "core" of earnest, moral intrigue-tragedy would not predictably imply Middleton and Rowley's theatrical embroidery. The reverse side of the same coin is the ambiguous effect of a truly naive "content" when treated by an artist of known accomplishment: an audience may well be pre-conditioned to look for far greater subtlety of meaning and effect in *Pericles* than in *Mucedorus* or even in *Alexander and Campasbe*.

Though post-classical experiments in style *per se* may hint at a later formal synthesis (as Fletcher points to Dryden or Rosso to Salviati), such art most frequently appears as a fragmentation of the parent synthesis—a split between style and content in which the former "shows off" and elaborates the technical sophistication absorbed from the classic, while the latter is merely "indicated," presuming upon the spectator's familiarity (or even boredom) with its established articulation. Fletcher's subjects and his notion of what plot and characterization might be all seem to be derived from his predecessors' standard practice. But here they are reduced to interchangeable parts in a machine which has as its *chief* function the display of operatic "passion" by means of rhetorically effective dialogue. The audience is to be "moved" *in vacuo*. Sometimes, at one remove further, a received content is overtly parodied, as in Euripides' *Electra*. Even then, the parody is often inconsistent and without an unequivocal thematic point. The Duke in *Measure for Measure* is obviously an ironically conceived version of the type of satirical, string-pulling "agents of Providence" represented by Marston's Altofronto and, more grandly, by Shakespeare's later Prospero. For all his blundering and impotent machinations, however, he is not clearly a butt of ridicule. Such tentativeness is rarely the case when a clever artist parodies naive material from a pre-classical phase of formal development; what is then parodied (however fondly) is naiveté itself, as in Peele's *Old Wives' Tale* no less than in Beaumont's *Knight of the Burning Pestle*.

We have, then, attempts to *force* engagement and to *curtail* engagement, neither of which is a major concern of artists confidently working in a fully integrated classic mode. Each of these diametrically opposite "strategies" results in a different kind of art (of which Susan Sontag has provided thumbnail sketches in her article, "Notes on Camp"[26]). Rarely, however, does any post-classical artist take such extreme postures *vis à vis* his classical models or the "strategy" opposite the one he elects. The experiments we should focus on as Manneristic are precisely those which give evidence of an attempt to encompass both poles at once, attempts which indicate the kind of formal (hence tonal) irresolution we first lit upon in *The Changeling*.27 Indeed, though Pontormo's asymmetry, shocking colors, and crowded, angular space often appear to exhibit the first "strategy" while the smooth, frozen denizens of Bronzino's courtly world suggest the second, neither can be said to represent a "pure" alternative.

Bronzino's *maniera* was suited not only to tense, icy portraits such as those of Eleanor of Toledo, Bartolommeo Panciatichi, and the anonymous, insolent "Young Man" in the Metropolitan Museum (all of whom could be characters from Fletcher). In *Christ in Limbo* and in *Venus, Cupid, Folly, and Time* the same sleek sophistication is applied to the disturbed collocation of thrusting bodies which Rosso had pioneered; what is more, the "elusive air of obscenity" in the latter picture is actually enhanced by Bronzino's detached dexterity.28 Fletcher again is brought to mind. Pontormo, even when his composition is most "Gothic" *(Joseph in Egypt)* or when his color and mood are most eerie *(Visitation, Deposition:* "crazed . . . as if lit by some monstrous aurora borealis"29), still puts enormous care into a complicated but "legible" *disegno* of focus and counter-focus—an evident intellectual deliberateness seemingly at odds with his "expressionistic" notes of hysteria. Parmigianino's famous *Madonna del Collo Lungo,* for all its bursting of the classical boundaries of weight-distribution, proportion, perspective, and visual "common sense," derives its very title from the cool, swan-like elegance into which the painter has forced his central figure.

The function of *contrapposto* in Giovanni Bologna's statuary is another case in point. In itself, exaggerated *contrapposto* ("counter-poise") represents a game-like approach to form: how twisting and multi-faceted, how apparently top-heavy and incapable of balance can I make a statue, without forfeiting gracefulness, movement, or support? Yet the most obvious effect of this appreciable virtuosity is to involve the spectator, at some length, in experiencing the object. He must see it from every possible angle, for each vista beckons him to the next, yet each angle of vision offers a surprise: a seemingly different statue, as interesting in its contours as the last. (Perhaps it is not too far-fetched to 'see this very *contrapposto,* proceeding ultimately from interwoven serpentine spirals in conflicting rhythms, as a concrete analogue of the serpentine arrangement of tones which our imagined model depicted for *The Changeling.*) Our two "strategies," conscious virtuosity at the possible expense of meaning and engagement, and forced engagement at the possible expense of formal coherence, become two ends of the same rubber band. The first keeps the second from ever becoming a Romantic (or expressionistic) anti-classicism; the second does not allow the first to become an art-for-art's-sake decorativeness.

The point is that the artist, working in the shadow of his classical teachers, cannot escape knowing what he is about. He cannot be naive about form and technique, nor can he afford to allow his spectators to think he is. Having had their own perceptions conditioned by a classic perfection of form, they are likely to give short shrift to an apparently genuine "primitive." He cannot whip up his own engagement with whatever confusing reality he perceives by simply "painting what he sees" or "writing what he feels," because both seeing and feeling have been colossally educated. He must, it seems, demonstrate to himself and his audience that he is a past master of good technique—at the same time that he casts doubt on technique's adequacy by "exploding" the general forms which it was previously developed to realize. This is a large generalization, but it provides a clue to the "heart" of Mannerism: the prototypical Mannerist painters and the most "Jacobean" of English playwrights are the ones in whose works we recognize an extreme tension between totally manipulative artifice (the *terminus ad quem* of *maniera*) and "the shock of recognition." As a result, their works inevitably appear "self-conscious." Irony, in its broadest critical senses, is their essential condition.

The best symbol of this ironic consciousness is the *repoussoir* in some Mannerist pictures, the man standing in the foreground glaring at the viewer and beckoning him into the "scene." He gestures to include us in the strangely affecting iconic world behind the picture-plane, and by so doing reveals himself as a painted device and the framed world itself a deliberate construction made for us to look at. Sypher has already noted that he corresponds to the *persona* of the satirist in Jacobean drama: Asper's "Macilente" mask, Altofronto's "Malevole." Functionally, the *repoussoir* parallels Gower in *Pericles*. That he should also suggest the Prospero of "Our revels now are ended" and the Epilogue is no wonder.

Mannered artifice and emotional engagement play the same unresolved tug-of-war in the plays as in the paintings. It is worth noting that the terms of the tension were familiar to seventeenth-century audiences no less than to ourselves. James Shirley, in his preface to the first folio of Beaumont and Fletcher's collected plays (1647), displays his understanding of how their dramaturgy managed to provoke both empathy and estrangement together. In the course of a typical scene, says Shirley, the spectator's passions are "raised . . . by such insinuating degrees" that he "shall not chuse but consent, and go along with them" to the point where he is in complete empathy with the character onstage: "grown insensibly the very same person." Yet, *"in the same moment"* (my emphasis), he cannot but "stand admiring the subtile Tracks of his engagement."[30]

A purely critical use of these formal concepts may easily transcend historical definition and provide insights into, say, Euripides' drama. It is not difficult to see also in Harold Pinter's *The Homecoming,* for instance, an analogous dramaturgy: his unnerving talent for detaching ostentatiously realistic dialogue from its conventional underpinnings in plot and "motivated" character. We might contrast Edward Albee's *Who's Afraid of Virginia Woolf?* with one of its apparent models, O'Neill's masterpiece of autobiographical realism, *Long Day's Journey Into Night.* In O'Neill, the relations among the characters can be schematized psychologically as a repetitious "game" (formula: "I hate you; no, I hate myself for saying that; therefore I love you; therefore don't hate me"). Yet in Albee, game-playing literally comprises the characters' relationships, a formal condition which leads with some plausibility directly to the revelation of George and Martha's fictitious child: a somewhat arbitrary "symbol." It is not that Albee's play is "unbelievable" (neither are Pinter's[31]), so much as that its patterns of suspense and surprise are so obviously a result of the playwright's conscious concern and (undoubtedly) of his ironic enjoyment in writing the play. Such is his manipulation of the interplay of our estrangement and our empathy, our accustomed sense of the "serious" and of the "funny," that we are never allowed to predict the tone of the next five minutes with any confidence.

We started with *The Changeling* and galloped far afield. Obviously, this exploratory excursus into Manneristic form was not necessary simply to elucidate that play. Rather, some such line of inquiry was suggested by the general problems *The Changeling* introduced. Though these problems of critical approach to a wide variety of late-Elizabethan and Jacobean plays have not by any means been "solved," we have reason, I think, to expect that the qualities of Manneristic form we have singled out for brief examination can continue to be refined as critical tools. If we are to adapt these categorical ideas appropriately (and not merely to "apply" them), we will, in our readings of the drama, have to persist in emphasizing subtleties of tone itself. It must be apparent that this critical route is neither easy nor, after a lapse of three and a half centuries, capable of leading to certainty.[32] But it may be hoped that in the long run a general approach of this kind will provide us with a fuller understanding of the interrelated modern enthusiasms for Mannerist painting, Euripides, the Jacobeans, and recent "Manneristic" dramatists like Albee and Pinter.

NOTES

1 It seems clear that the latter was intended by the authors: "Your only smiles have power to cause re-live/ The dead again . . ." (V.iii.224-25).

2 However, the play was entered in the Stationers' Register (Oct. 19, 1652) as "a Comedie . . . written by Rowley."

3 See N. W. Bawcutt, ed., *The Changeling*, Revels edn. (London 1958), pp. xxxixff. Line for line, Rowley may have written more of the play than Middleton (1073 lines to 1018 lines). Dorothy M. Farr, in *Thomas Middleton and the Drama of Realism* (Edinburgh, 1973), believes Middleton had ultimate control over the entire composition, even over the scenes (including the subplot) which Rowley penned (p. 131n, p. 133n). If this is true, at least it reinforces my argument that we ought not to separate the two authors' work when discussing the play's structure.

4 Empson, *Some Versions of Pastoral* (London, 1935), pp. 48-52; Bradbrook, *Themes and Conventions of Elizabethan Tragedy* (London, 1935), pp. 213-24, and *The Growth and Structure of Elizabethan Comedy* (London, 1955; rpt. Baltimore: Penguin, 1963), p. 165; Holzknecht, "The Dramatic Structure of *The Changeling*," *Renaissance Papers, A Selection of Papers Presented at the Renaissance Meeting in the Southern States*, ed. Allan H. Gilbert (Orangeburg, S. C., 1954), pp. 77-87. Richard Levin, in *The Multiple Plot in English Renaissance Drama* (Chicago, 1971), proposes a linkage on the basis of Aristotle's four kinds of causality: material (characters of both plots related to each other as friends, kinsmen, or neighbors), effective (characters or events from one action influence happenings in the other), formal (plots separate but related by parallel or contrast), and final (an "affective relationship between plots" is created by their qualities of tone, emotion, and sensibility). Yet for his scheme to work in *The Changeling*, Levin posits a "missing" scene: the wedding-masque brawl logically occurring before Act V.

5 Note also the internal evidence that the part of Franciscus was written to be played by the same actor who played Jasperino. This is not only an indication that Middleton and Rowley worked together but also a contributing factor to the lameness of the subplot. In IV.iii a letter is substituted for the (preferable) presence of Franciscus, who cannot appear until late in the scene because Jasperino has just exited in costume at the end of IV.ii.

6 Quotation from Brustein, *Seasons of Discontent* (New York, 1967), p. 253. Cf. Eliot, *Essays on Elizabethan Drama* (1932; rpt. New York: Harcourt Brace, 1956), pp. 85-86; Ellis-Fermor, *The Jacobean Drama* (London, 1936), p. 146.

7 Bawcutt, pp. lxv, lxvii. See also Richard Hindry Barker, *Thomas Middleton* (New York: Columbia Univ. Press, 1958), p. 121.

8 Eugene Ionesco has noted, for example, that any tragedy becomes comic simply if it is speeded up. See Susan Sontag, *Against Interpretation and Other Essays* (New York, 1969), p. 123.

9 This polarity corresponds generally to "transparent" vs. "opaque" as used by Bernard Beckerman, *Dynamics of Drama* (New York, 1970), pp. 31-33. Beckerman, when he speaks of "credibility" and "artificiality," uses a narrower focus, the former approaching the notion of stylistic realism, the latter referring to dramatic "conventions" such as the soliloquy. Obviously, a "convention" can be "transparent" (or, in my terms, "credible") to the extent that the audience is accustomed to it and accepts it simply as a way to express the fictive "content" of a dramatic event. Here, as in most such discussions, my judgments about what "engages" and what "estranges" in Jacobean drama are based on my assessment of a Jacobean audience's sensibilities in this regard, although scenes are singled out for comment on the basis of the problems they might have for us today.

10 Brustein, p. 253.

11 Jordan, "Myth and Psychology in *The Changeling*," *Renaissance Drama*, n.s. 3, (1970), 157-66.

12 In this and in all further observations about Fletcher's dramaturgy I am much indebted to Eugene M. Waith, *Patterns of Tragicomedy in Beaumont and Fletcher* (New Haven: Yale Univ. Press, 1952).

13 Alfred Harbage has drawn attention to the obvious parallels between "intrigue" tragedies, beginning with *The Spanish Tragedy*, and their near relatives (and perhaps immediate ancestors), the neo-Plautine comedies: "Intrigue in Elizabethan Tragedy," *Essays on Shakespeare and Elizabethan Drama in Honor of Hardin Craig* (Columbia: Univ. of Missouri Press, 1962), pp. 37-44. *The Changeling*, although unusual in this respect, is not the only "serious" play to take the comic potential inherent in such plotting the one crucial step further, to the emergence of an overt comic tone; cf. *The Jew of Malta*.

14 By far the most interesting topic explored by recent Elizabethan scholars has been this very perception of "Verfremdungseffekten." See, for example, Maynard Mack, "Engagement and Detachment in Shakespeare's Plays," *Essays . . . in Honor of Hardin Craig*, pp. 275-96; Anne Righter, *Shakespeare and the Idea of the Play* (New York, 1962); and Michael Shapiro, "Children's Troupes: Dramatic Illusion and Acting Style," *Comparative Drama*, 3 (1969), 42-53, and "Toward a Reappraisal of the Children's Troupes," *Theatre Survey*, 13, no. ii (Nov. 1972), 1-19. Jackson I. Cope, in *The Theatre and the Dream: From Metaphor to Form in Renaissance Drama* (Baltimore: Johns Hopkins Press, 1973), approaches many of these questions in a different but complementary perspective. His notion of the "Baroque" in drama includes some of the formal notes others have discussed as "Manneristic."

15 My debt to Kenneth Burke in all this should be apparent. See "Lexicon Rhetoricae," *Counter-Statement* (New York, 1931), pp. 157-61. In Burkean terms, the formal principle I find *The Changeling* exploiting (often by inversion) is that of "qualitative progression": a sequence of qualities which evoke audience-responses that seem "appropriately" to follow one another. Madeleine Doran's commentary is excellent: *Endeavors of Art: A Study of Form in Elizabethan Drama* (Madison: Univ. of Wisconsin Press, 1954), pp. 21-23. Burke's "qualitative progression" has much in common with Levin's "final causality"; the "parodic" interpretation of the plot-linkage would, at its simplest, highlight Burke's "repetitive form" and Levin's "formal causality."

16 Alsemero's earlier speeches are full of "forebodings." But heard in the context of the first scene's artificial rhetoric, they can provide no firm expectation that the play will not turn out to be—if not an outright comedy—a tragi-comedy or a romance of the lightest sort; cf. *The Malcontent.*

17 Waith, for example, says flatly (p. 41) that *A King and No King* (in this typical of the corpus of Fletcher's plays) "has no meaning."

18 The extremes of criticism pertaining to these plays, dating back to the eighteenth century, are well known. Only recently have the possibilities of Shakespeare's tonal manipulation (including parody) been concentrated on; see William Empson, *The Structure of Complex Words* (London, 1951), pp. 270-84; Joseph G. Price, *The Unfortunate Comedy: A Study of All's Well That Ends Well and Its Critics* (Toronto, 1968); and Jonathan R. Price, *"Measure for Measure* and the Critics," *Shakespeare Quarterly,* 20 (1969), 179-204.

19 Friedlaender, *Mannerism and Anti-Mannerism in Italian Painting* (New York, 1957). Friedlaender first advanced his views in a lecture at Freiburg in 1914.

20 Shearman, *Mannerism* (Harmondsworth: Penguin, 1967). Shearman's historical care is mirrored in the excellent essays on French literary Mannerism by Marcel Raymond: "La Pléiade et le Maniérisme," *Lumières de la Pléiade* (Paris, 1966); "Aux frontières du Maniérisme et du Baroque," *Etre et dire* (Neuchatel, 1970); *La Poésie française et le maniérisme 1546-1610* (Geneva, 1971).

21 Dvořák, *Geschichte der italienischen Kunst im Zeitalter der Renaissance* (Munich, 1927-29), vol. II; Hauser, *The Social History of Art,* trans. by the author with Stanley Godman (New York, 1951), vol. I; Sypher, *Four Stages of Renaissance Style* (Garden City, N.Y.: Doubleday, 1955). See also Douglas A. Russell, "Mannerism and Shakespearean Costume," *Educational Theatre Journal,* 16 (1964), 324-32; D. B. Rowland, *Mannerism—Style and Mood* (New Haven: Yale Univ. Press, 1964); and Roy Daniells, "The Mannerist Element in English Literature," *University of Toronto Quarterly,* 36 (Oct. 1966), 1-11.

22 My premises about the evolution of artistic forms are derived from George Kubler, *The Shape of Time* (New Haven: Yale Univ. Press, 1962). Kubler's concepts effectively supersede both the "organic" (growth-decay) metaphor and Friedlaender's "action-reaction" pattern. For a finely nuanced discussion of Mannerism in the context of historical "flow," see Blake Lee Spahr, "Baroque and Mannerism: Epoch and Style," *Colloquia Germanica,* 1 (1967), 78-100. Spahr reconciles the "historical" and "trans-historical" approaches to Manneristic style.

23 States, *Irony and Drama: A Poetics* (Ithaca, N.Y., 1971), pp. 126-38.

24 See Morse Peckham, *Man's Rage for Chaos* (Philadelphia, 1965).

25 See Shapiro, op. cit.

26 Sontag, pp. 288-89. Sontag's articles, "On Style," "Marat/Sade/Artaud," "Happenings: an art of radical juxtaposition," "Notes on Camp," and "One Culture and the New Sensibility," all provide remarkable insights into the range of artistic forms we are touching upon here.

27 See Davy A. Carozza, "For a Definition of Mannerism: The Hatzfeldian Thesis," *Colloquia Germanica,* 1 (1967), 66-77.

28 Michael Levey, *A Concise History of Painting from Giotto to Cezanne* (New York, 1962), p. 118.

29 Levey, p. 116.

30 See Maynard Mack, pp. 276-77.

31 The plausibility of Pinter's plays is argued by Martin Esslin, *The Peopled Wound* (Garden City, N.Y.: Doubleday, 1970).

32 See n. 9 above.

"Framing" as Collaborative Technique: Two Middleton-Rowley Plays

Michael E. Mooney

The nature of Renaissance dramatic collaboration remains a blind spot in the study of its dramaturgy. Although many explanations have been offered, we have yet to adequately describe a practice which employed nearly every Renaissance playwright, from Shakespeare and Jonson to Beaumont and Fletcher and a host of others, among them William Rowley and Thomas Middleton. Commentators, sifting among the possible divisions of labor in a collaborative work, project four main theories: (1) the dramatists partitioned their work by acts, with either one playwright writing Acts I, II, and III, another Acts IV and V; or with each playwright alternating in composing Acts I through V; (2) one playwright wrote a play's tragic scenes, his joint author the comic or satiric ones; (3) the dramatists divided shares along plot lines, with one writer responsible for the main plot, his collaborator for the subplot(s); and (4) one playwright added to or emended another's work, that is, certain plays are the products of revision.[1] But while each theory (or combination of theories) would seem to describe certain plays, it may be shown to be false in other cases; investigations into dramatic collaboration seem only to prove that we cannot, descriptively or prescriptively, account for this process.[2] As a result, the whole issue has become a critical quicksand where few dare to venture, the sheer number of explanations, in effect, explaining away the question.

An implicit premise underlies this investigation: I do not believe one can safely make a judgment about the collaborative *process* without considering each play individually, as a separate work. Given the possible permutations in dramatic form, it is conceivable that each play, in even so large a corpus as Beaumont and Fletcher's,[3] was written according to a different plan.

However, I do believe that from the evidence of two Middleton-Rowley plays, *A Faire Quarrel* (1617) and *The Changeling* (1622), emerge several generalizations, each of which sheds fresh light on the protean nature of dramatic collaboration.

What I would suggest is that, in writing these two plays, Middleton and Rowley employed a technique we may call "framing"—a collaborative *procedure* implying a division of labor by which William Rowley wrote, solely, Acts I and V and the plays' subplots, Thomas Middleton the main plot scenes in Acts II, III, and IV. I think these two plays provide instructive cases, not only because the Middleton-Rowley plays represent a successful collaborative partnership and because the playwriting shares in each case have been convincingly demonstrated,[4] but especially because Rowley's ability as a writer of bawdy subplots balances precisely the psychologically-oriented, tragic interests of Thomas Middleton.

The following analysis of the process by which *A Faire Quarrel* and *The Changeling* were written subsumes the first three of the four collaborative theories we have outlined. I assume that as a last step a final, joint revision of certain scenes was necessary to mold these plays into their final shapes, into forms where their verbal resonances might be finely heard. The effect that "framing" has on two plays, however, bears additional implications for the whole of Renaissance drama by illuminating the most elusive of literary practices. With our critical eyes trained on product, our efforts designed to measure plays by the procrustean bed of prescriptive forms, we often neglect the very process by which language is captured in the mold of form. In describing the way plays were composed to affect their audiences, then, rather than the relative effectiveness of the forms which result, "framing" asserts the primacy of process over product.

I

Although both tragic and comic elements appear in Middleton and Rowley's first collaboration, *The Old Law* (c.1615-1618), providing a basis for allocating the playwrights' shares,[5] a clear collaborative pattern does not emerge until *A Faire Quarrel*. In writing *The Old Law,* however, the playwrights designed the tragicomedy according to a plan that would help determine the process by which subsequent plays would be written. As even a cursory reading reveals, Middleton's main "tragic" action, involving the different responses Cleanthes and Lysander have to the "old law" condemning each one's parents to death, is balanced by the "comic" antics of Rowley's clown Gnotho, who wishes to rid himself of an aging wife to gain her fortune and enable him to marry a young courtesan.6 The serious action occupying Act I is comically undercut in Act II, when Gnotho makes his first appearance. From this point, scenes from each plot alternate, amplifying the contrasts between situations and, by analogy, reinforcing them, until the final act, when both courtier and clown stand before the Duke of Epire, keeper of law. The resultant play is a double-plotted "tragicomedy," not only because it observes the prescriptive rules of the genre, but also because it contains both a "tragic" and a "comic" plot, whereby the comedy intensifies the significance of the potential tragedy through the use of linguistic and thematic echoes as well as by the basic congruence shared by parallel plots.

This description, of course, closely resembles the one Richard Levin provides for *A Faire Quarrel,* a "tragi-comedy" having a "three-level hierarchy" of plots,7 linked imagistically through the repetition of the central concepts, *fair* and *honor,* and thematically by the singleness of their thrusts: on each plot level we see a character's honor tested in a quarrel. Scenes from each of the plots alternate until the final act, when all conflicts are resolved. Such a critical approach, however, does have its limitations. While "formal" analysis can dissect a play as a finished product, it cannot begin to describe a drama as we might see it unfold in space and time, as, in short, an experiential process in the open air of Middlesex. Nor can such an analysis take into account the fact that *A Faire Quarrel* is a collaboration designed to affect the viewing audience. With the advent of David J. Lake's statistical study of Middleton's canon,8 we are again reminded that Rowley's share here was greater than the play's "domestic" and farcical third "comic" levels: he also wrote the opening and closing scenes of the play.

With what affective result? The "formal" interplot relationships may demonstrably be seen in terms of a ratio:

	Insulter :	Object of Insult:	Defender
Main Plot :	Colonel :	Lady Ager :	Captain Ager
Domestic Subplot:	Physician :	Jane :	Fitzallen
Clown Scenes :	Chough &	Meg & Priss :	Captain Albo
	Trimtram :		

If we analyze the play as an integral unit, we find that *A Faire Quarrel* is structured along plot lines, with each character in a configuration duplicated on a separate plot level. Images, echoed on each level, draw arresting vertical lines of relief in the play's temporal movement.9 The analytical result is a blueprint outlining a perspective treatment of the theme of honor, telescoped toward the audience by different characters from their own different angles of vision, themselves converging in Act V's harmonious close. However, if we express the form of *A Faire Quarrel* diagrammatically, in terms of the playwright's shares, we learn something new about the way this play was designed:

Act I	II III IV	V
Rowley	Middleton Main Plot	Rowley
Rowley	Domestic Subplot	Rowley
Rowley	Clown Scenes	Rowley

Here we see "framing," the design which reveals the collaborative plan by which *A Faire Quarrel* was written to elicit audience applause. Rowley's exposition raises the conflicts to be explored in the play and resolved in his conclusion. The Fitzallen and Jane and Chough and Trimtram subplots, in mirroring the concerns of the main plot on "lower" levels, provide a structural base upon which the play's action and language resonate. Middleton scenes, like the celebrated interview (II.1) between Captain Ager and his mother about the Colonel's charge that Ager is the "son of a whore," are contrasted in subplot scenes, when, for instance, the Physician alleges that Jane is a "strumpet" and a "whore" (III.2; V.1) and when the clowns engage in a mock fair quarrel with Captain Albo and two true whores, Meg and Priss (IV.4). At apparently predetermined junctures, in fact, main plot scenes are replayed in the subplots to reinforce their significance.

As we imaginatively reconstruct this play in performance, four elements shared by each plot are visible. The first is the insult, which occurs in I.1 for the main plot; in III.2 and V.1 in the domestic quarrel; and in IV.1 and IV.4 in the clown episodes. The second element, an actual quarrel, is the precipitate of the insult, and appears in III.1 (main plot), in IV.4 (clown plot), and in V.1 (domestic plot). The third and fourth elements, the reconciliations and marriages, predictably occur in

Act V for all three plots. What these shared elements indicate
is a conscious patterning of the action. Each insult and quarrel
provides a commentary on the others; and as playgoers we anticipate this unfolding because of the conflicts set in motion in
Act I.

But perhaps it is important to show how this mirroring is
worked out in the language of the play. Ager and the Colonel's
serious quarrel in III.1, which results in an apparently mortal
wound for the Colonel, is verbally articulated in terms of the
concepts *fair, noble, valiant,* and *honor.* The training in the art
of roaring the clowns receive in IV.1 and the actual brawl they
engage in with Albo in IV.4 are also articulated by the use of
these same concepts—with the addition of the language of the
"Londonian roar," a parodic version of the language of the noble
quarrelers. When Jane's father, Russell, prepares to defend his
daughter's honor against the physician's charge that means "to
make her a whore" (V.1.160), this pattern is complete. Indeed,
we might trace a main, sub, and clown plot linguistic pattern
for the images of "arms," "good names," and "good words" as
well.[10] What results, through the juxtaposition of the language
and action of the main plot quarrel with the clown episodes
and with the domestic scenes, is patterning by contrast. Again
and again Middleton's rhetoric echoes in subplot scenes.

Such patterning, I submit, is more than a matter of the multiple plotting of language and gesture. It is a question not only
of form, but also of process, of the arrangement by the playwrights of the acts and scenes in the play. Indeed, what would
be readily apparent to a discerning contemporary audience—
the repetition of language and idea, and the mirroring of action
through the juxtaposition of scenes and situations—is often lost
when we read plays as products, as dramatic poems captured in
print. What is more interesting in its implications, however, is
that this arrangement by contrast is not an isolated example,
for Middleton and Rowley were to "frame" another play.

II

Now it is time to recall that Middleton and Rowley's *The
Changeling,* arguably the finest Renaissance dramatic collaboration, is also arranged according to this plan. According to the
findings of several generations of commentators, ranging from
Pauline Wiggin's early speculations to N. W. Bawcutt's careful

determinations, Rowley's share is all of Act I, the madhouse
subplot scenes, and the play's closing scene. Middleton's hand,
in contrast, has been traced in main plot scenes in Acts II, III,
and IV; and in Act V, scenes 1 and 2.11 Importantly, this
division coincides with the division of *A Faire Quarrel* in terms
of acts and scenes, of plotting, and of the separation of both
plays into their comic and tragic modes. The single exception
to this division, the granting to Rowley of IV.2.1-17, is an
expected and significant one: the lines provide an important
link between the main and sub-plots since they, as many readers
have noted, explicitly connect the Beatrice-Joanna-Alonzo and
Alsemero-De Flores tragic triangle with the Isabella-Albius-
Antonio and Franciscus-Lollio comic intrigue.12

In short, the play is a "framed" collaboration that can be
divided between the playwrights in terms of acts and scenes,
plots, and modes, with the addition of one interwoven section.
The collaborative form of *The Changeling* is clear:

Act I	II III IV V, 1, 2	V, 3,
Rowley	Middleton	Rowley
	Main Plot	
Rowley	Madhouse Subplot	Rowley

And it parallels my earlier diagram of the shares in *A Faire
Quarrel.*

As many readers, most notably William Empson, Muriel
Bradbrook, Karl Holzknecht, and Richard Levin,13 have realized, the madhouse scenes are in direct contrast to the courtly
plot and echo it at each important juncture in the action. The
subplot thus retains its dramatic distinctiveness as a conventional
comic tale of attempted cuckoldry at the same time it provides a
choric commentary on the main plot by describing concretely
and literally what occurs on a psychological level between
Beatrice and De Flores. While the difference between the plots
clearly is a difference in modes, the playwrights were able to
blend their styles so thoroughly that *The Changeling,* unlike
other collaborative plays, achieves a unique integral consistency.

Few readers of the play would quarrel about the degree of
formal unity here. What is most clear is the way the language of
the plots serves to recall and to mutually reinforce their separate
actions. Less noticed is the way the subplot leads us to the unfamiliar concretization of psychological behavior. For Rowley's
subplot literalizes what is adumbrated in main plot scenes: we

think immediately of the madmen's cries, the allusions to the game of barley-break, the images of hell, and the physical transformations in the characters of Franciscus and Antonio, the literal changeling of the play's title—each of which either articulates or makes visible the stages in Beatrice-Joanna's fall into corruption. When the language and imagery of the subplot do converge with the language in the main plot, they appropriately become part of Beatrice's self-realization and of De Flores' boast about cuckolding Alsemero:

> Vandemero.   . . . Joanna! Beatrice! Joanna!
> Beatrice.   O come not near me, sir, I shall defile you:
> I am that of your blood was taken from you
> For your better health; look no more upon't,
> But cast it to the ground regardlessly:
> Let the common sewer take it from distinction.
> Beneath the stars, upon yon meteor
> Ever hung my fate, 'mongst things corruptible;
> I ne'er could pluck it from him: my loathing
> Was prophet to the rest, but ne'er believed;
> Mine honour fell with him, and now my life.
>   . . .
> Alesemero.   Diaphanta!
> De Flores.   Yes; and the while I coupled with your mate
> At barley-brake; now we are left in hell.
> Vandemero.   We are all there, it circumscribes here.
>   (V.3.148ff)

Appropriately, the language of the subplot converges with that of the main plot in the final, framed scene in the play.[14]

It is fitting, in this sense, that the texture of the comic subplot be rich and colorful, full of bawdy innuendo, punning and allusion, rife with concrete representations of "love's tame madness." We need only glance at any of the annotated editions of *The Changeling* to see how dialogue in the subplot provides a wealth of comic richness—in stark contrast to Middleton's sparse, underplayed, and elliptical speeches between Beatrice and De Flores. For if, on the one hand, Middleton leaves much unsaid, suggests rather than reveals, Rowley's comic set pieces are meant to clarify what his collaborator deliberately implies. Indeed, the consecutive alternation of paired sets of scenes, of one main plot scene with another subplot scene, stresses this interrelationship.

But let us test this difference in modes. When De Flores, in the celebrated scene (III.4) in which he successfully blackmails

Beatrice, begins to impose himself ("All things are answerable, time, circumstance,/ Your wishes, and my service" [24-25]), he recalls Lollio's transparent attempt to persuade Isabella to bed with him in the immediately preceding scene (III.3). When Isabella refuses his kiss, Lollio reminds her of the conversation he overheard between her and Antonio, and threatens to expose her to Albius unless she gives him a kiss:

> Come sweet rogue; kiss me, my
> Little Lacedemonian. Let me feel how thy pulses beat;
> Thou hast a thing about thee would do a man pleasure,
> I'll lay my hand on't. (234-37)

Lollio's words match with De Flores' "Come, kiss me with a zeal now" (III.4.92), of course; but in his sexual candor Lollio also makes obvious what De Flores does not and need not say, that the intention of his blackmail attempt is a tryst. Yet, coming hard on the preceding scene, De Flores' wishes require no clear enunciation. And if Lollio does not realize his "share," we have a keener sense of the wages for De Flores' "service."

As Mr. Bawcutt has noticed,[15] Isabella counters Lollio's threat with one of her own:

> . . . be silent, mute,
> Mute as a statue, or his [Antonio's] injunction
> For me enjoying, shall be to cut thy throat:
> I'll do it, though for no other purpose,
> And be sure he'll not refuse it. (240-44)

The lines remind us that Beatrice commissioned De Flores to murder her betrothed, Alonzo. Here, reciprocal commentary reinforces both plots. But here, also, the parallel between Isabella's comic dilemma and Beatrice's tragic plight ceases. Isabella tells Lollio she will bed with Antonio only to foil him; Beatrice is forced, on the other hand, to accept De Flores' embrace. At this crux, seemingly similar situations become contrasting ones: Beatrice and Isabella will now course separate paths.

What I have identified as the interaction between modes in a pair of scenes may be confirmed by recalling that, in the structure of the play, scenes from each plot alternate from Act I, scenes 1 and 2; through Act III, scenes 3 and 4; and Act IV, scenes 2 and 3; to Act V, scenes 2 and 3. In each set the scenes reinforce and comment upon the action in both plots, with the madman's bestial cries amplifying the contrasts and suggesting the reality of love-become-lust. As in *A Faire Quarrel,* complexity emerges through contrast. In a deeper sense, however, it is important to realize that the subplot contributes to our response to the main plot; and that such contrasts are technical features, part of both the process of writing and of the experience of viewing *The Changeling.*

We might, of course, consider other subplot scenes, for example Act IV, scene 3, with Franciscus' mad cries about the moon and Isabella's fears about "the waiting moon," which turns lovers into fools and madmen. Clearly, Isabella anticipates Alsemero's final speech, "What an opacous body had that moon/ That last chang'd on us" (V.3.196-97), with its recognition of the transformations in character caused by the moon, the way it "shapes and transshapes, destroys and builds again" (IV.3.21). Indeed, many readers have elaborated the numerous patterns of imagery that weave throughout *The Changeling.* Certainly even a quality like "beauty"—which Isabella denies possessing after Antonio fails to perceive that she is the counterfeit woman before him (IV.3.130ff)—takes added significance when it is used to describe Beatrice-Joanna, whose "beauty is chang'd/ To ugly whoredom . . . is blasted . . . to deformity" (V.3.197-98, 32). The point is that imagery serves not only as a reinforcement between paired sets of scenes, brief intervals in the dramatic action, but also as part of a network that spans the play. Formal analysis, of course, points out such imagistic patterns, but certainly we need to remind ourselves that these are aural effects, written down to be heard and reheard by an audience.

The most vivid visual and aural collaborative effect in the play, the madmen's crazed dance across the upper stage in Act III, scene 3, provides us with a case in point. After seeing the madmen, Isabella cautions Antonio that they are "Of fear enough to part us." She continues:

> Yet they are but our school of lunatics,
> That act their fantasies in any shapes
> Suiting their present thoughts; if sad, they cry;
> If mirth be their conceit, they laugh again;
> Sometimes they imitate the beasts and birds,
> Singing, or howling, braying, barking; all
> As their wild fancies promt'em. (192-98)

Isabella's recognition here of her own whimsical infatuation with Antonio, who will readily change "shape" to suit her fancy, will later help her to avoid falling prey to his advances. But when Alsemero discovers Beatrice-Joanna's "deformity," he will confine both her and De Flores in his closet, where he will serve as their "keeper." Significantly, his language here echoes that which Isabella used in describing the madmen:

> I'll be your pander now; rehearse again
> Your scene of lust, that you may be perfect
> When you shall come to act it to the black audience
> Where howls and gnashings shall be music to you. (114-17)

When Vandemero questions, "What horrid sounds are these," this pattern which links Beatrice and De Flores to the madmen is complete. Language taken from the subplot once again emerges in the final framed scene; indeed, the "horrid sounds" emanating from the closet and Vandemero's question about them remind us of the cacophonous "howling" of the animalistic madmen and of the "wild fancies" that precipitate such "deformity."

But what does such analysis tell us, finally, about collaborative technique? Was a set of words, a prepared lexicon, used by the playwrights to develop their themes? Were these images added or reinforced in a final joint revision? Is it significant that images related to the game of barley-brake, to transformation, to the moon, and to sight and judgment aggregate in scenes written by Rowley; and that images related to blood and service appear in scenes acknowledged to be by Middleton?[16] Although answers to these questions are inherently uncertain, such patterning suggests that the playwrights gave *The Changeling* a thick internal consistency. But did the playwrights expect a carefully modulated image to be heard by their audience? And was it not a collaborative decision which made the subplot determine, in part, our response to the main plot?

Certainly, much of any audience's affective response to the play is dependent upon its feelings about the play's last scene. What would appear to be an unusual feature of *The Changeling* is that Rowley was entrusted with the writing not only of the comic subplot but also of the play's opening and closing scenes. It is easier, surely, to accept that the play was divided along plot lines; such a view would accord with our notions of Middleton's and Rowley's individual talents. It is not so surprising a fact, however, in light of the evidence of *A Faire Quarrel,* which is written according to the same plan. Indeed, as many readers have realized, the language in Act V, scene 3, serves to frame the language in Act I, scene 1, in many ways, most notably in its repetition of the religious and Garden imagery, of the image of the temple in which Alsemero first saw Beatrice, in his use of demonic tropes to describe her, and in his own awareness of the failure of his vision; these images coalesce in his anguished cry, "oh cunning devils!/ How should blind men know you from fair-fac'd saints?" (V.3.108-09).

What has not been seen is that a conversation between Alsemero and Jasperino in I.1 parallels an identical conversation between Beatrice and Alsemero in V.3—with one crucial difference. In the opening scene, Jasperino questioned his friend's melancholy state in terms of his "health"; he responded to Alsemero's fear that the "temple's vane" had turned "full in my face":

> *Jas.*　　　Against you?
> 　　　Then you know not where you are.
> *Als.*　Not well indeed.
> *Jas.*　Are you not well, sir?
> *Als.*　　　Yes, Jasperino.
> 　　—Unless there be some hidden malady
> 　　Within me, that I understand not. (20-25)

In the final scene, however, that which throughout the play has been the source of Alsemero's hidden malady becomes evident; the source is Beatrice, now emerging into his clearer view:

> *Bea.*　Alsemero!
> *Als.*　　　How do you?
> *Bea.*　　　　　How do I?
> 　　Alas! How do you? You look not well.
> *Als.*　You read me well enough. I am not well.
> *Bea.*　Not well, sir? Is't in my power to better you?
> 　　　　　　(V.3.14-17)

Through the use of the unique device of "cue-catching," a term Dewar M. Robb coined to describe Rowley's use of repeated echoes to modulate dialogue,[17] as well as by the obvious similarities in language, these paired conversations are linked. A few moments after this conversation, Beatrice will admit to Vandemero that she has been the source of illness in Alicante, the reason why the citadel and its inhabitants are "not well":

> Oh, come not near me, sir, I shall defile you:
> I am that of your blood was taken from you
> For your better health. . . . (149-51)

III

What has not yet been acknowledged by readers of *The Changeling* is that these effects are both "formal" *and* collaborative in nature. This is so in part because we continue to write about collaborative plays in a critical shorthand that makes them, for all purposes, plays of single authorship—plays by Thomas Middleton or by John Fletcher—and in part because we continue to think of plays as generic products, a tendency which helps to label them as tragedies, comedies, tragicomedies, and histories. Hence T. S. Eliot identified Beatrice's famous cry, "I am that of your blood was taken from you/ For your better health," as perhaps Middleton's finest dramatic verse, when in fact the lines have been positively identified as being by William Rowley.18 In much the same way, we doggedly maintain that the correct prescriptive and generic label to apply to *The Changeling* is "tragedy," reading only the tragic half of the play with any incisiveness and often dismissing the comic subplot as incidental. The irony, of course, is that if we approached this play organically, as a product, we would have to account for the comic scenes. The disreputable publisher of the play's first edition, Humphrey Mosley, was clearly wrong in describing *The Changeling* as "a comedy . . . by William Rowley."19 But he was, I believe, no more in error than contemporary critics, who by and large view the play as a tragedy by Middleton. The point should be self-evident: *The Changeling,* like *A Faire Quarrel* and *The Old Law,* holds two modes in equipose, the comic and the tragic, with the play's conclusion determined by the contrasting thrusts of comedy and tragedy. The main tragic plot concludes with Beatrice-Joanna's self-discovery and with her own and De Flores' deaths, and the comic subplot resolves itself in the final unmaskings of Antonio, Franciscus, and Albius to the delight and salvation of virtue in Isabella. The use of "changeling" to describe not only Beatrice, but also Antonio, Franciscus, and Albius makes this distinction clear.

This view of *The Changeling* raises a larger set of questions concerning an author's canon and concerning the nature of dramatic collaboration. As the division of labor inherent in both *A Faire Quarrel* and *The Changeling* suggests, Rowley was responsible for the structural organization of the plots, while to Middleton was given responsibility for the main plot rhetoric and development. In both cases, that is, Rowley constructed the plays, while Middleton, more competent a poet and writer of dramatic verse, tapped the potential psychological tensions implicit in situations such as those between Captain and Lady Ager and between Beatrice and De Flores. This view of the plays cannot be grounded on coincidence, nor on the prevailing view of Rowley as a hack playwright given the opportunity to collaborate with a leading playwright: both plays are patterned through structural contrasts, both blend comic and tragic elements into a unified whole. Though the plays may be read differently in the twentieth century, clearly they were written this way by Renaissance playwrights.20 And by 1617, the date of *A Faire Quarrel,* Rowley could hardly be said to have the status of a novice: he had been active for ten years, had written three independent plays, had established himself as a comic writer, actor, and manager of Prince Charles' men—and could look forward to joining the King's men and to collaborating with John Fletcher in *The Maid in the Mill* and with John Webster in *A Cure for a Cuckold.*21 Given the division of labor in these two plays, it is clear that Middleton and Rowley found a successful symbiotic formula, one which allowed each playwright to draw from his own strengths and from his partner's. This allocation of labor resulted in multiple-plotted "tragicomedies" (if the term will serve), where the main action is either paralleled or contrasted on other plot levels. In this sense, Rowley's clowns, fools, and madmen provide alternative models of behavior which contrast with or literalize the behavior of main plot characters. His women—Jane, Meg and Priss, and Isabella—perform the same function: their behavior throws into relief the actions of both the main plot women and, reflexively, their own actions. The result in these plays is a widening pattern of characterization and concept, a perspectival presentation of a theme crucial to a drama's unfolding action.

The presence of Rowley's hand in the opening and closing scenes of these two plays is another distinguishing aspect of his collaboration with Middleton. It suggests a plan of operation that recognized the need for a unified tone at the beginning and at the end of a collaborative work. The interconnections among plots, characters, and concepts might then be initially sketched by one hand and finally reinforced, without a loss of consistency, by bringing main and subplots into harmonic conjunction.

Perhaps the above evidence may also support a final argument about the nature of Renaissance dramatic collaboration. The process by which these plays were written was decided upon not because it conformed with the mold of a specific genre, but because it put to best use the individual talents of the collaborative partners. Renaissance dramatic form is too often the constricting concern of the critic, not the artist, who seeks rather to translate individual expression into affective dramatic art. It may well be that it is individual talent which determines the design of a collaborative play.

NOTES

[1] See Samuel Schoenbaum, *Internal Evidence and Elizabethan Dramatic Authorship: An Essay in Literary History and Method* (Evanston, 1966), pp. 225-30, for a slightly different outline. Schoenbaum also cites several contemporary documents pertaining to the question of collaboration.

[2] Schoenbaum, p. 230, suggests the scholarly work necessary before a critical assessment can be made. The orthographic and statistical studies by Cyrus Hoy, "The Shares of Fletcher and his Collaborators in the Beaumont and Fletcher Canon," *SB*, 1956-62, and by David J. Lake, *The Canon of Thomas Middleton's Plays* (Cambridge, 1975), would appear to provide the necessary scholarship. Although Hoy's and Lake's findings depend perhaps too heavily on orthographic evidence, their divisions add support to earlier conjectures, based on similar character types and language usage as well as on various kinds of external evidence. Hoy also made a call for critical response at the 1975 meeting of the *MLA*'s Renaissance Drama Seminar, devoted to "Critical and Aesthetic Problems of Collaboration." His comments are to be balanced with those made by Norman Rabkin; see *RORD*, 19 (1976), 3-6, 7-13 for the texts of their papers.

[3] Hoy's work on the Fletcher canon served as a model for Lake's investigation of the Middleton corpus; see Hoy, *SB*, 13 (1960), 78-88.

[4] See R. V. Holdsworth, ed., *A Faire Quarrel*, New Mermaid Edition (London, 1974), pp. xix-xxii; and N. W. Bawcutt, ed., *The Changeling*, Revels Plays (Cambridge, 1958), pp. xxxix-xliv, for summaries of the critical arguments dividing each play. Although these views predate Lake's survey, Lake's division of the two plays substantially supports earlier findings; see Lake, pp. 200-02; 204-05. All references to the plays will be taken from the editions of Holdsworth and Bawcutt. If we are to accept the findings of Hoy, Lake, Holdsworth, and Bawcutt, the conclusions I draw seem inescapable.

[5] I do not wish here to enter the debate concerning the shares of Middleton, Rowley, and Phillip Massinger in *The Old Law;* see Lake, pp. 206-11, for a current division of the shares. More pertinent to my argument is the fact that Lake separates the play among the playwrights by assigning the opening, the second half of the closing, and all subplot scenes to Rowley, the main plot scenes to Middleton, and the first half of V.1 (possibly) to Massinger. This view suggests that *The Old Law,* like *A Faire Quarrel* and *The Changeling,* is a "framed" collaboration.

[6] See George E. Rowe, *"The Old Law* and Middleton's Comic Vision," *ELH,* 42 (1975), 189-202, for a recent analysis of the play.

7 *The Multiple Plot in English Renaissance Drama* (Chicago, 1971), pp. 66-75.

8 *The Canon of Thomas Middleton's Plays,* p. 201. R. V. Holdsworth divides the play as follows: to Middleton he assigns I.1.1-93; II.1; III.1; III.3; IV.2 and IV.3 (substantially); to Rowley, I.1.93-424; II.2; III.2; IV.1; IV.4; V. George R. Price, in his edition of the play for the Regents' Renaissance Drama Series (Lincoln, 1976), gives all of Act I to Rowley.

9 See Levin, pp. 68-74.

10 See my essay, " 'The Common Sight' and Dramatic Form: Rowley's Embedded Jig in *A Faire Quarrel*," forthcoming in *SEL,* for an analysis of these images.

11 Bawcutt, p. xxxix.

12 See Levin, p. 35.

13 *Some Versions of Pastoral* (London, 1935), pp. 48-52; *Themes and Conventions of Elizabethan Tragedy* (Cambridge, 1935), pp. 213-24; "The Dramatic Structure of *The Changeling*," *Renaissance Papers,* 1954, pp. 77-87; *The Multiple Plot in English Renaissance Drama* (Chicago, 1971), pp. 34-48.
Three recent studies are Raymond J. Pentzell, *"The Changeling:* Notes on Mannerism in Dramatic Form," *Comparative Drama,* 9 (1975), 3-28; Penelope B. R. Doob, "A Reading of *The Changeling,*" *ELR,* 3 (1973), 183-206; and Joseph M. Duffy, "Madhouse Optics: *The Changeling,*" *Comparative Drama,* 8 (1974), 184-98. What Pentzell terms "Mannerist" in the play's tone and style I would call a function of the collaborative techniques of two *different* playwrights. Doob sees the subplot madness as a product of original sin, and bases much of her reading on Burton's *Anatomy of Melancholy.* For convenience, both Pentzell and Doob refer to Middleton as the author of the play. I am in agreement with Duffy's assessment of the madhouse scenes: "The great metaphor of *The Changeling* . . . is the asylum and it is short-sighted to cavil about the relevance of the subplot" (194). His recognition that we "see" the tragic action with "Madhouse Optics" supports my view of plot interaction.

14 And significantly, in that these images which echo throughout are now recalled and reinforced.

15 Bawcutt, p. lxiv.

16 See Christopher Ricks, "The Moral and Poetic Structure of *The Changeling,*" *Essays in Criticism,* 10 (1960), 290-306, for an analysis of the images of service and blood. This dimension of collaboration has not, to my knowledge, been recognized.

17 "The Canon of William Rowley's Plays," *MLR,* 45 (1950), 133.

18 *Essays on Elizabethan Drama* (New York, 1932), p. 94.

19 W. W. Greg, *A Bibliography of the English Printed Drama to the Restoration,* I, 60.

20 A fine example of patterning by structural contrast and of the blending of apparently unrelated modes can be found, of course, in Shakespeare's *A Midsummer Night's Dream.* See Robert Weimann, *Shakespeare and the Popular Tradition in The Theatre: Studies in the Social Dimension of Dramatic Form and Function* (Baltimore, 1978), pp. 237-52, for full development of this argument.

21 See G. E. Bentley, *The Jacobean and Caroline Stage* (Oxford, 1941-68), V, 1015-18.

The Language of Cruelty in Ford's
'Tis Pity She's a Whore

Carol C. Rosen

Though Antonin Artaud has been popularly deified as the mad martyr of the modern theater, his critical *The Theater and Its Double* deserves careful consideration not merely as an essential element in the bizarre alchemy of contemporary drama, but also as a provocative approach to orthodox dramatic theory. Indeed, Artaud's infamous "First Manifesto" of the Theater of Cruelty culminates in an apparently traditional program to stage "an adaptation of a work from the time of Shakespeare, a work entirely consistent with our present troubled state of mind" or other "works from the Elizabethan theater." Notions of traditional revivals are shattered, however, with Artaud's revolutionary stipulation that these "apocryphal plays" be performed not only "without regard for text," but that they be "stripped of their text and retaining only the accouterments of period, situations, characters, and action."[1] By offering John Ford's *'Tis Pity She's a Whore* as a paradigm of his proposed theatrical epidemic (TD 28-32), Artaud provides us with a convenient pivot about which we may examine the efficacy of his approach to the Elizabethan drama on the modern stage.

Surprisingly, except for his disdain for Elizabethan verbosity, Artaud's discussion of *'Tis Pity She's a Whore* is primarily a passionate affirmation of the appraisals of more reserved commentators.[2] But Artaud uses the incestuous union consecrated in the course of Ford's play as a simile for his own concept of the theater of revolt. His focus upon the excessive cruelty of Ford's play and his emphasis upon the "paroxysm of horror, blood, and flouted laws" (TD 29) lead Artaud to his awesome analogy:

> If the essential theater is like the plague, it is not because it is contagious, but because like the plague it is the revelation,

the bringing forth, the exteriorization of a depth of latent cruelty by means of which all the perverse possibilities of the mind, whether of an individual or a people, are localized.

Like the plague the theater is the time of evil, the triumph of dark powers that are nourished by a power even more profound until extinction. (TD 30)

By means of this circuitous syllogism, Artaud alludes to the cathartic value of the violated taboo in *'Tis Pity She's a Whore*. Consequently, Paul Goodman's facile summation of this section of Artaud's manifesto—"And he ends with a rhapsody on Ford's *Whore*, whose content seems to him to be the plague itself"3— misses the metaphoric point. Artaud's obsession is far from rhapsodic; the aptness of Ford's play for Artaud's essay is demonstrated by the broken taboo at its core. As Brian Morris notes in his Introduction to the New Mermaid edition of *'Tis Pity She's a Whore*, though plays about incest were not uncommon in the Jacobean period, *'Tis Pity She's a Whore* "is the only play which makes incest its central theme, and explores to the full the nature and consequences of the relationship."4 The content of Ford's play is, in essence, the plague itself.

Seeking to revive rather than to recall the primordial theater "whose only value is in its excruciating, magical relation to reality and danger" (TD 89), Artaud suggests an intensely savage stage which would externalize through grotesque images, exaggerated movements, stylization, and distortion the pervading cruelty of all human acts. He wants "to break through language in order to touch life . . . to create . . . the theater" (TD 13); like Cocteau, he longs to substitute a vital "poetry of the theater" for the impotent "poetry in the theater."5 But by dismissing the text of *'Tis Pity She's a Whore* as benign and obtrusive, Artaud undercuts Ford's dependence upon caustic language as dramatic texture. For it may be suggested that this crucial dramatic instance of overwhelmingly cruel forces exemplifies Artaud's theatrical concerns *most* concretely by means of its brutal language.

Artaud's base metaphor of the plague is itself anticipated in the language of *'Tis Pity*.6 In the first scene of Ford's play, in fact, the Friar counsels Giovanni:

> Beg Heaven to cleanse the leprosy of lust
> That rots thy soul. . . . (I.i.74-75)

This motif of internal decay echoes throughout the play. Its incremental effect is intensified as well as counterpointed by antithetical stage action. In Act IV, scene iii, for example, this grotesque image of the plague contrasts with the stage presence of Annabella, an innocent involved in a double edged action. Soranzo berates his wife for her "hot itch and pleurisy of lust" (IV.iii.8), he vows to drag her "lust-be-lepered body through the dust" (IV.iii.61), and he calls her "a damned whore" who "deserves no pity" (IV.iii.78-79). Yet Annabella remains pure; she braves the harsh sound of Soranzo's ravings, and finally, she rebels against the cruelty of his words. To Soranzo's threats of torture ("I'll rip up thy heart,/ And find it there" and "with my teeth/ Tear the prodigious lecher joint by joint" [IV.iii.52-55]), Annabella responds with sarcasm and laughter. In response to his furious physical attack ("I'll hew thy flesh to threads" and "Thus will I pull thy hair, and thus I'll drag/ Thy . . . body" [IV.iii.57-61]), she staunchly sings to the Heavens. But Soranzo's belittling of a lover who trifled with lesser parts than "the part I loved, which was thy heart,/ And . . . thy virtues" (IV.iii.127-28) hurts Annabella to the quick. For her brother's incestuous love she cries out now in anguish:

> O my lord!
> These words wound deeper than your sword could do.
> (IV.iii.128-29)

Clearly, the language of this scene intensifies its cruelty. For the angry, savage epithets hurled by Soranzo are the dark double of the innocent action of the siblings off-stage. Also, the horrible visual conclusion of the play is foreshadowed by Soranzo's verbal abuse of Annabella's torn heart. In this scene, Annabella's appeal for the audience is heightened by Soranzo's words perhaps even more than by his blows.

Citing this scene (IV.iii) as the crux of cruelty in 'Tis Pity, Artaud alludes to the antithetical stage effect of shrieks and songs:

> With them we proceed from excess to excess and vindication to vindication. Annabella is captured, convicted of adultery and incest, trampled upon, insulted, dragged by the hair, and we are astonished to discover that far from seeking a means of escape, she provokes her executioner still further and sings out in a kind of obstinate heroism. It is the absolute condition of revolt, it is an exemplary case of love without respite which makes us, the spectators, gasp with anguish at the idea that nothing will ever be able to stop it.

> If we desire an example of absolute freedom in revolt,
> Ford's Annabella provides this poetic example bound up with
> the image of absolute danger. (TD 28-29)

Artaud's visceral approach to the play compels him to call attention to this scene. Here, the tension between lawful cruelty and pure yet criminal rituals shreds the action in a conflict of energies. A vital paradox of deeds and demeanor, Annabella is guilty of incest and adultery, yet she stands as an image of innocence before us. Though Artaud is struck by the double nature of the action at the heart of *'Tis Pity,* he strikes out the words which parallel the poetic duplicity of the action.

The power of words to inflict as well as to aggravate wounds echoes throughout *'Tis Pity,* particularly in coarse allusions to blood and lust. A verbal distortion of love's image is, in fact, invoked by Florio, whose first angry utterance, though aimed at Grimaldi and Vasques (a soldier and a servant), nonetheless suggests the oral abuse to be hurled by an entire society at the incestuous love shared by his children, Annabella and Giovanni. Florio confronts the brawlers outside his home with the demand, "Have you not other places but my house/ To vent the spleen of your disordered bloods?" (I.ii.21-22). This image reinforces the Friar's early admonitions concerning the seductive bonds of "lust and death" (I.i.59), and it also anticipates Annabella's final profanation of her love as "lust" (V.i.9).

When spoken by Soranzo and his betrayed mistress, Hippolita, however, the lusty language of *'Tis Pity* is more precisely suited to the actions and characters being depicted. Hippolita's accusation of Soranzo as her seducer, whose "distracted lust" and "sensual rage of blood" have combined to wrong her (II.ii.27-28), for example, puts this verbal image in its proper visual perspective. For the language of blood in *'Tis Pity* has a double nature. At once it applies both to the violence and lust of Parma and to the blood-ties and rites of purification enacted by Giovanni and his sister.

Like Annabella's note of warning, the central action of Ford's drama is "double-lined with tears and blood" (V.i.34). Indeed, the incestuous lovers seem to have heeded the Friar's advice to "wash every word thou utter'st/ In tears (and if't be possible) of blood" (I.i.72-73). On one level their actions are termed monstrous, lewd, and unnatural. On a more symbolic level, however, the language of lust and blood is consistently undercut by the actions of tears and cleansed blood. For example, Hippolita's curse, when she is poisoned at the wedding of Soranzo and Annabella, proves ironically prophetic:

> Take here my curse amongst you: may thy bed
> Of marriage be a rack unto thy heart,
> Burn blood and boil in vengeance—O my heart,
> My flame's intolerable—Mayst thou live
> To father bastards, may her womb bring forth
> Monsters. . . .   (IV.i.93-98)

This burning speech not only foreshadows Soranzo's realization that his own "blood's on fire" (V.ii.25) and "blood shall quench that flame" (V.iv.27), but it also creates a strong verbal contrast with the pure visual image of the final monstrosity presented on stage. Similarly, Florio's early comments to Vasques bear a prophetic double-edge:

> I would not for my wealth my daughter's love
> Should cause the spilling of one drop of blood.
> Vasques, put up, let's end this fray in wine.
> (I.ii.60-62)

Verbally turning blood to wine, Florio fosters a motif of sacrilegious communion which, like Hippolita's bloody curse following a drink of deadly wine, culminates in the final scene of *'Tis Pity*. Here the potent image of wine is transformed back to the symbolic blood of childbirth as one heart is untimely ripped (V.vi.60) and another is broken (V.vi.63), suggesting a double pagan sacrifice when Giovanni attends a last banquet "trimmed in reeking blood,/ That triumphs over death" (V.vi.9-10).[7]

Constituting a cruel coup de théâtre, Giovanni's appearance with the essential prop of *'Tis Pity* fuses poetry and plot into the vital poetry of the theater. For the heart of Annabella, which her brother bears as an offering at the last banquet, serves the drama concretely as well as emblematically. Bringing to fruition Artaud's modern concept of the stage as a magical "concrete physical place which asks to be filled, and to be given its own concrete language to speak," the overwhelming reality of Annabella's heart envelops the action in a concrete physical language which, according to Artaud, is "truly theatrical only to the degree that the thoughts it expresses are beyond the reach of the spoken language." Thus, the stage property of Annabella's heart exemplifies Artaud's ideal of a solidified and sensual "poetry in space" (TD 37-38).

Annabella's heart is also more than a visible metaphor. It is the real "fragile, fluctuating center" of *'Tis Pity* (TD 13); it is, in effect, the life obscured by language in dramatic form. As such, it illustrates the elusive double nature of theater and its magical core postulated by Artaud. In his preface to *The Theater and Its Double,* "The Theater and Culture," Artaud asserts:

> Every real effigy has a shadow which is its double; and art must falter and fail from the moment the sculptor believes he has liberated the kind of shadow whose very existence will destroy his repose.
>
> Like all magic cultures . . . the true theater has its shadows too, and, of all languages and all arts, the theater is the only one left whose shadows have shattered their limitations. . . .
>
> But the true theater, because it moves and makes use of living instruments, continues to stir up shadows where life has never ceased to grope its way. (TD 12)

In Ford's *'Tis Pity,* Annabella's lifeless heart suggests that "real effigy" insulated by the shadow of its form.

Though it is carried out upon the tip of a bloody dagger, the double significance of Annabella's heart (even on Artaud's metaphysical terms) is ultimately tied to the text as if it were a stake. First, it is, as its deliverer stresses, "a heart,/ A heart, my lords, in which is mine entombed" (V.vi.27-28). To Giovanni, then, his sister's heart symbolizes their union in blood. Their marriage bed has become a coffin, and Annabella's heart is now Giovanni's grave. Secondly, Annabella's heart is a concretization of the lovers' bond and the ripened product of their love. For Giovanni has "ripped this heart" from Annabella's bosom as his dagger's point "ploughed up/ Her fruitful womb" (V.vi.32-33). So Giovanni also equates Annabella's heart with the miscarried fruit of her womb; and his emblematic gesture, as he bears in his "fists . . . the twists of life" (V.vi.72), becomes a sacrificial birth rite. Finally, the brutal interruption of a banquet visually recalls the Friar's foreboding words at a previous feast. Witnessing the murder of Hippolita, the Friar expresses his fear to Giovanni that "marriage seldom's good,/ Where the bride-banquet so begins in blood" (IV.i.109-10). The celebration of the marriage of Soranzo and Annabella which begins Act IV of *'Tis Pity* thus prefigures the ritualistic content of the interrupted final banquet. Whereas the first feast is halted by the masked entrance of Hippolita and ladies in white robes, with garlands of willows (IV.i.

36), the last feast ends with the sudden appearance of Giovanni. Each entrance inverts the purity of a ritual by means of unexpected murder. For in the course of the first banquet, the bloody happenings of its crueler double are foreshadowed as Hippolita takes a poisoned cup of wine as a token of charity. Clearly, then, Annabella's heart embodies the ripened seeds of death which have been verbally acknowledged throughout prophetic actions. As various meanings merge in a single moment, Annabella's heart's blood compresses the ritualistic occasions of 'Tis Pity into a single ceremony of innocence, combining aspects of communion, childbirth, and marriage rites.

Indeed, metaphoric language transforms symbolic action into ritual throughout Ford's play. In Act I, for example, gestures made in childish games are infused with ominous portent through the language of intuition. The game-world is established by the comments of secondary characters: the Friar describes choosing between degrees of sin as risky because "in such games as those they lose that win" (I.i.63), Florio reassures Soranzo of his "word" by reminding him that "Losers may talk by law of any game" (I.ii.55), and Donado strikes the central chord of 'Tis Pity as he rhetorically inquires of his foolish nephew, "wilt make thyself a may-game to all the world?" (I.iii.46-47) Likewise, the real-world of Parma is immediately established, as R. J. Kaufmann observes in his essay on "Ford's Tragic Perspective," as a "carefully contrived world . . . in which marriage is debased, sacraments are violated, vows are disregarded, churchly and secular sanctions are loosened and enfeebled."[8] Before this distorted mirror of their actions, the children of Florio invent a double-game of deadly vows and tragic promise.

The interplay between Giovanni and Annabella in Act I, scene ii of 'Tis Pity may thus be approached as the "real effigy" of actions by sacrosanct shadows in acceptable society. Giovanni first appears to his sister as "some shadow of a man" (I.ii.132), and he admits that he is already suffering from "incurable and restless wounds" (I.ii.143). He offers his own heart as well as his dagger to his sister:

> And here's my breast, strike home.
> Rip up my bosom, there thou shalt behold
> A heart in which is writ the truth I speak.
> (I.ii.205-07)

With these words, Giovanni verbally reverses the play's final image of his sister's heart wrenched in ritualized murder. Similarly, Annabella anticipates future repercussions of their mimetic actions when she joins her brother in an eerie game of simonsays. Instinctively kneeling in an imitation of the marriage-game, Annabella charges her brother with a vow. "Love me, or kill me, brother," she intones for him. And in a microscopic inversion of the play's progression, Giovanni responds in kind. "Love me, or kill me, sister," he swears as he kneels beside Annabella and they kiss in a mock consummation of the marriage vows (I.ii.252-58).

While they improvise miniature representations of the rituals by which they will be destroyed, Giovanni and Annabella also perform symbolic acts of sensuality (the offering of the sword and the simultaneous rising after the exchange of vows, for example). In addition, they recognize the insufficiency of language to purge an inner pain. Having shared the anguish of enforced silence, they now share a scorn for words used to define roles. Giovanni asserts that he "must speak, or burst" (I.ii.153), and Annabella admits that she has sighed and cried "not so much for that I loved, as that/ I durst not say I loved, nor scarcely think it" (I.ii.246-47). Now they dismiss the import of words like "brother" and "sister" (I.ii.228-30), and they become bound to each other by the "links/ Of blood . . . to be ever one,/ One soul, one flesh, one love, one heart, one all" (I.i.31-34).

Ironically, however, as Giovanni and Annabella free themselves from the bounds of Parma propriety, they are faced with more complex entanglements. In their first scene together, they form the pattern for *'Tis Pity,* naively anticipating the traps as well as the macabre trappings of parallel rituals to follow. Vows and bonds of blood take on the double nature of crueler actions, and ultimately they negate themselves in a pattern turned inside out.

Foremost among these doubles of the original ritual is Act III, scene vi. This scene opens with Annabella kneeling and whispering to the Friar. Immediately, the positioning of the actors in Act I, scene ii is recalled in a distorted form, because Annabella now repents her incestuous vows and she seeks forgiveness. Upon completion of his graphic lecture on Annabella's wretchedness, the torment of "raging lust," and the condemnation of "secret incests" (III.vi.7-26), the Friar warns Annabella: "Then you will wish each kiss your brother gave/ Had been a dagger's point" (III.vi.27-28). By echoing, yet significantly distorting Giovanni's first sacrificial offer, the Friar foreshadows the final movement of *'Tis Pity*. With these words, the Friar does "work/ New motions in [Annabella's] heart" (III.vi.31-32), for he twists the "love or kill" vow towards its final malignant form.

Another counterpart to the basic ritual of *'Tis Pity* is to be found in the double scene of Act III, scene ii. Echoing Giovanni's claim, Soranzo pronounces himself "sick to th' heart" (III.ii.34). He also pleads to Annabella for grace, even offering, as did her brother, to show her his heart (III.ii.21-26). This scene is performed not only before the audience, but also beneath Giovanni, whose voyeurism concretizes the double nature of his love and obsessive uncertainty. While watching this "looking glass" of his own actions (III.ii.40), Giovanni overhears his sister telling Soranzo, "If I hereafter find that I must marry,/ It shall be you or none" (III.ii.61-62). This double-talk is necessitated by Annabella's new "sickness."9 For Annabella's early sickness caused by silence has been changed into a more concrete morning sickness. She has, herself, become double, pregnant with another life inside her. Puzzled by Annabella's peculiar remarks and by her subsequent fainting spell, Soranzo, too, is "doubly . . . undone" (III.ii.76). And now, Hippolita's opinion of Soranzo ("You are too double/ In your dissimulation" [II.ii.51-52]) can come to fruition.

The ritualistic ceremonies of Act I, scene ii are finally most emphatically negated when the less innocent participants awaken from their "dream" and "night-games" (V.v.36 and 2). They can no longer play their marriage-games of exchanging vows and rings (II.vi.36-42). Instead, the cycle is completed; the dark side of Giovanni's vow is fulfilled as he kills his sister "in a kiss," repeating "Thus die, and die by me, and by my hand" (V.v.85) in what might be called a frenzied chant.

The concept of the feast is also negated in the final action of the play. Previously viewed as a celebration of fertility, the idea of a feast has gradually changed. As Richardetto foresaw, "And they that now dream of a wedding-feast/ May chance to mourn the lusty bridegroom's ruin" (III.v.23-24). Now, a supposedly redemptive rite portends evil; this feast is a funeral; this banquet is, as Annabella suggests, "an harbinger of death" (V.v.27). Giovanni arrives late. Recalling the image of Hippolita, who arrived like a spectre at an earlier marriage-feast, Giovanni belittles numbed spectators:

> You came to feast, my lords, with dainty fare;
> I came to feast too, but I digged for food
> In a much richer mine than gold or stone
> Of any value balanced; 'tis a heart,
> A heart, my lords, in which is mine entombed:
> Look well upon't; d'ee know't?   (V.vi.24-29)

When Vasques asks, "What strange riddle's this?" (V.vi.30) he is startled by Giovanni's coldhearted reply. " 'Tis Annabella's heart" (V.vi.31). The game is over.

Perhaps the most significant parallels in the play may be drawn between the ritualistic action of the main plot and that of the subordinate plot which also depicts a bloody stylized revenge for an unlawful love. The two plots, merging in Soranzo's "sensual rage of blood" (II.ii.28), counterpoint each other even to the mimesis of a "second death" (II.v.61). In the sub-action, the substitute murder of Bergetto in the place of Soranzo is a mistake; the irony of this dual revenge is intensified by the fact that the revenger himself (Richardetto) is playing a double role of doctor and destroyer. This bloody revenge by a man in disguise in Act II, scene iii serves as a counterpart both to Hippolita's deception (revealed in the removal of her mask during the masque) and to Hippolita's mistaken trust in the double nature of Vasques, who betrays her shortly afterwards (IV.i.35-63).

The fusion of the two plots is most clearly demonstrated in the final confrontation between Giovanni and Soranzo. Here, Giovanni's ecstatic proclamation that "Now brave revenge is mine" (V.vi.75) almost parodies the conscious motivations of Soranzo, Hippolita, and Richardetto. Twisting mad logic to his own ends, Giovanni declares his rage to be "the oracle of truth" (V.vi.53), and he offers to objectify the union of revenge by exchanging the heart of Annabella for the blood of her husband, Soranzo (V.vi.74). The torment of physical particularity which pervades the main action of *'Tis Pity* (especially IV.iii and V.vi) is also grotesquely burlesqued in the subplot of comic pain recounted by Bergetto (II.vi.69-85).

Obviously, the clearest indication of ritualized cruelty in silhouette is to be found in the balance between Ford's intertwined actions. Hence an emphasis upon the bloody nature of the double plot might be offered as a tentative defense for Artaud's dismissal of Ford's potent words. But a consideration of Maeterlinck's translation and adaptation of *'Tis Pity She's a Whore*, the version of Ford's play with which Artaud was familiar,10 invalidates this defense. For there is no doubled subplot in Maeterlinck's *Annabella*. In his preface to the play, Maeterlinck denounces the "melodrame" of Hippolita, and he derides the "grosse comédie" of Bergetto and his "obscène valet," Poggio. Deciding that "Ces scenes sont illisibles," Maeterlinck proceeds to eliminate them from his text.11

A reading of Maeterlinck's version of *'Tis Pity* also eliminates the possibility of justifying Artaud's scorn for Ford's piercing language on the basis of a faulty adaptation lacking the cruel images of the original text. On the contrary, Maeterlinck's translation is more than occasionally accurate; rather, it is almost literally exact. Yet its poetic force is ruthless as well, particularly in the crucial scene of IV.iii and in the concluding scene (which Maeterlinck ends, appropriately enough, with Giovanni's final speech and his death [V.vi.108]). Indeed, Maeterlinck's analysis of the dark workings of *'Tis Pity* foreshadows (and almost overshadows) Artaud's attempt at articulating the efficacy of ritualizing a drama dealing with the broken taboo. Maeterlinck writes:

> Ford est descendu plus avant dans les ténèbres de la vie intérieure et générale. . . . *Annabella* est le poème terrible, ingénu et sanglant de l'amour sans merci. C'est l'amour charnel dans toute sa force, dans toute sa beauté et dans toute son horreur presque surnaturelle. . . . Les mots qui le déclarent ont déjà sur leurs lèvres le goût âcre et sombre du sang.12

Like Artaud, Maeterlinck cites scene iii of Act IV as the crux of ruthless cruelty in the play. Asserting, "Je ne crois pas qu'il y ait dans la littérature une scène plus belle, plus douce, plus tendre, plus cruelle et plus désespérée," Maeterlinck also notes that Annabella braves the attack of Soranzo "avec des mots magnifiques arrachés comme des pierreries dans une tempête, aux abîmes éternels de l'âme humaine."13 So although, like Artaud, he stresses the inner horrors implied by Ford's *'Tis Pity*, Maeterlinck recognizes moreover the necessity for the language of the play. The words are hurled like bricks; in *'Tis Pity*

> la moindre parole que l'on prononce alors a une signification et une vie qu'elle n'a jamais ailleurs. Le ton du drame, là où ce ton existe, se modifie aussi.14

Maeterlinck, then, unlike the revolutionary Artaud, is not care-less with traditional texts. "Les vieux dramatistes," writes Maeter-linck in his preface (perhaps anticipating Artaudian theatrics), "n'avaient pas peur des mots."15

Taking Artaud's theories and Ford's play in a complementary context, it becomes increasingly apparent that Artaud's choice of *'Tis Pity* as a conceit for and as an instance of the theater of cruelty is more than understandable; it is unquestionably apt. Indeed, the action of *'Tis Pity* emphatically illustrates Artaud's extreme notions about a double drama of painful exposure. Nevertheless, if the action of *'Tis Pity* were simply to be mimed, as Artaud suggests (TD 99-100), then the edge of its essential weapon would be severely dulled. For the torrential language of *'Tis Pity* engulfs the drama in cosmic anguish as both the sound and the fury of ceremonies of innocence reverberate in the twisted redundancies of ruthless words. This balance be-tween the word and the unspeakable deed makes Ford's *'Tis Pity She's a Whore* the quintessential drama of cruelty.

NOTES

1 Antonin Artaud, *The Theater and Its Double*, tr. Mary Caroline Richards (New York: Grove Press, 1958), pp. 99-100. Subsequent page references to *The Theater and Its Double*, henceforth "TD," will appear in the text.

2 See, for example, Fredson Bowers' examination of tainted revenge in *Eliza-bethan Revenge Tragedy* (1940; rpt. Princeton: Princeton Univ. Press, 1971), pp. 208-11; M. C. Bradbrook's discussion of the sensual implications of Ford's language in *Themes and Conventions of Elizabethan Tragedy* (Cambridge: Cambridge Univ. Press, 1935), p. 253; T. S. Eliot's provisional acceptance of Ford's "double-stressing the horror" of *'Tis Pity She's a Whore* in *Essays on Elizabethan Drama* (1932; rpt. New York: Harcourt, Brace and World, 1960), p. 130; Ralph J. Kaufmann's analy-sis of the obsessive core and "delicately achieved balance" of "Ford's Tragic Perspec-tive," *Texas Studies in Literature and Language*, 1 (1960), 522-37, reprinted in *Elizabethan Drama: Modern Essays in Criticism*, ed. R. J. Kaufmann (New York: Oxford Univ. Press, 1961), pp. 356-72; Clifford Leech's recognition of the cultiva-tion by Ford of the "horrible and the shocking" in "The Last Jacobean Tragedy," in *Shakespeare's Contemporaries: Modern Studies in English Renaissance Drama*, 2nd edition, ed. Max Bluestone and Norman Rabkin (Englewood Cliffs, N.J.: Prentice-Hall, 1970), pp. 387-99; and Mark Stavig's discussion of the inversion of Christian rituals in *'Tis Pity She's a Whore* in *John Ford and the Traditional Moral Order* (Madison: Univ. of Wisconsin Press, 1968), pp. 95-121.

3 Paul Goodman, "Obsessed by Theatre," in *The Theory of the Modern Stage*, ed. Eric Bentley (Baltimore: Penguin, 1968), p. 77.

4 John Ford, *'Tis Pity She's a Whore*, ed. Brian Morris (New York: Hill and Wang, 1969), p. x. For convenience, this edition of *'Tis Pity She's a Whore* has been used as the source of quotations and citations in this paper. .

5 Jean Cocteau, "Preface: 1922" to "The Wedding on the Eiffel Tower," trans. Michael Benedikt, in *Modern French Theatre: The Avant-Garde, Dada, and Surrealism,* ed. Michael Benedikt and George E. Wellwarth (New York: Dutton, 1966), pp. 96-97.

6 It is important to note, however, that Artaud's choice of *'Tis Pity She's a Whore* as a model for his theater of cruelty has its basis in the play's obsessive quality, use of ritual, and breaking of taboo. This is substantiated by a consideration of the similar qualities exhibited by *Arden of Feversham,* the only other Elizabethan or Jacobean play Artaud mentions (TD 99). Though the image of the plague echoes throughout *'Tis Pity,* it is also understandably common in other plays of the period (e.g., Beaumont and Fletcher's *The Maid's Tragedy* [IV.i.38, 196]).

7 For a discussion of Ford's "hypnotic" use of the word "blood," see Brian Morris' introduction to *'Tis Pity She's a Whore,* pp. xxiv-xxv.

8 Kaufmann, "Ford's Tragic Perspective," in *Elizabethan Drama,* p. 366.

9 This guessing-game of incest, reminiscent of *Pericles* (I.i), is another instance of childish play which oversteps its bounds in *'Tis Pity.* For an illuminating discussion of play which may be applied to Artaud's concept of Ford's drama, see Johan Huizinga, *Homo Ludens: A Study of the Play Element in Culture* (1949; rpt. Boston: Beacon Press, 1968), pp. 107-11. Huizinga describes play as lying "outside morals" (p. 213) in a magic circle which absorbs "the player intensely and utterly" (p. 13) with a savagely poetic game which tends to be beautiful. Huizinga states, "All true ritual is . . . played. We moderns have lost the sense for ritual and sacred play. Our civilization is worn with age and too sophisticated" (p. 158). Huizinga's theories seem to support Artaud's quest for savage terms of artistic expression.

10 Artaud began his acting career under the direction of Lugné-Poe, who founded the Théâtre de l'Oeuvre (where Maeterlinck's adaptation of *'Tis Pity* was first performed on November 6, 1894). See Naomi Greene, *Antonin Artaud: Poet Without Words* (New York: Simon and Schuster, 1970), p. 18.

11 John Ford, *Annabella ('Tis Pity She's a Whore),* traduit et adapté par Maurice Maeterlinck (Paris: Paul Ollendorff, 1895), p. xviii. For a discussion of the weakness of the subplot of *'Tis Pity,* see also H. J. Oliver, *The Problem of John Ford* (New York: Cambridge Univ. Press, 1955), p. 97. For a defense of the subplot, however, see M. Joan Sargeaunt, *John Ford* (1935; rpt. New York: Russell and Russell, 1966), p. 108.

12 Maurice Maeterlinck, "Préface" to *Annabella,* pp. xii, xvi. See also Maurice Maeterlinck, quoted in Clifford Leech, "The Last Jacobean Tragedy," p. 398.

13 Maurice Maeterlinck, "Préface" to *Annabella,* pp. xviii, xvii.

14 *Ibid.,* p. xiii.

15 *Ibid.,* p. x.

Criticism and the Films of Shakespeare's Plays

Marvin Felheim

I

Among the other technical and artistic developments of the twentieth century, the motion picture camera, with its inherent capabilities for sound and color, was an inevitable step; equally unavoidable was the filming of the plays of Shakespeare. The greatest literary works in English, they have dominated the stages of the western world for the past 300 plus years. The union of film and Shakespeare was as natural and ordained a combination as bread and butter or life and breath. No other oeuvre has so consistently lent itself to experimentation and to translation, in every sense of those terms. Finally, and of necessity, in the wake of the films there came the criticism, both academic and journalistic.

The major problem with the criticism of Shakespearean films is that the critics are, in the main, Shakespeareans rather than film critics, and their chief concern is for the texts of the plays. Here we encounter the first real issue: language vs. visual imagery as a device for conveying Shakespeare's ideas and values. For purists, there can be no compromise: Shakespeare was a poet and his language is pre-eminent. But there have always been dissenters from this point of view. Indeed, a recent conference at Brooklyn College (January, 1974) raised one perennial confrontation: between those who see Shakespeare primarily as a dramatist, a practical playwright writing for a living theatre, and those who study the works primarily as dramatic poetry. Cinematic versions seem only to exacerbate the issue, especially in the case of such a stunning film as Kurosawa's *Throne of Blood*.

So, the first and chief and most traditional problem of film criticism vis-à-vis Shakespeare in the cinema is one of the oldest issues: what to do about the poetry in production. As Charles

Eckert has framed the conflict (in the Introduction to his collection *Focus on Shakespearean Films*) it is "between those who feel that fidelity to Shakespeare's text is of prime importance and those who are willing to allow the director and adaptor creative authority both in cutting the original and in imposing simplistic or even eccentric interpretations upon it" (the very words he uses are, of course, loaded). The former are, generally, academicians; the latter, with exceptions naturally, film buffs and enthusiasts who feel that the plays must be rendered in cinematic terms, people who want neither to delete Shakespeare from the contemporary repertoire nor to clutter the films with excessive, frequently unnecessary, verbiage.

This issue has been addressed by eminent authorities; I refer here only to two, the first of whom is Allardyce Nicoll, distinguished historian of the theater, who was, however, among the first (see his *Film and Theatre,* 1936) academicians to attempt to understand the nature of cinema. Defending Reinhart's *A Midsummer Night's Dream,* he pointed to its demonstration of "what may be done with imaginative forms on the screen"; he then isolated two notable aspects of the film: 1) "certain passages which, spoken in our vast modern theatres with their sharp separation of audience and actors, become mere pieces of rhetoric . . . were invested with an intimacy and directness they lacked on the stage"; 2) "the ease with which the cinema can present visual symbols to accompany language"; what Shakespeare's audience possessed, a capacity to "hear," we have lost ("owing to the universal development of reading"); the cinema can restore, visually, that loss, making us see what the Elizabethans literally visualized (the candle, the shadow and the player of Macbeth's speech, for example).

This argument has been extended by Henri Lemaitre (in his *Etudes Cinématographiques*) who finds no disharmony between the art of languages ("which triumphs in conferring all the puissant magic of the image upon the word"), and the cinematic art of the image ("which triumphs in conferring all the allusiveness of the word upon the image"), for they "are joined in a communion within the same dramatic aesthetic." Shakespeare and the cinema, he maintains, have transcended these two opposing concepts, thereby increasing the intensity of the drama. In other words, the principle is not in doubt, only the practice which falls short of the intention. For Lemaitre, the sense of sight is paramount (he calls on Shakespeare and Saint Thomas for support, quoting from *Troilus and Cressida* and the *Summa Theologica*); "Shakespearean drama, so concise were its material means of production, came to expand the visual values latent in words themselves; which is why dramatic presentation so often owes its power to what the words—their rhythm and their arrangement—are designed to produce. Before the inner eye of the spectator occurs the rich unreeling of an imaginary film."

His argument continues, for he sees the essence of Shakespeare's genius in such a passage as Caliban's "The isle is full of noises." Here in words is "a presentiment of the dreamlike magic of darkened cinemas." And "thus the pre-cinematic desire to *show,* which explains the visual density, and the energetic *tempo* of Shakespearean drama, leads to the use of multiple means of *perfected illusion*; much like those which the cinema achieves with its techniques. This illusion" (Shakespeare's, the cinema's) "is the opposite of *literary allusion,* which arose from a renunciation of a technique of showing, and, through the medium of the word, led to a perfection of the more indirect act of *saying.*" The Romantics, especially Vigny and Stendahl, perceived this distinction, Lemaitre points out, as he quotes Stendahl: "I feel that these brief moments of perfect illusion are found more often in Shakespeare's tragedies than in those of Racine." The cinema has the same capacity: it is as ubiquitous as the theater was in Elizabethan times; it can equally well produce that "passionate temperature" of the play; it can satisfy "the extraordinary hunger for space" and "desire for a temporality that is dense, multiple, infinitely expansive and various." (I am indebted here to Charles Eckert's translation.)

One must admit that, despite Nicoll and Lemaitre, problems do continue to exist. A provocative one relates to actors, to personality. A "star" playing any role, even a Shakespearean one, is, in his or her own person, an image. And in close-up, that image may become overwhelming. And so, it is difficult, one must agree, to concentrate upon all the subtleties of language, of a soliloquy for example, when the face of the star, with its superb make-up, is there before us, the lips and eyes moving, the whole image alight with all the technical skills which the camera can manage. Peter Brook felt this conflict so distracting that for his *Lear* he shot profiles and backs of heads rather than

full-face close-ups in order to play down the visual and play up
the verbal, to eliminate the "barrier between the little private
screen in one's head, in which Shakespeare's evocative words
are making pictures, and the real screen in the cinema" (Manvell, p. 138).

II

Perhaps we should digress a moment here for some bibliographical information. Two major studies exist which treat the
history of Shakespeare on film. The earlier, *Shakespeare on
Silent Film* (1968) by Robert H. Ball, is a major contribution
to Shakespearean studies; thorough, wise and eminently useful,
the work is a model of scholarship and sense. In the second
section of the book, designed specifically for "film buffs and
scholars," Ball has given "explanations and acknowledg-
ments" for 299 (out of some 400) silent film versions from
Tree's *King John* of 1899 to Neumann's *A Midsummer Night's
Dream* of 1925. In a final chapter to the first section, he enumer-
ates the problems (silence, a "ridiculous" condition for Shakespeare; the conflict between business and art) as well as the
achievements, not altogether minor, of those silent films: 1) they
educated an enormous, world-wide and generally unprepared
audience; 2) they exploited the strong narrative and visual elements which are essential aspects of Shakespeare's plays; further
they exalted the spectacular over the historical and/or realistic
elements; 3) they experimented with those technical details
which the camera could do well (focus, close-up, range) and
thus paved the way for a new art form, the color and sound film,
which would ultimately add a major dimension to the history of
Shakespearean production. Surely, as Ian Johnson points out,
Shakespeare and the Bible (those two noble Renaissance literary products) have "done well by the cinema"; the phrase
can be interpreted either way, that the cinema has used these
works extensively as sources or that the cinema has provided
new insights into these challenging stories.

The second study, which concentrates largely on sound films,
is Roger Manvell's *Shakespeare and the Film* (1971). He deals
with the period from 1929 (the date of Mary Pickford and
Douglas Fairbanks' *The Taming of the Shrew*) to 1970 (Peter
Brook's production of *King Lear*), during which time fewer than
fifty Shakespearean films appeared. Manvell makes no preten-

tions to the kind of meticulous scholarship which characterized Ball's work. But he is concerned, as Ball was, with establishing the validity of the films he discussed.

His points are: 1) that the conditions which prevailed in the Elizabethan theatre (the great variety of plays, the nature of the audience and its responses) were remarkably parallel to those of contemporary film and television; 2) that the thought and emotion (the range of understanding) in Shakespeare's mature works are fantastically modern; 3) that the dramatic structure of his plays closely resembles the structure of a screen-play; 4) that Shakespeare, like any screenwriter today, was ready to make free with history and was constantly on the watch for subjects which suited his company and his audiences; 5) that a film must exploit those aspects of Shakespeare's plays—the fluidity and excitement of the action—which are best adapted to the new medium, and especially important is what we see rather than what we hear; 6) finally, that the director must judiciously mix the spoken poetry of Shakespeare's stage with the visual imagery of the cinema (and he offers a concluding suggestion: that Shakespeare's plays may stand their best chance in those places farthest removed—such as Japan—from his verbal influence).

III

Many issues have intruded themselves into the criticism of Shakespearean films. Next to the question of language, probably the most important, from the perspective of film, is the whole area of technique. Few film critics of any sort deal in depth with these areas (either for want of expertise themselves, or else from the notion that readers easily become bored in the presence of too much cinematic know-how), and especially critics of Shakespearean films. But there are problems nevertheless. One that struck me most forcibly as I read through the "literature" was the almost complete absence of any reference to music. Most films have music of some sort, frequently particularly composed for the production. For example, all three of the Olivier films—*Henry V* (1944), *Hamlet* (1948), and *Richard III* (1955) — had music especially created by the distinguished composer Sir William Walton. Yet, in the reviews I have consulted, there are few, if any, references to the music, and only token acknowledgment of sound effects (true, in a footnote,

Manvell refers us to his book, *The Technique of Film Music,* for an analysis of music for *Henry V*). This failure to deal with such an integral aspect of film as sound (Kurosawa's *Throne of Blood* is a notable exception, but was occasioned by the fact that the Japanese director eliminated practically all language and used sound effects very subtly) exposes one of the major shortcomings of much film criticism: the technical deficiencies of many film critics and their lack of ability to deal with such significant aspects of film-making as sound, color, editing, lighting, etc. But it is also a failure of awareness, of sensitivity, since many of these same critics will deal with settings, costuming, even acting, all subjects about which they may lack professional knowledge.

The related problem of the rhythm of a film is another matter more often neglected than noted. A film running 90 to 120 minutes must have a tempo if it is to succeed, and this applies particularly to the films of Shakespeare's plays, which must substitute the dynamic structure and movement of film for the five-act pattern which today governs the printed text. Stage productions generally break this pattern in half or into thirds. Yet even here critics rarely comment on the resultant tempo. The film version enables us to see in the same way as Elizabethans watched the play: in one sweeping movement. But the film director, by virtue of the editing and through such techniques as montage, panning and the like is able to manipulate time and space in new ways. Concern for the text and preoccupation with characterization frequently occupy the whole of the reviewer's attention. He never tells us about the overall pacing, the climaxes, minor or major, and the skill or lack of it of the film's basic patterns. Film can juggle time and space in a way the modern theatre simply cannot; it is constantly shifting its point of view, forcing the audience to go along with the camera, again in ways that the theatre cannot manage; and it can use objects and actors with more inventiveness than can the stage: it can pan around or even through things, it can withdraw from an actor, approach him slowly or fast and can use breath-taking close-ups; these objects and these actors even take on metaphorical significance, but again many film critics are not alert enough to note the details, especially where objects and/or people are also identified with sound and/or music.

And to keep the record straight, we can insert here Eric

Bentley's assertion (in *The Playwright as Thinker*) which, far from emphasizing these accomplishments, merely relegates movies, as well as plays for that matter, to the realm of business. He allows only a few films and a few stage productions the quality or name of art. And that's that. In his view, there's no need for the critic to develop any awareness, any knowledge of technical matters.

Fortunately, most critics have more openness to film than Mr. Bentley. But his dismissal of most film as business rather than art does raise issues of concern to the critic. Since Shakespeare's plays must be translated in order for them to be made into movies, then we are faced with an issue which Shakespeare himself encountered: how much can be "lifted" from one art form to another? And how is the "sea-change" to be accomplished? Further, what is the goal of the adaptation: to make money or to provide entertainment? And finally, are all of these seemingly antagonistic factors really in opposition or can they be reconciled? Obviously no single production can satisfy everyone; even Olivier's *Henry V,* generally the most praised Shakespearean film, has its detractors, whereas most Shakespearean films have been more condemned than praised; indeed, the body of Shakespearean film criticism is largely negative; only here and there do we find critics making some attempt to defend or even to interpret imaginatively a Shakespearean movie.

Yet one must, I think, regard these films more creatively. Every film, as every stage production, can indeed be regarded as another interpretative essay written about the play in question. But, unlike the standard scholarly works, they do not ordinarily get buried in libraries. Alfred Harbage recently commented, anent the deluge of Shakespeare commentary, that the criticisms "eventually cancel each other out." But the movies seldom do that. For one thing, they are international, being produced wherever films are made. For another, they are various, even when one derives some details from another (as Polanski's *Macbeth* certainly had echoes of the earlier version by Orson Welles). In addition, they are more widely viewed than an article or an edition and so their impact is greater. But they are, finally, in the tradition of Shakespearean interpretation. Just as an editor or a textualist labors over the words and lines of a play to give them meaning, just as a scholar works and reworks his essay, so a stage or screen director is continually preoccupied with the central theme of his production; only the film director has more control over the audience: they can see only what he has chosen to show them. The film, as Stanley Kauffmann has pointed out, has certain obvious advantages (in the handling of time, for example; in the use of deep focus and montage) but it also is ultimately fixed in time (like an article or an edition); it cannot be changed or have a performer replaced after a while; and many films are seen once and never again. Kauffmann adds a telling and "crucial historical difference" between theater and film: "the theatre began as a sacred event and eventually included the profane; the film began as a profane event and eventually included the sacred."

His comment raises an important question: most film critics know little of the origin of film or its history. They are content to accept the immediacy of the film, a shortcoming which the cinema itself seems to foster: it is difficult to see older films, films as it were in retirement; silent films, further, are, in essential ways, different from sound films; most films are difficult to assess as they go by so quickly. They engage us so absolutely and the darkness and silence of the movie theater isolate us not only from one another but from our note pads, even when we are inclined or prepared to take notes.

Film is a special art, an art of the twentieth century. It has ventured to produce Shakespearean plays because they are still viable and valid in the twentieth century. It has taken most liberty with the text which, however sacred to scholars, may be the element which alienates people most vis-à-vis Shakespeare. And so we are back where we started, with the language of the plays, their glory and their problem. If, ultimately, we have to translate the plays into modern idiom, à la Chaucer (as Robert Graves has already done with *Much Ado*), then perhaps film will ironically turn out to be the only way to preserve Shakespeare's plays in anything like the originals. Then, as now and as in the past, we will have a choice: to film a stage production, even a dramatic reading in the exact words of the bard (so far as we know them) or to imaginatively create new and provocative versions of the plays for living audiences in tomorrow's world. Experimentation, as Garrick and Poel, Zefferelli and others have shown, is the name of the game.

IV

Two areas of investigation have recently emerged as having potential for reconciling the aspects inherent in Shakespearean films.

One is the study of rhetoric, especially as manifest in current structuralist investigations. We have long been familiar with classical rhetoric, which deals largely with language. Recent research, especially in linguistics, has tended to expand this interest into the larger area of communication in general and to incorporate other aspects, human as well as non-human, into the experience. Film thus becomes an all-inclusive form in which all the elements fall into place. Such a requirement, as in the case of the stage, places enormous responsibility upon both the intelligence and sensibility of the director; he is the one who can ultimately coordinate all the rhetorical elements (such as those of the film: frame, shot, scene, and sequence; as well as those of traditional concern: speaker, audience, subject) into one magnificent whole. In this system, color, sound, as well as the camera's point of view are all significant rhetorical aspects.

Another, closely related kind of study which is becoming an all-embracing system is semiotics. As Peter Woollen says (in the Introduction to his *Signs and Meaning in the Cinema*), "the study of film must keep pace with and be responsive to changes and developments in the study of other media, other parts, other modes of communication and expression." And he includes, most definitely, not only linguistics and montage but Marxist concepts of dialectic.

Index